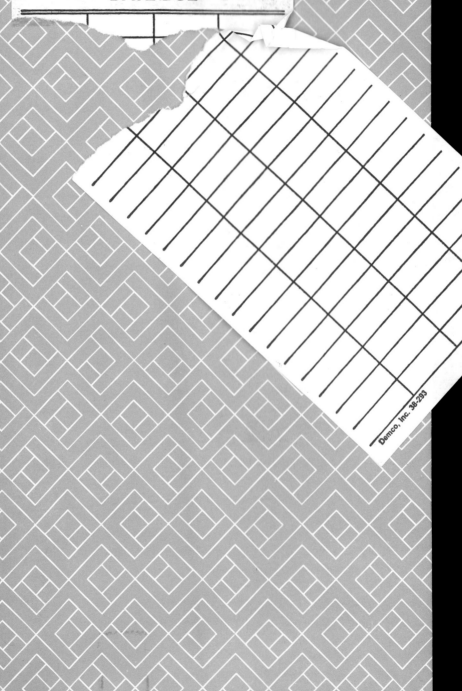

A Companion to Twentieth-Century German Literature

A Companion to Twentieth-Century German Literature

Raymond Furness and Malcolm Humble

London and New York

First published 1991
by Routledge
11 New Fetter Lane, London EC4P 4EE

Simultaneously published in the USA and Canada
by Routledge
a division of Routledge, Chapman and Hall, Inc.
29 West 35th Street, New York, NY 10001

Printed in Great Britain by T.J. Press (Padstow) Ltd, Padstow, Cornwall.

British Library Cataloguing in Publication data
A companion to twentieth-century German literature.
  1. German literature, 1900– Critical studies
  I. Furness, Raymond, II. Humble, Malcolm
  830.900912

Library of Congress Cataloging in Publication Data
  A Companion to twentieth-century German literature / by Raymond
  Furness and Malcolm Humble.
        p.   cm.
    Includes index.
    1. German literature – 20th century – Bio-bibliography. 2. Austrian
  literature – 20th century – Bio-bibliography. 3. Swiss literature
  (German) – 20th century – Bio-bibliography. I. Furness, Raymond
  II. Humble, Malcolm.
  Z2230.C65 1990
  [PT401]
  830.9′0091–dc20 90–35826

ISBN 0–415–01987–7

Preface

Writing some twenty-five years ago in *Encounter*, Erich Heller spoke of the modern mind as being beholden to the hegemony of the German cultural spirit: Germany, he writes, having been defeated in two World Wars, has invaded vast areas of the world's consciousness. 'The modern mind speaks German', Heller claimed, citing Marx, Freud and Nietzsche as its most illustrious tutors. This present Companion enumerates those twentieth-century literary figures who have contributed a distinctive voice; as Germany becomes the focus of Europe once more so its writers become increasingly interesting as interpreters of and commentators on the modern world. We have sought to do justice to the undisputed masters (Thomas Mann, Bertolt Brecht, Franz Kafka, Rilke, Hauptmann, Döblin, Günter Grass and Heinrich Böll) as well as to include a whole host of other established writers and to list the more obscure names. We have no particular axe to grind, but attempt to assess the importance of women writers, writers in the territories formerly known as the German Democratic Republic and those who are perhaps peripheral but nevertheless have an original tone. And 'German' must mean 'German-speaking' here: the Austrian contribution is, of course, incalculable and the Swiss, although of lesser stature, is equally fascinating. As the twentieth century enters its last decade, and Germany enters upon a new and daunting adventure, it is surely appropriate to have at one's fingertips concise and up to date information on those authors who, writing in German, have produced a body of literature which engages (and sometimes captivates) the modern reader. Our tastes are catholic, and only limits on time and space prevented the volume from exceeding acceptable dimensions. We apologize for the omission of those names which the reader seeks in vain.

Raymond Furness
Malcolm Humble
St Andrews
3 October 1990

A

Achleitner, Friedrich (1930–)

Achleitner studied architecture in Vienna, becoming an architecture critic (*Nieder mit Fischer von Erlach*, (1986) is a collection of his criticisms for the press) and in 1983 Professor of the history and theory of architecture at the Vienna Academy of Fine Arts (*Österreichische Architektur im zwanzigsten Jahrhundert* (1980–85)). Achleitner joined the *Wiener Gruppe* in 1955, writing in collaboration with other members and taking part in group performances in the 'literarische cabarets'. Achleitner's mild experimentalism finds expression in 'Konstellationen' in the style of **Gomringer**, dialect poems, montages and the *quadratroman* (1973), in which techniques of concrete poetry are applied in such a way that the square becomes the central motif of a *Bildungsroman*, undergoing numerous transformations into objects and sights the reader must identify and interpret according to his own whim.

Achternbusch, Herbert (1938–)

Achternbusch, whose roots lie in the small peasant communities of the remote Bavarian forest, began his writing career, after studying painting, with *Hülle* (1969), which dispensed with pagination and conventional divisions and was ignored. His breakthrough came in 1973 with *Der Tag wird kommen*. Since then he has produced a series of prose works all marked by radical subjectivity and a mixture of standard German and Bavarian dialect, fact and fantasy, some of which (*1969, Die Atlantikschwimmer* (1975) and *Die Alexanderschlacht* (1978)) have been revised and republished in collected form. Since 1975 he has written the scenarios for and directed films closely related to his other work, including *Das Andechser Gefühl* (1974), *Die Atlantikschwimmer* (1975), *Bierkampf* (1976), *Servus Bayern* (1977), *Der junge Mönch* (1978), *Der Komantsche* (1979) and *Das Gespenst* (1983), while since 1978 he has also branched into drama with plays which in their portrayal of 'geschundene Existenzen' from the Bavarian backwoods resemble some of the works of Franz Xaver **Kroetz** (*Ella* (1978), *Susn* (1979), *Plattling* (1982), *Der Frosch* (1982), *Mein Herbert* (1983), *Sintflut* (1984), *Gust* (1984), *Linz* (1987), *Heißer Stier* (1987) and *Heilt Hitler/Wohin* (1988)). The film *Herz aus Glas* (1976), directed by Werner Herzog, is based on a story in *Die Stunde des Todes* (1975).

Aichinger, Ilse (1921–)

Aichinger was born and grew up in Vienna, studied medicine, worked for a time at the *Hochschule für Gestaltung* in Ulm, married Günter **Eich** in 1953 and has lived since his death in 1972 near Salzburg. Her novel *Die größere*

1

Hoffnung (1948) was one of the first treatments of a Jewish fate during the Third Reich by one who had had direct experience of the system, yet it differs from contemporary 'Trümmerliteratur' in its concentration on the central character's existential situation, which is presented as detached from a concrete historical context. Her later works are marked by a tone and technique ranging between the bleak absurd (cf. Ionesco and Beckett) to playful whimsy, and include short stories ('Der Gefesselte' (1953), which appeared the previous year in Austria under the title 'Rede unter dem Galgen', and 'Spiegelgeschichte' (1954) have attained classic status, the latter being awarded the prize of the *Gruppe 47* in 1952) and radio plays (*Knöpfe* (1953), *Auckland* (1969) and *Gare maritime* (1973)), as well as collections of short dialogues and scenes (*Zu keiner Stunde* (1957, extended 1980)) and poems (in *Verschenkter Rat* (1978)). Her essay 'Aufruf zum Mißtrauen' encapsulated the mood of the time when it appeared in July 1946.

Altenberg, Peter (pseudonym of Richard Englaender, 1859–1919)

The pseudonym derives from the nickname 'Peter', the girl to whom Englaender was briefly engaged and who came from the town of Altenberg. This 'Verlaine d'Autriche', son of a wealthy Jewish family, frequented the Viennese cafés, where he associated with Egon Friedell, Alfred Loos and Karl **Kraus**, on whose recommendation the collection of impressionistic sketches *Wie ich es sehe* was published in 1896. 'Ich möchte einen Menschen in einem Satze schildern, ein Erlebnis der Seele auf einer Seite, eine Landschaft in einem Wort': this was Altenberg's programme. He edited with Adolf Loos the short-lived periodical *Kunst* from 1903–4; his novel *Prodromos*, 'der ersten Versuch einer physiologischen Romantik', appeared in 1906. *Was der Tag mir zuträgt*, a collection of sophisticated, often satirical sketches had been published in 1901, followed by *Märchen des Lebens* (1908), *Bilderbogen des kleinen Lebens* (1909), *Vita Ipsa* (1918) and *Mein Lebensabend* (1919). Altenberg's *Nachlaß* was published by Alfred **Polgar** in 1925: a selection of his writings, *Ausgewählte Werke*, appeared in 1961. Although Altenberg excelled at pithy and trenchant comments on the demimonde of Viennese night life his quizzical and frequently sardonic gaze encompassed Austrian (and German) society as a whole. *Das große Peter Altenberg Buch* was published in 1977, and the *Ausgewählte Werke* (two vols) in 1980. *Gesammelte Werke* began to appear in 1987.

Alverdes, Paul (1897–1979)

Born in Strasburg, Alverdes was a member of the German youth movement, joined the war in 1915 and suffered a severe wound to the larynx. His *Novelle*, *Die Pfeiferstube*, published in 1927 and reaching sales of 263,000 by 1948, is based on this experience and tells of the friendship between German soldiers and an English prisoner who all suffer the same wound. During the Third Reich Alverdes published, with Karl Benno von Mechow, the journal *Das innere Reich*, which propagated a conservative rather than a radical standpoint. Alverdes's poetry at this time is characteristic of much 'Blut und Boden' writing ('O meine Erde, meine liebe Erde,/es treibt, von Vatergeist ins Blut geschauert,/die Flamme namenlos mich fortzustürmen . . .') Other *Novellen* include *Der Kriegsfreiwillige Reinhold* and *Reinhold im Dienst* (1931). Alverdes also wrote radio plays (*Die Freiwilligen* (1934), dealing with the outbreak of war in 1914) and also *Märchen* (*Das Männlein Mittenzwei* (1937)). He was a frequent guest of Rudolf **Binding** at the latter's house near Starnberg. After 1945 Alverdes turned increasingly to fables and children's stories (*Grimmbarts Haus* (1949) and *Legende vom Christ-Esel* (1953)).

Amery, Carl (pseudonym of Christian Mayer, 1922–)

Amery is the author of novels in which an idiosyncratic historical awareness and elements of science fiction achieve a remarkable fusion. In the most important of these (*Das Königsprojekt* (1974)) a secret Vatican council sends a colonel of the Swiss Guard in a Wellsian time-machine back into the past in order to secure the re-Catholicization of Britain and the installation of the Wittelsbachs as the heirs to the Stuart pretenders. Amery's Bavarian patriotism also finds expression in *An den Feuern von Leyermark* (1979) in which Leyermark (Bavaria) wins the war of 1866 against Prussia with American help. In *Die Wallfahrer* (1986) the time-travelling device is reintroduced in order to bring together pilgrims from different periods of Bavarian history and allow them further progress into the future. The author offers alternative endings, the first preceding and the second following the apocalypse. His other novels are *Der Wettbewerb* (1954), *Die große deutsche Tour* (1958), against the *Wirtschaftswunder*, *Der Untergang der Stadt Passau* (1975), science fiction. A critical Catholicism is present in all Amery's essays (*Deutscher Katholizismus heute* (1963), *Fragen an Welt und Kirche* (1967), *Das Ende der Vorsehung. Die gnadenlosen Folgen des Christentums* (1972)), but in his more recent work he shows a growing concern with ecological issues (*Natur als Politik* (1976)) and criticizes the contemporary obsession with high technology (*Die starke Position oder Ganz normale MAMUS* (1985)).

Améry, Jean (pseudonym of Hans (Chaim) Mayer, 1912–78)

A Viennese Jew, Améry escaped to Belgium in 1938, only to suffer repeated internment and persecution on racial and political grounds in the following years, including confinement in the concentration camps Auschwitz,

Buchenwald and Belsen. These experiences and the influence of Sartre have left their mark on almost all his work, which can be divided into primarily autobiographical writings (*Jenseits von Schuld und Sühne* (1966), *Unmeisterliche Wanderjahre* (1971)), philosophical essays (*Über das Altern, Revolte und Resignation* (1968), *Hand an sich legen* (1976)), cultural, literary, critical and biographical essays (*Der integrale Humanismus* (1985)), and fiction (*Lefeu oder der Abbruch* (1974), the autobiographically based story of a painter whose will to live is broken by the Holocaust, and *Charles Bovary, Landarzt* (1978), a sympathetic portrait of the husband of Flaubert's Emma). He committed suicide, a theme of several works.

Anders, Günther (pseudonym of Günther Stern, 1902–)

Having studied philosophy under Cassirer, Husserl and Heidegger, Anders began the anti-Nazi novel *Die molussische Katakombe* in 1930, but failed to find a publisher when he was forced to flee to Paris in 1933. He turned to philosophy with *Pathologie de la liberté*, the principal thesis of which influenced Sartre, and moved on to the United States in 1936, where he associated with other *émigrés* in California. Since returning to Europe in 1950 he has settled in Vienna and been active in the various antinuclear movements of the following years, and his later philosophical works have been written against the background of the historical turning-points represented by Hiroshima (*Der Mann auf der Brücke* (1959), diary of a visit to Hiroshima and Nagasaki, *Off limits für das Gewissen* (1961), an exchange of letters with Claude Eatherley, one of the Hiroshima bomber pilots, *Endzeit und Zeitenende* (1972), *Hiroshima ist überall* (1982)) and the Holocaust (*Besuch im Hades* (1978), *Nach 'Holocaust'* (1979), *Wir Eichmannsöhne* (1964), an exchange of letters with Adolf Eichmann's son Klaus), culminating in his *magnum opus: Die Antiquiertheit des Menschen. Über die Seele im Zeitalter der 2. industriellen Revolution* (Part I (1956), Part II (1980)). He has also produced fables (*Der Blick vom Turm* (1968)), dialogues (*Ketzereien* (1982)), poems (published in *Tagebücher und Gedichte* (1985)), further diaries (*Die Schrift an der Wand* (1967)) and literary criticism (*Kafka – pro und contra* (1951) and the collection *Mensch ohne Welt* (1984)).

Andersch, Alfred (1914–80)

Andersch belonged to the generation of **Böll**, **Schnurre** and **Bender**, marked by involvement in a war which challenged their humanitarian instincts, but he can also be linked to the slightly older **Koeppen**, **Eich**, **Huchel**, as, like they, he began writing well before Germany's defeat. Andersch's early life was further complicated by his upbringing in a conservative household (his father was a businessman, soldier and supporter of Ludendorff) and schooling (one of his teachers was the father of Heinrich Himmler and his Greek class forms the substance of *Der Vater eines Mörders* (1980)). Having obtained a responsible position in the communist youth organisation, Andersch was briefly incarcerated in Dachau after the Nazi seizure of power, avoided further political involvement on his release, and did various odd jobs until his call-up in 1943. On 6 June 1944 he deserted on the Italian front, a decision which he later endowed with crucial political and existential significance and made the turning-point of his autobiographical work *Die Kirschen der Freiheit* (1952), the original version of which, devoid of existentialist overtones, appeared in 1950 under the title *Flucht in Etrurien* and was re-published in 1981. Returning from POW camp in the USA, he founded and edited with Hans Werner **Richter** *Der Ruf* (1946–7) until the threat of suppression by the American occupation authorities made its continuation under their editorship impossible, then worked for radio, developing new broadcasting forms such as the feature and the radio essay and opening the medium to younger writers. He performed a similar role as editor of the bimonthly *Texte und Zeichen* (1955–7). Settling in Ticino in 1958, he became a Swiss citizen in 1972.

Andersch's first novel *Sansibar oder der letzte Grund* (1957) assembles a small group affected in different ways by Nazi persecution: Judith is Jewish, Knudsen's wife is threatened by the euthanasia programme, Helander represents the church and its accommodation with the regime, Gregor stands for the communist underground and a statue by Barlach symbolizes spiritual freedom and 'degenerate art'. Knudsen and Judith succeed in fleeing to Sweden with the statue, while Helander falls victim to SS bullets. In confining narrative perspective to each of the characters in succession, the novel bears a technical resemblance to Gerd Gaiser's *Schlußball*. In *Die Rote* (1960, revised version 1972) the red-haired Franziska escapes the conflicting demands of her marriage and an affair by travelling to Venice, where after becoming involved in the revenge of an Irish victim of Nazism against his former Gestapo interrogator she finds the emotional fulfilment she seeks in a relationship with an ex-communist musician. The revision removes the last part, which presents her happiness with her lover's family in Mestre in a working-class idyll. In *Efraim* (1967) Andersch focuses on Georg(e) Efraim, a modern Ahasverus, who at the time of the Cuban missile crisis returns to his Berlin roots as a British journalist with the task of tracing his employer's daughter and begins an affair with a Marxist actress from East Berlin. When both the mission and the relationship fail, he moves to Rome and abandons journalism for novel-writing. The title of *Winterspelt* (1974), Andersch's principal work, refers to its setting, a village in the Eifel close to the Belgian frontier, where a German major, confronted by the Americans towards the end of 1944 and convinced of the futility of further combat, plans to surrender his battalion with the assistance of a school-teacher, a Czech communist and an art historian. The last of these, having saved a picture by Paul Klee from Nazi sequestration, undertakes to act as an intermediary in negotiations with the American side, but he is arrested and shot by a homosexual corporal who hopes thus to protect himself. The surrender plan comes to nothing after the major receives a secret order to withdraw in preparation for the imminent Ardennes offensive. The situation, the constellation of characters and the symbolical role of the work of art recall *Sansibar*, but the larger scale of the later novel allows Andersch to analyse the interaction of personal motivation and political duress with much greater subtlety. Andersch also produced a number of short story collections (*Geister und Leute. Zehn Geschichten* (1958), *Ein Liebhaber des Halbschattens* (1963), *Mein Verschwinden in Providence* (1971)), travel writings (*Wanderungen im Norden* (1962), *Hohe Breitengrade* (1969)), radio plays and poems (*empört euch der himmel ist blau* (1977) containing 'Artikel 3(3)', which unleashed a storm of controversy by its implication that government measures such as the 'Radikalenerlaß' challenged constitutionally guaranteed democratic freedoms).

Andreas-Salomé, Lou (1861–1937)

Of Russian and French descent, Lou Salomé was one of the first emancipated women to be associated with modern German literature. She studied at Zurich university, and later became associated with Nietzsche, who wished to marry her, with **Rilke**, **Gerhart Hauptmann**, Frank **Wedekind** and other notable literary figures. During her stay in Berlin she wrote articles on Ibsen and the modern stage for the *Freie Bühne*; her book on the Norwegian dramatist (1892) established her reputation. She travelled widely and accompanied Rilke to Russia twice, visiting Tolstoi at his country estate. A restless and intensely demanding woman, Lou Salomé portrayed in her stories (particularly in *Ma*, *Ruth*, the cycle *Im Zwischenland* and *Das Haus*, all written at the turn of the century) the problematic relationship between men and women. Her early story *Ein Todesfall* may have encouraged Gerhart Hauptmann to complete his *Michael Kramer*, performed in 1900, the rehearsals of which Lou Salomé attended with Rilke; her own *Ruth* may, in turn, have been inspired by *Hanneles Himmelfahrt*. Lou Salomé later became an associate of Sigmund Freud, and contributed to psycho-analytical discussion, writing articles on this and other related topics. Her *Lebensrückblick* (ed. Pfeiffer) was published in 1968; *Ausgewählte Texte* appeared in 1988.

Andres, Stefan (1906–70)

Born in the Moselle area, with Italy the setting of many of his works, Andres, after a period as a Capuchin novice and as a student, settled in Positano, where he spent the years 1937–49; in his later years he lived in the Rhineland (until 1960) and in Rome. Andres owed his popularity, which reached its height in the 1950s and has since much abated, to numerous unpretentious novels and stories with rural and Mediterranean settings, in which a Catholic morality, tolerant of the healing forces of time and nature, sees the characters through to a positive resolution of their problems (*Der*

Mann von Asteri (1939), *Der gefrorene Dionysos* (1941) – also under the title *Die Liebesschaukel* (1951), *Die Hochzeit der Feinde* (1947), *Ritter der Gerechtigkeit* (1948), *Die Reise nach Portiuncula* (1954)). More ambitious and substantial works include *Wir sind Utopia* (1943), dramatized as *Gottes Utopia* in 1950, and *El Greco malt den Großinquisitor* (1936), the former dealing with problems of conscience against the background of the Spanish Civil War, the latter the artist's duty to reveal to his subject his true nature as in a mirror; both are typical works of the Christian 'innere Emigration' (cf. **Bergengruen**, **Langgässer**, **Klepper**, **Reinhold Schneider**). A large-scale trilogy *Die Sintflut* (I, *Das Tier aus der Tiefe* (1949), II, *Die Arche* (1951) and III, *Der graue Regenbogen* (1959)), an attempt to treat the Third Reich in the form of a futuristic fantasy on the foundation of the legend of Noah, was less successful, but Andres came closer to the Old Testament in 1963, when in *Der Mann im Fisch* he offered his own version of the story of Jonah, who while inside the whale encounters a man whose guilt convinces him of his duty to answer God's call. One of several plays, *Sperrzonen* (1958), and the novel *Der Taubenturm* (1966) represent a more realistic approach to the Third Reich and its aftermath than *Die Sintflut*. Andres returned to the theme of commitment after a struggle with conscience in the posthumously published *Die Versuchung des Synesios* (1963), centred on a fifth-century bishop of Cyrene.

Andrian-Werburg, Leopold Freiherr von (1875–1951)

A Viennese aristocrat of partly Jewish descent (he was related to the composer Meyerbeer), Andrian was associated with **Hofmannsthal** and Stefan **George**, to whose *Blätter für die Kunst* he contributed (1894–1901). Andrian wrote polished, exquisite verse of wincing sensitivity; George dedicated the poem 'Den Brüdern' to him in the collection *Lieder von Traum und Tod*. A frequent theme in Andrian's poetry is a lament for the passing of Old Austria, whose beauty and refinement can only, apparently, be captured in poetic incantation: the sonnet 'Besinnst du dich, wie einst im Abendwind' exemplifies this. In 1893 Andrian published his *Novelle, Der Garten der Erkenntnis*, subtitled 'Das Fest der Jugend', a lyrical and haunting piece of writing; a second edition appeared in 1919. Andrian entered the diplomatic service, travelled widely and became (briefly) governor-general of Poland. Hofmannsthal was instrumental in his appointment as director of the *Hoftheater*, but the November revolution of 1918 abruptly terminated this. Andrian turned increasingly towards religion and a conservative stance, viz. *Die Ständeordnung des Alls. Rationales Weltbild eines katholischen Dichters* (1930) and *Österreich im Prisma der Idee* (1937). During the Second World War Andrian lived in exile, meeting Georges Bernanos in Brazil; he returned to Europe in 1945. Andrian stands very much under the shadow of Hofmannsthal, whose death in 1929 seemed to him to signify the death-knell of Austrian culture. The correspondence with Hofmannsthal was published in 1968.

Arendt, Erich (1903–84)

Arendt became a communist and a member of the communist-led *Bund proletarisch-revolutionärischer Schriftsteller* in 1926 when his earliest poems were appearing in later issues of the expressionist periodical *Der Sturm*. However, although his exile experiences in Spain, where he took part as a non-combatant in the Spanish Civil War (1936–9), and in Colombia, where he spent the years 1939–50, inspired poetry of a political dimension, he rarely conformed to socialist realist norms then or later. The poems inspired by Spain were eventually published in *Bergwindballade* (1952), including portraits of Lorca, Goya and Don Quixote, while the thirty Colombian poems of *Tolú* (1956) first appeared as a section of *Trug doch die Nacht den Albatros* (1951), in which the exile experience is embodied in the figures of Odysseus, Rimbaud and the bird of the title. Arendt's most important verse, both from a formal and thematic point of view, is to be found in *Flug-Oden* (1959), on the scientific view of the world and its positive and negative consequences, and *Ägäis* (1967), on the landscape and ancient monuments of Greece, which he visited in the early 1960s in order to prepare commentaries for photographic volumes. *Über Asche und Zeit* (1956), which traces the course of his relationship to his wife Katja, reappeared in *Gesang der sieben Inseln* (1957), set on the Baltic island of Hiddensee and in Italy. The free-verse forms developed in *Flug-Oden* and *Ägäis* become more laconic and concentrated, the tone increasingly dark and pessimistic, with the recurrence of a few basic images (stone, sand, lava and dust) in Arendt's last years, as is shown in *Feuerhalm* (1973 – Greece again), *Memento und Bild* (1977), *Zeitsaum* (1978) and *Starrend von Zeit und Helle* (1980), but in his last collection, *entgrenzen* (1981, extended 1983) he adds to his themes the eroticism of old age in poems of remarkable intensity.

Arp, Hans, (or Jean (1886–1966))

Born in Strasburg, Arp enjoyed a mixed cultural environment, and wrote in both French and German; he was talented enough to feel at ease as both graphic artist and lyric poet. His first poems were published by René **Schickele** in the *Neues Magazin* in 1905. In 1911 Arp exhibited his paintings and became associated with the *Blaue Reiter* group. He contributed also to the *Sturm* periodical (ed. Herwarth **Walden**) and attempted to emulate the effects of abstract art in literature. In the First World War he lived in Switzerland: he was invited by Hugo **Ball** to join the newly-formed Dadaist group in the Café Voltaire in Zurich. Arp also worked on the Tyrol Dada pamphlet *Dada Intirol Augrandair*. The first volume of his collected poetry, *Die wolkenpumpe*, appeared in 1920 and was characterized by grotesque and startling imagery, automatic writing and the deliberate cultivation of absurdity. (His most famous poem, 'Kaspar ist tot', appeared as a prose poem in the periodical *Dada* in 1919: it underwent many revisions.) Arp's 'absurd' and 'surrealist' poetry (he also exhibited his painting in the first general surrealist exhibition) exemplified the view that reason and progress had irretrievably alienated man from his basic integrity: poetry and painting should attempt to restore innocence and pre-rational expressiveness. After the death of his wife Sophie Taeuber, the designer, in 1943, Arp's poetry achieved an intensity and earnestness hitherto unknown, particularly in the *Sophie* cycle (1943–5), as well as in *Der vierblättrige Stern* (1945–50). Arp explained: 'Den zu Tode Getroffenen beschäftigten die Formprobleme nicht mehr. Er will sich dem unkörperlichen Raum nähern'. Arp is generally grouped with Hugo Ball and Richard **Huelsenbeck** as one of the founders of Dadaism; his painting is generally described as surrealist. The collection *Wortträume und schwarze Sterne* contains a collection of early work; *Gesammelte Gedichte* I (ed. Marguerite Arp-Hagenbach) appeared in 1963, volume II in 1974 and volume III in 1982. An interesting collection, *Unsern täglichen Traum* (1955) contains much autobiographical material.

Artmann, Hans Carl (1921–)

Born in a suburb of Vienna, Artmann spent five years as a soldier on the eastern front before capture by the Americans and has lived in Malmö, Berlin, Vienna and Salzburg. A brilliant linguist – he claims to understand twenty-six languages in addition to the eight from which he has translated – and master of stylistic masks, he is also a connoisseur of black romanticism, surrealism, baroque formalism and dialect. His best-known book remains that by which he became known: *med ana schwoazzn dintn* (1958), and his work done in collaboration with other members of the *Wiener Gruppe*, to which he ceased to claim allegiance before its eventual dissolution, includes besides *Montagen* (1964) further dialect poems, *hosn rosn baa* (1959). Because Artmann prefers the short form and the fragment, he is best approached through collections and anthologies such as *The Best of H. C. Artmann* (1970), in which all genres are represented, and *ein lilien-weißer brief aus lincolnshire, gedichte aus 21 jahren* (1969). Thirty-two mini-plays are assembled in *die fahrt zur insel nantucket* (1969) and all the prose until 1979 in *Grammatik der Rosen* (three vols). Readers in search of exuberant fantasy, verbal prestidigitation and the ludic transmutation and promiscuous juxtaposition of every conceivable form, tone, register, genre and trivial topos, need look no further; those after spiritual or psychological depth, reflection on serious contemporary issues, realistic depiction of milieu and genuine historical awareness must look elsewhere.

Arx, Cäsar von (1895–1949)

A Swiss theatrical producer and prolific playwright, Cäsar von Arx is associated particularly with festival drama and historical plays. *Die Geschichte vom General Suter* (1929) and *Der Verrat von Novara* (1934) were immensely popular, the latter play enjoying over two thousand performances. Cäsar von Arx learned his skill as *Dramaturg* at Leipzig (1920–3), being renowned as a 'Feinmechaniker and Kalkulator'. From this period stems his antipathy to **Brecht** and his methods; his statement 'Wer das Theater will, muß das Drama wollen' should be seen as a deliberate criticism of Brecht. Von Arx, in his *Moritat* (typed as a manuscript in 1928, but probably written two years before) satirizes Brecht's *Baal* and also **Wedekind**; his *Der kleine Sündenfall* (1938) demonstrates a similar concern. He befriended Georg **Kaiser** during the latter's exile in Switzerland during the Second World War, when Kaiser advised him to turn his attention to film scripts and novels. Feeling estranged from modern developments in the theatre, and failing to understand Kaiser's admiration for Brecht, he committed suicide.

Ausländer, Rose (1907–88)

Rose Ausländer spent her early life in the German-speaking, largely Jewish enclave centred on Czernowitz, Bukovina. She worked from 1921 in New York but returned to her homeland in 1931, only to be caught up in the political upheavals in the course of which Bukovina first became part of Romania, then in 1940 was absorbed by the Soviet Union, then after occupation by German troops rejoined Romania when that country entered the war on the German side in 1941. She narrowly escaped deportation, and was forced to spend the years 1941–4 in hiding in the ghetto. After returning to the USA in 1946, where she worked as a secretary and translator, she settled in Düsseldorf in 1963. She was associated in Czernowitz with a circle of writers in German and Yiddish, which included her mentor Alfred Margul-Sperber and Paul Celan. Thanks to Margul-Sperber her first collection of poems, *Der Regenbogen* (1939), was published; written in the manner of the early **Rilke** and **Hofmannsthal** it was later rejected by her as an epigonal work. Her second and most important collection, *Blinder Sommer*, did not appear until 1965 and was scarcely noticed; the title poem, containing reflections on the post-Holocaust situation, is followed by poems evoking New York, poems on language and the art of poetry, autobiographical poems and poems of identification with the Jewish spiritual heritage. The theme of exile with its multiple meanings is here already present and is repeated in further variations in the subsequent collections which appeared almost yearly throughout the 1970s and 1980s. *Gesammelte Gedichte*, drawn from five volumes (1976, extended 1977) and the *Gesammelte Werke in sieben Bänden* (1984–6) present sum and substance of her work, to be followed finally by *Ich spiele noch. Neue Gedichte* (1987) and *Und preise die kühlende Liebe der Luft* (1988). The *Gedichte aus dem Nachlaß. Jeder Tropfen ein Stein* appeared in 1990.

B

Bachmann, Ingeborg (1926–73)

Born in Klagenfurt, Ingeborg Bachmann studied philosophy from 1945 to 1950, concentrating on Wittgenstein and Heidegger and gaining a doctorate for a dissertation on the latter. She spent long periods in Rome, where she died of the effects of a domestic fire accident. She first became known in the 1950s for poems read at early meetings of the *Gruppe 47* (which awarded her its prize in 1953) and collected in *Die gestundete Zeit* (1953) and *Anrufung des Großen Bären* (1956), which whether in free-verse forms or in regular rhymed stanzas combined a high level of abstraction with rich imagery in a distinctive musical tone. Although her use of imagery from nature can be related to the romantic tradition of the *Stimmungsbild*, behind the majority of her poems lies the concrete experience of a damaged childhood in the Austrian provinces during the Third Reich. A melancholy sense of loss and fear that personal relationships are not only doomed to transience but threatened by socio-political forces pervade her work, even when a note of fulfilment is present as in the love poems of the second collection, at the end of which she also expresses faith in the transcending power of art. This faith, however, eventually yields to an awareness of the impotence and doubtful justification of 'fine' lyrical expression, which finds expression in the few remaining poems she wrote. At the end of the 1950s, in which Bachmann also produced radio plays (*Zikaden* (1955, music by Hans Werner Henze) and *Der gute Gott von Manhattan* (1958), in which the growing intensity of the love between Jan and Jennifer is symbolized by the gradual move to the top of a skyscraper hotel in New York and only Jennifer is granted by 'der gute Gott' the privileged *Liebestod*) and libretti for a ballet and an opera by Henze, her work underwent a critical transformation on the nature and necessity of which she reflected in the Frankfurt poetry lectures of 1959–60 by reappraising what she had written so far.

The following works, two collections of short stories (*Das dreißigste Jahr* (1961) and *Simultan* (1972)) and what was realized of a planned trilogy of novels (*Todesarten*), represent a breakthrough to a feminism of disturbing psychological depth. (Only the first part, *Malina* (1971) was completed before Bachmann's death; fragments and finished chapters of the other two, which were to have received the titles 'Der Fall Franza' and 'Requiem für Fanny Goldmann', were assembled in the complete edition.) In *Malina*, what appears at first to be an account of the course of a triangle involving the female narrator, the mysterious Malina and her lover Ivan turns out to be a form for the analysis of a deep psychic wound with the help of Jungian categories. It emerges that Malina does not represent a real person, but the narrator's 'animus' or male element, who, detached from her as sober listener and counsellor assists her to gain clarity. Yet this same detachment exposes and increases her vulnerability, leaves her unable to resist the terrifying fantasies of the chapter 'Der dritte Mann' and hold on to the utopia adumbrated in the *Märchen* 'Die Geheimnisse der Prinzessin von Kagran'. Ivan's betrayal leads to the identification of him with the father-figure of 'Der dritte Mann' and the loss of the narrator's creative identity, while Malina survives.

The burden of this novel and of the remaining fragments of the rest of the trilogy, as well as of the stories in *Das dreißigste Jahr* and *Simultan* – that men blindly ignore or brutally exploit the feelings of women, who are thereby doomed to betrayal, despair and the extinction of their personality – however dubious as a generalization from the facts of individual relationships, however extreme or obscure the form (realism, myth, psychic allegory) in which it is conveyed, is suffused with such a sense of agonized commitment that the reader is forced to recognize in Bachmann the presence of a writer able to carry over beyond the period of its inception the existentialist revolt of the first post-war generation and apply it to new themes. A complete edition, *Werke* in four volumes, appeared in 1978.

Bahr, Hermann (1863–1934)

Primarily an Austrian critic and essayist, Bahr also wrote novels and plays; an *habitué* of Viennese cafés, he was at the centre of the newest literary developments or, indeed, one step ahead. Maximilian Harden called him the 'Philosoph der Moderne', also 'der Mann von Übermorgen, welcher immer in der Zukunft lebt, in der Temperatur des übernächsten Tages'. In *Zur Kritik der Moderne* (1890) Bahr sensed that naturalism was on the wane, and in *Die Überwindung des Naturalismus* (1891) he called for a new 'nervöse Romantik', 'eine Mystik der Nerven'. Bahr was regarded as the spokesman for the 'Jungwien' cult of sensitivity and neo-romanticism; he was, however, cruelly lampooned by Karl **Kraus** in *Die demolirte Literatur* where he appears as 'ein Herr aus Linz', characterized by 'eine Linzer Gewohnheit, Genialität durch eine in die Stirne baumelnde Haarlocke anzudeuten'. Bahr later championed expressionism in his 1916 essay of the same name. The dramatist Bahr worked briefly under Max Reinhardt in Berlin, and was *Dramaturg* at the *Burgtheater*: his plays were meant as entertainment, and *Das Konzert* (1909) is probably the most successful, with its amusing portrayal of the idolatry enjoyed by the pianist Gustav Heink. Bahr's novels tend towards the impressionistic and the cultivation of moods and subtle personal interrelationships: he attempted a cycle of twelve to portray the cultural scene in Vienna, and these include *O Mensch* (1910), *Himmelfahrt* (1916) and *Die Rotte Korahs* (1918) with its fulsome insistence on Austria's significance for post-war Europe. As a young man Bahr had spoken at the notorious funeral oration for Richard Wagner (5 March 1883) and had been expelled from the university for being excessively 'deutschnational'. In 1909 he married the Wagner-singer Anna Mildenburg. Bahr's essays are indispensable reading for an understanding of Viennese cultural life at the turn of the century, despite the strictures of Karl Kraus. Bahr also discovered d'Annunzio, Maeterlinck, Unamuno, Ortega and Whitman; he encouraged the reading of late Stifter and, above all, drew attention to the young prodigy **Hofmannsthal**. Bahr was also one of the initiators of the Salzburg Festival. The *Ausgewählte Werke* were published in 1968, and the correspondence with his father in 1971; the *Tagebücher 1888–1904* appeared in 1987.

Ball, Hugo (1886–1927)

Ball, one of the co-founders of Dadaism, originally studied acting at the Max Reinhardt school in Berlin and, shortly before the First World War, became director of the Munich *Kammerspiele*. He met Richard **Huelsenbeck** in the Berlin Café des Westens (or 'Café Größenwahn'), turned to poetry and published in the expressionist journals *Die Aktion* and *Die Revolution*; the latter only survived two months but contained such violent poems as Ball's 'Die Revolution' and 'Der Henker'. Ball greeted the outbreak of war as a welcome cataclysm and sought to enlist. He was rejected, but managed to witness trench warfare in Belgium: he reacted in disgust and horror. In Zurich he performed in the Café Voltaire, reciting the first 'sound poem' dressed in cardboard tubes and cape ('Verse ohne Worte in kubistischem Kostüm'). The Dadaist antics of Ball and others mirrored the chaos raging in Europe, yet also sought to recover spontaneity and an 'absurd' playfulness (for example in such poems as 'jolifanto bambla ô falli bambla'). After a nervous breakdown Ball turned his back on Dada, took up journalism and also contributed to René **Schickele's** *Die weissen Blätter*. After the war he attacked the arrogance of the German intellectual tradition in *Zur Kritik der deutschen Intelligenz* (1919), turned increasingly to religion (*Die Folgen der Reformation* (1924) and *Byzantinisches Christentum*, (1923)) and befriended Hermann **Hesse**. The publication of Ball's diaries *Flucht aus der Zeit* (new edition 1946) gave much information on the Dada years. *Gesammelte Gedichte* appeared in 1963 and the 'fantastical novel' *Tenderenda der Phantast* (written 1914–20) in 1967. The less personal, more flippant novel *Flametti oder vom Dandysmus der Armen* had appeared in 1918. Ball's wife, Emmy Ball-Hennings (1885–1948) was a famous soubrette and cabaret artiste: she took part in the Dada evenings at Zurich. She wrote on this period in her life, also on her later life with Ball, in *Hugo Balls Weg zu Gott* (1931), *Der Kranz* (1939) and *Ruf und Echo* (1953). *Damals in Zürich. Briefe aus den Jahren 1915–1917* were published in 1978.

Barlach, Ernst (1870–1938)

Sculptor, graphic artist, dramatist and novelist, Ernst Barlach was without doubt the most gifted of those expressionists (Arnold Schoenberg and Oskar **Kokoschka** were others) who enjoyed a rich diversity of talent. Hailed as one of the greatest German sculptors of the twentieth century, Barlach also achieved considerable acclaim for his plays, and he was awarded the Kleist prize in 1924 for his outstanding literary gifts. His sculptures are characterized by a tension between an earth-bound solidity and a yearning for some transcendental reality: Barlach's journey to Russia in 1906 was an experience akin to the mystical, and the hunched figures of peasants which he modelled, who seem to partake of both realms, furthered his reputation. The plays contain a similar dichotomy between 'Diesseits' and 'Jenseits', a common theme being the need for redemption or 'excarnation'. *Der tote Tag*, begun after the Russian journey and published in 1912, contains an autobiographical element, namely, Barlach's own struggle to gain possession of his illegitimate son. The play is mystical and sombre, exploring the conflict between the principle of transcendence (the Father) and that of immanence (the Mother), with the son as the battlefield. A brooding atmosphere prevails throughout as the son attempts to escape the clinging maternal influence; although he perishes in the struggle the knowledge of an immaculate spiritual conception is gained. *Der arme Vetter* (1918) continues the theme of mystical illumination, but against a realistic background: Barlach demanded 'Milieuechtheit', for physical reality, although ultimately inauthentic, is 'organisch auf dem Wesentlichen gewachsen'. The scene on the heath by the River Elbe, and the arrival of a party of Easter trippers at the country inn, is plausibly portrayed; humour is also provided by 'Frau Venus' and 'Kapitän Pickenpack'. The 'poor cousin' of the title, Sieben-mark, struggles in vain to appreciate spiritual values, yet he develops enough to admit: 'Mir fehlt der Abglanz vom Jenseits'. The original title of the play, *Osterleute*, emphasizes the concept of resurrection which is central to it; the father-son relationship is also significant. *Die echten Sedemunds* (1920) describes a fight for genuine values and religious awareness within a family; *Der Findling* (1922) is a mystery play which shows the power of love to redeem and transform. *Die Sündflut* (1924) is a reworking of the biblical account of the Flood; *Der blaue Boll* (1926), perhaps Barlach's most successful play dramatically, is of interest in that it describes the dramatic tension between the two halves of 'Gutsbesitzer Boll' in a manner which anticipates **Brecht**. *Die gute Zeit* (1929) is another 'Erlösungsdrama', imbued with a knowledge of guilt and evil but which also describes man's longing for ultimate goodness. *Der Graf von Ratzeburg* was unfinished and published posthumously in 1951: the statements 'Es geht nicht ums Gelten, es geht ums Sein!' and 'Ich habe keinen Gott, aber Gott hat mich' belong quintessentially to Barlach. Most of the plays are 'Stationendramen', portraying in an expressionist manner the soul's struggle for self-transcendence. The North German atmosphere prevails throughout most, and a wry, often clumsy, humour is often prevalent. Barlach frequently published lithographs and woodcuts, illustrating his plays (those for *Der Findling* are especially successful): these complement the work he did in wood, stone and bronze. Two unfinished novels, *Der gestohlene Mond* and *Seespeck* (both published in 1948), contain passages of striking descriptive power: *Seespeck* has a literary portrayal of Theodor **Däubler**, whom Barlach had befriended in Florence in 1909. (Barlach also did a wood-carving of Däubler's massive form, entitled *Ruhender Däubler*, in 1922.) In 1933

Barlach's work was declared 'entartet' ('degenerate'): the sculptures were impounded and the plays vilified. He died in complete isolation in Güstrow in 1938. His eminence in both sculpture and drama is now assured: *Das dichterische Werk* (three vols) appeared between 1956 and 1959, was reprinted between 1968 and 1976, and two volumes of letters in 1968 and 1969. (See also the novel by Alfred **Andersch**, *Sansibar oder der letzte Grund* (1957), for a description of Barlach's wood-carving *Der lesende Kloster-schüler*.)

Bartsch, Rudolf Hans (1872–1952)

An Austrian writer of popular novels, Bartsch achieved great success with his *Zwölf aus der Steiermark* in 1908: critics wrote that 'Die Erfindungen in der Fabel sind von Gottfried Keller, der Gedankengehalt von Jean Paulscher Üppigkeit . . .'. Bartsch described the life of the peasants in south-west Styria and the threat of Slav encroachment; other novels (he published over twenty) were characterized by excessive sentimentality and pretentiousness. *Schwammerl* (1912) is a facile portrayal of the life of Schubert; *Lukas Rabesam* (1917), dedicated to Peter Rosegger, and with its motto 'Mein Reich ist nicht von dieser Welt', is a pallid imitation of Gerhart **Hauptmann**'s *Emmanuel Quint*, with Graz ('wo alles Wunderliche möglich ist') the venue for Christ's appearance. Bartsch wrote with a facility which impaired his earlier reputation. His plays include *Ohne Gott* (1915) and *Fernes Schiff* (1934). *Vom sterbenden Rokoko* is a collection of *Novellen*. Bartsch's sentimental portrayal of Austrian life has made him the favourite of undiscriminating readers; social problems are hinted at in some of the early works, but the bulk of Bartsch's writing is escapist and insipid.

Bauer, Wolfgang (1941–)

Bauer was born in Graz, where he studied and has continued to live. Impressed by Ionesco, he began with over thirty one-act plays ('Mikro-dramen') influenced by the theatre of the absurd, then turned to an increasingly idiosyncratic portrayal of sordid bohemianism, achieving scandalous fame with *Magic Afternoon* (1968) and *Change* (1969). However, he cannot be bracketed with a dated pop culture, as he uses its trappings for his own purposes, sharing with the early Handke and other Austrians a concern with appearance and reality and a stage method which demonstrates delusion and deception in ever more sophisticated variations through the way in which characters adopt roles and force them on one another through manipulation. Bauer's more recent work has been much criticized for its supposed impenetrability and triviality; in fact from *Magnetküsse* (1976) onwards he adopts a new approach to the same themes by presenting events through the eyes of central characters who are insane (Ziak in *Magnetküsse*, Toni in *Memory Hotel* (1980)). While the plays of 1967–75 (including also *Party for Six* (1967), *Film und Frau* (1971), *Silvester oder Das Massaker im Hotel Sacher* (1971) and *Gespenster* (1975)) can be understood as naturalistic evocations of milieu and attitudes in the tradition of the *Volksstück* and **Horváth** or simply as provocations of a conventional audience, the later plays (including also *Pfnacht* (1980), *Batyscaphe oder Die Hölle ist oben* (1982), *Woher kommen wir? Was sind wir? Wohin gehen wir?* (1982), *Ein fröhlicher Morgen beim Friseur* (1983), *Das kurze Leben der Schneewolken* (1983) and *Herr Faust spielt Roulett* (1987)) present a Monty Python world in a manner which marks to some degree a return to the style Bauer had developed in the 'Mikrodramen' of 1962–4. A complete edition, *Werke* in seven volumes (1986–), is in progress.

Baum, Oskar (1883–1941)

A Prague novelist and lifelong friend of Franz **Kafka**, Oskar Baum was blinded as a boy during a fight between German and Czech nationalists. His *Uferdasein* (1908) is a collection of short stories concerned with blindness: those who cannot see are able to explore, writes Baum, an inner world of sensations and mystic awareness with a greater facility. His first novel, *Das Leben im Dunkeln* appeared in 1909; a later work, *Die Tür ins Unmögliche* (1920), portrays a supernatural experience. Baum also attempted to write drama (*Das Wunder* (1920), *Der Feind* (1926) and *Der pünktliche Eros*, 1927), but was more at home in prose fiction. He later became a contributor to Herwarth **Walden**'s *Der Sturm*, veering towards expressionism in the wake of **Werfel** and **Brod**. Kafka's comment on Baum is most telling: 'Der Jude Oskar Baum verlor sein Sehvermögen also Deutscher. Als etwas, was er eigentlich nie war und was ihm nie zuerkannt wurde. Vielleicht ist Oskar nur ein trauriges Symbol der sogenannten deutschen Juden in Prag.'

Baum, Peter (1869–1916)

Baum was one of the associates of Elsa **Lasker-Schüler** and Peter **Hille**; he was later introduced to the *Sturm* circle. His prose style is reminiscent of that of E. Th. A. Hoffmann, and his predilection for the macabre (he intended to write a *Grabenbuch*) looks back to Edgar Allan Poe. He was called up in 1914 and published his *Schützengrabenverse* in 1916 (reprinted as *Und alles war anders* in 1955). This collection contains varied verse forms: 'Am Beginn des Krieges stand ein Regenbogen' is a pseudo-sonnet. The war is seen in many poems as a fight to the death between wild animals ('Leuchtkugeln aus gesträubtem Tigerhaar'). Baum was killed by a stray piece of shrapnel in 1916.

Baum, Vicki or Vicky (1888–1960)

Normally, but unjustly, regarded as a writer of light, sentimental novels, Vicki Baum worked in the editorial office of Ullstein in Berlin and soon reached a wide readership with the publication of *Die Tänze der Ina Raffay* in 1921. *Welt ohne Sünde* (the 'Roman einer Minute' (1922)) demonstrated that the authoress was able to handle the technique of interior monologue; *Hell in Frauensee* (1927), subtitled 'Ein Sommerbuch von Liebe, Sport und Hunger' is a by no means trivial analysis of interpersonal relationships. The erotic is handled with sensitivity and skill in Vicki Baum's more successful novels, and the social scene, together with contemporary problems, is also invoked, as in *Stud. chem. Helene Willfüer* (1929). That same year saw the publication of *Menschen im Hotel*, one of the most characteristic novels of the Weimar Republic. A thinly veiled description of the Hotel Adlon, it cleverly enmeshes the destinies, pathetic and frequently sordid, of the guests staying beneath its roof. Filmed in America as *Grand Hotel* it consolidated Vicki Baum's success; she settled in America and died in Hollywood in 1960. She wrote her later novels in English: *Berlin Hotel* (1943) attempted unsuccessfully to regain the popularity of the earlier novel, although the descriptions of air-raids over Berlin have a certain graphic quality. Her autobiography *Es war alles ganz anders* appeared in 1962.

Bayer, Konrad (1932–64)

A member of the *Wiener Gruppe*, Bayer remained until his death the most wilfully experimental of the five in his work and his life style. **Artmann** was his mentor, with whom he shared a taste for surrealism and black romanticism. The works performed at the 'literarische cabarets', some of which were done in collaboration with other members of the group, consist of language divorced from its conventional meaning and social context and reorganized according to abstract, sometimes mathematical principles (e.g. the montages of extracts from a nineteenth-century language primer (1964), with Artmann; *der vogel singt. eine dichtungsmaschine in 571 bestandteilen* (1957–8), based on series and intervals), or the exposure of everyday linguistic stereotypes in such a way that the audience/reader becomes aware of language as a mode of social conditioning and integration (e.g. the plays *kasperl im elektrischen stuhl* (1968) and *der boxer* (1971), which can be related to the early plays of Handke). Bayer's career was marked by a growing scepticism concerning language as an instrument of communication, combined with an anarchistic individualism which showed the influence of Max Stirner. His last works, two novels (see below), indicate the desire to expand consciousness beyond the limits imposed by the need for social interaction and the rational ordering of experience and to reinstate sensual awareness – an aim achieved at the cost of a solipsism and loss of identity which undoubtedly contributed to Bayer's suicide. *der kopf des vitus bering* (1965, radio play 1964, film 1970) portrays the eighteenth-century Russian polar explorer in eighty-seven sections which consist of a montage of extracts from various sources touching in various ways on Bering's role as discoverer of new territory, both in objectivity reality, through his voyages of exploration, and in consciousness, through his euphoric experiences as an epileptic. *der sechste sinn* (1966, 1969), centred on the autobiographical figure of Franz Goldenberg and, left incomplete at Bayer's death, is a mosaic of fragments ending significantly in the disappearance of its protagonist. *Das Gesamtwerk*, edited by fellow *Wiener Gruppe* member Gerhard **Rühm**, appeared in 1977.

Becher, Johannes R. (1891–1958)

Son of a wealthy Bavarian judge, Becher revolted against his family, became a pacifist, joined the *Spartakus-Bund* in 1918 and, later, the Communist Party. His early poetry is ejaculatory and fervent: 'Der Dichter meidet strahlende Akkorde' and 'Verfluchtes Jahrhundert! Gesanglos! Chaotisch!' are two representative poems. Grotesque hyperbole and abysmal bathos reduce much of Becher's poetry to the preposterous. Kasimir **Edschmid** described him thus: 'Bei Johannes R. Becher verströmt die große Explosion. Im Herauswurf gerät ihm das Gedicht in Fetzen. So ungeheuer ist das Gefühl aufgestanden in ihm.' The collections *Der Ringende* (1911), *An Europa* and *Verbrüderung* (1916) show the influence of **Werfel**; the increasingly revolutionary stance of his poetry and its hymnic fervour well exemplify the committed, left-wing aspect of expressionism. A confessional drama, *Arbeiter, Bauern, Soldaten* appeared in 1921. Becher became a Communist deputy in the Reichstag in the Weimar Republic, fled Germany in February 1933 and eventually settled in Moscow. The autobiographical novel *Abschied*, published in Moscow in 1941 (Germany in 1945) is an account of Becher's rejection of the bourgeoisie and his subsequent faith in the ultimate triumph of communism. The *Ausgewählte Dichtung aus der Zeit der Verbannung. 1933–1945* (1945) is predictable in sentiment, yet also demonstrates a return to formal discipline; form now becomes 'Sinnbild einer Ordnungsmacht'. The *Neue deutsche Volkslieder* (1950) and *Deutsche Sonette* (1952) are undistinguished. Becher was Minister of Culture in East Germany, and given a state funeral in November 1958. Editions of his work include *Auswahl* (four vols, 1949); *Auswahl* (six vols, 1952); *Gesammelte Werke* (18 vols, 1966–81). A three-volume *Werke* appeared in 1971.

Becher, Ulrich (1910–90)

Becher's first publication, the collection of stories *Männer machen Fehler* (1932, reissued in extended form in 1958), was burned by the Nazis, and he was forced into emigration, first to Austria, then to Switzerland (1938),

Brazil (1941), New York (1944), returning to Vienna in 1948 and later moving to Basel. His exile works include *Niemand* (1934), a modern mystery play inspired by the drawing 'Christus in der Gasmaske' by George Grosz, a further story collection *Die Eroberer* (1936) and the anti-Fascist satire *Das Märchen vom Räuber, der Schutzmann wurde* (1943). (Grosz was an early mentor and is portrayed in the novel *Das Profil* (1973)). Becher achieved success in 1948 with the première of the 'tragic farce' *Der Bockerer*, written in collaboration with the actor Peter Preses; in it the title-figure, a Viennese butcher, develops his own Schweikian form of resistance to the Third Reich, despite the presence of committed Nazis in his own family. Of Becher's other plays *Samba* (1950) and *Feuerwasser. Deutsch-amerikanische Chronik* (1951) portray the struggle of exiles to survive in the Brazilian jungle and in New York. Becher's reputation is based on his novels, which are influenced by American writers of the 1920s and 1930s and apply the techniques of film in a rich, exotic and sometimes artificial style. Of these *Kurz nach 4* (1957) and *Murmeljagd* (1977) deal with the tribulations of exiles on the run, either viewed retrospectively or experienced directly, while *William's Ex-Casino* (1973) is set in a divided France during the Algerian war of independence, combining elements of the political thriller with reflections by the narrator on the life and death of Ernest Hemingway.

Becker, Jurek (1937–)

Becker spent his childhood in the ghetto of Lodz, Poland, and in two concentration camps before settling in Berlin in 1945. In the upheavals within the GDR writing community following the expatriation of Wolf **Biermann** Becker was expelled from the SED and resigned from the Writers' Union, and he has lived in the West since the end of 1977. Becker achieved prominence in 1969 with the appearance of *Jakob der Lügner*, which commemorates the unheroic heroism of the title-figure forced to lie in order to maintain morale in a Polish ghetto in the closing phase of the Second World War after accidentally hearing on police radio of the Red Army's approach. Seen from a pragmatic point of view, Jakob's lies have a positive effect; seen from an absolute point of view, they emerge as the line of least resistance. The title of Becker's next novel, *Irreführung der Behörden* (1973), points to the continuity of the theme of deception, of oneself and others, in Becker's work. Apparent too is its connection to the subject of story-telling, which is an abiding preoccupation of the central characters, who usually narrate their own story. In his account of his successful career as a writer Georg Bieneck reveals himself as a careerist, opportunist and above all as a fraudulent manipulator of all those with whom he comes into contact. When his estranged wife confronts him with the truth about himself, he accepts that he has flouted socialist principles. Other novels focus on Jewish victims of the Holocaust whose inability to come to terms with the traumas left by their experiences renders them unwilling outsiders in either German state (*Der Boxer* (1976), *Bronsteins*

Kinder (1986)), or similar figures whose failure to accommodate themselves to the expectations of their professional and social milieu leads not to active protest but to withdrawal, illness and attempted suicide (*Schlaflose Tage* (1978), *Aller Welt Freund* (1982)). Neither these novels, nor the twenty-five stories of the collection *Nach der ersten Zukunft* (1980), were published in the GDR.

Becker, Jürgen (1932–)

Becker has spent most of his life in Cologne, where he has been employed in radio play supervision. His early prose writings (*Felder* (1964), *Ränder* (1968) and *Umgebungen* (1970)) draw on Joyce and Helmut **Heißenbüttel** to challenge the traditional novel with its emphasis on plot and character. In them reality in the form of particles of everyday life is filtered through the subjectivity of the author, who then carefully arranges these often fragmentary and disparate perceptions, occasionally conveyed in deliberately ungrammatical and punctuation-free form, in measured proportions to form a symmetrical whole. Faithful to the view that the old generic divisions are no longer valid, Becker combines lyrical, anecdotal and dramatic elements, exposes the stereotyped nature of the language associated with particular activities, in order to indicate how jargon hinders access to reality. (cf. concrete poets and *Wiener Gruppe*.) Unity is provided by the topography of Cologne and its surroundings, which remains the author's standpoint. The lyrical impulse present in these early prose works becomes dominant in the poetry collections *Schnee* (1971), *Das Ende der Landschaftsmalerei* (1974), *Erzähl mir nichts vom Krieg* (1977), *In der verbleibenden Zeit* (1979) and, combining the poems in these volumes with unpublished pieces written between 1974 and 1980, *Gedichte 1965–1980* (1981), all of which, like the prose, register perceptions by means of free association like diary jottings. In concentrating on the effects of industrial activity in the urban landscape these poems become the vehicle of regret for the loss of the idyll represented by pre-industrial nature and fear of environmental catastrophe. *Erzählen bis Ostende* (1981) presents the biography of a radio editor in the now familiar atomistic style, placed within the framework of a railway journey to Ostende, and the same impressionism is the principal feature of his most recent prose (*Die Türe zum Meere* (1983)) and verse (*Odenthals Küste* (1986) and *Das Gedicht von der wiedervereinigten Landschaft* (1988)). Becker is also the author of numerous radio plays.

Beer-Hofmann, Richard (1866–1945)

A Viennese writer of Jewish descent, Richard Beer-Hofmann was one of the most influential of that group of authors associated with the Café Griensteidl and exemplifying 'Jung Wien' neo-romanticism. A fastidious craftsman

(Karl **Kraus** lampooned him as a writer who 'seit Jahren an der dritten Zeile einer Novelle arbeitet, weil er jedes Wort in mehreren Toiletten überlegt'), he published little: two short stories (*Camelias* and *Das Kind* (1893)); a slim novel, *Der Tod Georgs* (1900), whose hero is a typical representative of *fin de siècle* Viennese decadence with his impeccable taste, refinement and morbid aestheticism; a five-act play *Der Graf von Charolais* (1904), based on Philip Massinger's *The fatal dowry* (the critic Alfred Kerr attacked its unequal quality, claiming that half had been written by Beer and the other half by Hofmann); a cycle of biblical dramas, including *Jaákobs Traum* (1918), *Der junge David* (1933) and *Das Vorspiel auf dem Theater zu König David* (1936); a handful of lyric poems, the most famous being 'Schlaflied für Miriam'; a commemorative piece (*Gedenkrede für Wolfgang Amadé Mozart* (1906)) and a book of memoirs for his wife, *Paula, ein Fragment*, published posthumously in 1949. Beer-Hofmann fled Austria after the *Anschluß* and settled in New York, where he died in 1945. *Der Tod Georgs* is his best achievement, generally regarded as the finest *Jugendstil* novel in the German language; it also contains, in the hero's final awareness of his Jewish blood, anticipations of Beer-Hofmann's later preoccupations. The *Gesammelte Werke* appeared in 1963, the correspondence with Hofmannsthal in 1972.

Bender, Hans (1919–)

Bender belongs to the generation of men who witnessed the Second World War and the collapse of the Third Reich as reluctant soldiers and disillusioned POWs (cf. **Andersch**, **Böll**, **Schnurre**, **Weyrauch**) and who transposed their experiences into fiction, usually in the form of short stories on the American model, which proved to be a suitable vehicle for the literary renewal represented by 'Trümmerliteratur'. Although such experiences form the background to some of Bender's best-known short stories ('Die Wölfe kommen zurück', 'Die Schlucht', 'Iljas Tauben' and 'Der Brotholer'), other themes (childhood and youth, travel, the West Germany of the early *Wirtschaftswunder* years) are present from the beginning. Bender's first novel *Eine Sache wie die Liebe* (1954, revised version with a more convincing ending 1965) concerns the growing pains of an eighteen-year-old student during the transition to a more independent existence and the first serious encounter with the opposite sex. More important is the more substantial novel *Wunschkost* (1959), which tells of the POW Ulmer, whose comrades ensure that he escapes death from pneumonia by collecting enough money to buy penicillin. His survival proves to be brief, as he eventually becomes the innocent victim of his Soviet captors' determination to implicate him in a war atrocity committed by men of the infantry division to which he had belonged.

From its foundation in 1954 until 1980 Bender was editor of *Akzente* (until

1968 with Walter **Höllerer**), a literary magazine with a remarkable openness to new talents from Germany and abroad which did much to bring about a climate in which West Germany was able to rejoin and draw from the mainstream of literary modernism. He has also been active as a poet (*Fremde soll vorüber sein* (1951), *Lyrische Biographie* (1957)), anthologist (*Mein Gedicht ist mein Messer* (1955), *Widerspiel. Deutsche Lyrik seit 45* (1961), *In diesem Lande leben wir. Deutsche Gedichte der Gegenwart* (1979)), and has recently returned to the short story (*Bruderherz* (1987)). *Worte Bilder Menschen* (1969) represents a cross-section of his early work.

Benn, Gottfried (1886–1956)

Generally acknowledged to be one of the most outstanding German lyric poets of the twentieth century, Gottfried Benn came from a family of Protestant parsons, studied medicine in Marburg and Berlin and published, shortly after graduating as a medical officer in 1912, a cycle of poems entitled *Morgue und andere Gedichte*. These brutal and frequently grotesque poems, which spoke of corpses and putrefaction, were welcomed by Ernst **Stadler** and established Benn's reputation as a poet of uncompromising modernity. He published in the major expressionist journals (*Die Aktion*, *Der Sturm*, *Neues Pathos* and *Die weißen Blätter*); the second volume of poems, *Söhne* (1913) was dedicated to Else **Lasker-Schüler**. In *Die weißen Blätter* there appeared in 1914 a short dramatic sketch entitled *Ithaka*, which tells of a violent and lethal confrontation between young idealists and professional authority; typically expressionist is the plea for atavistic vitalism: 'Wir wollen den Traum. Wir wollen den Rausch. Wir rufen Dionysos und Ithaka!' Benn's primitivism is derived largely from Nietzsche; it is also the realization of the man of science that life is suffused with powerful instincts that cannot be suppressed. During the First World War Benn was in charge of an army brothel in Belgium; he also witnessed the shooting of Nurse Edith Cavell. Benn came into contact with Carl **Sternheim**, Otto **Flake** and Carl **Einstein**. Einstein particularly was an admirer of Benn's poetry, and this is seen above all in his review of the latter's *Gesammelte Gedichte* of 1927 (he singled out Benn's 'durch keine Wirklichkeit vorbestimmte(s) Sprachspiel' and his 'halluzinativ autistisches Wortgeschehen' for high praise). The collection *Fleisch* appeared in 1917, *Schutt* and *Spaltung* in 1924 and 1925 respectively. Benn's poetry of the 1920s (he settled as a medical practitioner in Berlin after the war) is characterized by a juxtaposition of deliberately modern, urban phrasing, of medical and scientific terms, deliberately 'unpoetic' and aggressive, with irrational longings for the exotic and the sensual. In an incomprehensible universe meaning is only achieved through the poetic act, the mysterious fusion of disparate parts: Broadway, interstellar space, the Parthenon, the cervical cortex. The montage effects of many poems, the concentration on substantives, the almost Alexandrian breadth of allusion and the sophisticated cynicism alienated those who regarded poetry as lyrical effusion; **Brecht**, however, esteemed Benn's modernity and presented him with a signed copy of *Die Hauspostille*. Benn moved in the same circle as **Klabund**, Oskar **Loerke** and **J. R. Becher**; he also appeared in court as a medical witness in the trial concerning the ostensible obscenity of the Dadaist journal *Jedermann sein eigener Fußball*.

Benn's primitivism, his disillusionment with democracy and his inability to sympathize with platitudinous humanism led him to throw in his lot with National Socialism; by no means an aberration, his welcoming the Nazi seizure of power was a natural development of certain tendencies which characterized his poetry throughout. His standpoint is clearly expressed in *Der neue Staat und die Intellektuellen* of 1933. Benn also replied to **Klaus Mann**, who demanded a statement concerning Benn's refusal to emigrate: the *Antwort an die literarischen Emigranten* extols the emergence of a new biological type of man in Nazi Germany. Benn found himself, however, out of favour with the authorities for his earlier poems, his formalism and modernism, and was attacked in 1936 as a purveyor of lewd pornography. He withdrew into 'inner emigration' and rejoined the army. In isolation he concentrated upon a definition of poetry as being an act of defiance in the face of absurdity and nihilism. The concept of the 'absolute poem', created *ex nihilo*, became of increasing importance for Benn during the Second World War: the poem 'Ein Wort', written in 1943 and published in the *Statische Gedichte* of 1948, emphasizes above all the impact, yet also the transience, of articulate utterance. Benn remained in Berlin after 1945; the brilliance, intensity, and also the tone of quiet resignation in his poetry attracted a growing readership who were prepared to condone his earlier political views. The *Novelle, Die Ptolemäer* (1947), is an account of the suffering and the dislocation experienced in Germany in the post-war period. In 1951 Benn delivered a famous lecture at Marburg University on problems of writing lyric poetry, a lecture quoted and discussed in Cambridge by T. S. Eliot. Benn's death brought forth tributes from all over Europe and America. Eight volumes of *Gesammelte Werke* (ed. **Wellershoff**) appeared between 1958 and 1961 (reprinted 1968); *Sämtliche Erzählungen* in 1970 and *Das Hauptwerk* (four vols) in 1980. A complete edition (Stuttgarter Ausgabe) began publication in 1986.

Bergengruen, Werner (1892–1962)

Born in Riga, Bergengruen fought in the First World War and in the subsequent campaign in the Baltic. In 1923 there appeared his first novel, *Das Gesetz des Atum*, a derivative (E. Th. A. Hoffmann) and pseudo-expressionistic account of student life in which Atum, an ancient Egyptian sun-god, acts as judge and paradigm. Collections of *Novellen* (*Rosen aus Galgenholz*) were also published in the 1920s, followed by the next novel

Das große Alkahest (1926, republished as *Der Starost* in 1938): like Atum, the alcahest or *acidum universale* of Paracelsus represents a supernatural power which invalidates human greed and aspiration. The undemanding nature of Bergengruen's style and the quasi-religious atmosphere invoked by many of his stories made him a very popular writer: extremely prolific, he published a succession of novels, *Novellen* and also poetry. His finest achievement is generally considered to be the novel *Der Großtyrann und das Gericht* (1935), an account of the corruption of power and the demoralization which infects a whole society. The story is set during the Italian Renaissance, but the book may be seen as a thinly veiled portrayal of conditions prevailing within Germany in the 1930s, the 'Großtyrann' being the arch-criminal. Surprisingly, the book was not banned by the Nazis. Bergengruen remained within Germany, although life became increasingly difficult for him: in 1937 he was removed from the *Reichsschrifttumskammer*, although he was allowed to publish *Am Himmel wie auf Erden* in 1940. A historical novel which is set in sixteenth-century Brandenburg, the book also hints at punishment and a higher destiny; Bergengruen, by now a devout Catholic, was not blinded by the initial successes of the German army. *Der Tod von Reval* (1939) is a grotesquely humorous *Totentanz*; *Der spanische Rosenstock* (1942) a delightful piece of escapism. After the war Bergengruen published his *Rittmeister* trilogy, and also collected his poetry and published it in two volumes, *Die heile Welt* (1950) and *Figur und Schatten* (1958). His religious belief insisted that the world, despite suffering and destruction, was 'heil' ('Was aus Schmerzen kam,/war Vorübergang./ Und mein Ohr vernahm/nichts als Lobgesang . . .'): a somewhat facile optimism, however, cannot be denied. Bergengruen's popularity has been eclipsed in recent years by more aggressively modern writers, but his uncomplicated style and religious belief still appeal to many.

Bernhard, Thomas (1931–89)

A dominant but eccentric figure in contemporary German letters, with Handke the best-known Austrian writer of recent decades, Bernhard has monomaniacally devoted himself to an ever more elaborate transposition of his bleak vision of the senselessness of human existence into a vast output of work in prose fiction, autobiography and drama, in which mental disturbance, physical decay and death are the permanent themes. The five volumes of his autobiography, *Die Ursache* (1975), *Der Keller* (1976), *Der Atem* (1978), *Die Kälte* (1981) and *Ein Kind* (1982) reveal a disturbed childhood, marked by illegitimate birth, the experience of two boarding-schools, one Nazi and one Catholic, both so oppressive that the boy was almost driven to suicide, illness which developed into tuberculosis and confined him for four years to hospitals, a period as a grocer's apprentice made barely tolerable by the discovery of music, the death of his loved grandfather the writer Johannes Freumbichler, years of poverty as a student of music and acting. After travels in Sicily, Britain and Poland Bernhard withdrew to a farm in the centre of Upper Austria which he turned into a hermitage for the production of the works (eighteen full-length plays, seven full-length novels, numerous stories and shorter prose in addition to the autobiographical series) which poured without interruption from his pen in the following twenty-four years.

Bernhard's *Weltanschauung* is encapsulated in the statement: 'Es ist nichts zu loben, nichts zu verdammen, nichts anzuklagen, aber es ist vieles lächerlich; es ist alles lächerlich, wenn man an den Tod denkt.' It prompts him to treat physical affliction and mental disturbance not as departures from a norm, but as testimonies to the general scheme of things, artistic and scientific achievements as meaningless attempts at distraction from this ultimate truth. Many of the figures in his novels and plays indulge in more or less literary forms of the *Schwadronade* (tirade or flyting monologue) characteristic of Austrian folk culture. Many of them are locked into inescapable family relationships defined by the dialectic of domination and servitude (e.g. the plays *Ein Fest für Boris* (1970), *Am Ziel* (1981)), others are obsessively engaged in artisitic or scientific projects which either fail to materialize (Konrad's study of hearing in *Das Kalkwerk* (1970), Rudolf's work on Mendelssohn in *Beton* (1982)) or are condemned by their creator to decay (Roithamer's concrete cone in *Korrektur* (1975), after his sister's death and his own suicide). Alternatively the discipline demanded by art turns its practitioners into performing machines indistinguishable from circus animals, as in the Salzburg plays *Der Ignorant und der Wahnsinnige* (1972) and *Die Macht der Gewohnheit* (1974). In setting all his novels in remote parts of rural Austria Bernhard challenges like several contemporary Austrian novelists the strong tradition of the *Heimatroman* as represented by e.g. Stifter, Rosegger and Waggerl, inverting its values to create black idylls. The formal principles of repetition and variation evident in the macrostructure of the novels can be traced to Bernhard's knowledge of music, while their microstructure is defined by complex sentences artfully constructed like a series of Chinese boxes. He often models his figures on real persons, making the connection more or less explicit (e.g. Ludwig Wittgenstein in *Korrektur*, Paul Wittgenstein in *Wittgensteins Neffe* (1982), the pianist Glenn Gould in *Der Untergeher* (1983), the philosopher in *Immanuel Kant* (1978), the actor in *Minetti* (1977)). The plays, several of which have been great successes on stage, come closer than the novels to the traditional satire of human foibles, especially intellectual and artistic vanity, as in the plays *Der Weltverbesserer* (1979), *Über allen Gipfeln ist Ruh* (1981) and *Der Theatermacher* (1984). Although to a high degree discursive and devoid of the kind of action which creates familiar theatrical effects, the plays are characterized by an increasingly light touch which makes their dark themes more palatable, even when these are the legacy of the Third Reich, as in *Vor dem Ruhestand* (1979) and *Heldenplatz* (1988), or a more generalized political satire, as in *Der Präsident* (1975). The task of making qualitative distinctions between individual works in an *œuvre* defined by such formal and thematic constants is difficult, but it is likely that Bernhard will be remembered more for the early novels *Frost* (1963) and *Verstörung*

(1967) than for the voluminous *Auslöschung* (1986), the culmination of his desperate attempt to exorcise his personal past and anathematize the 'black' Austria which the traumas of his early life fixed in his imagination.

Bichsel, Peter (1935–)

Bichsel was awarded the prize of the *Gruppe 47* in 1965 for the twenty-one prose miniatures of *Eigentlich möchte Frau Blum den Milchmann kennenlernen* (1964) in which ordinary people confined by the restrictions and routines of everyday life secretly yearn for a change of scene and more human contact. His prose is spare and pointed, conveying static situations without dramatic conflict. The eight *Kindergeschichten* (1969) are not only for children; the strange but harmless obsessions of the aged eccentrics who populate them are portrayed with sympathy, while a few stories, in which the withdrawal to a private world leads to the invention of a private language, recall the inspired nonsense of Lear and Carroll. Bichsel's sole longer prose piece *Die Jahreszeiten* (1967) shares with **Jonke** a concern with the relation between reality and invention, whether the former can ever be fully rendered and whether and in what sense the latter can be said to have a life of its own. Bichsel has attacked Swiss conservatism in combative newspaper articles, essays and speeches collected in *Geschichten zur falschen Zeit* (1979) and *Schulmeistereien* (1985). *Der Busant* (1985) marks a return to the short story, which forms the subject of the Frankfurt lecture *Der Leser. Das Erzählen* (1982).

Bieler, Manfred (1934–)

Bieler began his career in the GDR with parodies, *Der Schuß auf die Kanzel oder Eigentum ist Diebstahl* (1958, extended and altered as *Walhalla*, 1987). *Bonifaz oder Der Matrose in der Flasche* (1963) recounts the picaresque adventures on land and sea of the title-figure. The original version of *Maria Morzeck oder Das Kaninchen bin ich* (1969) was produced and filmed in the GDR; however, neither book nor film reached the public and Bieler left the GDR for Prague in 1966, eventually settling in Munich in 1968. The West German version has, like Bieler's first novel, picaresque features, but gains by having as its narrator the central character Maria, a sympathetic East Berlin barmaid whose conflicting loyalties to brother and lover motivate her story. The title-story of the collection *Der junge Roth* (1968) – of the eleven stories five had already appeared in the GDR as *märchen und zeitungen* (1966) – can be related to the central section of Bieler's next novel *Der Passagier* (1971); both deal with crimes committed by seamen. His work since consists of four bestsellers, two of which trace family fortunes over several decades in Prague (*Der Mädchenkrieg* (1975)) and Munich high society (*Der Kanal* (1978)), while the others are set in the GDR (*Ewig und drei Tage* (1980), *Der Bär* (1983)). Bieler is also the author of numerous radio plays, some of which are collected in *Drei Rosen aus Papier* (1967, 1970).

Bienek, Horst (1930–90)

Born in Silesia, Bienek had contacts with **Brecht** and the *Berliner Ensemble* until, after taking part in an anti-Stalinist protest in West Berlin, he was deported to the Soviet Union, where he spent the following four years in the Gulag. He subsequently lived in the West, mainly in Munich and its environs. Although he produced prose (*Traumbuch eines Gefangenen* (1957), two stories in *Nachtstücke* (1959), *Die Zelle* (1968)) and poetry (*was war was ist* (1966)) on his prison experiences, he became best known for the 'Gleiwitzer Tetralogie', *Die erste Polka* (1975), *Septemberlicht* (1977), *Zeit ohne Glocken* (1979), *Erde ohne Feuer* (1982). Each of volumes I–III focuses on one day in the lives of the Piontek family and their friends: 31 August 1939, 4 September 1939, Good Friday 1943, while in volume IV the action is divided between the occupation of Gleiwitz by the Russians and the destruction of Dresden in February 1945, an episode into which Bienek introduces the unnamed but clearly identifiable figure of **Gerhart Hauptmann**. Together the novels throw much light on everyday life during the Third Reich and in particular on German-Polish-Jewish relations in a frontier area plagued by communal strife. Childhood and growing up in Silesia are also the subject of *Beschreibung einer Provinz. Aufzeichnungen, Materialien, Dokumente* (1983) and *Reise in die Kindheit* (1988), and his other volumes of poetry (*Gleiwitzer Kindheit* (1976) and *Die Zeit danach* (1974)) are autobiographically based. *Bakunin. Eine Invention* (1972) traces the failure of a researcher to uncover the truth about the declining years of the nineteenth-century anarchist revolutionary, while *Königswald* (1984) presents eight aristocratic ladies and their maid trapped for a time in a castle in Bohemia with a group of SS troops as the Americans and Russians advance from different directions.

Bierbaum, Otto Julius (1865–1910)

Poet, novelist, playwright and co-founder of the art journal *Pan* (1895) and the literary journal *Die Insel* (1899), from which the Insel-Verlag was to develop, Bierbaum demonstrated a restless talent which perfectly exemplified the disparate and often confused tendencies of the literary scene of the 'Jahrhundertwende'. Briefly editor of *Die freie Bühne* (1893) and contributor to *Die Gesellschaft*, he stood in the vanguard of modernism; naturalism, however, did not suit his playful and capricious temperament, and he turned to poetry, frequently gallant and frivolous, which appeared in the Munich journals *Simplicissimus* and *Jugend*, the latter journal, and Bierbaum's poetry in particular, creating the so-called *Jugendstil* mentality. Collections such as *Nemt, Frouwe, disen Kranz* (1894), *Irrgarten der Liebe* (1901) and *Maultrommel und Flöte* (1907) contain many poems characterized by a pseudo-anacreontic and 'Karneval' mentality ('Ringel-ringel-rosenkranz,/Ich tanz mit meiner Frau . . .', 'Zu Flöten und Geigen/Hier tanz ich im Reigen . . .' and the famous 'Faunsflötenlied' are good examples). In Bierbaum's novels the satirical element comes to the fore: *Stilpe* (1897) is a 'Roman aus der Froschperspektive' and portrays the life and fortunes of a megalomaniac writer of the Berlin Bohemia (there are sketches of Richard **Dehmel**, Peter **Hille**, Johannes **Schlaf** and Maximilian Harden) who finally commits suicide. The description of the Utopian cabaret MOMUS inspired Ernst von Wolzogen's *Überbrettl*; from 1898 onwards Bierbaum worked in the Munich cabaret *Die elf Scharfrichter* (other contributors included Frank **Wedekind** and Hanns von **Gumppenberg**). *Prinz Kuckuck. Leben, Taten, Meinungen und Höllenfahrt eines Wollüstlings* (1906–7) parodies the Nietzschean antics struck by many would-be *Übermenschen* and the pathetic attempts at amoralism indulged in by its hero. Bierbaum's work is illuminating for any attempt to understand the prevailing literary tendencies of the first decade of this century: the *Irrgarten der Liebe* was, in fact, the most popular book of poetry of its time, with 40,000 copies sold in five years. His works for the stage, and further novels, were not so successful. The *Gesammelte Werke* (ten volumes) appeared between 1912 and 1921.

Biermann, Wolf (1936–)

Poet, singer, composer and guitar virtuoso, Biermann, whose communist father was murdered in Auschwitz in 1943, was born into a working-class family in Hamburg. Moving to the GDR in 1953 he studied philosophy and worked for **Brecht**'s *Berliner Ensemble*. He soon fell foul of the authorities for his criticisms of blinkered dogmatism, residual Stalinism (which, like Heiner **Müller**, he links with the regimentation fostered by the Prussian ethos) and failure to allow scope for revolutionary idealism and a personal fulfilment grounded on spontaneous feeling. From 1965 until September 1976 he was forbidden to perform in the GDR and all his publications and records appeared only in the West (*Die Drahtharfe* (1965), *Mit Marx- und Engelszungen* (1968), *Deutschland. Ein Wintermärchen* (1972), *Für meine Genossen* (1972)). Having been given permission to take part in a concert tour of the Federal Republic he was deprived of his citizenship on 16 November 1976 after performing with spectacular success in Cologne. The event divided the GDR writers into opposed camps and, after protests by such prominent figures as Christa **Wolf**, Heiner **Müller**, Stephan **Hermlin** and **Jurek Becker**, led to an exodus of writing talent (incl. Thomas **Brasch**, **Sarah Kirsch**, Bernd Jentzsch, Reiner **Kunze**, Günter **Kunert**, Jurek Becker, Stefan **Schütz**, Karl-Heinz **Jakobs**, Erich **Loest**, Klaus **Schlesinger**, which, although not every decision to leave can be linked directly to the Biermann case, was not reversed before 1989.

While it is difficult to separate Biermann's notoriety from his achievement and assess his influence in the GDR precisely, there is no doubt that he has succeeded in reaching a wide audience without making any concessions to pop culture and its commercialism. He belongs both to an international line of poet-musicians (incl. Carl Michael Bellman and Francois Villon) and to the strong tradition of German political poetry represented by Heine, Herwegh and Brecht. Ideas and images are drawn from these and other sources (Bible, folk and worker's songs, *Bänkelsang* and *Moritat*, *Märchen*, French chansons) and adapted to the combative expression, usually in the form of regular strophes with refrains, of his views on subjects which have expanded from the GDR and the opposition between the two German states as symbolized by the Berlin Wall to include freedom movements throughout the world (incl. Spain, South and Central America, Czechoslovakia, Poland), student movements in France and Germany in poems on the *événements* and the German student leader Rudi Dutschke, and East European dissidents, incl. Robert Havemann in the GDR and Yuli Daniel in the Soviet Union, whose *Report from the socialist camp* he has translated (1972). Despite the difficulties of maintaining his role in the West and the occasional signs of resignation (e.g. in the late Hölderlin poems) he has held consistently to a rejection of capitalism and has become active in efforts for peace and nuclear disarmament in the 1980s.

A journey to Hamburg in 1964 inspired the 400 stanzas of *Deutschland. Ein Wintermärchen* (1972), a brilliant adaptation of Heine's model with which it shares the form and the theme of a return to roots, with the significant difference, however, that the transition from new home to old provides the opportunity to criticize both. The same effort to apportion even-handed blame is present in Biermann's interpretation of the adaptation he made of Evgeni Schwarz's *The Dragon* (*Der Dra-Dra* (1970)), that the forces represented by the title-figure can be found in both East and West. The collections which have appeared since Biermann's return to the West (*Preußischer Ikarus* (1978), *Verdrehte Welt – das seh' ich gerne* (1982) and *Affenfels und Barrikade* (1986)) are marked by self-criticism and a predilection for more private themes. Yet even birthday poems for his children are given a political dimension in the context of the nuclear threat. The pre-1976 collections are assembled in *Nachlaß I* (1977).

Billinger, Richard (1893–1965)

Born in Upper Austria, from peasant stock, Billinger trained for the priesthood but later turned to writing. His novels deal with the interaction of the sacred and the profane, generally in a rural setting: *Die Asche des Fegefeuers* (1931) established his reputation. This novel is characterized by its full-blooded evocation of the Bavarian Alps, but also strains for effect with pretentious and frequently overladen images ('Nebelzähre in der

Wange des Sommers', meadows as 'müde Mägde des Herrgotts' etc.); the portrayal of the 'Riesin' verges upon the bizarre. *Das Schutzengelhaus* (1934) deals with the experiences of Philomela Spielhahn, a town-dweller, during a holiday in the country, a situation somewhat akin to that of *Cold Comfort Farm*. Billinger was considered a 'safe' writer by the Nazis because of his description of peasant life, although the baroque excesses, particularly of many of the plays, are hardly exemplary. *Perchtenspiel* (1928, first performed at the Salzburg Festival) mixes natural and supernatural, modern and mystical, in an uncomfortable manner; *Rauhnacht* (1931) and *Spiel vom Knecht* (1932) anticipate the theatre of Franz Xaver **Kroetz**. In 1937 Billinger achieved great success with *Der Gigant*, a depiction of Bohemia and Prague which was filmed as *Die goldene Stadt* (the 'giant' of the title referring to the big city). His Agnes Bernauer play *Der Herzog und die Badestochter* (1937) should be mentioned, also his *Paracelsus* (1943). Billinger also wrote poetry: *Über die Äcker* (1923) and *Sichel am Himmel* (1931) deal mostly with the landscape he knew best; later collections include *Der Pfeil im Wappen* (1932), *Nachtwache* (1935), *Holder Morgen* (1941) and *Lobgesang* (1953). The *Gesammelte Werke* (twelve volumes) appeared between 1955 and 1960. *Würfelspiel* (a selection, plus bibliography) was published in 1960; six volumes from the *Nachlaß* followed between 1972 and 1982.

Binding, Rudolf (1867–1938)

An author known primarily through his *Novellen* and war diary, Rudolf Binding was a late developer as a writer and did not publish until he was over forty. *Der Opfergang* (1912) is a moving story which tells of the magnanimity of a wife who overcomes jealousy and saves her husband's mistress from certain death; a tale of adultery is transfigured by this final act. Other stories show Binding's traditionalism, which he shares with writers like Hans **Carossa** and Rudolf Alexander **Schröder**; a classical sense of form and a refusal to follow modernist experimentation characterize his writing. Most effective is the short story *Wir fordern Reims zur Übergabe auf*, which has an almost Kleistian intensity and economy; it is an 'Anekdote aus dem großen Krieg', as is *Unsterblichkeit* (1921), which was inspired by the death of the fighter pilot Baron von Richthofen but also suggests mystical, archetypal dimensions (the lure of the sea and the suicide therein of the married woman who sought to join her dead lover who had been shot down in the Channel). Binding's war diary *Aus dem Krieg* (1925) is possibly the finest account of the First World War in German literature; two years later various autobiographical sketches appeared as *Erlebtes Leben*. The *Reitvorschrift für eine Geliebte* appeared in 1926 and is a charming (and accurate) account of horse-riding: Binding's expertise in equestrian matters has a refinement which is lacking in the more elemental relationships between horse and man in the work of Hans Henny **Jahnn**. Binding's poetry is generally unremarkable, although the *Sonette der Verschmähten* possess a quiet dignity. In later life Binding settled near Starnberg in Bavaria and cultivated the friendship of such writers as Paul **Alverdes**, Georg **Britting** and Ernst **Penzoldt**. Rudolf Alexander **Schröder** held his funeral oration in 1938. The *Gesammelte Werke* (two volumes) appeared in 1954, with *Die Briefe* in 1957.

Blass, Ernst (1890–1939)

Born in Berlin, Blass studied law there and in Heidelberg; he became bank-clerk, film critic and publisher's reader. He was friendly with Kurt **Hiller** and formed with Hiller the *Neuer Club* in 1909; he also read his poetry in the 'Neopathetisches Cabaret'. Blass may be seen as one of the founder members of early expressionism: his first collection of poems, *Die Straßen komme ich entlanggeweht*, appeared in 1912. The tone is generally that of Van **Hoddis** and **Georg Heym**: 'Vormittag' and 'Ende' are typical, with their concatenation of disparate and disturbing images. Blass edited the Heidelberg journal *Die Argonauten* from 1914 to 1921: the emphasis in his poetry shifted from 'Großstadtlyrik' to a style which was manifestly influenced by Stefan **George**, a poet whom Blass greatly admired and upon whom he wrote a dissertation. Blass did not sever his links with Berlin, however, and would later write nostalgically of the 'Café des Westens' and its *habitués*. *Die Gedichte von Trennung und Licht* appeared in 1915, followed by *Die Gedichte von Sommer und Tod* in 1918 and *Der offene Strom* in 1921. Kasimir **Edschmid** praised Blass as being the poet 'der an erster Stelle das Gedicht zu revolutionieren begann'; Kurt Hiller called him 'der erste seit Goethe, der, ohne epigonal zu sein, ganz goethesch wirkt'. The Nazis forbade him to write because of his expressionist poetry; he died almost completely blind. A painting of Ernst Blass by **Kokoschka** hangs in the Kunsthalle, Bremen. The *Sämtliche Gedichte* appeared in 1980.

Blei, Franz (1871–1942)

Blei, a versatile critic, essayist and writer, was most influential in the literary life at the turn of the century, founding various journals, of which *Hyperion* was the most famous. (Blei was also briefly editor of *Die weißen Blätter*.) His ironic stance led him to satirize the literary figures of his day, and his most skilful and amusing book is the *Bestiarium Literaricum*, published in 1920 under the pseudonym 'Dr. Peregrinus Steinhövel' and in a later, more extended edition in 1924 with the title *Das große Bestiarium der modernen Literatur*. This is a brilliant and scurrilous anthology or 'bestiary', which lampoons the European writers of the time, Blei himself included: 'Der Blei ist ein Süßwasserfisch, der sich geschmeidig in allen frischen Wassern tummelt (. . .) Gefangen und in einen Pokal gesteckt, dient er oft Damenboudoirs als

Zimmerschmuck.' An intermediary for French literature, Blei specialized in piquant and erotic writing, frequently with a rococo setting. He had met Oscar Wilde in Paris, translated him and also Beardsley (*Venus und Tannhäuser*). His most famous collections of essays include *Von amoureusen Frauen* (1906), *Die Puderquaste* (1909) and *Der Geist des Rokoko* (1923). Blei also wrote poetry and plays, some conventional (*Der dunkle Weg* (1906) and *Logik des Herzens* (1915)), but *Die Welle*, produced by Hugo **Ball** in the Munich Kammerspiele (1913), with Blei himself acting in it, demonstrated his links with more experimental theatre. Blei's house in Munich became a meeting-place for the literary Bohemia of that city, and Blei became renowned as bibliophile and artistic mentor. He moved to Mallorca in 1933, then, after the Spanish Civil War, to Vienna, Marseilles, Lisbon and finally New York, where he met Hermann **Broch**, Albert **Ehrenstein** and other *émigrés*. He died in Westbury, Long Island. Six volumes of *Vermischte Schriften* were published from 1911 to 1912; the *Schriften in Auswahl*, with an essay by A. P. Gütersloh, appeared in 1960.

Blunck, Hans (1888–1961)

A writer of prose, poetry and plays, Hans Blunck (born in Altona) became identified with *Blut und Boden* literature and the cult of North-German earnestness, mission and superiority. The trilogies *Das werdende Volk* (1920–3), *Die Urvätersaga* (1925–8) and *Märchen von der Niederelbe* (1922–30) continue the tradition of the *Heimat*-novel and contain familiar stereotypes. From 1933 to 1935 Blunck was president of the newly-formed *Reichsschrifttumskammer*; relations between him and Josef **Goebbels** became strained, and Hanns **Johst** replaced him. A ten-volume edition of his writings appeared in 1938: he received the Goethe medal in the same year. Blunck's poetry (*Balladen und Gedichte* (1937) and *Die Sage vom Reich* (1941–2)) is generally undistinguished and extols Teutonic greatness and North-German peasant life. Blunck was pronounced a Nazi sympathizer and collaborator by the Denazification Tribunal in 1949: he insisted that the verdict was unjust. *Buch der Balladen* appeared in 1950, *Unwegsame Zeiten* in 1952 and *Sagen vom Rhein* in 1957. The *Gesammelte Werke in Einzelausgaben* (fifteen vols) appeared from 1950 to 1956; *Dramen und Lustspiele* (two vols), also in 1956; *Das Gesamtwerk* (four vols) between 1960 and 1961. A *Gesellschaft zur Förderung des Werkes von Hans Friedrich Blunck* exists in Plön, Holstein.

Bobrowski, Johannes (1917–65)

Bobrowski was born in Tilsit and grew up in Memel, and all his poetry and much of his prose results from the effort to reconstruct through memory the landscape and childhood experiences of this frontier area, in which Poles,

Lithuanians, Russians and Jews had lived in close proximity for generations. The war took him further east into the Soviet Union, where he remained a POW until 1949, when he settled in East Berlin and became a publisher's reader. Bobrowski was both conservative in his debt to poets such as Klopstock mainly ignored in the twentieth century and, in the context of GDR writing, in his Christian commitment, and modernist in his development of free verse and of a fragmentary prose form which allows several voices and perspectives to emerge. Along with Peter **Huchel** he is a master of the humanized landscape. Despite his circumscribed themes his influence is present in the work of several writers, incl. Christa **Wolf**, Helga **Schütz**, Rose **Ausländer** and **Sarah Kirsch**.

Bobrowski wrote his earliest poems as a soldier in Russia, some of which appeared in the periodical *Das Innere Reich* before the end of the war, but the majority of his poems can be dated to the years 1954–62. The award in the latter year of the prize of *Gruppe 47* after his second reading before the group and the publication of his first collection *Sarmatische Zeit* (1961) made him known in the West. Other collections followed, three of them posthumous (*Schattenland Ströme* (1962), *Wetterzeichen* (1967, 1980), *Im Windgesträuch* (1970), *Literarisches Klima. Ganz neue Xenien* (1977), the last a series of satirical epigrams on figures in the contemporary German literary landscape). Bobrowski's novels *Levins Mühle. 34 Sätze über meinen Großvater* (1964) and *Litauische Klaviere* (1966) are set in 1874 and 1936 respectively, i.e. in periods of strong German nationalist sentiment and consequent communal tension in his homeland, of which the second, with its stress on the healing power of art and its utopian ending, is the more conciliatory. His thirty-six stories are collected in *Mäusefest und andere Erzählungen* (1965), *Boehlendorff und andere Erzählungen* (1965) and *Der Mahner* (1967), and a four-volume complete edition, *Gesammelte Werke*, ed. E. Haufe, appeared from 1987.

Böll, Heinrich (1917–85)

Böll is not only the sixth German to receive the Nobel Prize for literature (and the first of German nationality since **Thomas Mann** in 1929), he can also be considered the most internationally famous post-war West German writer, his sales having reached seventeen million in 1977. The attitudes which find consistent expression in both his fiction and his public writings (e.g. *Hierzulande* (1963), *Neue politische und literarische Schriften* (1973), *Einmischung erwünscht* (1977), *Vermintes Gelände* (1982), *Ein- und Zusprüche* (1984), *Die Fähigkeit zu trauern* (1986)) have their roots in the nonconformity ('anarchism', to use his own term) of his Cologne petty bourgeois family, his Catholicism and his experience of the war (mainly on the Russian front) as an ordinary infantry recruit throughout its duration. Anti-fascism inspired by left-wing Catholicism was an unconventional and, in view of Adenauer's status, an unpopular position before the advent of liberation theology, but it is to be found in his work from the beginning of his career and may be summed up in the phrase 'die subversive Madonna' (the title of a critical account of his work).

The early short stories *Wanderer, kommst du nach Spa . . .* (1950), *Die Verwundung* (1983, but written in the late 1940s) and the novels and longer stories *Der Zug war pünktlich* (1949), *Wo warst du, Adam?* (1951), *Das Vermächtnis* (1982, but written 1947–8) belong firmly to the 'Kahlschlag' phase of the post-war period, which he supported in the essay 'Bekenntnis zur Trümmerliteratur' (1952). All present the senselessness of war by adopting the perspective of the ordinary soldier whose only escape from the horrors of combat, the total subordination to his superiors and the soul-destroying boredom of military routine is the memory or fantasy of private happiness. Böll adopts in *Der Zug war pünktlich* the technique of inner monologue which he develops further in *Ansichten eines Clowns* and combines with multiple narrative perspectives in *Billard um halb zehn* and the semi-dramatic form of *Frauen vor Flußlandschaft*, while the portrayal of the military system as a machine beyond human control destroying its servants looks forward to other images of futility such as the statistical work in the story 'An der Brücke', the vision of a society in which the function of packaging is to ensure an endless supply of litter in the story 'Der Wegwerfer', and the revolving wheels of the jacked-up jeep in the novel *Ende einer Dienstfahrt* (1966).

In the 1950s Böll turns to the domestic and social problems of the transition from the material shortages and political vacuum of the 'Trümmerjahre' to the brash commercialism and political stagnation of the 'Wirtschaftswunderjahre'. In *Und sagte kein einziges Wort* (1953) the predicament of the soldier come home, forced by inadequate housing to meet his wife in hotel rooms, is exacerbated by the unsympathetic attitude of the better off and contrasted with ecclesiastical pomp and tasteless advertising. Here the narrative is assigned to man and wife alternately, a technique elaborated in *Haus ohne Hüter, Billard um halb zehn, Gruppen-bild mit Dame* and *Fürsorgliche Belagerung*. In *Haus ohne Hüter* (1954) two boys, whose fathers have died in the war, fail to find understanding from their mothers who attempt to escape their fear of the present by means of nostalgia or a series of casual affairs. *Das Brot der frühen Jahre* (1955) is a love-story confined to a single day in which the empty life of a young man, whose humdrum job, repairing washing-machines, has followed a deprived childhood symbolized by hunger for bread, is transformed by his meeting with his future wife. Satire of the materialism and frenetic activity of the economic miracle finds expression in *Doktor Murkes gesammeltes Schweigen und andere Satiren* (1958), while Böll's growing awareness of a conflict between private and institutional catholicism, present already in the 'Brief an einen jungen Katholiken' (1958), is conveyed through the nonconformity of the clown Hans Schnier, whose perspective dominates the next novel *Ansichten eines Clowns* (1963), revealing him as the isolated opponent of a church-state alliance and of the upper middle class which provides it with solid support. In *Billard um halb zehn* (1958) the seventieth birthday of the architect Heinrich Fähmel, which coincides with the dedication of an abbey rebuilt by his grandson Joseph, forms the framework for a series of reminiscences by Heinrich and members of his family, which trace the fortunes of three generations and their involvement with or resistance to Nazism and the war. The abbey Heinrich had built in 1908 is destroyed by his son Robert in 1945 as a protest against the church's acceptance of the regime, while other forms of resistance are represented by the flight into madness of Heinrich's wife Johanna and the activities of Robert's school-friends. The dramatic sequence of events in the narrative present culminates in Johanna's attempt to assassinate an official guest at the birthday party and the decision by Robert to adopt Hugo, the lift-boy with whom he regularly plays billiards, and bequeath to him the Fähmel property.

Böll returns to light satire in *Ende einer Dienstfahrt*, in which protest against the military is masked as a happening, which takes the form of setting on fire a Bundeswehr jeep, a claim upheld by the court on secret instructions from above when those responsible, a carpenter and his son, are brought to trial. Böll's most substantial novel, *Gruppenbild mit Dame* (1971), reconstructs the life of Leni Pfeiffer, a living symbol of his most cherished values, by means of interviews conducted by the narrator, whose attitude of impersonal pedantry is conveyed by the abbreviation 'Verf.', with more than twenty persons who knew her. Their accounts, in throwing light on the separate stages of her biography, add up to a panorama of the period 1936 to 1966, placing *Gruppenbild* firmly in the tradition of the *Zeitroman*.

The seventies brought with them a series of events which put severe pressure on Böll's ideal of a community moulded by the personal spontaneous morality of its members and free from interference by institutions. Acts of terrorism by the *Rote Armee Fraktion* (better known as the Baader-Meinhof group) forced the authorities in the Federal Republic to mobilize state power to an extent unprecedented in its history in order to arrest, try and convict them. While the anti-terrorist campaign undoubtedly had the support of public opinion, it occasionally led to excesses which undermined rights guaranteed by the constitution as those suspected of sympathizing with or sheltering terrorists were subjected to police surveillance and vilified by sections of the press. After Böll had criticized the attitude to the Baader-Meinhof group maintained by the *Bild Zeitung*, West Germany's principal tabloid, he found himself branded as a 'Sympathisant'. He responded with three works: *Die verlorene Ehre der Katharina Blum oder: Wie Gewalt entstehen und wohin sie führen kann* (1974), *Berichte zur Gesinnungslage der Nation* (1975) and *Fürsorgliche Belagerung* (1979), in which his targets are the police, the press and the secret service, in the last instance the general atmosphere of paranoia and mistrust fostered by the activities of all three and its corrupting effect on personal relations. Also in *Fürsorgliche Belagerung* Böll over-simplifies political tensions within a constellation of characters similar to that of *Billard um halb zehn*, just as in his last posthumously published novel or 'Lesedrama' *Frauen vor Flußlandschaft* (1985) he gathers together and repeats topoi of several earlier works no longer valid in a more complex age. In *Die verlorene Ehre der Katharina Blum*, however, he combines a devastating critique of witch-hunting journalism's invasion of the private sphere with another portrait of female integrity and a tense, carefully constructed plot.

Böll rejected the phrase 'conscience of the nation' as a description of his work as 'Moral und Ästhetik erweisen sich als kongruent, untrennbar'. For all his faults, parochialism, sentimentality, black-and-white characterization, he demonstrated that the novel is still able to show how people relate to one another as members of a family, a community and a nation.

A collected edition, *Werke* in ten volumes, appeared in 1978.

Bonsels, Waldemar (1880–1952)

Traveller, publisher and writer of popular novels and stories, Bonsels made his reputation with *Die Biene Maja und ihre Abenteuer* (1912), a charming account of a queen bee and the adventures that befall it. Bonsels had attempted serious novels (*Blut* (1909) and *Der tiefste Traum* (1911)), but felt more at east with naïve portrayals of the natural world. For a time he had been associated with writers connected with expressionism (he also published Heinrich Bachmair's book on Detlev von Liliencron), but was aware of the facile nature of his own writing and became unashamedly a popular writer. His *Indienfahrt* (1916) continued the example set by Melchior Lechter (designer for the typeface and for illustrations of Stefan George's poetry) and Hermann Graf Keyserling, both of whom had visited the subcontinent. *Das Anjekind* (1913) and *Himmelsvolk* (1915), the latter being 'Ein Buch von Blumen, Tieren und Gott' were, like *Die Biene Maja*, enormously successful, appealing above all to those who delighted in fanciful (and fey) descriptions of nature. Bonsels was greeted thus by the *Münchener Zeitung*: 'Weil in ihm die Sehnsucht nach Erneuerung des Lebens Stimme wird, und er zugleich als wirklicher Dichter seine Sehnsucht zu Gestalten zu zwingen vermag, – deshalb grüßen wir Waldemar Bonsels als einen Pfadfinder zu neuen Zielen.' Bonsels's pantheism gave way in later life to a confused nature-mysticism. A year before his death he republished, under the title *Das vergessene Licht*, an earlier pseudo-Christian novel.

Borchardt, Rudolf (1877–1945)

An author remembered for his essays and translations, Borchardt was one of a group of writers (R. A. **Schröder** was another) who insisted upon a conservative, classical stance in his approach to literature. The neo-romantic aspects of his earlier poetry (*Jugendgedichte* (1913)) increasingly gave way to classical forms. Borchardt was an accomplished linguist and translated from Greek, English and Italian: his *Dante Deutsch* (1922–30) is an acknowledged masterpiece. Borchardt was a close associate of Hugo von **Hofmannsthal**. His *Rede über Hofmannsthal* was published in 1905, although his vehement and frequently uncompromising insistence on formal perfection and literary excellence was not always expressed with tact, and Hofmannsthal did not always feel at ease in his presence. The essay *Gegen das Moderne*, with its indiscriminate attack on all modern developments in literature (the terms

'Fäule' and 'Siechtum' occur frequently) is reminiscent of Max Nordau. *Vermischte Gedichte* appeared in 1924. Borchardt had little dramatic talent, and his plays (including *Päpstin Jutta* (1920) and *Die Staufer* (1936)) were unsuccessful. Like Hofmannsthal, Borchardt insisted upon a 'conservative revolution' (this is expressed in the essay *Die Aufgaben der Zeit gegenüber der Literatur* (1929)), and used terminology which, in its reactionary earnestness, contains a somewhat dubious ring. The novel *Vereinigung durch den Feind hindurch* (1937) was published in Vienna: the title refers to an essay on military tactics. Borchardt, who was partly Jewish, was arrested by the Gestapo, but later released; he died in the Tyrol at the end of the war. The *Gesammelte Werke in Einzelbänden* (fourteen so far) appeared from 1955 to 1982; the *Gesammelte Erzählungen* (three vols) in 1977.

Borchert, Wolfgang (1921–47)

Borchert, an unwilling soldier from 1941, suffered periods of imprisonment under the Nazis, the rigours of which contributed to his early death one day before the première on 21 November 1947 of his sole play *Draußen vor der Tür* (a radio version having been heard on 13 February of the same year). This evocation of the social and existential solitude of the soldier come home, Hans Beckmann, also introduces the allegorical figures of death, the river Elbe and God as well as 'der Andere', Beckmann's positive *alter ego*. After these, together with real persons – a girl, his colonel, a theatre manager, the repulsive Frau Kramer, all of whom have left him 'draußen vor der Tür' – pass by him in a closing vision, Beckmann remains without an answer to his questions and without the hope inspired by 'der Andere' which had prevented a return to thoughts of suicide. Beckmann is intended to represent Borchert's own generation whose aspirations he expressed in programmatic statements such as 'Das ist unser Manifest'.

Borchert's short stories can be divided according to theme (war in 'Vier Soldaten', 'Jesus macht nicht mehr mit', 'An diesem Dienstag'; homecoming in 'Die drei dunklen Könige', 'Die lange lange Straße lang', 'Der Kaffee ist undefinierbar'; imprisonment in 'Schischyphusch', 'Die Kirschen', 'Der Rahmbonbon') or according to their formal characteristics (stories with conventional structure and stories which are more impressionistic and reflective). He also wrote numerous poems, only a few of which were eventually published.

Borchert was a transitional figure, the initiator and archetype of the 'Kahlschlag' phase of literature after the Second World War and at the same time one whose debt to expressionism is evident in his rhetoric and in his adoption of the quest theme presented in a series of stations.

Das Gesamtwerk (1949) brings together all Borchert's published work (the poems *Laterne, Nacht und Sterne* (1946), the stories *Die Hundeblume* (1947), *An diesem Dienstag* (1947) and the play), and some unpublished stories and poems. *Die traurigen Geranien* (1962) made available further unpublished material.

Born, Nicolas (1937–79)

Born was one of fifteen authors who contributed to *Das Gästehaus* (1965), a project initiated by Walter **Höllerer**. His first novel *Der zweite Tag* (1965), in which the impressions received on a train journey are registered in minute detail, bare of symbol and metaphor, can be associated with the Cologne school of realism (including **Wellershoff**, **Herburger**, **Elsner**). The poems, eventually collected in *Gedichte 1967–1978* (1981), show the influence of the Americans W. C. Williams, Robert Creeley and Frank O'Hara (cf. **Brinkmann**), place the clichés of politics and the media in a personal context or contain snapshots of everyday life or memories of past experiences and deceased friends. Politics, reflection on the function of poetry and moments of satisfaction and hope contrasted with fear of the impersonal forces of the state are further topics in the later poems.

Born's other novels, *Die erdabgewandte Seite der Geschichte* (1976) and *Die Fälschung* (1979) both suffer from uncontrolled emotional impressionism, the former in its concentration on the shipwreck of the narrator's personal relations, a German variant of the psychological introspection which characterized much writing in the 1970s. *Die Fälschung*, however (successfully filmed by Volker Schlöndorf in 1981), convincingly links the private and professional problems of its central figure, a journalist, and the confused inferno of the civil wars in Lebanon. In taking up a Third World theme, it marks a significant departure from what was in danger of becoming a new provincialism and can be compared with similar works by Uwe **Timm** and F. C. **Delius**.

Brasch, Thomas (1945–)

Brasch was born in Britain, where his Jewish communist parents spent the war years. His early life in the GDR, where his father became a prominent SED functionary, was marked by the conflict of a vital, anarchistic talent with prevailing aesthetic and social norms and is partly reflected in variations on the generation gap (*Vor den Vätern sterben die Söhne* (1977)). A resemblance to Büchner, expressionism and the early **Brecht** is apparent in the poems (eventually published in *Der schöne 27. September* (1980)), prose (*Vor den Vätern* and *Kargo* (1977), both collections of anecdotal prose fragments) and dramas Brasch brought with him to the West in 1976 following the expatriation of Wolf **Biermann**. The play *Rotter* (1977) concerns the self-imposed conformity of an under-privileged figure determined to prove himself in both the Third Reich and the early years of reconstruction. Brasch's treatment of a common theme of GDR literature owes much to Heiner **Müller** and a dramatic tradition which includes surrealism and the Theatre of Cruelty in its development of possibilities beyond Brecht's epic theatre. The move to the West has not resulted in any firm political commitments and the rebellion of Brasch's characters, many of whom are disturbed artists, drop-outs and criminals (the poet Georg Heym in *Lieber Georg* (1980), Lackner in *Rotter*, Rita in *Lovely Rita* (1977)) is more existentially than politically motivated. Brasch has more recently concentrated on adaptations (Shakespeare, Chekhov) and films (*Engel aus Eisen* (1981), *Domino* (1982), *Welcome to Germany/Der Passagier* (1988)).

Braun, Felix (1885–1973)

A fervent literary disciple of **Hofmannsthal**, Felix Braun was a minor writer associated with the Viennese cultural scene at the turn of the century (his autobiography *Das Licht der Welt. Geschichte eines Versuches, als Dichter zu leben* (1949) gives a sympathetic and informative account of meetings with Hofmannsthal, **Rilke**, **Wildgans**, **Ginzkey**, **Mell**, **Stefan Zweig**, **Werfel** and others). Braun's poetry is quintessentially neo-romantic: collections such as *Gedichte* (1909) and *Das Haus der Berenike* (1919) extol the inner world of beauty at the expense of the outer ('Geheimnis, dessen Sinn ich nie verstand:/Sich über Worte atemlos zu neigen/Und zu vernehmen in gespanntem Schweigen,/Was einer dachte, fühlte und erfand'). In 1953 Braun published his collected poems under the title *Viola d'amore*. He travelled widely, living in Italy and also in exile in England. His verse dramas betray much sensitivity but little dramatic talent: themes are derived from classical antiquity (*Tantalos* (1917), *Aktaion* (1921) and *Der Tod des Aischylos* (1946)) and from the history of the house of Habsburg (*Kaiser Karl V* and *Rudolf der Stifter*). Braun's most ambitious prose work is *Agnes Altkirchner* (1927, renamed *Herbst des Reiches* in 1959), a detailed portrayal of the Austro-Hungarian Empire in the years between 1913 and 1919. Braun was also an accomplished anthologist: *Der tausendjährige Rosenstrauch* (1948) and *Die Lyra des Orpheus* (1952). His *Ausgewählte Dramen* appeared in two volumes between 1955 and 1960; a selection of his work, *Unerbittbar bleibt Vergangenheit*, was published in 1957. Braun's sister, Käthe Braun-Prager, published translations, delicate poetry and collections of aphorisms (*Reise in die Nähe* (1954)).

Braun, Volker (1939–)

Braun's importance lies in his successful cultivation of all three major genres and in his concern to contribute to a more humane and genuinely democratic socialism in the GDR. His early poems (*Provokation für mich* (1965), an extended version of which appeared with the title *Vorläufiges* in the Federal Republic in the same year) proclaimed attitudes and described experiences typical of the first generation to grow up in the GDR without direct awareness of the Third Reich or the West. The collections *Wir und nicht sie* (1970), *Gedichte* (1972, extended 1976) and *Gegen die symmetrische Welt* (1974) are marked by mastery of numerous short forms and a critical dialogue with earlier German poets. *Training des aufrechten Gangs* (1979) and *Langsamer knirschender Morgen* (1987) show a predilection for longer cyclic forms mixing verse and prose, which allow a more tentative process of self-examination combined with a wide-ranging exploration of man's nature and prospects as a social being. The dialectic of past and present, of utopian hope and reality is treated in manifold variations, culminating in the last volume in fragmentary forms which appear to reflect a fear of stagnation.

The stories 'Der Schlamm', 'Der Hörsaal' (1964) and 'Die Bretter' (1968), collected in *Das ungezwungene Leben Knasts* (1972, extended 1979 by the addition of 'Die Tribüne') are based on personal experience as a worker and student and mark a break with the earlier 'Aufbauliteratur' and the work which emerged from the Bitterfeld movement. *Unvollendete Geschichte* (1975) is still more openly critical of government mistrust of the people; its publication in the GDR's leading literary periodical *Sinn und Form* was one of the earliest signs of a change in policy at the top adumbrated in Honecker's programmatic anti-taboos speech of 1971.

Braun's early dramas, like those of **Hacks** and Heiner **Müller**, adapt the forms and themes of **Brecht** to similar historical situations (e.g. *Der große Frieden* (1979), set in ancient China, builds on *Turandot*) or to the problems faced by the worker in the industrial process after the transition to socialism in the GDR (*Kipper Paul Bauch* (1966, revised as *Die Kipper* 1972), *Tinka* (1975), *Schmitten* (1981)). More recently he has widened this latter theme to embrace revolutionary change elsewhere and at different periods and developed more radical approaches to it: in *Guevara* (1978) the story of Che is told in reverse, *Simplex Deutsch* (1980) owes as much to Brecht and Beckett as to Grimmelshausen, and *Lenins Tod*, although written in 1970, received its première only in 1988. The perpetuation of the master-servant relationship in 'der real existierende Sozialismus' is present in all Braun's treatments of the Hinze Kunze theme: the play *Hinze und Kunze* (1973, originally called *Hans Faust*), the prose anecdotes *Berichte von Hinze und Kunze* (1983) and the *Hinze-Kunze-Roman* (1985), while similar authoritarian structures as found in the context of industrial employment are linked to sexual relationships in *Tinka* and *Schmitten*, whose eponymous heroines, like Lisa Hinze in the novel, testify to Braun's growing interest in feminist issues. His continuing debt to his literary predecessors is evident in his other plays: *Dmitri* (1982), a Brechtian reworking of Schiller's last incomplete play on the Russian pretender, *Übergangsgesellschaft* (1987), based on Chekhov, and *Transit Europa* (1988), based on Anna **Seghers**'s novel *Transit*.

Brecht, Bertolt (1898–1956)

Brecht was one of a group of young dramatists who emerged during the early years of the Weimar Republic and whose works (frequently awarded the Kleist prize) created theatrical scandals by their fearless outspokenness and reluctance to conform to accepted standards. *Baal* (1918, first performed in 1923) derives from Hanns **Johst**, particularly the latter's *Der Einsame*, but eschews pathos and hyperbole to a large extent: the brutal vigour of the language, the **Wedekind**-like ballads and the anarchic tendency make it very much a young man's play. Through collaboration with **Feuchtwanger** and others Brecht, with cunning and undeniable talent, kept abreast of the modern techniques of a man like Piscator, and produced a corpus of work which was to mark a watershed in Weimar theatrical history. As the *enfant terrible* of Berlin, Brecht, abrasive, cynical, witty and nonchalant in turn, deliberately rejected all the manifestations of bourgeois culture, particularly the naturalist's 'well made play'; he also scorned the formlessness, rodomontade and pretentiousness of much expressionist writing, although certain of the anti-illusionist techniques he later perfected were derived from writers like Georg **Kaiser**. The hero with a vision was ousted by the cynical Kragler in *Trommeln in der Nacht* (1923); the expressionist 'Stationendrama' gave way to a balladesque, almost flippant, structure; the baleful moon falls from the stage, an obvious prop. The exhortation 'Glotzt nicht so romantisch!' was a deliberate attempt to break any sense of illusion and later, more subtle, alienation techniques would encourage the stimulation of critical thought. Leaving behind those plays which extolled individuality above all else and which portrayed struggles to communicate in a hostile and even absurd environment (such as *Im Dickicht der Städte* (1923) with its obvious echoes of Upton Sinclair's novel of Chicago life *The Jungle*, and the adaptation, with Feuchtwanger, of Marlowe's *Life of Edward II of England*), Brecht turned increasingly towards a Marxist interpretation of human life: the loss of a certain exuberance, particularly at the beginning of the 1930s, was the price he had to pay for a growth of ideological commitment. Brecht's greatest success during the years of the Weimar Republic was *Die Dreigroschenoper* (1928); this play, together with Carl **Zuckmayer**'s *Der fröhliche Weinberg* (which anticipates Brecht's later play *Herr Puntila und sein Knecht Matti* (1948)) was the most famous theatrical event of the 1920s. This adaptation of John Gay's *A Beggar's Opera*, plus ballads derived from Kipling and Villon, owes much of its success to Kurt Weill's music, but the grotesque *Moritat*, with its cheeky equation of capitalism and criminality, is very much Brecht's own. It was after the enormous success of this work, a work that the audience seemed bent on enjoying at all costs, that Brecht tended to the extremes of dogmatism which he felt were necessary to convey his social message: the need for a new society, free from exploitation and privilege. Fortunately this period was a transient one, and the well-rounded, plausible, deeply human characters that his dramatic flair never tired of creating asserted themselves after the cardboard sterility of the *Lehrstücke*. What makes *Mann ist Mann* (1926), the *Dreigroschenoper* and *Aufstieg und Fall der Stadt Mahagony* (1928–9) such good entertainment is the plenitude of ebullient characters, rooted in a fantastic Victorian, Anglo-American (or Anglo-Indian) world never found in reality but culled from the legends of the roaring twenties, or the heyday of the British Raj; Brecht never ceased to admire the world of boxers, lumberjacks, colonial soldiers and gangsters, which he may, in part, have derived from the expressionist cult of vital, atavistic forces. The theme of survival, likewise, is a central one for Brecht, found from *Baal* through to *Galilei*; tragic inevitability was alien to Brecht, for whom metamorphosis, development and change preclude dramatic clash, and 'epic' theatre, with its working out of a particular fable, was seen as providing a far more satisfactory mode of portrayal than conventional drama. Brecht needed also the stimulus of collaboration, which stemmed from a sincere desire to discuss and learn rather than from paucity of invention, as the critic Alfred Kerr claimed, who sought constantly to detect plagiarism. Brecht wrote closely with **Klabund**, who would later give Brecht the idea for *Der kaukasische Kreidekreis*. Brecht's first book of poetry, *Die Hauspostille* (1927), parodies the popular anthologies of such writers as J. P. Hebel with their moralizing homilies; Brecht's tone is cynical, modern, *sachlich* and urban, his realism oblique to the real.

The increasingly Marxist tendency of Brecht's work in the early 1930s meant that flight was inevitable (he was fifth on the Nazi blacklist); the dramatic cantata *Die Maßnahme* (1930) testified to the need to obliterate individuality should the work of the Communist party be jeopardized. The adaptation of Gorki's *Mutter*, performed early in 1932 under great difficulty, was overtly propagandistic; the film *Kuhle Wampe* (also 1932) was immediately banned by the government because of its uncompromising portrayal of the life of the unemployed. After the burning of the Reichstag Brecht fled to Vienna; he attended the meeting at Sanary-sur-mer of exiled writers, and thence moved to Denmark, to the province of Svendborg, where he watched events in Germany most closely. Brecht continued to work relentlessly: 'Das Entsetzen über die Reden des Anstreichers' (i.e. Hitler), described in the poem 'Schlechte Zeiten für Lyrik', kept him at his writing-desk in an unceasing vigil. The resultant works range from the tediously predictable *Die Rundköpfe und die Spitzköpfe* (1933–4) and *Die Horatier und die Kuriatier* (1934) through the successful description of fear, menace and betrayal (*Furcht und Elend des Dritten Reiches* (1935–8)) to the undisputed masterpieces written between 1939 and 1945 which, due to a parabolic approach, achieve universality and greatness. The view that Brecht, deprived of a theatre, turned his attention to formulating a Marxist aesthetic of drama, a theoretically determined system, is erroneous: the subsequent theorizing was an attempt to explain to himself as well as to others how it happened that this or that particular work had been written and produced in a particular way. His theoretical writings reflect the way in which he meditated upon his own work: there is nothing rigid nor inflexibly ideological about his speculation. The tone is light, frequently wryly humorous, often curious, but always allowing for movement and renewal; a rare intelligence is at work which questions, worries, retreats, adapts and restates. Theatre, literature and politics, society and even landscape are discussed: Brecht's *alter ego*, Herr Keuner, examines his own personal attitudes, and Ziffel and Kalle, the refugees of the *Flüchtlingsgespräche*, range in their discussions from the mentality of 'Wieheißterdochgleich', the then ruler of the German people, to military virtues, passports, *Ordnung* and the potential for humorous irreverence latent within Hegelian dialectics. The *Messingkauf* dialogues, a four-handed conversation piece, relate more directly to theatrical problems, and stress above all the need for lightness of touch, *Spiel*, and a kind of elegance in acting which contains sobriety within it. The rapier thrust is preferred to the sabre blow, the elliptical precision of Chinese art to Germanic ponderousness and an athletic form of acting to the pretentiously histrionic.

In 1940 Brecht left Europe for America; in the following year the *Zürcher Schauspielhaus* staged his *Mutter Courage und ihre Kinder*, a 'Chronik aus dem dreißigjährigen Krieg'. This was to be the play with which the *Berliner Ensemble* opened in 1948; it has remained in the repertoire ever since and has been staged by the leading theatres throughout the world. It provides an excellent example of 'epic theatre', that form of theatre which eschews Aristotelian forms of drama and concentrates instead upon a 'Fabel', a tale which narrates and offers a nucleus for possible discussion. In the *Kleines Organon für das Theater* (1948) Brecht insisted upon the importance of this 'Fabel' ('Auf die Fabel kommt alles an, sie ist das Herzstück der theatralischen Veranstaltung'). 'Spruchbänder' stretched across the stage provide the various 'chapter' headings. The importance of alienation is found here in the choice of historical subject, in the encouragement to the actors to 'imitate' and 'represent' their parts, rather than identifying with them, and by the use of songs (music by Paul Burkhard, later Paul Dessau) to interrupt the action and drive the several points home. Every scene, and there are twelve of them, is supposed to stand as a self-contained unit (indeed, in theory they should be virtually interchangeable), but a cumulative effect is undeniable, and there are moments that are conventionally dramatic, which enthral, rather than alienate, the audience. At the climax of Brecht's creativity magnificently observed characters are brought to life, characters as well drawn as the best of those of **Gerhart Hauptmann**. Yet the audience, composed of 'Kinder des wissenschaftlichen Zeitalters', must assess Mother Courage's actions and motives coolly and impartially. Brecht did not approve of the reactions of the audience after the first performance: in notes to the play he added certain modifications which were intended to emphasize the more negative qualities of the central character. 'Dem Stückeschreiber (his favourite term for 'playwright') obliegt es nicht, die Courage am Ende sehend zu machen . . . ihm kommt es darauf an, daß der Zuschauer sieht.'

In his 'Aus einem Brief an einen Schauspieler' Brecht himself admitted that several misconceptions had arisen concerning his theoretical practices. He had been forced, he claimed, to overstate the differences between the conventional theatre and his own in order that certain abuses be rectified: there was nothing sacrosanct or dogmatic about his suggestions. As early as *Aufstieg und Fall der Stadt Mahagony* he had, in fact, stressed that an overschematic differentiation between dramatic and epic was unsuitable: it was simply a matter of emphasis. In 1937 he had written a conventional play – admittedly not one of his best – on Aristotelian lines, *Die Gewehre der Frau Carrar*, which provided opportunity for splendid acting on the part of the heroine. Brecht turned on the critics and admonished them to look at his plays *as plays*, without preconceived ideas or theories. The year 1943 saw a performance of two plays in Zurich which demonstrated once more Brecht's skill in creating memorable characters, roles which have entered the standard theatrical repertoire: the heroine of *Der gute Mensch von Sezuan* and Galileo in *Das Leben des Galilei*. The former, a parable play set in modern China, deals with the virtual impossibility of doing good in this world; the kindness of Shen Te has to be tempered by the ruthlessness of Shui Ta, her 'other self', to prevent the importunate demands of spongers and parasites. Brecht utterly rejected the Christian idea of original sin: it is the nature of man to be good ('freundlich' is an epithet used with ever greater frequency in his later works); the poem 'Die Maske des Bösen' emphasises this. The epilogue to *Der gute Mensch von Sezuan* exhorts the audience to think of a better solution to the play, which terminates in Shen Te's despair at not being able to meet the conflicting demands of charity and self-survival; a society which has not found a solution to this must make way for one which can. *Leben des Galilei* had been admired as Brecht's masterpiece; he worked at it intermittently for over seventeen years. His initial concern was to show Galileo as a man determined to live, whose cunning recantation enables the truth to be heard despite the strictures of the Church. Yet Brecht's faith in the ultimate triumph of reason suffered a severe setback at the time of the exploding of the atomic bomb; with its detonation Brecht saw that the submission of the scientist to the state could have fearful consequences. In the third version of the play Galileo, in a crucial declaration, explains what submission (previously a virtue in Brecht's eyes) could mean, and what knowledge divorced from morality must lead to. The issues are intellectual, but the play provides magnificent theatre, especially in the scene of the dressing of the Pope, the transformation of man to institution as each layer of clothing is added. Brecht chose to ignore the obviously dramatic scene, that of the recantation itself (normally used as a climax as, for example, in Jakob Bührer's *Galileo Galilei* (1933)), but the sense of dramatic inevitability which accompanies the action shows yet again that Brecht did not adhere to any rigid scheme of 'epic theatre': he created living characters in conflict at a crucial time of man's intellectual history.

Brecht's *Arbeitsjournal* (published 1973) and his return to poetry to express a more personal reaction to the world around him reflect his misgivings and sense of crisis at this time. The Soviet purges sickened him, as did the American situation: the work on the film *Hangmen also die* with Fritz Lang made him entirely disillusioned with the American film industry. There is undoubtedly a sense of isolation, but not of paralysis: he reworked the *Galileo* material and took over Hašek's figure of *The Good Soldier Sveyk* to exemplify yet again (in *Schweik im Zweiten Weltkrieg* (1941–4)) the need for survival and cunning; he turned to the American underworld to see a parallel between Hitler and Arturo Ui, a Capone-like gangster (in *Der aufhaltsame Aufstieg des Arturo Ui* (1941)); he had brought from Finland *Herr Puntila und sein Knecht Matti*, a rumbustious portrayal of the drunken landowner who completely steals the play; he worked with Feuchtwanger again on *Die Gesichte der Simone Machard* (1941–3), another St Joan travesty, as had been *Die heilige Johanna der Schlachthöfe* (1930). But the most tender and perennially successful of the plays which he wrote in the mid-1940s was *Der kaukasische Kreidekreis* (1944–5), based on Klabund's adaptation of the old Chinese tale. The theme of goodness occupied him once again, but the basic theme concerns the rightness of giving the child, or the disputed land to those best able to tend or cultivate it. The play is most successful in the portrayal of the judge Azdak, a figure compounded of the vitality and amoral zest of Baal, of Puntila and, to a lesser extent, of Galileo himself.

Brecht returned to Europe at the end of 1947. The setting up of his own *Theater am Schiffbauerdamm* brought little comfort: the *Berliner Ensemble* was boycotted by the orthodox critics, the workers made up only a small percentage of the audience, and government pressure was brought to bear at every point. *Das Verhör des Lukullus*, which Brecht had written in 1939 and which condemned war, had to be modified at the behest of the authorities who demanded that war against aggressors be permitted, indeed praised. It is perhaps significant that Brecht wrote nothing of original merit for the theatre after his return to East Berlin; he adapted, produced and modified, turning his attention, amongst other things, to *Waiting for Godot* and *Pineapple Poll*. He withdrew again into poetry and wrote, in the *Buckower Elegien*, some of his finest. With economy, grace and sobriety he evoked a world of trees and water, silence and serenity, far from the turmoil of Berlin. Before his premature death in 1956 he had suggested that his epitaph might contain the lines: 'Er hat Vorschläge gemacht, Wir/haben sie angenommen.'

Brecht's influence on the theatre has been enormous. His narrative prose is best exemplified by the short stories *Kalendergeschichten* (1949) and *Geschichten von Herrn Keuner* (1958); the novels *Dreigroschenroman* (1934) and *Die Geschäfte des Herrn Julius Caesar* (1957) are uneven and, apart from flashes of wit, undistinguished. The collections of poetry (*Die Hauspostille* (1927), *Svendborger Gedichte* (1939) and *Buckower Elegien* (1953)) are of a consistently high standard, ranging from 'Gebrauchslyrik' to haiku and tanaka. His theoretical writings may be rated alongside Schiller's and Richard Wagner's as those of a man obsessed with the potentialities of the theatre. The following editions of his work should be noted: *Versuche* (fifteen vols, 1930–57); *Stücke* (fourteen vols, 1953–67); *Sinn und Form Sonderhefte* (1949 and 1957); *Gedichte* (nine vols, 1960–9); *Gesammelte Gedichte* (four vols, 1976; ten vols, 1960–76); *Gedichte aus dem Nachlaß* (two vols, 1982); *Schriften zum Theater* (seven vols, 1963f); *Prosa* (five vols, 1965); *Gesammelte Werke* (twenty vols, 1976) (an eight-volume edition appeared also in 1967); *Werke* (five vols, 1973); *Die Stücke* (four vols, 1978); *Gesammelte Prosa* (four vols, 1980); *Gedichte über die Liebe* in 1982; *Texte für Filme* (1969); *Tagebücher 1920–1922. Autobiographische Aufzeichnungen 1920–1954* (1978); *Werke (Große kommentierte Berliner und Frankfurter Ausgabe)* (1988–).

Brinkmann, Rolf Dieter (1940–75)

Brinkmann, whose early death in a road accident on a visit to London put an end to a career which may or may not have been in the doldrums, began in association with the Cologne realists (**Wellershoff**, **Herburger**, **Elsner**, etc.) and developed quickly during the 1960s to become Germany's principal advocate of American pop culture (especially in the poems of *Die Piloten* (1968), in the translation of Frank O'Hara's *Lunch Poems* (1969) and in the anthologies *ACID* (1969, with Ralf-Rainer Rygulla) and *Silver Screen* (1969)) and the *poète maudit* of the German alternative scene. Never political, he combined crude vitalism, linguistic virtuosity and an obsession with the surface detail of everyday life; only the last of these features, however, was taken up and developed by others (e.g. **Born, Theobaldy, Jürgen Becker**). While his poetry already seems dated and undisciplined, his final major prose work *Rom.Blicke* (1979) may prove to be a seminal work in its combination of verbal and photographic commentary, besides maintaining the strong German tradition of literature portraying the metropolis.

Britting, Georg (1891–1964)

Poet, playwright and writer of narrative prose, Britting started to write after the First World War (he was badly wounded in 1918). He collaborated on many expressionist journals (*Die rote Erde*, *Der Sturmreiter*, *Der silberne Spiegel*) and edited his own, *Die Sichel*, with Josef Achmann who contributed the graphic designs. Britting greatly admired **Georg Heym**; he also wrote grotesque versions of biblical themes (*Hiob*, *Kain*, *Jor auf der Flucht* etc.). A one-act play *Der Mann im Mond* (a 'Schattenspiel' (1921)) is a piece of expressionist pantomime-theatre, as is *Das Storchennest* (1923); *Das Herz* ('Ein Tanz auf einem Seil' (1923)) is greatly indebted to **Wedekind**. *Michael und das Fräulein*, a collection of short stories, appeared in 1927; *Gedichte* in 1930. Britting's best-known work is the novel *Lebenslauf eines dicken Mannes, der Hamlet hieß* (1932). Britting provides an 'anti-Hamlet' (one is reminded of Wilhelm Meister's description of a fat Hamlet) who kills Claudius in a 'Freßduell', has a son by Ophelia and finally retires to a monastery. Hamlet's long periods of vegetative apathy anticipate certain passages in Samuel Beckett (*Molloy* in particular). During the Second World War Britting turned increasingly to nature poetry, leaving behind the excesses of expressionism and the parodistic elements of *Hamlet*. *Der irdische Tag* (1935) evokes in striking images the landscape of South Germany ('Bayerischer Sonntag' is a good example). Short stories also appeared: *Der bekränzte Weiher* (1937), *Das gerettete Bild* (1938) and *Der Schneckensweg* (1941) (the picture of the snail which creeps into its shell seemed to Britting to describe his own apolitical stance). *Lob des Weines*, a collection of twenty poems, appeared in 1944: more were added after the war (1947). Britting turned to traditional themes and structures, although his imagery remained fresh and striking. *Unter hohen Bäumen* was published in 1951. *Geschichten und Gedichte* appeared in 1956; the *Gesamtausgabe in Einzelbänden* (eight vols) between 1957 and 1967; *Das große Georg Britting Buch* in 1977; *Sämtliche Werke* began to appear in 1987.

Broch, Hermann (1886–1951)

Son of a wealthy Viennese textile manufacturer, Broch studied mathematics, philosophy and economics, and turned to writing shortly before the First World War (in 1913 he contributed to Ludwig von Ficker's periodical *Der Brenner*). Broch insisted upon an intellectualization of the novel, on working out, by sheer intellectual effort, the troubles of the world. Theoretical essays alternated with works of imagination: philosophical, mass-psychological and socio-economic investigations return ultimately to a religious realization of the fallenness of man; the inability to love is the root cause, for Broch, of human unhappiness. Both Broch and **Musil** embarked upon vast novels that would encompass the problems of the age, combining rationalism and mysticism. The *Schlafwander* trilogy (1931–2), encyclopaedic and polyhistorical novels, have as their concern the disintegration of values and the decay of European civilization in the period 1888–1918. The first, *Pasenow oder die Romantik*, has been compared with Fontane, but the secure ground of the nineteenth century has been left far behind: the age seems bent on radical solutions, and the symbol of the uniform seems an apt one. The second, *Esch oder die Anarchie*, portrays the insubstantiality of the existence of the small book-keeper Esch, who is able neither to escape from Europe nor to come to terms with it; the third, *Huguenau oder die Sachlichkeit*, portrays violence and anarchic forces which destroy the narcissistic world of the heroine. A series of theoretical chapters discuss the 'Zerfall der Werte'; a passage of blank verse is also included, the 'Geschichte eines Heilsarmeemädchens in Berlin'. The fusion of prose and poetry anticipates the technique used in Broch's third novel, *Der Tod des Vergil* (1945), a beautifully modulated portrayal of the last eighteen hours of the dying Virgil in Brindisi: the novel is essentially an interior monologue, and calls into doubt the whole meaning of art for, apparently, the poet has little wisdom to offer in times of turbulence. (The realization of the helplessness of the word when faced by the unspeakable will be a concern of many writers in the twentieth century, especially in German-speaking countries.) Broch's second novel, *Die unbekannte Größe* (1933) is his weakest, an overschematic account of the need for both rational and irrational experiences. The fourth novel, *Die Schuldlosen* (1950) treats twentieth-century themes and uses certain dates (1913, 1923 and 1933) as points of reference: the dangers of solipsism are analysed with considerable sensitivity. Broch's last novel, *Der Versucher* (1953, posthumous) exists in several drafts (it is sometimes called *Der Bergroman*): basically the work is a parabolic description of the evils of National Socialism; the pseudo-mystical demagogue Marius Ratti who tempts the inhabitants of a mountain village to savagery and sacrificial murder is an obvious portrayal of Adolf Hitler. The novel is uncomfortably suspended between political allegory and romantic myth. The character of Mutter Gisson with her Demeter-like qualities fails to convince, the symbolism being forced and obtrusive, but the description of mass psychology is masterful. The speculative study on *Massenpsychologie* stands comparison with the essay *Masse und Macht* by Elias **Canetti** as one of the most perceptive analyses of the relationship between the individual self and the corporate whole.

Broch, of Jewish parentage, was arrested when the Nazis invaded Austria, but was released on the intervention of writers like James Joyce. He settled in America and wrote his last novels there. His work is often compared with that of Robert Musil, but Broch's ponderous earnestness lacks the humour and relativizing irony of his Austrian contemporary. Broch died in New Haven, USA, in 1951. The *Gesammelte Schriften* (ten vols) appeared between 1952 and 1961 (reprinted 1968); the *Kommentierte Werkausgabe* (13–17 vols) appeared from 1974 to 1981.

Brod, Max (1884–1960)

Chiefly remembered as friend and literary executor of Franz **Kafka**, Brod was influential among the avant-garde circles in Prague in the early years of this century and became a prolific critic, journalist and littérateur. His early story *Tod den Toten!* (1906) exemplifies the expressionist cult of violence: the disused theatre, full of works of art, is to be dynamited together with its eccentric owner. The novel *Schloß Nornepygge* (1908) was much read at the time, and demonstrates the transition between decadence and early expressionist concerns: the hero's 'Indifferentismus' is an amorality which stems from debased Nietzscheanism. Brod turned away from portrayals of degenerate aestheticism to the writing of novels which extolled involvement with others and a healthy sensuality (*Ein tschechisches Dienstmädchen* (1909); *Franzi* (1922); *Leben mit einer Göttin* (1923)). As a Jew, Brod became a Zionist in 1913, and he became especially interested in the more conservative faith of his co-religionists from the eastern provinces of the Austro-Hungarian Empire. His best book is acknowledged to be *Tycho Brahes Weg zu Gott* (1916), a portrayal of the Prague of Rudolf II and the two types of scholar, the god-inspired seeker for the truth (Tycho) and the coolly analytic finder (Kepler); it is the greatness of the former that he recognizes the latter's intellectual superiority. Brod's best selling novel was *Eine Frau, nach der man sich sehnt* (1927). His poetry is undistinguished (*Der Weg des Verliebten* (1907); *Tagebuch in Versen* (1910); *Das Buch der Liebe* (1921)); he only achieved success on the stage with adaptations of Hašek and Kafka (*Das Schloß* and *Amerika*). Brod emigrated to Tel Aviv in 1939 and died there in 1960. In that year his autobiography *Streitbares Leben* appeared, which contains enlightening references to Kafka and also to Franz **Werfel**, of whose conversion to Christianity (see *Das Lied von Bernadette*) Brod did not approve. The *Ausgewählte Romane und Novellen* (six vols) appeared in 1919.

Bröger, Karl (1886–1944)

A worker-poet and socialist like **Engelke** and **Lersch**, Bröger served on the Western Front through most of the First World War. He produced three volumes of war poetry, *Aus meiner Kriegszeit. Gedichte* (1915), *Kamerad, als wir marschierten. Kriegsgedichte* (1916) and *Soldaten der Erde. Neue Kriegsgedichte* (1918). A war novel, *Bunker 17. Geschichte einer Kameradschaft* (1929) was widely read (it was translated into English as *Pillbox 17*). Bröger's collected poems appeared under the title *Sturz und Erhebung. Gesamtausgabe der Gedichte* in 1943. Bröger's most famous poem is 'Bekenntnis' with the last lines: 'Herrlich zeigte es aber deine größte Gefahr/daß dein ärmster Sohn auch dein getreuester war./Denk es, o Deutschland.' These words were quoted by Chancellor Bethmann-Hollweg in the *Reichstag* in 1917; Adolf Hitler was also fond of them. Bröger's patriotism was used by the Nazis for their own aims (a *Feldpostausgabe* of his poems appeared in 1941), but he did not openly support them. Other memorable war poems include 'Nachtmarsch' and 'Gesang der Granaten'. *Bekenntnis. Eine Auswahl der Gedichte*, appeared in 1954.

Bronnen, Arnolt (originally Bronner, 1895–1959)

Dramatist and novelist, Bronnen was one of the most extreme of the young talented writers who made the opening years of the Weimar Republic a fascinating and often disturbing experience. His play *Vatermord* (written in 1915, performed in Berlin in 1922) was the first of many scandals that surrounded his name; the portrayal of brutal violence and uninhibited sexuality outraged the audience. The son murders his father and then rejects the incestuous advances of his mother ('Geh deinen Mann begraben, du bist alt/Ich bin jung aber/Ich kenn dich nicht'). *Die Geburt der Jugend* (1922) is a chaotic description of anarchic youth; the older generation is annihilated by sexually demented adolescents. Bestiality is extolled: Bronnen's manifesto *Jugendkunst* explains that 'tiefstes menschentum ist tiefstes tiertum'. In his comedy *Die Exzesse* (1923) the erotic desires of the woman, Hildegarde, finds satisfaction in contemplation of intercourse with a goat. *Katalaunische Schlacht* (1924) looks back to the war as a time of frenzied (and erotic) ecstasy. Bronnen's exultant cult of violence and primitivity led him to greet National Socialism with enthusiasm. *Rheinische Rebellen* (1925) is an overtly nationalist play; *Ostpolzug* (1925), a monodrama, fuses ancient and modern in its portrayal of Alexander the Great. The novel *O.S.* (1929) praises the exploits of the *Freikorps*, and *Rossbach* (1930) glorifies Hitler's Munich putsch. Bronnen worked for the film industry in the 1930s, also the *Reichsrundfunkgesellschaft*. His relations with the Nazis were, however, strained. He had difficulty in proving his Aryan ancestry, and a man who once confessed that his ego was a 'Gewirr der sexuellen Planetoiden' was an uncomfortable fellow-traveller. During the Second World War Bronnen joined the communist opposition in Austria and briefly became mayor of Goisern (Oberösterreich). His autobiography *Arnolt Bronnen gibt zu Protokoll* appeared in 1954; *Tage mit Brecht* posthumously in 1960. *Viergespann* (*Dramen*) was published in 1958; *Stücke* in 1977; *Werke* in 5 volumes in 1989.

Bruckner, Ferdinand (pseudonym of Theodor Tagger, 1891–1958)

Primarily a dramatist, Bruckner achieved fame in 1928 with his play *Krankheit der Jugend*, a crass and naturalistic portrayal of adolescent sexuality, much indebted to Freud. Youth itself is 'ein Gefahrenherd. Jugend ist latente Todesnähe.' *Die Verbrecher* (1929) attempts to uncover the true criminals, those without love or compassion: the action takes place alternately between the two halves of the stage, representing a split between the storeys of a house, a juxtaposition of ostensible criminals and apparent judges. Bruckner used techniques made famous by Erwin Piscator; his greatest success was *Elisabeth von England* (1930), where the stage is again split between the two realms, Catholic Madrid and Protestant London, with both antagonists praying to the same god for victory. Bruckner also turned his attention, with less success, to classical themes (*Timon* (1932) and *Pyrrhus und Andromache* (perf. 1952)); he also arranged Kleist's *Die Marquise von O.* (1933). A very successful play was *Die Rassen* (1933), one which exploits the generation conflict and also the tension between Jew and Aryan. Bruckner sees the attraction of Nazism for a disenchanted generation, and the myth of the *Führer* is seen in all its sinister magnetism. His early poetry, *Der Herr in den Nebeln* (1917) and his novels *Die Vollendung des Herzens* (1917) and *Auf der Straße* (1920) are largely forgotten. Bruckner emigrated to America in 1936 and returned to Europe in 1951, spending the last years of his life in Berlin. The play *Früchte des Nichts* (1952) is a final statement on the apparent hopelessness and despair felt by young people after the Second World War, a complement to *Krankheit der Jugend*. *Dramatische Werke* and *Schauspiele nach historischen Studien* were both published in 1956. Bruckner also translated Arthur Miller (*Der Tod des Handlungsreisenden* (1945)).

Brust, Alfred (1891–1934)

An East Prussian playwright distantly related to Heinrich von Kleist, Brust was encouraged to write by the Lithuanian dramatist Vilius Storasta and his early plays, *Der Irrtum* and *Das kleine Tier* were produced in Tilsit in 1910. It was a reading of Nietzsche, however, which turned Brust's attention to elemental, drastic situations; during and immediately after the war he made the acquaintance of expressionist writers and painters (Schmidt-Rottluff greatly admired him). Brust was helped by Kurt Wolff; he lived in isolation in Memel and moved to Cranz after the Lithuanian occupation. His reputation was established by the play *Die Wölfe* (1921), a so-called 'Winterstück' which juxtaposes East and West, sensuality and intellect in a series of violent contrasts: the play was notorious for its portrayal of bestiality. Brust shares with many expressionists a predilection for crass and often shocking climaxes. *Die Wölfe* was meant as a trilogy: other plays which include Pastor Tolkening are *Die Würmer* (a 'Tragödie im Feuerofen') and *Der Phönix* ('Ein Märchenstück'). Brust turned towards a portrayal of pseudo-religious experiences in a series of other plays (*Cordatus. Ein dramatisches Bekenntnis* (1927); *Gnade für Gomorra. Fünf*

BURCKHARDT, CARL JAKOB 51

Akte aus der Tiefe, never performed). Brust also wrote poetry (*Ich bin* (1929)) and a 'Hörspiel' (*Der Friedhof von Sankt Johann*). He died in obscurity, isolation and poverty at the age of forty-three; the Nazis initially tolerated his writing, believing him to be an acceptable poet of East Prussian life, although later his work was condemned as degenerate. His complete *Nachlaß* was destroyed in Königsberg in 1945. The *Dramen 1917–1924* (ed. Horst Denkler) appeared in 1971.

Bruyn, Günter de (1926–)

De Bruyn began with a novel *Der Hohlweg* (1963) on the impact of the Third Reich and its aftermath on a young man in search of a meaningful role in a new society; this muted example of a genre much cultivated in the early years of the GDR was later criticized by its author but is in many ways superior to the archetypal 'Ankunfstromane' of Max Walter Schulz and Dieter Noll. Since then he has written stories (*Ein schwarzer, abgrundtiefer See* (1963, extended 1966) and *Babylon* (1977) and novels which concentrate on human foibles and idiosyncrasies in domestic and professional contexts, although social and political pressures, implicitly criticized, are present in various forms. *Buridans Esel* (1968) presents the triangle of a librarian, his wife and the woman with whom he conducts a tentative affair; *Preisverleihung* (1973) and *Märkische Forschungen* (1978) gently expose party *dirigisme* in the literary life of the GDR (in the second by contrasting two approaches, disinterested and ideologically orthodox, to the investigation of the past, here represented by a forgotten eighteenth-century writer), while *Neue Herrlichkeit* (1984) depicts life in an official writers' retreat. De Bruyn has done much to make accessible the work of past authors, as a parodist (*Maskeraden* (1966), *Das Lästerkabinett* (ed., 1970)), a biographer (*Das Leben des Jean Paul Friedrich Richter* (1975)), an adapter (a version of Gottfried von Straßburg's *Tristan und Isolde* (1975)) and a critic (*Lesefreuden. Über Bücher und Menschen* (1986)).

Burckhardt, Carl Jakob (1891–1974)

A Swiss diplomat and politician (he was briefly High Commissioner for Danzig and later President of the International Red Cross), Burckhardt was also a historian and man of letters. Of interest in this latter context is volume V of his *Gesammelte Werke* (1971), which contains his narrative prose work (*Erzählungen*); volume IV is also relevant here, the *Porträts und Begegnungen*, which recount Burckhardt's friendship with Hugo von **Hofmannsthal**, and meetings with Rudolf Alexander **Schröder**, Annette **Kolb** and Werner **Bergengruen**. An informative document on Burckhardt is the Festschrift which appeared on his seventieth birthday, *Dauer im Wechsel* (1961).

Burger, Hermann (1942–89)

Burger studied in Zurich, wrote dissertations on Paul **Celan** and contemporary Swiss literature and taught for a while at the Federal Technical University in Zurich. His chief works, *Schilten*. *Schulbericht zuhanden der Inspektorenkonferenz* (1976) (in which a village schoolteacher reports on his work to the educational authorities) and *Die künstliche Mutter* (1982) (in which the central figure seeks salvation in psychotherapy administered by women in a womb-like sanatorium beneath the Saint Gotthard pass and, failing to adjust to reality finds death in a state of artistic euphoria) are both phantasmagorias on death, sickness and the inescapable influences of family life in childhood and adolescence. Burger shares with the Austrian Thomas **Bernhard** and with other contemporary Swiss writers (e.g. E. Y. Meyer) the theme of death as the ultimate threat to personal identity, which he treats with an even greater degree of linguistic virtuosity and reflective intensity. Other works include the story collections *Diabelli* (1979) and *Blankenburg* (1986), the poems *Kirchberger Idyllen* (1980), a brilliant recreation of a form associated with German classicism, and further fiction, *Der Schuß auf die Kanzel* (1988) and *Brenner* (1989). He committed suicide in 1989.

Burte, Hermann (pseudonym for Hermann Strübe, 1879–1960)

Painter, dramatist, poet and novelist, Burte made his reputation above all with the immensely successful novel *Wildfeber, der ewige Deutsche* (1912). This 'Geschichte eines Heimatsuchers' with its belief that 'Meinen, das heißt: lieben aus dem Blut heraus', and the cult of the swastika (the 'uralte(s) Hakenkreuz – Ha, wenn das wieder lebendig würde!') perfectly exemplifies the link between 'Heimatkunst' and incipient nationalistic irrationalities. Burte's most famous play was *Katte* (1914), a portrayal of the execution of the close friend of Frederick the Great of Prussia. Burte's poetry is generally mediocre: the collection *Anker am Rhein* extols the 'Krist am Holz und in der Esche Woden' (a Germanic Christ was also praised in *Wildfeber*); the poem 'Nibelungen-Handschrift' (1941) explains: 'Gerührter trat ich kaum zum Abendmahl/Als vor die Liederschrift der Nibelungen'. (*Der unsichtbare Held*, a Nibelungen drama, appeared in the same year.) Burte published poems in Alemannic dialect (*Madlee* (1923)); a further anthology appeared in 1950 (*Die Seele des Maien*). Burte received much acclaim for his work, the Kleist prize (for *Wildfeber*) and other distinctions during the Third Reich.

Canetti, Elias (1905–)

Born in Bulgaria into a family of Sephardic Jews, Canetti's first language was Spanish. At the age of six he was brought to Manchester; the family moved to Vienna after the father's death in 1913. Canetti's first book (and only novel) is *Die Blendung* (1935), a somewhat prolix study of *idées fixes* and manic encapsulation. The sinologist Peter Kien, obsessed by his own private library, and retreating ever further into a state of solipsism, is ultimately destroyed by fire, ancient symbol of transformation. (The other characters, Pfaff, Theresa Krumbholz and Fischerle, are also utterly self-centred and convinced of their own importance.) The idea for the novel came to Canetti in 1927 when he witnessed the burning of the Palace of Justice by a mob in Vienna. Canetti moved to Paris in 1938 and to London in the following year, where he still lives. In 1960 he published *Masse und Macht*, a sociological, anthropological study of crowds and power: here fire is interpreted as a symbol for the crowd. In 1964 Canetti's plays were published (*Hochzeit* (1932); *Komödie der Eitelkeit* (1950); *Die Befristeten* (1956)): they are the weakest part of his *œuvre*, combining pseudo-expressionism, copulative merry-go-rounds and an existentialist preoccupation with freedom. A collection of aphorisms made between 1942 and 1944, *Aufzeichnungen*, appeared in 1965. *Die Stimmen von Marakesh* (1967) is a personal account of a journey to North Africa; *Der andere Prozeß* (1969) is a study of Franz **Kafka**'s letters to Felice Bauer and suggests yet another interpretation of Kafka's novel. (Canetti also holds that Kafka is the greatest expert on power; he also attempts to see Kafka as a 'Chinese' writer, that is, one who avoids the pretentious and concentrates upon the apparently insignificant and the peripheral.) *Der Ohrenzeuge – fünfzehn Charaktere* appeared in 1974. The first part of Canetti's autobiography, *Die gerettete Zunge*, was published in 1977; the second part, *Die Fackel im Ohr*, in 1980; the third part, *Das Augenspiel*, in 1985. *Das Geheimnis der Uhr. Aufzeichnungen 1973–1985* appeared in 1987. In 1981 Canetti was awarded the Nobel prize for literature.

Carossa, Hans (1878–1956)

Son of a doctor, Hans Carossa studied medicine in Munich and Leipzig, then settled as a medical practitioner in Bavaria. He served in the medical corps during the First World War, and his *Rumänisches Tagebuch* (1924, republished in 1935 as *Tagebuch im Krieg*) was a volume of reminiscences, showing the author to be a man of humane values. *Eine Kindheit* (1922) is a popular autobiographical account of the first ten years in the life of a Bavarian doctor's son; Goethean wisdom is imparted and the need for transformation and acceptance is frequently stressed, the author's goal being 'anderen ein Licht auf ihre Bahn zu werfen, indem ich die meinige aufzeigte'. *Verwandlungen einer Jugend* (1928) is a (less successful) sequel. *Der Arzt Gion* ('Gion' is the Rhaeto-Romansch for 'Hans') (1932), tells of the calling and profession of a young doctor after the First World War. The novel *Geheimnisse des reifen Lebens* (1936) uses the diary form to explore human relationships. During the Second World War Carossa withdrew into 'inner emigration', attempting to keep alive the memory of the finer elements in the German cultural tradition; he was, however, nominated by **Goebbels** in 1941 as President of the *Europäische Schriftstellervereinigung*. After the war Carossa attempted to explain his situation at that time in *Ungleiche Welten* (1951). Further autobiographical details of his life appeared in *Aufzeichnungen aus Italien* (1947); a scattering of short stories appeared in the 1950s. His poetry is unassuming and traditional: the famous *Abendländische Elegie* ('Wird Abend über uns, o Abendland?') laments in restrained and dignified language the collapse of civilized values in Germany and elsewhere, yet hopes for a better future. In his work Carossa eschews modernist experimentation; he appealed to the educated middle-class German reader with his cultivation of humanistic values derived from Goethe. *Sämtliche Werke* (two vols) appeared in 1962; *Werke* (five vols) in 1978; *Ausgewählte Gedichte* also in 1978.

Celan, Paul (pseudonym of Paul Antschel, 1920–70)

Celan's roots lay in the German-Jewish cultural enclave centred on Czernowitz, Bukovina, which passed from the Austro-Hungarian empire to Romania and finally to the Soviet Union, but he gained contact with international modernist trends before settling in Paris in 1948, where he remained until his suicide as a teacher at the *École Normale Supérieure*. Unlike his parents Celan escaped deportation when his home was occupied by the Nazis, but awareness of the Holocaust is at the centre of his work, his approach to the problems of language and communication in general (long a preoccupation of writers from the linguistic melting-pot of Central Europe and the Balkans) being linked to the impossibility of conveying the extreme physical and existential exposure of the persecuted. The unprecedented combination of topical theme and modernist technique predestined the early 'Todesfuge' for anthologization and a fame which has distracted attention from the rest of Celan's work and its development towards increasing fragmentation. Thirty poems from the quickly withdrawn *Der Sand aus den Urnen* (1948) reappeared in *Mohn und Gedächtnis* (1952) with which he first came to the attention of a broad public, to be followed by *Von Schwelle zu Schwelle* (1955), *Sprachgitter* (1959), *Die Niemandsrose* (1963), *Atemwende* (1967), *Fadensonne* (1968), *Lichtzwang* (1970) and *Schneepart* (1971). These, together with translations of twenty-one sonnets by Shakespeare and poems by Char, Supervielle, Michaux, Yessenin, Mandelstam, Block and others, were assembled in the provisional *Gesammelte Werke* (1983) in five volumes. Some aid to an understanding of Celan's work is offered in speeches (e.g. 'Der Meridian' on award of the Büchner prize in 1960), commentaries in letters, in *Der Traum vom Traume* (1948) on eight lithographs by Edgar Jené and in the essay 'Gespräch im Gebirg', written in 1959 (in *Ausgewählte Gedichte* (1970)). Despite the increasing number of exegeses (see the *Celan-Jahrbuch* :1987–)) there is still uncertainty on the question whether his work may be interpreted by reference to the Bible and the esoteric Judaism in which he was partly educated, or whether it represents an ever more private exploration and probing of language and its elements on the edge of silence. He was a man of mystical tendency whose experience of the Holocaust placed obstacles in the way to religious enlightenment; the distortion and reversal of normal syntactical relationships which is a marked feature of his work is related to this central paradox. However, he remained attached to Jewish culture, as is evident especially in late poems set in Jerusalem. Although these and other poems have an identifiable autobiographical content or trace his relation to such congenial figures as Hölderlin, Büchner and Rosa Luxemburg, and although he claimed that he hoped for a dialogue with the reader, most of his work represents a dialogue with the elements of language in which the latter sets the topics and the tone.

Chotjewitz, Peter O. (1934–)

Having studied law, Chotjewitz qualified as a professional advocate in 1966. His defence of members of the Baader-Meinhof group during the seventies influenced (along with **Kafka**) the fragmentary novel *Die Herren des Morgengrauens* (1978). The disintegration of conventional narrative structures and experience of the growing radicalism of Berlin intellectual circles in the initial phase of the *Studentenbewegung* mark *Hommage à Frantek* (1965) and *Die Insel. Erzählungen aus dem Bärenauge* (1968). Chotjewitz sought his way to a new style in the story collection *Durch Schaden wird man dumm* (1976) and may be said to have found it in the realism of *Der dreißigjährige Friede. Biographischer Bericht* (1977), which tells the life-story of an arsenist, *Die mit Tränen sehen* (1979), the travel diary of a visit to Israel, and *Saumlos* (1979), the reconstruction in fictional form, but with the help of documents, of the lives of a number of Jews in a small Hessian village during the Weimar Republic and the Third Reich. He has also produced works which owe their origin to experiences in Italy (*Malavita. Mafia zwischen gestern und morgen* (1973) and *Briganten* (1976)), a play on Mayakovsky (*Weltmeisterschaft im Klassenkampf* (1971)) and radio plays.

Csokor, Franz (1885–1969)

Csokor is known primarily as an Austrian expressionist dramatist. He worked in theatres in St Petersburg before settling in his native Vienna: his early work, particularly *Die rote Straße* (1916) shows the great influence of Strindberg, the fourteen scenes representing a 'Stationendrama' and the characters exemplifying types ('Die Dirne', 'der Grundbesitzer', etc.). In *Die Sünde wider den Geist* (1915) **Wedekind** is detected as well as Strindberg (the woman as vampire); *Die Stunde des Absterbens* (1916) is an expressionist Everyman. After the First World War Csokor turned to historical and social problems: *Gesellschaft der Menschenrechte* (1929) is a play on Büchner; *Besetztes Gebiet* (1930) deals with the French occupation of the Ruhr; *Dritter November 1918* (1936) takes place in a snowed-up sanatorium where the disintegration of Austria-Hungary is acted *in nucleo*. After 1938 Csokor fled into eastern Europe; he was finally arrested in Yugoslavia, and interned. His experiences are described in *Als Zivilist im Polenkrieg* (1940) and *Als Zivilist im Balkankrieg* (1946). His novel *Das Reich der Schwärmer* (1933) is a depiction of the Anabaptists in Münster: it was republished in 1955 as *Der Schlüssel zum Abgrund*. Csokor's poetry was published in the collections *Der Dolch und die Wunde* (1917), *Ewiger Aufbruch* (1926), *Das schwarze Schiff* (1944) and *Immer ist Aufbruch* (1952). He published his plays under various groupings, a trilogy and a 'dramatisches Diptychon' among them. A selection of his works, *Du bist gemeint*, with a foreword by Erhard Buschbeck, appeared in 1959. The *Zeuge einer Zeit. Briefe aus dem Exil 1933–1950* (1964) provides informative documentation of Csokor's relationship with many modern Austrian writers (particularly Ödön von **Horváth**). *Ein paar Schaufeln Erde. Erzählungen aus fünf Jahrzehnten* appeared in 1965.

Czechowski, Heinz (1935–)

Czechowski witnessed the destruction of Dresden, which became the subject of several poems and autobiographical sketches. After verse which owed much to Peter **Huchel** and Erich **Arendt** he has become one of the more original voices in contemporary GDR poetry. His melancholy free verse belongs to a tradition of nature poetry which originates in the eighteenth century and is imbued with an awareness of how his predecessors have responded to the same mainly Saxon landscapes and the effects on them of industrial development. He has been grouped with **Volker Braun**, Karl Mickel, **Rainer Kirsch** and Reiner **Kunze** in the so-called Saxon or Dresden school of poets. The selection *An Freund und Feind* (1983) is drawn from his first four volumes *Nachmittag eines Liebespaars* (1962), *Wasserfahrt* (1967), *Schafe und Sterne* (1974) and *Was mich betrifft* (1981), while the selection *Ich und die Folgen* (1987) includes poems from *Ich, beispielsweise* (1982) and *Kein näheres Zeichen* (1987). In all these one can detect a movement from a positive depiction of everyday life in the

GDR and a straightforward autobiographical approach to the expression of a more complex subjectivity, sceptical of conventional views of progress.

D

Däubler, Theodor (1876–1934)

Born in Trieste, Däubler was bilingual and turned to German as a medium for his poetry after an overwhelming performance of Wagner's *Siegfried*. His vast epic *Das Nordlicht*, which took him twelve years to write, was published in 1910: some thirty thousand lines long, it is a vast cosmogony, characterized by frequently bizarre neologisms. The central idea would seem to be the yearning of the earth for identification with the sun, the desire to become a radiant star; in the polar realms of ice and darkness the intense striving for the sun kindles a 'Nordlicht'. The first part, entitled 'Das Mittelmeer', has a cosmic sweep reminiscent of Whitman; the section 'Hymne der Höhe' is a portrayal of a sunrise indebted to Nietzsche's *Also sprach Zarathustra*, and stretches language to an extreme intensity. In the second part, 'Sahara', Däubler's hyperbole exceeds all limits: gigantic images of mass destruction verge on the bathetic. 'Der Weltbruch' attempts to fuse Nietzsche, Mahler and the Book of Revelations; an 'Astraler Gesang' is reminiscent of *Faust II*. The final section, 'Der Geist', is a vision of ultimate redemption. This cataract of verses (spread over 1,200 pages in the 'Genfer Fassung') alienates many by the grotesque excesses of its language; the rare moments of tenderness (the descriptions of the Tuscan landscape) bring welcome relief. The works that follow *Das Nordlicht*, particularly the collection of sketches *Mit silberner Sichel* (1916), contain much talented writing: monstrous hyperbole gives way to an unsuspected delicacy. Däubler met the Austrian poet **Trakl** in 1912, and certain poems ('Vertändelt ist das ernste Gold der Garben') are reminiscent of Trakl; Däubler also befriended Ernst **Barlach**, who gives a perceptive account of Däubler in the fragmentary novel *Seespeck* (he also sculpted a 'Ruhender Däubler'). Däubler travelled widely and admired such modern painters as Chagall, Klee and Munch: his essay *Expressionismus* is an important one. His collections of poems include *Der sternhelle Weg* (1915), *Päan und Dithyrambos* (1924) and *Attische Sonette* (1920). Prose works include *Wir wollen nicht verweilen* (1915), *L'Africana* (1928) and *Die Göttin mit der Fackel* (1931). Däubler was a member of the Prussian *Akademie der Künste* and was President of the German PEN club. *Dichtungen und Schriften* appeared in 1956, and *Gedichte* in 1965.

Dauthendey, Max(imilian) (1867–1918)

Dauthendey, son of a photographer in Würzburg, studied painting before starting to write poetry. In Berlin (1891) he came into contact with Julius and Heinrich Hart, Bruno Wille and Hermann Bölsche (the so-called

'Friedrichshagener Kreis'), and absorbed their monistic doctrines; his receptivity to the sensuous appeal of colour and light, together with the neo-Darwinism of the Berlin writers, led to the writing of his first novel *Josa Gerth* (1892), a book very reminiscent of Jens Peter Jacobsen. In the following year his best-known work appeared, *Ultra Violett. Einsame Poesien*, an impressionistic, *Jugendstil* concoction where colours are extravagantly flaunted ('Ultra Violett' is, apparently, the spirit of loneliness which promises ultimate rapture). In 1895 a cosmic 'Drama im Hirn eines Menschen' appeared, *Sehnsucht*, but Dauthendey was more successful in his poetry: *Singsangbuch* (1904) and *Lusamgärtlein. Frühlingslieder aus Franken* (1909). He travelled extensively; a collection of *Novellen* (again, greatly influenced by *Jugendstil* topoi) appeared in 1911: *Die acht Gesichter am Biwasee. Japanische Liebesgeschichten* (it was reprinted in 1953 and was extremely popular). In the same year his second novel, *Raubmenschen*, was published: the descriptions of Mexico and other countries are little more than travelogues. Dauthendey responded sensitively to the Orient and popularized the culture of the Far East: he was interned in Java during the First World War and died there. *Erlebnisse aus Java* (1924) and *Letzte Reise* (1926) appeared posthumously. Walter von Molo described him as 'ein Punkt in der goldenen Mantelschnalle, die die germanische Dichtkunst in der Nähe ihres Herzens trägt'; his cultivation of the exotic is akin to that of Lafcadio Hearn. His *Gesammelte Werke* (six vols) appeared in 1925.

Degenhardt, Franz Josef (1931–)

Degenhardt became known in the 1960s as author, composer and performer to his own guitar accompaniment of protest songs, of which there have been numerous recordings and publications, incl. *Spiel nicht mit den Schmuddelkindern* (1967 and 1969), *Im Jahr der Schweine* (1970), *Laßt nicht die roten Hähne flattern ehe der Habicht schreit* (1974), collected in *Kommt an den Tisch unter Pflaumenbäumen* (1979). His early songs were anarchist-romantic in the tradition of Villon and the anonymous *Bänkelsang* (broadsheet ballad), but after 1967 he showed increasing commitment to politically radical causes (against nuclear weapons, the war in Vietnam, emergency laws in the Federal Republic, unemployment, the 'drift to the right'). As a novelist he is associated with the realists published by the Autoren-Edition (incl. **Fuchs, Timm**), who aim to raise political consciousness in a wide readership by showing how political forces impinge on the lives of ordinary people. In *Zündschnüre* (1973) working-class youths join an anti-Nazi resistance group in 1944, in *Brandstellen* (1975) a community protests against the use of local land as a Nato exercise area, in *Die Mißhandlung* (1979) a state prosecutor undergoes a change of heart while dealing with a case of child abuse, in *Der Liedermacher* (1982) the title figure suffers the conflict of commercial pressures and political commitment during the election of 1980, and in *Die Abholzung* (1985) a middle-class woman overcomes political apathy by chaining herself to a beech-tree in protest against the clearing of forest land for a motorway.

Dehmel, Richard (1863–1920)

A student of the natural sciences, philosophy and economy, Dehmel took up writing in the Berlin of the 1890s and reflected in his poetry the main preoccupations of the following two decades: Nietzscheanism, naturalism, impressionism, *Jugendstil* and a latent expressionism. He achieved great popularity during his lifetime (hailed by Liliencron and others as Germany's greatest living poet: 'Nietzsche philosophus, Dehmel poeta'). His poetry is marked by a powerful sensuality, compassion and a keen intellect. In 1890 there appeared *Erlösungen: eine Seelenwanderung in Gedichten und Sprüchen* (certain poems, 'Der Rächer' and 'Landung' with their stock-in-trade swan imagery, also the Kaspar Hauser motif, are very much of their time; the 'Nachruf an Nietzsche', rapturous and ecstatic, transcends neo-romantic velleity). *Aber die Liebe* (1893) explores the relationship between the sexes with passion and sensitivity; the famous 'Der Arbeitsmann' demonstrates social awareness without being crudely political. Dehmel stresses in many poems the joy to be found in sexual love, together with hope for true emancipation in the future. *Die Verwandlungen der Venus* (1907), a cycle of poems ('Venus Primitiva', 'Venus Homo', 'Venus Domestica', 'Venus Adultera', 'Venus Perversa', 'Venus Sapiens', etc.) caused Dehmel much difficulty with the censor. Dehmel's love for Ida Auerbach (he divorced Paula Oppenheim in 1901) is reflected in his masterpiece *Zwei Menschen* (1903), a cyclical epic poem (a 'Roman in Romanzen'): Schönberg's *Verklärte Nacht* derives from it. Dehmel also wrote plays: *Der Mitmensch* (1895, a naturalist work), *Die Menschenfreunde* (1917) and *Die Götterfamilie* (published posthumously in 1921), but it is as a poet that his reputation is established. His work is at its best in the portrayal of sensuous love and in its sincere, humanitarian beliefs. Although exempt from enlistment (due to injuries received at school after a fall from a horizontal bar), Dehmel joined the army in 1914 (he was over 50 at the time): his experiences are described in *Zwischen Volk und Menschheit* (1919). Dehmel was in close contact with the major writers of his day; he contributed to the leading literary journals. *Gesammelte Werke* (ten vols) appeared from 1906 to 1909 (a three-volume selection in 1913). A posthumous autobiography *Mein Leben* was published in 1922. In 1963 appeared *Dichtungen, Briefe, Dokumente*.

Delius, Friedrich Christian (1943–)

Delius lived during the years 1963–78 mainly in West Berlin and his work of the period reflects and propagates the many causes associated with the student movement and the APO (*außerparlamentarische Opposition*). He first became known as the author of laconic and reflective poems in the manner of **Brecht** (*Kerbholz* (1965), *Wenn wir bei rot* (1965), *Ein Bankier auf der Flucht* (1975), *Die unsichtbaren Blitze* (1981)) and of documentary satires (*Wir Unternehmer* (1966), *Einige Argumente zur Verteidigung der*

Gemüsefresser (1985)) of which the most notorious, *Unsere Siemens-Welt* (1972), led to a libel action. His awareness of the forces at work in contemporary society and of how their interaction affects individual lives underlies all his novels. *Ein Held der inneren Sicherheit* (1981) is a fictional projection of the situation created by the murder in 1977 by the *Baader-Meinhof-Gruppe* of Hans-Martin Schleyer, chief of the West German directors' organization; it centres on the assistant of an equivalent figure who, after unleashing a publicity campaign for the interests represented by his dead superior, experiences a crisis of loyalty which is only overcome by his transfer to another position. In *Adenauerplatz* (1984) a security guard employed to watch over a shopping and business complex in an anonymous German city is forced to confront the contradictions of his position as a refugee from Chile after the fall of Allende when he is drawn into collusion with a plot by friends to burgle an international wheeler-dealer with a stake in the political *status quo* in South America; having become aware of the ramifications of Third World exploitation he decides to abandon his job and return to Chile. *Mogadischu Fensterplatz* (1987) is a fictional treatment from the perspective of an ordinary passenger of the hijack carried out by members of the Baader-Meinhof group in Somalia in 1977 and reflects a deepening concern with Third World topics evident also in the work of **Born** and **Timm**.

Derleth, Ludwig (1870–1948)

Ludwig Derleth studied philosophy and theology in Munich, and published hieratic and highly stylized poems in the bibliophile quarterly *Pan* and *Blätter für die Kunst*; his reputation was made, however, by *Die Proklamationen*, read to a group of initiates on Good Friday, 1904. This work, a collection of highly charged utterances, preaches an extreme form of militant catholicism: *Christus Imperator Maximus* calls for the destruction of the world and the need to expunge millennia of human domesticity ('Badet euch in Blut. Sättiget euch mit Blut. Berauschet euch mit Blut (. . .)'). This cult of aesthetic violence links Derleth's name with that of Schuler and Klages. Derleth led an itinerant life, moved to Rome and embarked upon *Der Fränkische Koran*, a work which occupied him for over twenty years and which grew so unwieldy that he was forced to publish Part One separately in 1932: the complete work was to consist of two thousand poems. It begins with the section 'Anrufungen und Gebete' (where Christian ritual is extolled); 'Weinlieder' and 'Liebeslieder' evoke pagan deities. Criticisms of modernity follow in 'Kritik der Wissenschaft' and 'Kritik der Geschichte'. The publication of Part One met with little interest, the exception being Karl **Wolfskehl**, who looked back on it with great pleasure during his New Zealand exile. Of the second part of the work only 'Der Tod des Thanatos' and 'Die seraphinische Hochzeit' were published in Derleth's lifetime: other sections ('Die Posaune des Krieges', 'Der chymische Herkules', 'Die apokalyptische Schlacht' and 'Von Wingert zur Kelter') are virtually unknown. *Das Werk* (six volumes) was published in 1971. A literary portrait of Derleth, under the name 'Daniel zur Höhe', appears in *Doktor Faustus* by **Thomas Mann**.

Dinter, Artur (1876–1948)

A student of the natural sciences, Dinter became a teacher, then turned to the theatre; he became increasingly anti-Semitic and reached notoriety with a trilogy of novels published between 1917 and 1922: *Die Sünde wider das Blut, Die Sünde wider den Geist*, and *Die Sünde wider die Liebe*. The first of these was much acclaimed and widely read; in crudely sensational terms it describes the poisoning of the blood of a German woman, Johanna, through once having had intercourse with a Jew. The child borne to Johanna and her husband Hermann, both blond and Germanic, is dark and of Jewish appearance. Hermann kills the Jew and returns to find that his wife has killed the child and has committed suicide. Certain passages of this book are on a level with Julius Streicher's *Der Stürmer*: 'Nun ermesse man den Schaden, der jahraus jahrein der deutschen Rasse durch die Judenjünglinge zugefügt wird, die alljährlich *tausende* und abertausende *deutscher* Mädchen verführen!' Dinter was another confused nationalist who attempted to prove that Christ was an 'Aryan'; he was briefly *Gauleiter* of Thuringia, but his bizarre fusion of religion and politics proved unpalatable even to the Nazis. He was expelled from the party, and his 'Deutsche Volkskirche' was disbanded in 1937.

Döblin, Alfred (1878–1957)

A doctor by training, Döblin worked first in a psychiatric hospital in Berlin before moving to his own private practice in the poorer part of the city. He came into contact with Herwarth **Walden**, Else **Lasker-Schüler** and Peter **Hille** in the Café des Westens and wrote for *Der Sturm*: his first novel, *Der schwarze Vorhang*, first appeared in instalments in this journal (in book form in 1919). Before the First World War he wrote a series of short plays, the best being *Lydia und Mäxchen* ('Tiefe Verbeugung in einem Akt'), which was performed in 1906; it anticipates Pirandello in many ways. A collection of *Novellen* appeared in 1913, bearing the title of the first story, *Die Ermordung einer Butterblume*, an account of mental disturbance and, in fact, little more than a catalogue of neuroses. In 1915 Döblin achieved his literary breakthrough with the novel *Die drei Sprünge des Wang-lun*: the theme is the question of how the individual should stand in relation to his environment (the 'three leaps' being a demonstration of decisive change in the life of the protagonist). Döblin's second major novel, *Wadzeks Kampf mit der Dampfturbine* (1918) concerns transformation, adaptability and assimilation in a modern (Berlin) setting. *Wallenstein* (two vols), which appeared in 1920, deals with the historical figures of the Thirty Years War but also hints at wider issues – the role of the individual during a time of massive upheaval. Döblin published two plays in 1920 (*Lusitania* and *Die Nonnen von Kemnade*); an amazing science fiction novel *Berge, Meere und Giganten* appeared in 1924, an attempt to describe the development of the industrial world up to the year 2500. (The book owes much to Marinetti's *Mafarka le futuriste*, which Döblin greatly admired.) Man and nature are locked in a gigantic struggle: with the help of energy gathered in 'turmaline veils' the ice of Greenland is melted, but monsters are generated which threaten man by their enormous proliferation. In great contrast is the 'epische Dichtung' *Manas* (1927), a work steeped in Buddhistic quietism and acceptance. Döblin's masterpiece is without doubt *Berlin Alexanderplatz* (1929), a novel hailed as the most radically modernist work of the 1920s. Comparisons have been made with *Manhattan Transfer* and *Ulysses* (Hans Henny **Jahnn** and others referred in their reviews to the Irish novelist): interior monologue, collage and montage convey the density as well as the fragmentary and elusive quality of life. The book documents Franz Biberkopf's passage through the roaring city in the form of an enormous *Moritat*. Biberkopf sinks from one stage of degradation to another: obstinate, gullible, and at times violent, he is crushed beneath a force stronger than he. Visions of Job, of the Great Whore of Babylon and 'der singende Tod' accompany this tale of one who ultimately gains insight; he cannot live for himself, but only as part of a teeming multitude. Some of the quietism of Wang-lun has been achieved, and the question at the end of *Die drei Sprünge* answered affirmatively.

In 1933 Döblin, of Jewish descent and well-known socialist views (he had earlier contributed satirical essays to the *Neue Rundschau* under the pseudonym 'Linke Poot') fled to Switzerland, thence to France. *Babylonische Wandrung* (1934) curses the sin of pride and portrays with grotesque humour the passage of the hero through the Babylon of Western civilization in a journey of self-exploration and expiation. The work appears formless (a fusion of mythology, history, modern events, statistical facts and popular songs), but an inexhaustible richness cannot be denied. In 1935 there appeared *Pardon wird nicht gegeben* and *Flucht und Sammlung des Judenvolkes*; Döblin became a French citizen and worked in France's Ministry of Information. In 1940 he escaped via Spain and Portugal to New York and thence to Hollywood. In 1941 he became a convert to Roman Catholicism and after the war he returned to Paris, working in the cultural department of the French military government (his son Wolfgang had been killed in the war, fighting as a French soldier). In 1946 Döblin founded the magazine *Das goldene Tor* and commenced work on *Hamlet oder die lange Nacht nimmt ein Ende*: this novel was probably inspired by James Hilton's *Random Harvest*, which Döblin had read in Hollywood, and tells of the return of a wounded soldier to a house of guilt. Questions are asked concerning the possibility of responsible action and the ultimate meaning of human existence. The trilogy *1918* (published 1950) was unsuccessful, a sceptical account of Germany's failed revolution; the ambitious *Amazonas Trilogie* (1947–8) attempts to explore the evils of colonialism.

Döblin wrote many essays on political and literary topics; the description of a journey to Poland (*Reise in Polen* (1925)) contains a moving account of a visit to Cracow. Among contemporary writers it is Günter **Grass** who has acknowledged the biggest debt to Döblin (in *Akzente* (1967)). *Ausgewählte Werke* (twenty-one vols) appeared from 1960 to 1982; a *Jubiläumssonderausgabe* (seven vols) in 1977.

Doderer, Heimito von (1896–1966)

Born near Vienna, Doderer enlisted in the Austrian army as a young man and became a Russian prisoner of war in 1916: his novel *Die Geheimnisse des Reichs* (1930), an account of the Russian civil war, is obviously based on his experiences (he returned to Austria in 1920). Doderer studied history at Vienna University, received his doctorate in 1925 and dedicated himself to creating an epic description of the city he knew so well. He had published a book of poems, *Gassen und Landschaften* in 1923, also a short novel *Die Bresche* in 1924, but Doderer felt that he needed the breadth of the full-scale novel to do his subject (Vienna) justice. After decades of preparation *Die Dämonen* appeared in 1956, with *Die Strudlhofstiege* (1951) as an introduction or prelude. (Other novels, *Ein Mord, den jeder begeht* (1938), *Der Umweg* (1940) and *Die erleuchteten Fenster* (1950), are best regarded as sophisticated detective stories and thrillers, meant for a wide readership.) *Die Strudlhofstiege* takes its name from the steps in the Ninth District of Vienna (connecting the Boltzmanngasse with the Liechtensteinstraße): many lives intersect at these steps, from different social strata. The hero is one Melzer, former imperial officer, now senior official in the new republic. The years 1910–11, and 1923–5 are compared and contrasted. Doderer's major achievement, however, is *Die Dämonen*: characters from the *Strudlhofstiege* are reintroduced, and the years 1926–7 are portrayed, 1927 being the year of the burning of the Palace of Justice (see **Canetti**). Doderer seeks to put Vienna on the literary map, like Joyce (Dublin) and Döblin (Berlin); it is generally felt, however, that his wordy exuberance, his long-windedness and his inability to convey the realistic weight (also the mythic presence) of the milieu prevent his being a 'city novelist' of the top rank. The book is felt to lack social awareness, despite the rich clutter of its scenario. Doderer is concerned with a process which he calls *Menschwerdung*: the threat to modern existence is seen in a 'second reality', that is, an ideology, which cuts the individual off from the random complexity of everyday reality about him: the 'first reality', that is, the experience of the 'Alltag' must be regained in a moment of rebirth or epiphany. A certain pretentiousness cannot be denied here, also much implausibility (the worker Leonhard Kakabsa, for example, who experiences Latin as an almost mystical illumination).

After this epic re-creation of Vienna Doderer turned to shorter narrative forms: *Die Posaunen von Jericho* (1958) and *Die Peinigung der Lederbeutelchen* (1959); a scurrilous portrayal of incest (somewhat akin to *Der Erwählte* by **Thomas Mann**) is found in *Die Merowinger oder Die totale Familie*

(1962). In 1963 there appeared *Die Wasserfälle von Slunj*, which gives an account of the years between 1877 and 1910 and the adventures which befall Robert Clayton, a technical adviser to an English engineering firm. The waterfalls at Slunj (Croatia) are meant to serve the same narrative function as the 'Strudlhofstiege', but it seems that the characters visit them in order to perform some symbolic function. This novel is meant to be part of a cycle bearing the title *Roman Nr. 7*, a monumental attempt to cover, in a 'totaler Roman', the period from roughly the end of the 1870s to the beginning of the 1960s (apparently even the volcanic eruption on Tristan da Cunha would have been described). *Der Grenzwald*, a fragmentary part of this cycle, appeared posthumously in 1967. *Frühe Prosa* appeared in 1968; *Die Erzählungen* in 1972 and *Das Doderer Buch* in 1976.

Domin, Hilde (pseudonym of Hilde Palm, 1912–)

Domin's long exile from 1932 to 1954, spent in Italy, Britain and Latin America, inspired her early work, begun in 1951, when she was a teacher of German in the Dominican Republic (from which her pseudonymous surname derives). She made her final return to Germany in 1961, since when she has lived in Heidelberg. Her *Gesammelte Gedichte* (1987) are drawn from the collections *Nur eine Rose als Stütze* (1959), *Rückkehr der Schiffe* (1962), *Hier* (1964), *Höhlenbilder* (1968) and *Ich will dich* (1970), and contain a hundred further poems. Marked by concentration and allusiveness, each poem is 'ein gefrorener Augenblick' and also a process of reflection which the reader may trace to a conclusion by way of the apparently stray thoughts and images preceding it. The central themes of language, exile and yearning for justice and peace relate her work to that of Rose **Ausländer** and Nelly **Sachs**. She has also produced autobiographical writings, *Von der Natur nicht vorgesehen* (1974), *Aber die Hoffnung. Autobiographisches. Aus und über Deutschland* (1982, 1987) and a novel on an emotional triangle *Das zweite Paradies. Roman in Segmenten* (1968, revised version 1980). Her editorial work includes the anthology *Nachkrieg und Unfrieden* (1970) and *Doppelinterpretationen* (1966), in which brief essays by readers and authors on poems by the latter are juxtaposed. The poetological reflections present in the introductions and epilogues to these volumes are continued in the Frankfurt lectures *Das Gedicht als Augenblick der Freiheit* (1968).

Dörmann, Felix (pseudonym for Felix Biedermann, 1870–1928)

A Viennese *fin de siècle* writer, Dörmann exulted in the neurotic, the decadent and the bizarre: his collections of poetry *Neurotica* (1891), *Sensationen* (1892), *Gelächter* (1898) and *Tuberosen* (1920) cultivate the exploration of perverse sensations. His best-known poem is 'Was ich liebe', with its climax: 'Ich liebe, was niemand erlesen,/Was keinem zu lieben gelang:/Mein eignes, urinnerstes Wesen/Und alles, was seltsam und krank'). Dörmann also wrote plays characterized by a crass naturalism (*Ledige Leute* (1897); *Zimmerherren* (1900); *Die Liebesmüden* (1905)). He also provided libretti for popular operettas: *Der Walzertraum* (1907); *Die liebe Unschuld* (1912); *Die goldene Markgräfin* (1912); *Der Liebling von London* (1924). Dörmann struggled to maintain the pose of the decadent, but lacked Oscar Wilde's energy and wit.

Dorst, Tankred (1925–)

Dorst served in the army at the end of the Second World War, was a POW until 1947, then studied German literature, art and drama in Munich, where he has continued to live. His plays since the early 1970s are the result of a close working partnership with his wife Ursula Ehler. In his early work the influence of the marionette theatre and the commedia dell' arte, of Beckett, Ionesco and Giraudoux marks it off from the German tradition of the stage as a place of debate. In *Gesellschaft im Herbst* (1960) a stately home is transformed into an asylum for waifs and strays during the search for a non-existent treasure, in *Die Kurve* (1962) two men profit from accidents on a mountain road and in *Freiheit für Clemens* (1962) a prisoner accommodates himself to his confinement. *Große Schmährede an der Stadtmauer* (1962) approaches Brecht in its handling of the play-within-a-play device in a Chinese setting. After adaptations of *Aucassin et Nicolette* in *Die Mohrin* (1964), of Dekkers's *The Shoemaker's Holiday* in *Der Richter von London* (1966), of Tieck's *Der gestiefelte Kater* (1963) and of Diderot's *Le neveu de Rameau* in *Rameaus Neffe* (1963) Dorst achieved prominence in 1968 with *Toller* on the role of the title-figure in the Munich Räterepublik of 1919, a montage of material from various sources composed in revue style. He then collaborated with the director Peter Zadek on the television film *Rotmord* (1969) based on this play, and on the revue *Kleiner Mann – was nun?* (1972) after the novel by Hans **Fallada**. The film scenario *Sand* (1971, radio play 1973) which explores the motives for a political murder in 1819 was followed by *Eiszeit* (1973) on an old man who can be identified as the unrepentant Nazi sympathizer Knut Hamsun; with his stubborn will to live he is contrasted with his would-be assassin who commits suicide. The late 1970s were occupied with the Merz cycle, an extensive chronicle in various media of a middle-class family between the late 1920s and the present consisting of *Auf dem Chimborazo* (1975, play, radio play and television film), *Dorothea Merz* (1976, novel and television film), *Klaras Mutter* (1978, story and television film), *Die Villa* (1980, play), *Mosch* (1980, film), *Fragment einer Reise nach Stettin* (1981, radio play), *Die Reise nach Stettin* (1984, scenario) and *Heinrich oder die Schmerzen der Phantasie* (1985, play and radio play) which together form a vivid panorama of German history. *Merlin* (1980), consisting of a prologue and two parts ('Die Tafelrunde' and 'Der Gral') lasting almost ten hours, demonstrates the catastrophic consequences of misplaced idealism in a dramatization of parts of the Arthurian cycle in which the title-figure appears as the son of the devil. Dorst's most recent work continues to show a preoccupation with the artist-intellectual in a time of political upheaval, as in *Goncourt oder die Abschaffung des Todes* (1977) set during the Paris commune in 1871 and in *Der verbotene Garten. Fragmente über D'Annunzio* (1982); and with the legend and the *Märchen*, as in the play *Ameley, der Biber und der König auf dem Dach* (1982, radio version 1983), the film *Eisenhans* (1982), the plays *Grindkopf* (1986) and *Korbes* (1988) and the story *Der nackte Mann* (1986), an offshoot from *Merlin* on Parzival's quest for God, while in *Ich, Feuerbach* (1986) he offers a sympathetic portrait of an ageing actor. The conflicts in Dorst's plays, whether between idealism and pragmatism, the general good and individual survival or fulfilment, role-playing and decision-making, the personal and the political, art and reality, all develop from an essentially theatrical concern with existence as a role which renders fluid the distinction between illusion and reality. A *Werkausgabe* has been in progress since 1985.

Drewitz, Ingeborg (1923–86)

Although she began as a dramatist, producing the first play to deal directly with the Nazi concentration camps *Alle Tore waren bewacht* (1955), Ingeborg Drewitz's reputation rests on five novels set in Berlin which combine a broad historical panorama with a sympathetic focus on the problems and conflicts of the principal female characters, who are usually also narrators. *Oktoberlicht* (1969) portrays a day in the life of a middle-aged woman who visits her scattered family after a stay in hospital; in *Wer verteidigt Katrin Lambert?* (1974) a reporter reconstructs the life of a social worker after she is found drowned; in *Das Hochhaus* (1975) the anonymity of the city is exemplified by the lives of tower block residents; *Gestern war heute – Hundert Jahre Gegenwart* (1978) traces the life of the narrator Gabriele M from 1923 to 1978 and develops the flashback technique introduced in *Oktoberlicht*; *Eis auf der Elbe* (1982) makes the diary a vehicle for a similar evocation of the past. *Eingeschlossen* (1986), in which Jesus and Prometheus confront one another as a social worker and an atomic physicist who have become the inmates of a mental hospital, represents a significant departure from the naturalism of her previous work.

Dürrenmatt, Friedrich (1921–90)

A son of the manse, Dürrenmatt studied in Berne and Zurich science, philosophy and German literature, wrote theatre criticism from 1951 to 1953 for the Zurich *Weltwoche* and sketches for cabarets, settled in 1952 in Neuchâtel, where he lived until his death. For many years he, together with **Frisch**, represented contemporary drama in German to the rest of the world.

Early influences consisted of the theology absorbed at home – he was especially in his early years exercised by theological problems in what he recognized as a post-religious age and therefore approaches existentialism – and the plays of Thornton Wilder and **Brecht**. In the course of his career his work was marked by consistency of theme and a formal development towards ever greater emphasis on the grotesque, prompted by his early realization that the anonymity of the forces which control human fate nowadays cannot be reconciled with the traditional conception of tragedy: 'Der heutige Staat ist . . . jedoch unüberschaubar, anonym, bürokratisch geworden . . . Kreons Sekretäre erledigen den Fall Antigone. . . . Schuld gibt es nur noch als persönliche Leistung, als religiöse Tat. Uns kommt nur noch die Komödie bei.' The guiding thread of his plays is the vulnerability of individual freedom and the failure to act responsibly in the face of power structures which arise from collective fear and mask themselves with ideologies which are invalid and harmful. Dürrenmatt began with historical dramas set during the Anabaptist rule in sixteenth-century Münster (*Es steht geschrieben* (1947), second version *Die Wiedertäufer* (1967)) and in the Thirty Years War (*Der Blinde* (1947)), the former on the claims of religion and its fraudulent practice in a time of political upheaval, the latter a mystery play in which the first of a series of courageous men makes his appearance, to be followed by the last Roman emperor in *Romulus der Große* (1949), Graf Übelohe in *Die Ehe des Herrn Mississippi* (1952), the beggar Akki in *Ein Engel kommt nach Babylon* (1953), Ill in *Der Besuch der alten Dame* (1956) and Alfredo Traps in the radio play *Die Panne* (1956); Möbius in *Die Physiker* (1962), who takes refuge in feigned madness in order to preserve moral integrity and save the world from the consequences of his discoveries, also belongs to this line. *Der Meteor* (1966), in which a Nobel Prize-winning author is resurrected against his will, was followed by a number of plays in which the symbiotic relationship between crime and political power is the subject, the Shakespeare adaptations *König Johann* (1968) and *Titus Andronicus* (1970), *Frank V* (1959) on a criminal banking dynasty, with similarities to Brecht's *Die Dreigroschenoper*, *Der Mitmacher* (1973) on corruption and opportunism in a murder syndicate and *Die Frist* (1977) on the slow death of a dictator and the intrigues amongst his potential successors. Dürrenmatt's disillusionment with ideology culminates in *Achterloo* (1983) in which a schematic treatment of the events in Poland in 1983 serves as a foundation for the ridicule of the panaceas represented by Napoleon, Richelieu, Franklin, Hus, Robespierre and Marx. In the context of the breakdown of ideological confrontation in the late 1980s, the play appears unwittingly prophetic. The radio plays occasionally were the testing ground for themes later dramatized for the theatre and are assembled in *Gesammelte Hörspiele* (1961). The most successful of the adaptations for the stage, which include besides Shakespeare Goethe's *Urfaust* and Lessing's *Emilia Galotti*, is *Play Strindberg* (1969). With the exception of the light comedy in prose *Grieche sucht Griechin* (1955) Dürrenmatt's fiction applies the detective story or 'Kriminalroman' (*Der Richter und sein Henker* (1952), *Der Verdacht* (1953), *Die Panne* (1956), *Das Versprechen* (1958), *Justiz* (1985) and *Der Auftrag* (1986)), the Kafkaesque anecdote (some of the stories collected in *Die Stadt: Prosa I–IV* (1952) and *Stoffe I–III* (1981)), the reinterpretation of myth ('Das Bild des Sisyphos' in *Die Stadt*, 'Das Sterben der Pythia' in *Der Mitmacher. Ein Komplex* (1976), the ballad *Der Minotaurus* (1985)) and the political thriller (*Der Sturz* (1971)) to devise variations on the theme of the struggle against evil in a labyrinthine world in which there is no permanently valid moral or judicial authority, elaborated in the *Monstervortrag über Gerechtigkeit und Recht* (1976) and the speech *Über Toleranz* (1977). His other writings include two volumes of *Theaterschriften und Reden* (1966, 1972), *Der Mitmacher. Ein Komplex* (1976), written in reaction to the failure of the play on stage, *Sätze aus Amerika* (1970), *Zusammenhänge. Essay über Israel* (1976), *Albert Einstein* (1979) and *Versuche* (1988). A *Werkausgabe* in thirty volumes appeared in 1980, *Gesammelte Werke* (8 volumes) in 1988 and *Das dramatische Werk* (17 volumes) in 1990.

E

Edschmid, Kasimir (pseudonym of Eduard Schmid, 1890–1966)

Edschmid studied Romance languages in Munich, Geneva, Paris and Strasburg; he rapidly associated himself with the young writers of expressionism and became a tireless propagator and theoretician of that movement. In a famous lecture (13 December 1917) he described the expressionists thus: 'Ihnen entfaltet das Gefühl sich maßlos. . . . So wird der Raum des expressionistischen Künstlers Vision. Er sieht nicht, er schaut. Er schildert nicht, er erlebt. Er gibt nicht wieder, es gestaltet. Er nimmt nicht, er sucht. Nun gibt es nicht mehr die Kette der Tatsachen: Fabriken, Häuser, Krankheit, Huren, Geschrei und Hunger. Nun gibt es die Vision davon.' In the previous year his *Die sechs Mündungen* had appeared, a collection of six *Novellen*, 'die die sechs Mündungen heißen, weil sie von verschiedenen Seiten einströmen in den unendlichen Dreiklang unsrer endlichsten Sensationen – des Verzichts – der tiefen Trauer – und des grenzenlosen Todes': the style is clenched, concentrated and highly charged. *Das rasende Leben* and *Timur* date from the same time; the poem 'Stehe von Lichtern gestreichelt' (1919) is typical in its portrayal of savage sexual encounter. Edschmid gave another speech on expressionism in Darmstadt (10 June 1920) entitled *Stand des Expressionismus*; he gradually distanced himself from the movement and became a prolific writer of popular novels, also travel books (*Glanz und Elend Südamerikas* (1931), *Zaubergröße des Mittelmeers* (1932), and *Italien* (1935–48) in five volumes). In later life he wrote on expressionism again (*Lebendiger Expressionismus* (1961)); his diary (*Tagebuch* (1958–60)) also contains reminiscences. *Frühe Satiren 1917–1920* appeared in 1960, and *Frühe Schriften* in 1970.

Ehrenstein, Albert (1886–1950)

Born in Vienna, son of Hungarian Jewish parents, Ehrenstein was discovered by Karl **Kraus** who published his poems and grotesque prose sketches in *Die Fackel*. His *Tubutsch*, a tragicomic narrative with twelve illustrations by **Kokoschka** made Ehrenstein's name widely known. Other prose works include *Selbstmord eines Katers* (1912), retitled *Bericht aus dem Tollhaus* (1919), *Nicht da, nicht dort* (1916) and *Den ermordeten Brüdern* (1919), a collection which also included poetry, and which lamented, among others, the death of Georg **Trakl**. Ehrenstein is known, however, primarily as a lyric poet; *Der Mensch schreit* (1916) is a collection of expressionist verse, pacifist, dynamic and urgent in tone: the poet, in isolation, laments the destructive fury of man ('Der Kriegsgott', 'Der Dichter und der Krieg', etc.). Other collections of poetry include *Die weiße Zeit* (1914) and *Die rote Zeit* (1917). The continent 'Barbaropa' seemed, to Ehrenstein, to be ripe for annihilation: the poem 'Ende' greets the prospect of the end of the world, a world free from human insanity: 'In den Tagen der Zukunft/rein von Menschenameisen, stürzest du ein/oder es schluckt dich, Erde, die Sonne . . .'. Ehrenstein went to Switzerland during the First World War; he led a restless life afterwards, travelling through Europe and Asia in an attempt to find and cherish the finest manifestations of human civilization. In the 1920s other collections of poetry appeared: *Die Nacht wird* (1920), *Wien* (1921), *Herbst* (1922); a collection of prose narratives, *Mörder aus Gerechtigkeit* was published in 1931: this purports to be a 'Roman aus dem Chinesischen' and consists of four stories, 'Mörder aus Gerechtigkeit', 'Die vier Frauen des treuen Liana', 'Sonderbare Geschichten' and 'Po Sung Ling'. Ehrenstein fled to New York, where he died in a hospital for the poor in 1950. *Gedichte und Prosa* (ed. Karl **Otten**) appeared in 1961; *Ausgewählte Essays*, with articles on, *inter alia*, **Gerhart Hauptmann**, Frank **Wedekind**, Franz **Kafka**, Oskar Kokoschka, Bertolt **Brecht** and **Thomas Mann** appeared in the same year.

Eich, Günter (1907–72)

Like **Huchel**, **Kaschnitz** and **Weyrauch** Eich belongs to the 'lost generation' of writers whose lack of ideological commitment made them dependent during the Third Reich on the few outlets for work in which Nazi cultural policy was not rigidly enforced, such as the short-lived periodical *Die Kolonne* and radio drama. Eich served in the army throughout the Second World War, then spent one year as an American POW, an experience which inspired the much-anthologized archetypal poem of 'Trümmerlyrik', 'Inventur'. His first collection of poems had appeared in 1930 and for some time he remained loyal to the nature lyric as cultivated by **Loerke** and **Lehmann**, but most of his post-war poetry in the volumes *Abgelegene Gehöfte* (1948), *Untergrundbahn* (1949), *Botschaften des Regens* (1955), *Zu den Akten* (1964) and *Anlässe und Steingarten* (1966) is characterized by an exploratory approach to reality and language's relation to it which breaks with the long romantic tradition in which nature is a vehicle for self-expression. Although he is remembered for lines from the radio play *Träume* (1951): 'Wacht auf, denn eure Träume sind schlecht! . . . Seid unbequem, seid Sand, nicht das Öl im Getriebe der Welt', this attitude of vigilant mistrust and suspicion of ideologies typical of the first two decades of West German writing is usually expressed in a less declamatory form, in which the influence of the haiku and Chinese poetry – Eich studied Sinology before the war – is present. After an excursion into wit and whimsy for which there are few precedents in German literature in *Maulwürfe* (1968) and *Ein Tibeter in meinem Büro, 49 Maulwürfe* (1970), consisting of aphorisms, proverbs, nonsensical fantasies prompted by gossip and verbal clichés, Eich returned to poetry in

Nach Seumes Papieren (1972). Eich also achieved prominence in the 1950s as the principal contributor, along with Ilse **Aichinger**, whom he married in 1953, Ingeborg **Bachmann** and Wolfgang Weyrauch to the renaissance of radio drama, composing some fifteen plays within the decade. In them he skilfully adapted the special effects developed in the medium at this time to present a picture of man in a state of existential exposure, in which dream and reality mix or alternate with one another, passive figures express themselves in monologues, some of which are addressed directly to the listener, as in *Der Tiger Jussuf* (1952), undergo metamorphoses of identity, as in *Die andere und ich* (1951), or undertake quests which end in a death they voluntarily accept as their fate, as in *Die Mädchen aus Viterbo* (1953) and *Die Brandung vor Setúbal* (1957). The problem of language as an instrument of knowledge and communication becomes more and more prominent; present already in *Der Tiger Jussuf*, it dominates *Die Stunde des Huflattichs* (1956) and *Man bittet zu läuten* (1964). An edition of Eich's *Werke* in four volumes appeared in 1973.

Einstein, Carl (1885–1940)

Son of a Jewish cantor in Neuwied/Rhein, Einstein studied philosophy and history of art in Berlin; from 1907 onwards he frequently visited Paris, where he associated with Picasso, Braque and Gris. From 1906 to 1909 he worked at *Bebuquin oder die Dilettanten des Wunders* (published 1912), a piece of fiction regarded as the earliest example of expressionist (or 'absolute') prose. It derives from nothing in German literature, rather from André Gide, to whom it is dedicated, and anticipates the utterances of the Dadaists. The short novel is 'logical', but Einstein's logic is utterly divorced from the norm: the hypercerebral and the ironic exist side by side. Diverting is the Eleanora Duse parody (the actress Fredegonde Perlenblick); one of the characters, Nebukadnezar Böhm, although dead, seems unaware of the fact. During the First World War Einstein fought on the Western Front and later worked with the civilian administration in Brussels, where he met Gottfried **Benn** and Carl **Sternheim**. In 1915 his treatise *Negerplastik* appeared, containing 119 illustrations of African masks and statues. Einstein pleaded for a new three-dimensionality, finding in African carvings a sense of spatial structure similar to that created by cubism. At the end of the war Einstein was involved in revolutionary activity in Brussels and Berlin; his rejection of scientific positivism, materialism and capitalism, and his new aesthetic programme (primitive art being defined as the 'Abheben der kapitalistischen Kunstüberlieferung') led him to sympathize with communism. He contributed to *Die Aktion*, and in later writings (*Die Kunst des XX. Jahrhunderts*) sought to combine the assessment of primitivism with social awareness. Einstein identified with the anarchists in the Spanish Civil War and fought with them; he returned to France, but was interned when the German armies invaded. Unable to return to Spain because of his previous involvement he committed suicide at Gave de Pau. *Gesammelte*

Werke (ed. Nef) appeared in 1962; *Werke I* (1908–18), *II* (1919–28) and *III* (1929–40), appeared in Berlin, in 1980, 1981 and 1985 respectively.

Eisenreich, Herbert (1925–86)

Eisenreich has lived in Vienna and Upper Austria, except for a period of war service, four years as a writer for the newspaper *Die Zeit* and the radio in the Federal Republic and a stay in France. He wrote numerous short stories assembled in the collections *Böse schöne Welt* (1957), *Sozusagen Liebesgeschichten* (1965), *Die Freunde meiner Frau* (1966, 1978) and *Die blaue Distel der Romantik* (1976). These and his novels show him to have been the last representative of a tradition of Austrian social fiction which reached its zenith in the work of **Joseph Roth** and Heimito von **Doderer**. *Auch in ihrer Sünde* (1953) relates the trials and tribulations of a widow and her son in the spiritual vacuum left by the collapse of the monarchy after the First World War and turns on doubts concerning the latter's parentage. *Der Urgroßvater* (1964) traces a search for ancestry and identity. *Die abgelegte Zeit* (1985) is the surviving fragment of a novel which originally had the title *Sieger und Besiegte* and presents from the standpoint of 1958 the efforts of a number of characters to adapt to the situation after the Second World War in the spirit advocated by a resigned and conciliatory Austrian general in the theory of retreat he devises in the last weeks of the war.

Elsner, Gisela (1937–)

Elsner achieved fame and notoriety at a stroke with the award of the Formentor Prize for her first novel *Die Riesenzwerge* (1964). The gruesome, grotesque effects conveyed here by mainly concentrating on the meal rituals of the petty bourgeois family can be related to the distanced distortions evident in the work of **Grass**, Jakov **Lind** and the early **Peter Weiss** rather than to the Cologne realists (**Wellershoff**, **Herburger**, **Born**) with whom she was initially associated. They are less manifest in her later novels, but she remains primarily a satirist of contemporary social and domestic mores in the Federal Republic, viewed from the committed standpoint of a member of the West German communist party.

In *Der Nachwuchs* (1970) the narrator is a repulsive child treated as a pet by its parents and forced to make a late discovery of the world beyond the confines of the stuffy family house; narrator, family and neighbours appear, as in *Die Riesenzwerge*, in the same jaundiced light. In the following novels the satire becomes more psychologically penetrating and socially specific: *Das Berührungsverbot* (1975) shows the impact of the sexual revolution on a group of couples whose half-hearted experiments fail to overcome the after-effects of a repressed upbringing, while *Der Punktsieg* (1977) exposes a manufacturer of lingerie with 'progressive' political views, who does not hesitate to sack workers in the interest of profitability. The story collection *Die Zerreißprobe* (1980) includes, in addition to satirical vignettes, 'Die Antwort Hermann Kafkas auf Franz Kafkas Brief an seinen Vater', in which Kafka's father rejects the role of judge devised by his son in order to confirm his self-image as suffering victim. *Abseits* (1982) updates the story of Flaubert's *Madame Bovary*, transferring it to a drab German satellite town in the present, while in *Die Zähmung* (1984) a husband is forced into the dependent role occupied in *Abseits* by the wife. *Das Windei* (1987) covers forty years in the lives of a couple determined to maintain an affluence they have been brought up to take for granted by means of a shady construction business which ends in bankruptcy.

Engelke, Gerrit (1890–1918)

From a working-class background, Engelke, apprenticed to a house-painter, turned early to poetry and in 1913 approached **Dehmel** for encouragement: the latter remarked that Engelke was a better poet than he was himself and recommended him to the so-called 'Werkleute auf Haus Nyland'. (This was a group of poets, formed in 1905, including Jakob Kneip, Joseph Winckler and Heinrich **Lersch**; Winckler's Westphalian farm gave the group its name.) With Kneip Engelke became quickly befriended; after enlistment in 1914 (the outbreak of the war found him writing his novel *Don Juan* in Denmark) Engelke grew closer to Lersch. He is normally considered to be an 'Arbeiterdichter', but the pantheistic, ecstatic element in his poetry is reminiscent of certain aspects of religious expressionism. The poem 'Schöpfung' portrays the creative act of God in declamatory, cosmic images; 'Mensch zu Mensch' is greatly indebted to Whitman and **Werfel**. An enthusiastic proclamation of a higher humanity pulsates throughout much of his work. A selection of his poems appeared in a volume entitled *Schulter an Schulter* (1916). Engelke refused, however, to write 'war poetry' as such: 'Im Marschieren' and 'An den Tod' eschew popular bombast. A projected 'faustische Kriegsdichtung' came to nothing. The 'Buch des Krieges' was written in 1917 in response to the news of the death of his best friend August Deppe. Engelke was killed near Cambrai on 13 October 1918; he is buried close to the spot where Wilfrid Owen was to die two weeks later. *Das Gesamtwerk. Rhythmus des neuen Europa* appeared in 1960 (reprinted 1979).

Engelmann, Bernd (1921–)

After service at the front Engelmann was confined to Dachau and other camps until 1945. He has worked for the news magazine *Der Spiegel* and for the television programme *Panorama* and has held office in the PEN centre of the Federal Republic and the VS (Union of German Writers). As one who owes much to the committed stand taken by such magazines as *Die Weltbühne* in the Weimar Republic he has, like **Wallraff**, turned investigative journalism into a (sort of) art, his sales reaching seven million in 1981. He offered an alternative view of German history in the *Deutsches Antigeschichtsbuch (Wir Untertanen)* (1974), covering the period from the Middle Ages to 1918, *Einig gegen Recht und Freiheit* (1975) on the Weimar Republic and the Third Reich and *Trotz alledem* (1977) on German radicals during the last two hundred years. Semi-documentary works exposing the rich and mighty include *Meine Freunde – die Millionäre* (1963), *Meine Freunde – die Manager* (1966), *Krupp* (1969), *Das Reich zerfiel, die Reichen blieben* (1972), *Ihr da oben – wir da unten* (1973). His three 'Tatsachenromane' ('faction') can be compared to those of **Degenhardt**: in *Großes Bundesverdienstkreuz* (1974) the investigation by an American lawyer of an inheritance problem leads to revelations concerning the Nazi past of a leading industrialist (who brought a libel action which went substantially in Engelmann's favour); in *Hotel Bilderberg* (1977), also modelled on the political thriller, a case of corruption based on the Lockheed affair is shown to be symptomatic of the activities of a right-wing alliance of politicians and industrialists which include former Nazis hastily rehabilitated by the occupation forces after the war; in *Die Laufmasche* (1980) the protest against enforced dispossession of a farm to make way for a satellite town is linked with the attempt to bring to justice those responsible for driving a couple to suicide in 1944, with the victimization of a guest-worker and with the activities of neo-Nazis.

Enzensberger, Hans Magnus (1929–)

Enzensberger grew up in Bavaria, studied in Germany and France from 1949 to 1954 and worked under **Andersch** for South German Radio. He has lived as a free-lance writer or as a lecturer in Norway (which inspired some bleak nature poems), Rome and the USA. A stay in Cuba prompted an interest in the Castro revolution and the attempt to reverse it in the Bay of Pigs invasion, which bore fruit in *Das Verhör von Habana* (1970), one of the last of the documentary plays which dominated the West German stage in the late 1960s. After writing a doctoral dissertation (1955), which was eventually published as *Clemens Brentanos Poetik* (1961), he came to the attention of the public with the poetry collections *verteidigung der wölfe* (1957), *landessprache* (1960) and *blindenschrift* (1964), which combine a Brechtian intellectual delight in and exposure of contradiction and paradox with an emotional reaction to hated phenomena in the West German and world scene in which rage and arrogance find expression in elaborate imagery sometimes reminiscent of Gottfried **Benn**. The poems in the first collection were introduced as 'Inschriften, Plakate, Flugblätter, in eine

Mauer geritzt' and divided into sections entitled 'Freundliche Gedichte', 'Traurige Gedichte' and 'Böse Gedichte', while the polemical note reached its climax in the long poems 'landessprache' and 'schaum' in the second collection. *Mausoleum. 37 Balladen aus der Geschichte des Fortschritts* (1975) presents portraits of major politicians, revolutionaries, scientists and inventors in a survey of the contradictions inherent in the development of humanity towards greater freedom and control of the environment, the darker aspect of which receives allegorical treatment in *Der Untergang der Titanic* (1978); here the threat to civilization in the twentieth century is explored on three time-levels, 1912 when the ship sank, 1969 when Enzensberger visited Cuba and 1977 when the book was composed. *Gedichte 1955–1970* (1971) adds to the first three collections thirty-three poems; the contents of this volume, together with *Die Furie des Verschwindens* (1980), fifteen poems previously published in book form and 'zehn Lieder für Ingrid Caven' are assembled in *Die Gedichte* (1983).

Enzensberger is a polemicist schooled in the dialectic of Hegel, Marx and Adorno, to the last of whom he owes insights developed in the essays collected in *Einzelheiten* (two volumes (1962 and 1984)) which rigorously analyse the West German media. He edited the periodical *Kursbuch* from 1965 to 1975 and presided over the notorious fifteenth and sixteenth issues in 1968 which rejected the mainstream of literary criticism and of politically uncommitted imaginative writing, while more recently he has been associated with the 'Journal des Luxus und der Moden' *Transatlantik*, modelled on the *New Yorker*. His journalism has been collected in the volumes *Politik und Verbrechen* (1964), *Politische Kolportagen* (1966), *Deutschland, Deutschland unter anderem* (1967), *Palaver* (1974), *Politische Brosamen* (1982), the seven travel reports *Ach Europa!* (1987) and the compendium *Mittelmaß und Wahn* (1988). With *Das Verhör von Habana*, the documentary collage *Der kurze Sommer der Anarchie. Buenaventura Durrutis Leben und Tod* (1972) on a Spanish anarchist shot in 1936 and the libretti for musical compositions by Hans Werner Henze, *El Cimarrón* (1970) and *La Cubana – oder ein Leben für die Kunst* (1975) form a Hispano-American complex, while the five prose biographies of *Der Weg ins Freie. Fünf Lebensläufe* (1975) mark a withdrawal from what he had come to recognize as the pseudo-authenticity of reportage. *Der Menschenfeind* (1979), a version of Molière's *Le misanthrope* and *Der Menschenfreund* (1984), a version of Diderot's *Est-il bon? Est-il méchant?* focus on intellectuals whose actions and attitudes reflect the contradictions of the social group to which they – then and now – and Enzensberger as their contemporary representative belong.

Enzensberger has been a key figure in the intellectual life of the Federal Republic from its foundation and his influence far transcends the reputation he has gained from his contribution to any single genre, even poetry. Occasionally derided as a chameleon figure he has demonstrated by his polemical talent, his wit, his cosmopolitanism, his versatility in several media and his ability to take a broad view of social and political developments and to assess their implications in a pragmatic spirit unusual in the German left, that, as in the days of Heinrich Heine, there is a place for positive subversion.

Ernst, Paul (1866–1933)

Coming from a working-class background (the family had traditionally been miners), Ernst studied philosophy and theology before moving (in 1886) to Berlin, where he became involved in socialist activity and associated with the literary-political society *Durch*, as well as contributing to the *Berliner Volkstribüne*. A visit to Italy turned his attention to questions of artistry rather than politics: a neo-romantic phase giving way rapidly to neo-classicism. As *Dramaturg* in Weimar (1903–14) Ernst wrote a series of historical plays (including *Demetrios* (1905), *Canossa* (1908), *Brunhild* (1909) and *Ninon de Lenclos* (1910)). After 1918 the patriotic tone in his writing became more pronounced, and his conservative stance more extreme; the basic human problems, Ernst believed, were revealed more clearly in rural, even feudal, society than amongst the urban proletariat. His literary reputation is founded on his prose rather than his dramas: his novel *Der schmale Weg zum Glück* appeared in 1904 and *Saat auf Hoffnung* in 1916; both contain autobiographical elements. The hero of the first, one Hans Werther, rejects social and political preoccupations and finds fulfilment in marriage and agriculture. Most well-known are the collections of *Novellen*: the *Komödianten und Spitzbubengeschichten* (1927) are comic tales with an Italian background similar to that favoured by Paul Heyse; *Geschichten zwischen Tag und Traum* (1930) contain exotic and supernatural elements; *Geschichten von deutscher Art* (1928) have patriotic themes, and the *Romantische Geschichten* (1930) evoke a pseudo-medieval world. Ernst's best-known stories are probably *Das Porzellangeschirr* and *Das Eisenbahnwägelchen*: both deal with problems of fate and responsibility. Ernst's insistence on classical severity frequently leads to a sparse and lifeless quality in his writing. His essays (including *Der Weg zur Form* (1906)) advocate restraint and order in writing and a hierarchical ideal in society. The attempt to rescue the verse-epic (*Das Kaiserbuch* (1922–8), and *Der Heiland* (1930)) was largely unsuccessful. Paul Ernst was deemed a 'safe' writer by the Nazis: his *Kassandra* had a prominent production in Berlin in 1938. Ernst had, in fact, been elevated to the *Dichter-Akademie* of the Third Reich, but died in May 1933. His *Gesammelte Werke* (now largely unread) appeared between 1928 and 1942 in twenty-one volumes.

Ewers, Hanns Heinz (1871–1943)

Ewers began writing poetry heavily indebted to neo-romantic and decadent modes; he later appeared in the Munich cabarets *Überbrettl* and *Die elf Scharfrichter*, where his grotesquely satirical humour was exploited to the full. His first literary successes were the two collections of bizarre stories *Das Grauen* (1907) and *Die Besessenen* (1908); the novel *Der Zauberlehrling oder die Teufelsjäger* (1909) shocked by its horrifyingly orgiastic scene in which a pregnant girl is crucified and her unborn child stabbed by a pitchfork. The second novel, *Alraune. Die Geschichte eines lebenden Wesens*

(1911) was immensely popular (a girl is born from the seed of an ejaculating victim of the hangman implanted in a certain Alma Raune in a nearby hospital): it reached sales of over a quarter of a million in ten years and was filmed twice, the 1928 version being provided by Henrik Galeen (who also wrote the film script for Murnau's *Nosferatu*, Ewers himself having provided the script for *Der Student von Prag* in 1913). *Vampir. ein verwilderter Roman in Farben und Fetzen* appeared in 1920; *Nachtmahr*, another collection of horror stories, followed in 1922. Ewers considered himself the herald of a fantastic Satanist movement that looked back to Poe and de Sade: the stories alternate between portrayals of algolagnia, stock-in-trade horror (spider-women etc.) and pornography, whilst the novels are characterized by a style compounded of journalistic reportage, sentimentality and commercialized nastiness. *Der Fundvogel* (1928) is a sensational account of an enforced sex change. Ewers was ready and eager to serve the Nazi cause; in 1932 he wrote the *Reiter in deutscher Nacht* (the story of the *Freikorps*) and then, probably on Hitler's recommendation, the biography of Horst Wessel, *Ein deutsches Schicksal*: 200,000 copies were sold in 1934. Ewers was appointed to the *Dichter-Akademie*, but the Nazis, finding his earlier writings incompatible with visions of Nordic health, prohibited further writing and pronounced Ewers degenerate. His work is primarily of interest in the link that it provides between decadence, Satanism and National Socialism. *Gesammelte Werke* (eight vols) appeared in 1928. *Die Spinne. Seltsame Geschichten* were published in 1964.

F

Fallada, Hans (pseudonym of Rudolf Ditzen, 1893–1947)

Ditzen adopted his pseudonym after the murdered horse Falada of Grimm's fairy-tale whose cut-off head continued to tell unpleasant truths to an unheeding world. His first successful novel was *Bauern, Bonzen und Bomben* (1931), a rambling and yet accurate account of a farmers' revolt, based on an actual event in Holstein which Fallada had witnessed: the novel was highly praised by Kurt **Tucholsky** as 'die beste Schilderung der deutschen Kleinstadt, die mir in den letzten Jahren bekannt geworden ist'. Fallada became instantly famous with *Kleiner Mann, was nun?* (1932), a moving (and at times sentimental) account of the struggles of a young couple to survive during the harsh years of unemployment and frustration. The protagonist Pinneberg attempts to defend his private happiness between the middle classes on the one hand and the proletariat on the other, dreading redundancy and the threat of impoverishment: the 'little man' fights a losing battle, but his wife ('Lämmchen') remains resilient and cheerful. *Wer einmal aus dem Blechnapf frißt* (1934) concerns the plight of the recidivist: the novel is compared often with *Berlin Alexanderplatz* by **Döblin**, but remains within the realist tradition in its narrative structure. *Wolf unter Wölfen* (1937) is a tragic account of the battle for survival in post-1918 Germany. Fallada, an alcoholic, wrote at frantic pace to provide himself with funds; during the Third Reich he turned to idyllic romances and folksy legends. *Damals bei uns daheim* (1942) and *Heute bei uns zu Hause* (1943) are little more than autobiographies. The Russians elected Fallada as mayor of Feldberg in Mecklenburg two years before his death. Posthumous novels of merit include *Jeder stirbt für sich allein* (1949) and *Der Trinker* (1950). Fallada is a powerful story-teller who succeeds best when describing the narrow, sentimental world of the *petite bourgeoisie*: he is less convincing when a fake folksiness and an exaggerated sympathy with the underdog intrude. The *Ausgewählte Werke in Einzelausgaben* appeared from 1962; *Gesammelte Erzählungen* in 1967.

Fassbinder, Rainer Werner (1946–82)

Although Fassbinder's fame rests on his work as the most controversial, successful, productive and original film-maker of the Federal Republic, his place in a survey of West German literature is ensured by his own contributions as author to the theatre and by his dependence on German (and foreign) authors in his adaptations. The three original plays later transferred to other media are *Katzelmacher* (1968 as a play, 1969 as a film), on the persecution of a Greek guest-worker by the young men of a village community, which can be related to the critical *Volksstücke* of **Kroetz** and **Sperr** in its debt to Marieluise **Fleißer**, to whom the film version is dedicated, *Bremer Freiheit* (1971, television version 1973) on the authentic case of a female poisoner in Bremen in 1820 and *Die bitteren Tränen der Petra von Kant* (1971, film 1972) on an exploitative lesbian relationship. Plays which never made the transition to film or television but were mainly performed at the Munich *antitheater* include *Preparadise sorry now* (1969) on the Moors murderers Brady and Hindley, *Werwolf* (with Harry Bär, 1969), *Anarchie in Bayern* (1969), *Blut am Hals der Katze* (original title *Marilyn Monroe contre les vampires* (1971)) in which a visitor from another planet is turned into a vampire, and the never-realized *Die schönen Tage der Faschisten* on Evita Peron. His productions of Ferdinand **Bruckner**'s *Die Verbrecher* (1967), Fleißer's *Pioniere in Ingolstadt* (1971 for both theatre and television), Goethe's *Iphigenie auf Tauris* (1968), Molnár/**Polgar**'s *Liliom* (1972) and **Heinrich Mann**'s *Bibi* (1973) as a revue are in some instances radical reworkings. His films include *Wildwechsel* (1972) by Franz Xaver Kroetz, *Fontane Effi Briest* (1974) (the nineteenth-century novel by Theodor Fontane), *Bolwieser* (1977) by Oskar Maria **Graf** and most important of all in a remarkably faithful rendering of a work to which Fassbinder was especially attuned *Berlin Alexanderplatz* by Alfred **Döblin**, televised in fourteen parts in 1980. His dramatization of *Der Mull, die Stadt und der Tod* (published in 1976, performed in New York in 1987) by Gerhard **Zwerenz** has yet to appear on the stage of the Federal Republic.

Fels, Ludwig (1946–)

Of working-class origin, Fels has more successfully than any other contemporary social realist, with the possible exception of **Kroetz**, encapsulated in his poetry and prose the sadness, frustration, anger and disorientation of the under-class in the urban environment. Neither the communist-inspired experiments in 'proletarian' writing of the 1920s nor the left-wing romanticism and theorizing of the 1960s appear to have had any influence and his association with the *Werkkreis Literatur der Arbeitswelt* (see **Wallraff**) was brief. Fels relies on experience and an unidealistic identification with his characters. His most important works to date are the novels *Die Sünden der Armut* (1976) and *Ein Unding der Liebe* (1981) and the plays *Lämmermann* (1983) and *Der Affenmörder* (1985).

Feuchtwanger, Lion (1884–1958)

Dramatic critic, playwright and novelist, Feuchtwanger made his reputation in the 1920s with a series of historical novels. He helped Bertolt **Brecht** with *Trommeln in der Nacht* (originally called *Spartakus*) and collaborated with him on *Leben Eduards des Zweiten von England*; Brecht in turn helped him to revise his *Warren Hastings, Gouverneur von Indien* (written 1915, published 1916) and, some twenty years later, wrote with him *Die Gesichte der Simone Machard*. Feuchtwanger's novel *Erfolg* (1930) gives a thinly disguised portrayal of Brecht as 'Kaspar Proeckl', a motor-car designer. His novels *Die häßliche Herzogin Margarete Maultasch* (1923) and *Jud Süß* (1925) made him internationally known: the latter was filmed by the Nazis with Ferdinand Marian in the leading role, while Werner Kraus played all the other Jews. A Jew himself, Feuchtwanger described as early as 1933 (in *Die Geschwister Oppenheim*) the sufferings and tribulations of his fellow Jews in Germany. He fled to France and also visited the Soviet Union; he became co-editor with Brecht and Willi Bredel of the anti-fascist literary review *Das Wort*, published in Moscow. He was interned in Vichy France (he had also been interned as a German in Tunisia in 1914), escaped to America, where he moved to Pacific Palisades and became one of the leading German writers in exile (he often used the pseudonym 'J. L. Wetcheek'). Novels written in his exile include *Die Brüder Lautensack* (1944), *Der Tag wird kommen* (1945) and *Waffen für Amerika* (two vols, 1947–8). His plays, mostly Old Testament and historical dramas, have not proved successful, apart from those written in collaboration with Brecht. Together with others, Feuchtwanger founded the Aurora publishing house in New York at the end of the war to bring out works in German for the reviving German market. In 1953 he was awarded the *Nationalpreis der DDR*. His *Gesammelte Werke* appeared from 1933–48; the *Gesammelte Werke* (twenty vols) from 1959 on, with a sixteen volume edition appearing in 1984.

Fichte, Hubert (1935–86)

The illegitimate son of a Jewish father, Fichte spent part of his childhood in a Catholic orphanage, an experience which formed the basis of his first novel *Das Waisenhaus* (1965). He then trained as an actor, but also worked on the land in North Germany and Provence before becoming a professional writer in Hamburg. Here he remained until his death, except for extensive journeys in South America and the Caribbean in connection with his later anthropological works. The novels *Die Palette* (1968), *Detlevs Imitationen 'Grünspan'* (1971) and *Versuch über die Pubertät* (1974) are all autobiographical and are set in the Hamburg alternative scene represented in two of these by the night-spots named in their titles; in them Fichte cultivates a fragmented prose style with cinematic features, including flashbacks to the Second World War like the bombardment of Hamburg in 1943 (cf. **Nossack**, *Der Untergang*) and references to the ritual practices of Afro-American religions. These form the subject of the following works: *Xango* (1976) (accompanied by a photographic volume with the same title), dealing with Bahia, Haiti and Trinidad, and *Petersilie* (1980), on Santo Domingo, Venezuela, Miami and Grenada, a development of the preoccupation with abnormal sexual practices and psychopathology which is reflected in his earlier work. The numerous works left unpublished on Fichte's death have been grouped together under the title *Die Geschichte der Empfindlichkeit*, forming eight volumes planned to appear between 1987 and 1991. His earlier works include *Der Aufbruch nach Turku und andere Erzählungen* (1963), fourteen episodes from the lives of young drifters, and *Wolli Indienfahrer* (1978), seven interviews offering a cross-section of the St Pauli community, Hamburg's red-light district. Although Fichte had little contact with literary groups his work is symptomatic of recent trends ('neue Subjektivität' and Third World themes).

Flake, Otto (1880–1963)

With René **Schickele**, Ernst **Stadler** and Hans **Arp**, Otto Flake was one of the leading representatives of the Alsatian literary circle which came together in 1901–2 and contributed to the periodical *Stürmer*. During the First World War he was in Brussels and was in close contact with **Sternheim**, **Einstein** and **Benn**. Flake is best known for his expressionist novel *Die Stadt des Hirns* (1919), a work which claims in its preface to be modern and difficult ('Hilflos sitzt Leser da wie er hilflos vor einem kubistischen gar abstrakten Bild steht. . . . Ihr sollt euch nicht drei Stunden mit einem Buch beschäftigen, sondern drei Wochen denkend verbringen'); the book is, however, facile in content and conventional in structure. The title refers to the hero's dream of wandering through a brain whose electrical impulses relate to the cosmos. Flake turned to traditional writing after the war and sought to promote understanding between France and Germany: the *Romane um Ruland* (five vols, 1926–8) concern the experiences of Ruland the modern European. In the 1930s Flake embarked upon a *Badische Chronik*: he also wrote essays on French literary figures, his best being on the Marquis de Sade (1930), whose preface attempts to explain that it is necessary to describe the perverse in order fully to appreciate the norm. After the Second World War Flake continued to portray the ideal European (*Ein Mann von Welt* (1947)). An autobiography appeared in 1960 (*Es wird Abend*). Flake's reputation rests with *Die Stadt des Hirns*: any attempt to compare Flake and Döblin as writers of polyhistorical novels is generally unconvincing. The *Werke* (five vols) appeared from 1973 to 1976.

Fleißer, Marieluise (1901–74)

Marieluise Fleißer studied at Munich and was encouraged to write by Lion **Feuchtwanger**, to whom she had shown a short story. In 1924 she met Bertolt **Brecht**, who had the most far-reaching influence upon her work. In 1926 her play *Fegefeuer in Ingolstadt* was produced through Brecht's intervention in Berlin (the original title, *Die Fußwaschung*, being forgotten).

It is a sultry, tormented account of the problems (sexual and religious) of puberty, and owes much to **Wedekind**, also the early plays of Brecht (the theme of unmotivated aggression owes much to *Im Dickicht der Städte*). More sober is *Pioniere in Ingolstadt* (1929), a hard-boiled portrayal of the effect on the young girls of the town of the arrival of a troop of soldiers. The succession of short scenes anticipates the theatre of Ödön von **Horváth**. A volume of short stories, *Ein Pfund Orangen*, appeared in 1929; in 1931 Fleißer published her novel *Mehlreisende Frieda Geier*, a laconic account of a young swimmer and the conflicting demands of job and lover: the tone is deliberately flat. Fleisser was not able to regain her earlier popularity: the shadow of Brecht loomed too large, and her indebtedness to his style was too pronounced. (*Avantgarde* (1962) is a thinly-veiled portrayal of Brecht.) Her play on Charles I, *Karl Stuart*, was first published in 1946. The *Gesammelte Werke* (three vols) appeared in 1972, a four-volume edition in 1988.

Flex, Walter (1887–1917)

Flex, who was killed in the fighting on the island of Ösel (Estonian Saaremaa) in the First World War, wrote one of the most popular best-sellers of that war, *Der Wanderer zwischen beiden Welten* (1916), a *Novelle* which exemplified many *Wandervögel* attitudes. The hero, Ernst Wurche, is Flex's *alter ego*: he carries with him into battle three sacred books (the New Testament, Goethe's poems and Nietzsche's *Also sprach Zarathustra*); he rejoices in comradeship, self-sacrifice and a glowing faith in Germany's greatness. The cult of youth and the latent homosexuality (the bathing scene *à la* Fidus) are also very much of its time, as is the quasi-religious cult of death. Flex had also published two volumes of poems before the war and a historical tragedy in verse, *Klaus Bismarck* (1913), dealing with an ancestor of the Prussian statesman (Flex had been a private tutor to the Bismarck family). After the war there appeared posthumously *Zwölf Bismarcks* (1925), a collection of sketches, some verging on the hagiographical, of other Bismarck ancestors. (This was reprinted in Riga as late as May 1944.) *Gesammelte Werke* (two vols) appeared in 1925. Flex's work, however, met with little favour after 1945, when a concept such as 'die welterlösende Sendung des Deutschtums' (a phrase used by Flex) was hardly permissible.

Fock, Gorch (pseudonym of Hans Kinau, 1880–1916)

Gorch Fock ('Fock' means foresail) was killed at the battle of Jutland in 1916 when the *Wiesbaden* was sunk. He was famous for short stories concerning the lives of North German fishermen (his father having been one): *Schullengrieper und Tungenknieper* (1911), *Fahrersleute* (1914) and *Nordsee* (1916). He reached a wide readership with his novel *Seefahrt ist not!*

(1913). Much of his writing is in *Plattdeutsch*, particularly the *Hamborger Janmooten* (1914). His plays, *Cilli Cohrs* (1914) and *Doggerbank* (posthumously, 1918) are less successful. Fock also published a collection of *Plattdeutsche Kriegsgedichte* (1914–15), many of them humorous: the poem 'De dicke Berta' is a droll account of the big gun ('Dicke Berta heet ik,/ tweeundveertig meet ik,/wat ik kan, dat weet ik,/söben Milen scheet ik!') The *Sterne überm Meer. Tagebuchblätter und Gedichte* (1917) and *Ein Schiff! Ein Schiff! Ein Segel* (1934) made popular reading in schools; the portentous and frequently melodramatic style of these two books is lampooned by Günter **Grass** in *Katz und Maus*. The *Sämtliche Werke* (five vols) were published in 1925. *Das schnellste Schiff der Flotte. Die besten Geschichten Gorch Focks* appeared in 1980. The West German training-ship for young cadets is named after him.

Fontana, Oskar Maurus (1889–1969)

A Dalmatian born in Vienna, O. M. Fontana made his name with a group of plays (including *Die Milchbrüder* (1912), *Der Studentengeneral* (1913) and *Marc* (1917)) which were characterized by an uneasy fusion of neo-romantic and expressionistic elements. During the First World War (1916) Fontana edited an anthology of Austrian expressionist poetry, *Die Aussaat*; his later essay *Der Expressionismus in Wien. Erinnerungen* is an informative and sympathetic document. The prose works *Erweckung* (1919), *Empörer* (1920) and *Insel Elephantine* (1926) are of interest in any account of Austrian expressionism. In 1920 Fontana contributed poems to a collection by E. A. Rheinhardt entitled *Die Botschaft*. Fontana turned increasingly to the novel: his *Die Gefangene der Erde* (1928) is a realistic yet also highly intensified description of the plight of a mother during and immediately after the First World War. In 1936 appeared *Der Weg durch den Berg*, a novel dealing with the building of the St Gotthard pass; another novel dealing with the advantages and disadvantages of modern technology (the use of gas) is *Der Atem des Feuers* (1954). Fontana's most interesting novel for British readers is *Der Engel der Barmherzigkeit* (1950), an account of the life of Florence Nightingale, who is seen by Fontana as the personification of *caritas*. In his later years Fontana devoted himself to theatre criticism. In 1948 he published *Wiener Schauspieler*, a portrayal of famous actors and actresses (from Mitterwurzer to Maria Eis). A selection of his writings, *Mond im Abendrot*, was published in 1962.

Forte, Dieter (1935–)

After working in advertising and television Forte settled in Basel, where his plays have received their premières. The first, the controversial *Martin Luther & Thomas Münzer oder Die Einführung der Buchhaltung* (1971) aims, like Martin Walser's *Das Sauspiel* (1975), to demythologize its subject and demonstrate the predominance of materialistic factors in history. In the second, *Jean Henry Dunant oder Die Einführung der Zivilisation* (1978), the rise and fall of the banker who became the founder of the International Red Cross is the unifying element in a panorama of the nineteenth century. In *Kaspar Hausers Tod* (1979) analogies to the situation in Germany in 1977 (anti-terrorist campaign) are indicated in the funeral of the famous foundling murdered in 1833. *Das Labyrinth der Träume* (1983) juxtaposes the careers of two mass murderers, Peter Kürten, the so-called vampire of Düsseldorf, and Adolf Hitler. Forte is also the author of numerous plays for radio and television in which everyday subjects are treated with original use of these media.

Frank, Bruno (1887–1945)

Frank can be associated with the generation of middle-class novelists active between the wars (**Heinrich** and **Thomas Mann**, Lion **Feuchtwanger**, Franz **Werfel**, Hermann **Broch**), who combined historical awareness, acute psychological insight and stylistic refinement and who were forced into emigration by the Nazis. Frank became a member of the Californian emigration close to Thomas Mann, the influence of whose *Der Tod in Venedig* is evident in the development to a tragic close of *Politische Novelle* (1928), a work inspired by the wish for Franco-German reconciliation and European unity. Like Feuchtwanger's historical novels centred on artists and intellectuals painfully embroiled in the political and religious tensions of their time (e.g. Goya, Josephus) Frank's most important work *Cervantes* (1934) draws a parallel between the trials and tribulations of an author of the past and the desperate struggle of his mid-twentieth-century equivalent to maintain his principles. Frank was drawn to proud solitary men with an Achilles heel and portrayed them with imagination and sympathy: Frederick the Great in *Tage des Königs* (1924) and *Trenck* (1926) (and the play *Zwölftausend* (1927)), the director Max Reinhardt in *Der Magier* (1929) and a fictional prince forced into exile in the Third Reich in *Der Reisepaß* (1937). His play *Sturm im Wasserglas* (1930), about an unscrupulous small-town careerist, was adapted by James Bridie as *Storm in a Teacup* in 1936.

Frank, Leonhard (1882–1961)

After training as a mechanic, Frank moved to Munich in 1904, where he studied painting. In Berlin he published his first novel, *Die Räuberbande* (1914) which met with considerable success: the title refers to the fantasy world indulged in by working-class children. A socialist and pacifist, Frank fled to Switzerland during the First World War; he worked with René

Schickele and in *Die weißen Blätter* published in 1916 the famous story *Der Kellner*, which tells of a waiter who, having lost his son in the war, devotes himself to the highest humanitarian ideals. It later appeared as the introductory story of the collection *Der Mensch ist gut* (1918). Frank had publicly slapped the face of a writer in the Café des Westens in Berlin who had rejoiced in the sinking of the *Lusitania* with the loss of 1,198 lives: the incident is recorded in the autobiographical novel *Links, wo das Herz ist* (1952). Another much-read *Novelle* was *Die Ursache* (1915), which Frank dramatized in 1928: it is an attack upon capital punishment. Frank returned to Germany after the war, and received the Kleist prize for *Der Mensch ist gut*. The novel *Das Ochsenfurter Männerquartett* (1927) can be compared with Fallada's *Kleiner Mann, was nun?* in its expression of pity for the underdog in inflationary times; *Der Bürger* (1929), dedicated to 'der bürgerlichen Jugend', pleads for understanding and fraternity. The novel *Karl und Anna* (1927) is an example of 'Heimkehrerliteratur'; it was successfully dramatized in 1929. In 1933 Frank escaped to Switzerland, France and finally America. He returned to Germany in 1950, published his autobiographical novel in 1952 and the *Deutsche Novelle* two years later. Some of the later writings (particularly *Traumgefährten* (1936)) tend to the introspective rather than the political. He received the East German *Nationalpreis* in 1955 and the West German *Großes Verdienstkreuz* in 1957. Frank is best regarded as a novelist who, through his left-wing political sympathies, remained on the fringe of the expressionist movement; his narrative prose is, however, traditional in structure. *Gesammelte Werke in Einzelausgaben* (five vols) appeared in 1936; the *Gesammelte Werke* (six vols) in 1957; *Die Summe* in 1982.

Franke, Manfred (1930–)

Having written a doctoral dissertation on the figure of Schinderhannes in the German folk-tradition, Franke went on to produce a documentation in 1977 and a demythologizing biography in 1984 of the same Robin Hood figure. In the anthology *Straßen und Plätze* (1967) he gave an account of a traumatic childhood experience which eventually prompted the writing of his best-known work to date *Mordverläufe 9/10.XI.38* (1973), which traces the course of the 'Reichskristallnacht' in a provincial town and consists of a collage of quotations from police records and newspaper reports, together with topographical information, statistics, etc. In aiming to demonstrate what is typical in this microscopic view of a particular case Franke can be associated with other documentary writers active in a similar spirit at the same time, especially Alexander **Kluge**. Franke has also written *Ein Leben auf Probe* (1967), the story of the struggle to survive of a child suffering from a rare illness, *Bis der Feind kommt* (1970), an autobiographical novel on the last days of the Second World War viewed from the perspective of a fourteen-year-old boy (cf. Gert **Hofmann**, *Unsere Eroberung* (1984)) and a biography of the Nazi 'martyr' Albert Leo Schlageter in 1980.

Frenssen, Gustav (1863–1945)

Born in Dithmarschen, Frenssen became a pastor there before turning to writing novels. His first, *Die Sandgräfin* (1896) is a facile account of an aristocratic family whose fortunes are restored by the daughters' marriage to bourgeois suitors; the second, *Die drei Getreuen* (1898), attracted little attention. The third novel, *Jörn Uhl* (1901) became enormously successful: an example of *Heimatkunst*, it tells of the struggle of the eponymous hero to keep his North German farm in the face of great opposition (indifference of siblings, military service, fire and storm damage). The farm is finally abandoned, but Uhl turns his attention to agricultural industry, builds dikes and continues to serve the community. The novel was enthusiastically reviewed by **Rilke**, who praised its 'Frische, Kraft und Menschlichkeit' ('Man befindet sich nicht so sehr einem Kunstwerk gegenüber . . . als vielmehr einem Menschen'). *Hilligenlei* (1905) tells of the attempt by the hero, Kai Jans, to write the 'Leben Christi des Deutschen'; Frenssen's Germanic Christianity has a disturbing quality which is reinforced by his later, pagan attitudes. *Peter Moors Fahrt nach Südwest* (1907) is an account of colonial adventure; *Klaus Hinrich Baas* and *Der Untergang der Anna Hollmann* followed in 1910 and 1911 respectively. In the 1920s Frenssen continued to write novels of life in Dithmarschen; in 1933 he was awarded an honorary doctorate at Heidelberg and became a member of the *Dichter-Akademie*. *Der Glaube der Nordmark* (1936) is his most extreme statement of belief: 'Weil der Führer und seine Bewegung ihr Werk aus der tiefsten Tiefe der germanischen Seele holten, so erscheint . . . deutlicher als jemals in der deutschen Geschichte der alte, urgermanische Glaube. . . . Das Christentum ist alt und welk geworden. Die Zeit ist erfüllt.' *Die Begegnung von Skagerak* appeared in 1918; *Lebensrückblick* (an autobiography) in 1940. Frenssen died, four weeks before the end of hostilities, in April 1945. *Gesammelte Werke* (six vols) were published in 1943.

Fried, Erich (1921–88)

Fried emigrated from Vienna to London at the time of the *Anschluß* after his father had been made the victim of Gestapo brutality. He remained in Britain until his death, employed for a time by the BBC World Service and active as a translator of Shakespeare, Dylan Thomas, Wilfred Owen and T. S. Eliot. His first collections (*Deutschland* (1944), *Österreich* (1945)) were typical products of exile literature, while *Reich der Steine. Zyklische Gedichte* (1963) incorporated the non-specific imagery characteristic of certain modernist trends. A political dimension emerges in the laconic word play of *Warngedichte* (1965) and becomes dominant in *und Vietnam und* (1966). Since then he has produced eighteen volumes of poetry, four collections of short stories and a novel on the delicate topic of guilt for Nazi crimes *Ein Soldat und ein Mädchen* (1960). Fried is the most skilled of those poets (including von **Törne**, **Delius** and **Zahl**) who have applied **Brecht**'s dialectical technique to the political problems which have arisen since Brecht's death. His relation to Brecht (and other poets) emerges in numerous quotations from them in contexts which provide occasion for challenge and elaboration, and the principle of paradox as a motor of thought is refined and extended to include puns and word games, phonetic experiments, parodies and montages of other poets' styles and a pragmatic analysis of the implications of clichés and slogans from all sections of the political spectrum.

Fries, Fritz Rudolf (1935–)

Born in Spain, the home of his maternal ancestors, Fries came with his family to Germany in 1942, went to school in Leipzig until 1953, studied there, was employed in the 1960s at the GDR Academy of Sciences and then became a full-time writer and translator. Fries was one of the first GDR writers to inject a strong element of fantasy conveyed by means of interior monologue into a story which otherwise conforms to conventional realism, thus heralding a trend in GDR writing of growing importance during the 1970s and 1980s, when the influence of the German romantics became ever more apparent (**Fühmann**, de **Bruyn**, **Christa Wolf**, **Morgner**). *Der Weg nach Oobliadooh* (published 1966 in the Federal Republic only) relates the picaresque adventures of the interpreter Arlec and the dentist Paasch, who yearn to discover a West which will conform to a fantasy image they have created with the aid of Dizzy Gillespie's song 'I knew a princess in the land of Oobliadooh'. They go no farther than West Berlin, from which they return to play the role expected of them by officialdom of disillusioned victims of Western intrigues aimed at undermining the GDR. *Das Luft-Schiff. Biographische Nachlässe zu den Fantasien meines Großvaters* (1974), inspired by Cervantes' *Don Quixote* and Jean Paul's *Der Komet*, portrays an eccentric inventor whose talents are exploited by an entrepreneur with a more realistic view of the potential of air power in the years up to the Second World War and whose plan for the construction of an airship is never realized. *Verlegung eines mittleren Reiches* (1984) is a futuristic fantasy set in a small town in the GDR after a nuclear war and *Alexanders neue Welten* (1983) provides a satirical confrontation of rationalism and imagination in the efforts of a scholar to get to grips with the colourful life of his friend in a report destined for the Academy of Sciences.

Frisch, Max (1911–)

Born in Zurich Frisch studied German literature, travelled extensively in Europe before the Second World War, studied architecture in Zurich, combined writing with the practice of this profession until 1954, when he decided to devote himself exclusively to the former. He has since been resident in Switzerland, Rome and New York. Initially influenced as a dramatist by **Brecht** with whom he had contact in 1947–8, he lacks his faith in class consciousness as a lever for political change but shares with him a critical view of those who out of ideological naïvety, moral blindness or myopic pragmatism accommodate themselves to prevailing norms or power structures and a parabolic approach to their presentation in drama. He began his career as a novelist with *Jürg Reinhart* (1934) and *J'adore ce qui me brûle oder die Schwierigen* (1943, second version 1957), but became internationally known as a dramatist with Friedrich **Dürrenmatt** after the war. His plays may be divided into three groups: *Nun singen sie wieder* (1946) and *Als der Krieg zu Ende war* (1949) have an explicit bearing on the Third Reich and the Second World War; *Die chinesische Mauer* (1947), *Graf Öderland* (1951, second version 1961) and *Biedermann und die Brandstifter* (1955, second version 1958) concern the relation of the intellectual or the blinkered bourgeois to totalitarian power, while *Don Juan oder die Liebe zur Geometrie* (1953, second version 1962) and *Andorra* (1961), the latter a parabolic treatment of the aetiology of anti-Semitism, deal with the conflict between the self-image ideally the subject of free development and the stereotyped view adopted and imposed by others. The last of these themes becomes central, especially in the novel *Stiller* (1954) on the determination of the title-figure to preserve his independence from those formerly close to him and from the representatives of officialdom. The question whether it is possible to alter the course of one's life receives formally original treatment in relation to death in the later plays *Biografie. Ein Spiel* (1967) and *Triptychon* (1978, radio version 1981). *Homo Faber* (1957) and *Montauk* (1975) offer more self-critical and existentially inspired examinations of human relationships, the former with overtones of Greek tragedy which add depth to a critique of technological rationality, the latter in a manner close to autobiography. *Mein Name sei Gantenbein* (1964) remains the most formally sophisticated of Frisch's works, in which a story of jealousy and adultery is made the vehicle for a further variation on the identity theme, this time by means of alternation between first and third persons. The most recent novels *Der Mensch erscheint im Holozän* (1979), in which an old man is marooned by freak weather in his Alpine hermitage, and *Blaubart* (1982), consisting of the inner monologues of a doctor accused and acquitted of the murder of his former wife and culminating in a confession of guilt after a confrontation with seven women in his life, are marked by a ruminative interweaving of memories and associations which increases in complexity at the expense of plot. Frisch's diaries *Blätter aus dem Brotsack* (1940), *Tagebuch mit Marion* (1947), *Tagebuch 1946–1949* (1950), *Tagebuch 1966–1971* (1972) and *Dienstbüchlein* (1974) throw much light on his working methods, the anecdotal origins of his other writings, his views of himself as artist and citizen of Switzerland and of the world. Other works include the stories *Antwort aus der Stille* (1937), *Bin oder die Reise nach Peking* (1945) and *Wilhelm Tell für die Schule* (1971), of which the last offers an alternative perspective on the Swiss national hero. *Gesammelte Werke in zeitlicher Folge 1931–1985* in six volumes (1976) were republished with an additional volume as a Jubiläumsausgabe in 1986.

Frischmuth, Barbara (1941–)

Barbara Frischmuth visited Turkey in 1961 and Hungary in 1963 after studying the languages of those countries at the Institute of Interpreters in Graz. Although a member of the *Grazer Autorenversammlung*, to which also **Handke**, Kolleritsch, **Gerhard Roth**, **Scharang** have belonged, she has lived in Vienna since 1977. *Die Klosterschule* (1968), the autobiographically inspired account of a boarding-school for girls run by nuns, and her early stories *Amoralische Kinderklapper* (1969) and *Tage und Jahre* (1971) concentrate on the experience of children and their relationships to adults. The novel *Das Verschwinden des Schattens in der Sonne* (1973), set in Istanbul, confronts an Austrian student with local conditions and traces her growing involvement with revolutionary activists which stops short of clear commitment.

The trilogy of autonomous novels *Die Mystifikationen der Sophie Silber* (1976), *Amy oder die Metamorphose* (1978) and *Kai oder die Liebe zu den Modellen* (1979) is held together by the theme of metamorphosis. The introduction of elementary fairy spirits whose origins lie in the Alpine regions results in a story on two levels: the realistic level traces the life of Sophie Silber who on the mythical level makes a descent to the mother and death goddesses with the assistance of the fairy godmother Amaryllis Sternwieser. The second volume concerns the transformation of Amaryllis into the totally human Amy Stern, whose personal and professional ambitions are realized, but at a price. The third volume places hope for a utopian future in Amy Stern's son Kai, as Amy wrestles with the problems of bringing him up, maintaining a relationship with her partner Klemens and realizing her writing ambitions. In *Bindungen* (1980), *Die Ferienfamilie* (1981), *Die Frau im Mond* (1982), *Herrin der Tiere* (1986) and *Über die Verhältnisse* (1987) and the story collections *Geschichten für Stanek* (1969), *Rückkehr zum vorläufigen Ausgangspunkt* (1973), *Haschen nach Wind* (1974) and *Entzug – ein Menetekel der zärtlichsten Art* (1979) Frischmuth supplies further variations on her preferred themes of domestic life in a rural setting and women struggling to realize themselves in situations and relationships not always of their own choice or coming to terms with the failure of relationships.

Fuchs, Gerd (1932–)

Fuchs studied in Cologne, Munich and London, qualified as a secondary school-teacher, wrote a doctoral dissertation on **Rilke** in England, then became a journalist for *Die Welt* and *Der Spiegel*. Since 1968 he has been a professional writer based in Hamburg and associated with the Autoren Edition publishing venture. The eleven stories of *Landru und andere* (1966) show him able to devise situations typical of certain historical phases. The title-figure murders women whose beauty in its contrast to the wretchedness of the time renders them guilty in his eyes. *Beringer und die lange Wut*

(1973), inspired by the upheaval of the Studentenbewegung, centres on a journalist who takes stock of his life, friendships and political stance during a visit to his parents, whose lives are illuminated by means of flashbacks to the war and the immediate post-war years. In *Ein Mann fürs Leben* (1978) a man with a wife and two children is made redundant at the age of thirty-nine. The consequent adjustment of roles within the family leads eventually to his departure. *Stunde Null* (1981) presents the situation in a Hunsrück village at the time of the defeat in 1945, concentrating on family divisions and disorientations. *Schinderhannes* (1986) places the story of the folk-hero in the context of the effects of the French Revolution in occupied Germany west of the Rhine at the end of the eighteenth century.

Fühmann, Franz (1922–84)

Fühmann's family belonged to the Sudeten German minority of pre-war Czechoslovakia, which became the first target of Nazi 'Heim ins Reich' propaganda, and most of Fühmann's work is inspired by his difficult transition from commitment to National Socialism to acceptance of socialism in the context of the GDR on return from POW camp in the Soviet Union. His early poems (*Die Fahrt nach Stalingrad. Eine Dichtung* (1953), an epic poem in free verse relating his three visits to the city, first as soldier, then as POW and finally as friend, and *Die Nelke Nikos* (1953)) proclaim in naïve emotional terms loyalty to the Soviet order. These are followed by a series of *Novellen* and stories in which the experiences of soldiers in occupied territory during the Second World War induce radical rethinking. Begun in *Kameraden* (1955), this theme reaches its fullest elaboration in *König Ödipus* (1966), which in a skilful juxtaposition of argument and action reveals how Nazi ideology had been rendered palatable to a number of educated and half-educated Germans and how the course of the war causes a reinterpretation of the ideology in relation to the Oedipus myth and the ancient civilization of which they consider themselves the defenders and heirs. The scope of Fühmann's treatment of Nazism is extended in the stories 'Das Gottesgericht' and 'Kapitulation' in *Stürzende Schatten* (1959) and in the cycle *Das Judenauto* (1962), which covers the Third Reich and its aftermath in a series of narrative snapshots taken at a number of historical turning-points. The four stories of *Der Jongleur im Kino* (1970) show a sensitive boy adapting to and adopting a pre-fascist mentality. Fühmann's later work is increasingly preoccupied with myth in its distinction from the *Märchen* and in its bearing on contemporary issues, especially the relation of individual and society under socialism, as in the account of a visit to Hungary in *Zweiundzwanzig Tage oder Die Hälfte des Lebens* (1973), and in *Saiänsfitschen* (1981), the projection of the present problems of 'der real existierende Sozialismus' into a future land of 'Uniterr' allows a critical view of the effect of surviving political hierarchies on everyday life to emerge. Fühmann retold and recast ancient Greek myths in *Der Geliebte der Morgenröte* (1978), *Prometheus. Die Titanenschlacht* (1975) and *Die Schatten*

(1986) and his thoughts on 'Das mythische Element in der Literatur', the most significant of the essays and speeches collected in *Erfahrungen und Widersprüche* (1975), amount to a challenge to prevailing views of socialist realism, as do his rehabilitations of E. T. A. Hoffmann in *Fräulein Veronika Paulmann aus der Pirnaer Vorstadt oder Etwas über das Schauerliche bei E. T. A. Hoffmann* (1979) and of Georg **Trakl** in *Der Sturz des Engels. Erfahrungen mit Dichtung* (1982), which appeared in the GDR in the same year under the title *Vor Feuerschlünden. Erfahrung mit Georg Trakls Gedicht*.

Fühmann deserves to be better known in the West because his work is of (almost) consistent merit and because his career is a paradigm of the general course of GDR literature during his lifetime.

Gaiser, Gerd (1908–76)

Gaiser, whose earliest work appeared during the Third Reich (stories in the periodical *Das innere Reich* and poems in *Reiter am Himmel* (1941)), is difficult to place in the context of the post-war revival of literature. While the stereotypes of *Blut und Boden* literature are absent from his fiction, there is nevertheless a clear difference between his conservative criticism of the vacuous provincial society of Neuspuhl in the novel *Schlußball* (1958) and the spirit imbuing the satire of **Koeppen** and the humane realism of **Böll** in works which reached the public at the same time. Gaiser's first post-war novel was the 'Heimkehrerroman' *Eine Stimme hebt an* (1950), but it was with *Schlußball* and *Die sterbende Jagd* (1953), which covers thirty-six hours in the last futile but heroic operations of a *Luftwaffe* squadron, that Gaiser prompted comparison with some of his contemporaries, thanks to the incorporation of changing narrative perspectives assigned to the principal characters. In *Das Schiff im Berg* (1955), the history of a mountain in the Schwäbische Alb, Gaiser's preoccupation with myth and a circular view of history is more evident. The thirteen stories of *Am Paß Nascondo* (1960) are based on allegorical contrasts comparable to those present in the fiction of Ernst **Jünger**. Further story collections are *Zwischenland* (1949), *Einmal und oft* (1956), *Revanche* (1959), *Gib acht in Damokosch* (1959) and *Mittagsgesicht* (1983).

Geissler, Christian (1928–)

Geissler, who has passed from Protestantism to Catholicism, communism and anarchism and edited the left-wing periodical *kürbiskern* from 1965 to 1968, has developed along with others a type of social realism adapted to conditions in the Federal Republic and able to deal with the Nazi legacy and the social and economic system in its effect on ordinary working people. *Anfrage* (1960) was one of the earliest novels to treat the theme of 'Bewältigung der Vergangenheit' by linking it to a conflict between father and son. *Kalte Zeiten* (1966) presents a day in the life of a young couple in a proletarian milieu. *Das Brot mit der Feile* (1973), set in the Federal Republic during the 1960s, traces the development of a young worker's political consciousness, while in *Wird Zeit, daß wir leben* (1976) a similar process culminates in a successful plot to release communists from a Nazi jail at the end of 1933. *Kamalatta* (1988) is one of several recent treatments of the terrorist phenomenon. Geissler has also produced poetry, *Im Vorfeld einer*

Schußverletzung (1980) and *spiel auf ungeheuer* (1983), which includes a section 'schottisches nächtebuch'.

George, Stefan (1868–1933)

George is generally acknowledged to be one of Germany's greatest modern poets, a writer of comparable stature to Baudelaire and Mallarmé, deriving much from French symbolism, but also indebted to Hölderlin, Goethe and Nietzsche. As a young man of private means, George went to Paris in 1889 and, having been encouraged by Mallarmé, later returned to Germany with a sense of mission: nothing less, in fact, than the vivification and purification of German poetry, its rebirth from the provincialism and stale romanticism of the 1870s and 1880s. Remarkable in George is the single-minded sense of dedication which would characterize his work for almost forty years; the cult of the dandy and the deliberate cultivation of remote sensibilities may be seen as a youthful extravagance, the later austerity and aloofness representing a triumph of order and discipline over passionate involvement. From *l'art pour l'art* attitudinizing George would advance to a vast imperious vision: a transformation of life through art, with Greek ideals (derived partly from Nietzsche, partly from Hölderlin) coming to the fore.

George insisted that poetry be given a quasi-religious status: orthography, punctuation and a stylized typeface should mark it off from banal communication. From the *symbolistes* George derived the idea that poetry should express the esoteric; he differed from them, however, in the utter rejection of free verse and in the compression of his images into predetermined poetic forms. An austere classicism prevails, with pure rhymes, faultless rhythms and a meticulous choice of consonants. The collection *Hymnen* (1890) appeared privately printed in a limited edition of one hundred copies: it stresses the isolation of the consecrated poet (the poem 'Weihe' insists upon his separateness and impresses with its use of assonance and interior rhymes). *Pilgerfahrten* (1891: dedicated to Hugo von **Hofmannsthal**) contains the little poem 'Die Spange' which praises the coolness of polished steel as against the gorgeous and the elaborate; George rejected the cult of ornamentation of certain circles in Munich and Vienna, and the monochrome hue and studied tread of much of his later poetry are deliberately opposed to the wayward and the *outré*. *Alagabal* (1892: dedicated to the memory of Ludwig the Second of Bavaria) is George's flirtation with decadence: the cruelty of Heliogabalus, the Nietzschean image of the spiritual aristocrat, remote in azure blueness, and the sterile opulence of Byzantium fuse to form a bizarre and deliberately amoral ethos. These *Algabal* poems have been called the finest example of German *décadence*, and may be regarded as a tribute to those French attitudes which seemed unavoidable in the 1890s.

In 1892 George's plan to form an exclusive journal entirely devoted to the cult of beauty came to fruition: the first number of the *Blätter für die Kunst* appeared. It insisted upon a 'geistige Kunst', utterly rejected naturalism and utilitarianism and emphasized purity of form above all. The *Blätter* appeared intermittently (together with the associated *Jahrbücher*) until 1919: the programme continued to extol the search for formal perfection and refused to contemplate any political or ideological commitment. It rejected the novel as an art form because of its social preoccupations and also the commercialized theatre. Poetry was regarded as the supreme art form, and a spiritual élite was called for, a sodality dedicated to the cultivation of ideal beauty and the expression of that beauty in the noblest verse. There was nothing narrowly patriotic in George's vision: he disdainfully rejected the vulgarity of the Second Reich and sought disciples in many European countries (in France, Belgium, Holland, Poland and England). Hofmannsthal contributed to the *Blätter*, but later withdrew, fearing that an all-too-close involvement was detrimental to his own art.

In 1895 appeared *Die Bücher der Hirten- und Preisgedichte der Sagen und Sänger und der hängenden Gärten*, a triple cycle of poems dealing with primitive forms of culture, pastoral, medieval and oriental. A dignified expression of restrained grief is 'Jahrestag': the language is elevated, and the mourning is ritualized; the scene is probably Grecian, but the meaning is universal as well as being strangely elusive. 'Der Herr der Insel', in stately blank verse, repeats the theme of the 'otherness' of art and the harmful effect of the banausic. 'Die Lieblinge des Volkes' adumbrates the classical world of which George was so fond, the world of naked wrestlers and inspired minstrels. The next collection, *Das Jahr der Seele* (1897), has a perfectly symmetrical construction of three parts in each of the three sections; the poems are basically crystallizations of the moods of the poet himself. The Byzantine accoutrements of some of the earlier poems have been replaced by a ghostly persona, and George's ability to create a clear, and yet elusive, situation with a possibly symbolic extension, is much in evidence: the famous 'Komm in den totgesagten park und schau' is a good example. The cult of self is paramount here, and George narrowly misses mannerism and pose (and not always misses: see 'Sprüche für die geladenen in T.'). 'Entflieht auf leichten kähnen' was hauntingly set to music by Anton von Webern. *Der Teppich des Lebens* (1899) is dedicated to Melchior Lechter, friend, illustrator and designer of George's typeface; it is a monumentally architectural collection, once more in triple form. The poem 'Der teppich' illustrates George's deeply felt belief that the formal structure of existence appears only to the few, and then only in rare moments of heightened awareness. 'Ich forschte bleichen blickes nach dem horte' tells of the naked angel of beauty who steps forth to greet the poet; 'Ich bin freund und führer dir und ferge' emphasizes the Hellenistic cult of beauty and its superiority to Christian morality. The poem 'Die fremde' (using the quatrains of the folk-song) describes a mysterious stranger whose presence in the village is disruptive and baleful, and who leaves behind a mysterious child: the anti-social, even disreputable nature of art is suggested. A masterpiece is 'Juli-Schwermut' (dedicated to Ernest Dowson), with its Keatsian evocation of the heaviness of summer; the mood-painting, however, is strictly controlled.

Der siebente Ring (1907) occupies a crucial position in George's *œuvre*. The collection falls into seven sections, each with poems to a multiple of seven. 'Nietzsche' is a poem of tribute to the thinker who had died, without regaining sanity, seven years before: Nietzsche's vision and agony are compared with those of Christ. 'Franken' portrays George's indebtedness to the 'Land of the Franks'; it is from the land of Mallarmé, Villiers and Verlaine (all mentioned by name) that George derived his inspiration, but Nietzsche and Böcklin remained dear to him. The poem ends with a line of pseudo-Old French. This collection is notorious, however, for the portrayal of the central experience in George's life: the meeting with the boy Maximilian Kronberger ('Maximin'), his worship, death and deification. The central section, 'Maximin', is dedicated to his memory; this ephebe represented (for George) the highest spiritual beauty, and the concept of a new élite of youth would come to predominate in George's poetry, a youth dedicated to the renewal of civilization. This deification of Maximin proved a stumbling-block to certain members of the George circle (to Verwey particularly), but George remained adamant. The collection also contains the mysterious poem 'Entrückung', used by Schönberg in the last movement of his F sharp minor quintet. *Der Stern des Bundes* (1914), again in tripartite form, provides poems which are hieratic and frequently prophetic: 'Wer je die flamme umschritt' rebukes those who sought to break from George's artistic hegemony to seek their own, eccentric paths. (Klages, **Derleth** and Schuler, *inter alia*, are meant here.) The dictatorial note becomes increasingly intrusive in George's writing at this time: the poem 'Mit den frauen fremder ordnung/sollt ihr nicht den leib beflecken' has a disturbing ring to it and seems to preach the need for racial purity. It must be remembered, however, that George's circle was international, and that he regarded **Wolfskehl** and Gundolf, both Jews, as his closest disciples. The outbreak of the First World War disturbed him greatly, and it was not until 1928 that he was able to publish his next poetic statement. *Das neue Reich* contains his most profound poem, 'Der Krieg', which praises the youth of all European nations, laments the unscrupulousness and ignorance of political leaders, and sees that the end of an epoch was somehow justified ('Erkrankte welten fiebern sich zu ende . . .'). The hope is expressed that the ideals of Ancient Greece will restore European civilization once more: North and South, as Hölderlin had described, would fuse to form a new realm of the spirit, a new Realm ('Reich'). This last collection also contains what is held to be one of the greatest love poems in the German language: 'Du schlank und rein wie eine flamme'.

George's cult of youth, discipline, order and a new 'Reich' easily played into the hands of the Nazis: certain lines of 'Der dichter in zeiten der wirren' seemed overtly fascist. Disgusted, however, by the excesses of the movement and the ignorance of its leaders, George (amongst whose admirers at that time may be numbered Claus Graf Schenk von Stauffenberg) refused the presidency of the *Dichter-Akademie*, and moved to Switzerland, where he died.

George's greatness lies in his utter dedication to the task of refining the German language, of treating poetry as the highest art and of seeking the ideal in the commonplace. The small poem 'Das wort' (in *Das neue Reich*) explains that articulation is everything: 'Kein ding sei wo das wort gebricht'. His work includes over five hundred pages of distinguished verse translations from seven languages: most remarkable is his version of the *Divine Comedy* and certain of the Shakespeare sonnets. His ability to inspire others to gain similar achievements and his sincere desire to assist other writers (Ernest Dowson, among others) render the occasional affectation unimportant. His own edition of his works, *Gesamt-Ausgabe* (eighteen vols) appeared from 1927 to 1934. A useful edition is the *Ausgabe in zwei Bänden* (Küpper, vormals Bondi, 1958, reprinted 1968 and 1976). *Werke in Einzelausgaben* appeared between 1964 and 1969; *Gesammelte Werke* 1982f.

Ginzkey, Franz Karl von (1871–1963)

Born at Pola, a former Austrian naval arsenal, Ginzkey studied in Fiume, Trieste and Graz before becoming an army officer in Salzburg, Braunau and finally Vienna, where he was employed in the Military Geographical Institute. Ginzkey first published poetry (*Das heimliche Läuten* (1906), which received the Bauernfeld prize; *Balladen und neue Lieder* (1910); *Vom Gastmahl des Lebens* (1921)); a verse epic *Die Erschaffung der Eva* appeared in 1941. The poetry is generally derivative and nostalgic. More important are Ginzkey's novels, although they appear unduly sentimental to many modern readers. *Jakobus und die Frauen* (1908) tells of the importance of a woman's love for the timid protagonist ('des Lebens bestes Wunder geschieht uns von den Frauen'); the painter Lernemann in *Geschichte einer stillen Frau* (1909) finds in his wife his truest companion. Ginzkey's best-known novel was *Der von der Vogelweide* (1912), which paints a plausible picture of the medieval poet; *Der Wiesenzaun* (1913) is a *Novelle* with Albrecht Dürer as its hero. Ginzkey published over fifty novels and collections of stories, many of them trivial. In his autobiography *Der Heimatsucher* (1948) he tells of the fusion of 'Volk' and 'Armee' in pre-1914 Austria-Hungary: the chapter 'Die Entdeckung Wiens' contains a description of soldiers and civilians streaming together across the 'Prater-Stern'; the narrator, sitting on the steps of the Tegetthoffdenkmal, perceives a mystical significance. Ginzkey also wrote a work on Mozart (*Mozarts unsterbliche Sendung* (1942)); his children's books are still read today (*Hatschi Bratschis Luftballon* (1904); *Florians wundersame Reise über die Tapete* (1928); *Tani-Wani* (1947)). The *Ausgewählte Werke* (in four volumes) appeared in 1962.

Glaeser, Ernst (1902–63)

Glaeser's psychological novel *Jahrgang 1902* (1928), with its motto 'La guerre – ce sont nos parents', was widely acclaimed: it is a sensitive and yet sober account of puberty, adolescence and the reactions of young schoolboys to the First World War. A certain grim humour is also present (the hero greets the news of the assassination in Sarajevo with relief as his own sexual peccadillo would be forgotten). In the following year Glaeser edited *Fazit. Ein Querschnitt durch die deutsche Publizistik*; in 1930 appeared the next novel *Frieden*, which deals with the problems confronting the young after the war. In 1931 he collaborated with F. C. Weiskopf on a documentary study of the successes of the Soviet economy (*Der Staat ohne Arbeitslose*). The novels *Das Gut im Elsaß* (1932) and *Der letzte Zivilist* (1933) were less successful. Glaeser went into exile in 1933 and published a collection of stories, *Das Unvergängliche*, in Amsterdam (1936). His decision to return to Germany in 1939 met with little understanding on the part of his fellow-*émigrés*; he attempted to explain his reasons later in the autobiographical novel *Glanz und Elend der Deutschen* (1960). He was viewed with suspicion by the Nazis, but was permitted to write as a journalist. *Köpfe und Profile* (1952) contains a series of literary sketches of Theodor Heuss, Kurt Schumacher, Robert Schumann, Ernst Reuter and others. The only book to be known outside Germany is his first; it was translated by Edwin and Willa Muir as *Class 1902*.

Goebbels, Josef (1897–1945)

Reichspropagandaminister, President of the *Reichskulturkammer* and thereby cultural dictator of the Third Reich, Goebbels deserves mention here because of his novel *Michael, ein deutsches Schicksal in Tagebuchblättern*, written in 1921 and published in 1929. Stephen Spender devoted a whole chapter to it in his book *European Witness* (New York, 1946): he notes that the copy in his possession had been taken out of the public library in Aachen on an average of once every two months between 1940 and 1943. The novel is loosely based on Goethe's *Werther*, but also bears a striking resemblance to *Der verbummelte Student* by Gustav **Sack**, written some four years earlier; there are also echoes of Nietzsche, Dostoevski, Scheffel, Liliencron and Schiller. Michael's struggle for self-fulfilment and self-identification is portrayed in an overwrought and pretentious manner. The culture of cosmopolitan cities is rejected, and the essential 'German' virtues are extolled: 'Während ein ganzes Volk im Sterben lag, proklamierte seine angefaulte Intelligenz, was modern ist: Film, Monokel, Bubikopf und Garçonne. Ich danke!' The rejection of modern developments in the arts, however, does not prevent Goebbels from allowing his hero to betray unmistakably expressionistic sentiments; a rather unsubtle definition of that movement is also suggested. Michael greets the industrial landscape of the Ruhr in ecstatic terminology; inspired by Van Gogh he seeks fulfilment in his work and is killed in a mining accident. The ending deliberately echoes *Werther*: 'Bergleute trugen ihn. Als Arbeiter, Student und Soldat wurde er begraben.' Michael's apotheosis is achieved in an urban, rather than an agricultural, milieu, but attempts are also made to describe the Frisian islands and the Bavarian Alps; the storm-girt and the elemental, apparently, are regarded as external correlations to the power of the German soul. Goebbels also wrote a drama entitled *Heinrich Kampfert*; sketches also exist of a play to be called *Judas Iscariot*. His play *Der Wanderer* was never published, although it was performed: it contains a prologue, eight scenes and an epilogue and may be called a 'Stationendrama'. Goebbels's poetry is derivative and full of neo-romantic topoi.

Goering, Reinhardt (1887–1936)

Goering studied medicine in Berlin and Munich; in 1912 his first poems appeared in an anthology entitled *Lyrisches Jahrbuch*, but are traditional in style and content and have nothing in common with the poetry published in the same year by Kurt **Hiller** (in the *Kondor*). In the following year a novel, *Jung Schuk*, appeared, a psychological novel in the manner of *Werther* which can be said to anticipate certain modern existentialist works. At the outbreak of the First World War Goering served as a military doctor in the Saar, but a tubercular lung necessitated a prolonged convalescence in Davos. It was here, in 1916, that Goering wrote his most memorable work, *Seeschlacht*, a play first performed in early 1918 in Dresden, when it caused a scandal; a later performance that year in Berlin under Max Reinhardt owed its success primarily to the changed war situation in Europe. The play takes place in a gun-turret of a battleship at the Battle of Jutland: it is highly stylized and tautly structured, the language compressed and ecstatic. The seven nameless sailors move towards inevitable death; the fifth sailor meditates on the possibility of mutiny, but as they prepare to do battle all are caught up in a death-intoxicated rapture. A huge explosion kills them all, and the fifth sailor, dying, explains: 'Ich habe gut geschossen, wie?/Ich hätte auch gut gemeutert! Wie?/Aber schießen lag uns wohl näher? Wie?/ Muß uns wohl näher gelegen haben?' The play is expressionistic in its reduction of men to types, its tendency to abstraction and its fervour: it is also classically controlled and concentrated (the critic Kerr wrote that 'Heute wirkt Goering als käme er von der Antike'). Goering's other plays include *Scapa Flow* (1918: Paul Fechter praised its 'Aeschylean' intensity) and *Südpolexpedition des Kapitän Scott* (1930), performed in Berlin under Leopold Jessner, with Veit Harlan playing Bowers. (This was performed as an opera in 1937 with music by Winfried Zillig; Goering's suggested title of *Die Pinguine* was changed by Zillig to *Das Opfer*: the work was banned by the Nazis.) Goering's disordered domestic life, his restlessness and attacks of mental instability led to his suicide in 1936. *Prosa – Dramen – Verse* appeared in 1961.

Goetz, Curt (1888–1960)

Curt Goetz, whom **Zuckmayer** called 'der eleganteste und geistreichste Komödienschreiber und -spieler der zwanziger Jahre', was famous above all for his comedies of manners in the style of Oscar Wilde. These plays were most effective when he took the leading role. *Ingeborg* (1921), written to mark the opening of the *Theater am Kurfürstendamm*, portrays the triangular relationship between two men and a spoilt, frivolous woman; *Hokuspokus* (1926) is a light-hearted thriller, as is his best-known play *Dr. med. Hiob Prätorius* (1932), where the fatal accident to the popular gynaecologist and its investigation provide the dramatic *sujet*. (The doctor, who believed that laughter was the best medicine, drove into a tree after laughing at a joke of his wife's. Sherlock Holmes also puts in a brief appearance.) *Die tote Tante* (1924) verges on the grotesque: the dead aunt stipulates in her will that the niece may only inherit if she produces, as the aunt had, an illegitimate child before the age of seventeen. *Der Lügner und die Nonne* (1929) tells of a cardinal whose son saves the reputation of a novice and later marries her. (It was he who was the father of a certain baby found in her possession; she was not the mother.) Goetz moved to Hollywood in 1939 and became a successful film writer. After the war he returned to Switzerland and consolidated his considerable reputation with the novel *Die Tote von Beverly Hills* (1951). His last works for the stage were the three one-acters *Miniaturen* ('Die Rache', 'Herbst' and 'Die Kommode' (1959)). His wife was the actress Valerie von Martens, who often took the leading part in his plays. The *Sämtliche Bühnenwerke* appeared in 1963 (enlarged 1977); *Werke* (three vols) were published also in 1977.

Goetz, Wolfgang (1885–1955)

Goetz made his reputation primarily as a nationalist dramatist whose plays deal mainly with themes from Prussian history: his greatest success was *Neidhardt von Gneisenau* (1925). The hero's words from the end of Act Five ('Wir sind ja Deutsche. Uns ward ein schwerer Weg: doch sitzt an seinem Ende Gott, und breitet seine Hände uns entgegen') were welcomed by patriotic circles eager to forget the humiliations of 1918. Goetz was in favour with the Nazis and became President of the 'Gesellschaft für Theatergeschichte' (1936–40). Bismarck is extolled fulsomely in *Der Ministerpräsident* of 1936; *Kampf ums Reich* (1939) continued to glorify German history. Goetz also wrote *Novellen*; a collection, *Der Herr Geheime Rat*, appeared in 1941. The story *Der Mönch von Heisterbach* tells of a medieval Rip van Winkle. After 1945 Goetz claimed, with conviction, that he had been a patriot and never a Nazi; he edited the *Berliner Hefte für geistiges Leben* from 1946–9. Eminently readable is his account of Berlin café life in *Im 'Größenwahn' bei Pschorr und anderswo. Erinnerungen an Berliner Stammtische* (1936).

Goll, Yvan, Iwan or Ivan (pseudonym of Isaac Lang, 1891–1950)

'Ivan Goll hat keine Heimat; durch Schicksal Jude, durch Zufall in Frankreich geboren, durch ein Stempelpapier als Deutscher bezeichnet': this is the autobiographical note which Goll provided for Kurt Pinthus's

Menschheitsdämmerung (1920). Goll published his first collection of poems, the *Lothringische Volkslieder*, in 1912; the same year saw the publication of *Der Panamakanal* – the canal symbolizing for Goll communication and fraternity. Goll, a pacifist, moved to Zurich in 1915; he associated with **Stefan Zweig**, Ludwig **Rubiner** and Hans **Arp**, and also knew James Joyce, assisting later to get *Ulysses* published in a German translation. In 1919 Goll moved to Paris and in the same year wrote a tribute to the French poet Guillaume Apollinaire, stressing the need for 'Überrealismus' or 'surréalisme'. The influence of Apollinaire's *Les mamelles de Tirésias* is seen in Goll's grotesque play *Methusalem oder Der ewige Bürger*, first performed in Berlin in 1922: characters split and multiply (Ego, Superego and Id), animals speak and a part is written for a joke-box. The 'Ur-Bürger' is mercilessly lampooned, yet Goll also admires his resilience, vulgarity and irremediable complacency. The décor for this 'satirical drama' was by Georg Grosz. Goll was also interested in the potential of film: his 'Filmdichtung' *Chaplinade* appeared in 1920. **Brecht** admired Goll, calling him 'der expressionistische Courteline'. In 1924 there appeared not only André Breton's famous surrealist manifesto but also Goll's (in the first and only number of his periodical *Surréalisme*). He wrote for the musical stage (*Der neue Orpheus* (1928)) but is known primarily as a lyric poet, able to express himself with ease in both French and German, and occasionally English. Of interest are the *Poèmes d'amour* written with his wife Claire (Marc Chagall sketched the two of them together), also *La chanson de Jean sans Terre*, a series of ballads (1935–44). Goll frequently published two versions of his poems, one in French, the other in German (the 'homeless one' is also called 'Johann Ohneland' or 'John Lackland'). The *Traumkraut* poems (published in 1951) are his finest in German: a preface written in hospital two weeks before his death, and read aloud to Alfred **Döblin**, explains that it was only at the point of death that Goll understood the true nature of things. Reference is made to the Japanese artist Hokusai; the cult of things of a poet like **Rilke** is also noticeable. Goll is of great interest as the link between expressionism and surrealism, also, later, as the exponent of a mystical humility *vis-à-vis* the natural world. In 1960 appeared the *Dichtungen*; *Œuvres* (vol. I) in 1968; *Briefe* (vol. I) in 1971.

Gomringer, Eugen (1925–)

The Swiss Gomringer has combined his experiments in concrete poetry with a career in advertising and design. His important theoretical statement 'vom vers zur konstellation' appeared in the periodical *augenblick* in 1954. The *konstellationen*, published in 1953, 1960 and 1963, together with *das stundenbuch* of 1965, were assembled in *worte sind schatten, die konstellationen 1951–1968* (1969) and *konstellationen, ideogramme, stundenbuch* (1977). Gomringer's type of concrete poetry consists of word games devoid of political engagement or a critical approach to human problems; words are brought together in patterns and variations in which the visual aspect takes precedence.

Graf, Oskar Maria (1894–1967)

Son of a Bavarian baker, Graf was largely self-taught; he refused to serve in the First World War, was imprisoned and briefly incarcerated in a mental home. He published revolutionary poetry in 1917 (*Die Revolutionäre*), associated with Kurt Eisner, Gustav Landauer and Erich **Mühsam** and, after the collapse of the Munich soviet, was again imprisoned. In 1920 he published *Ua-Puah! Indianergeschichten*; his first success, however, was the autobiographical novel *Wir sind Gefangene* (1927), a novel praised by Gorki and compared by him to Grimmelshausen. The account of the hardship of youth, of family relationships and poverty also brings Ludwig **Thoma** to mind. (It was translated into English as *Prisoners All* in 1928.) The years 1927–9 were prolific ones and Graf consolidated his reputation by tales of Bavarian peasant and small-town life, *Das bayerische Dekameron* (1928) being the best known. Graf was hailed as 'der bedeutendste erotische Schriftsteller des Bauerntums'. *Kalendergeschichten* appeared in 1929. The novel *Bollwieser: Roman eines Ehemanns* (1931) successfully portrayed small-town life: it was translated into English as *The Station Master* in 1933 and, in 1977, was filmed by Rainer Werner **Fassbinder**. Graf's portrayal of peasant life was originally approved by the Nazis; Graf, however, incensed by the fact that his books had not been burned by them, demanded (in the *Volksstimme*, Saarbrücken, 1933) that they should also be destroyed rather than be approved by such a regime: 'Vergebens frage ich mich, womit ich diese Schmach verdient habe. . . . Nach meinem Leben und meinem ganzen Schreiben habe ich das Recht, daß meine Bücher der reinen Flamme des Scheiterhaufens überantwortet werden und nicht in die blutigen Hände und die verdorbenen Hirne der braunen Mordsbanden gelangen'. Graf was in exile in Czechoslovakia, Russia and then America: he became co-editor of the *Neue deutsche Blätter*. From 1938–40 he was president of the German-American Writers Association in New York. Works written in exile include *Unruhe um einen Friedfertigen* (1947), *Das Leben meiner Mutter* (1946), *Die Flucht ins Mittelmäßige* (1959), *Der große Bauernspiegel* (1962) and *Der Quasterl und andere Erzählungen* (1965). Graf's writing tends to the episodic, and the shorter stories are generally considered to be better than the novels. An 'Arbeitskreis für O. M. Graf' was formed in 1974. The *Gesammelte Werke in Einzelausgaben* appeared from 1975; *Ausgewählte Werke* (seven vols) in 1982.

Grass, Günter (1927–)

Grass was just old enough to experience the Third Reich through school indoctrination and military service before he was forced to leave his birthplace Danzig at the end of the Second World War. He became a POW, then worked in a china clay mine before training as a monumental mason. From 1948 to 1951 and from 1953 to 1956 he studied sculpture and graphic art in Düsseldorf and Berlin, joining the *Gruppe 47* shortly before the appearance of his first poems and plays. Having married in 1954 he moved in 1956 to Paris, where during the following three years he completed *Die Blechtrommel*, for part of which he received the prize of *Gruppe 47*. Its publication in 1959 marked a turning-point in the development of the literature of the Federal Republic and made him internationally famous.

The three volumes of what has come to be known as the Danzig trilogy share a single setting and a preoccupation with 'Bewältigung der Vergangenheit', but they differ in length, narrative technique and the manner in which they focus on their respective principal characters. A distinctive amalgam of social realism and grotesque fantasy is present throughout, together with variations on the device by which the past is reflected in the present consciousness of a witness. However, the *Novelle Katz und Maus* (1961) gives relatively little attention to the post-war period, while in *Hundejahre* (1963) the strict chronology of Oskar Matzerath's picaresque progress through more than two decades is replaced by a more flexibly handled structure which allows commentary by three distinct narrators.

örtlich betäubt (1969) provides in the confrontation of the teacher Starusch and his pupil Scherbaum Grass's answer to the challenge of the student movement, while in *Aus dem Tagebuch einer Schnecke* (1972) he tells his children of his experiences as a campaigner for the SPD during the election of 1969. *Der Butt* (1977) may be considered with *Die Blechtrommel* his masterpiece; in it the stories of nine female cooks in various periods between the stone age and the present are made the vehicles of a pro-feminist view of history according to a reinterpretation of the well-known *Märchen* 'vom Fischer und syner Frau'. In *Das Treffen in Telgte* (1979) the meeting of a group of poets in a small Westphalian town towards the end of the Thirty Years War enables Grass to reflect on the essential role but limited power of the artist-intellectual then and now. *Kopfgeburten oder Die Deutschen sterben aus* (1980) and *Zunge zeigen* (1988) bring out the contrast between the West and the Third World, in the first through the medium of a 'modern' couple on a visit to India, in the second more directly in an account of Grass's stay in Bengal from August 1986 to January 1987. The novel *Die Rättin* (1986) had a mixed reception although it contains many features characteristic of his more successful earlier works; however, the nostalgia of a central episode in which Oskar Matzerath, now a video tycoon, returns to Danzig to join in the celebration of his grandmother's birthday is overshadowed by the dystopian vision of a nuclear catastrophe after which the narrator and the title-figure remain encircling a devastated earth in a space capsule.

Grass's early plays *Hochwasser* (1957), *Onkel, Onkel* (1958), *Noch zehn Minuten bis Buffalo* (1959) and *Die bösen Köche* (1961) can be associated, like the plays of **Hildesheimer**, with the theatre of the absurd. In *Die Plebejer proben den Aufstand* (1966) he presents in the figure of the Chef, whose rehearsal of a version of Shakespeare's *Coriolanus* is interrupted by workers hoping for his support in their demands for reform, a portrait of **Brecht** at the time of the uprising of 17 June 1953 in East Berlin, while *Davor* (1969) is a dramatization of parts of the novel *örtlich betäubt*. Grass's poems in *Die Vorzüge der Windhühner* (1956), *Ausgefragt* (1967) and

Gleisdreieck (1960), collected in the *Gesammelte Gedichte* of 1971, contain in miniature form some of the fantasies elaborated with such inventive *élan* in the novels. His essays and speeches consist of declarations of support for the SPD in *Über das Selbstverständliche* (1968), *Der Bürger und seine Stimme* (1974) and *Denkzettel* (1978), more recent speeches made mainly on behalf of the peace movement in *Politische Gegenreden 1980–1983* (1983) and *Aufsätze zur Literatur 1957–1979* (1980), which contains the important declaration of allegiance 'Über meinen Lehrer Döblin'. A *Werkausgabe* in ten volumes appeared in 1987. *Deutscher Lastenausgleich. Wider das dumpte Einheitsgebot. Reden und Gespräche* (1990) expresses Grass's concern at the process of unification.

Gregor-Dellin, Martin (1926–88)

After a brief period of active service on the Western Front and as a POW, Gregor-Dellin became at different times a publisher's reader, radio editor and professional writer, moving from the GDR in 1958. He is perhaps best known for his writings on the Wagner circle, including a major biography (*Richard Wagner. Sein Leben, sein Werk, sein Jahrhundert* (1980)) and his edition of Cosima Wagner's diaries. His novels, however, span his whole career, from *Jakob Haferglanz* (1956), on the suicide of a Jew in the Third Reich (cf. Friedrich **Torberg**, *Der Schüler Gerber hat absolviert* (1929)) to *Schlabrendorf oder die Republik* (1982), about a German aristocrat who throws in his lot with the French Revolution, and include also *Der Kandelaber* (1962), which exposes the totalitarian bureaucracy of the Ulbricht regime in the GDR, *Einer* (1965), the fictional biography of an ordinary man who somehow survives a disadvantaged upbringing and a series of personal and professional failures before, during and after the Third Reich, written by himself as self-justification for his employer, and *Föhn* (1974), a work of faction on a bank robbery in Munich.

Grimm, Hans (1875–1959)

After studying banking in London, Grimm worked in South Africa until 1910; in 1913 he published the *Südafrikanische Novellen*, stories characterized by vivid landscape description. He returned to Germany to study law; during the First World War he served in the artillery until being seconded to write on alleged French atrocities in German Togoland. A fictional diary, *Der Ölsucher von Duala* (1918) is based on these experiences. It was with *Volk ohne Raum* (1926) that Grimm achieved enormous popularity; despite its length the book sold almost half a million copies by 1940 (a new edition appeared as late as 1956). Grimm became the leading exponent of German colonialism, and 'Volk ohne Raum' became one of the slogans of the Third Reich. The book tells of the adventure of Cornelius Friebott who leaves his farm in Lower Saxony, works briefly in a steel-mill, then emigrates to South-West Africa where he volunteers for the

Boer War and, after imprisonment by the British on Saint Helena, returns to champion the German cause. After the collapse of 1918 he escapes to Portuguese Angola and, in the early 1920s, leaves for Germany to awaken his countrymen to their lack of space and the need for them to expand. It is only the novelist Hans Grimm (who appears as a character in the book) who realizes the full importance of his message and is determined that Friebott, killed by a stone flung by a political enemy, should not have died in vain. The readers of *Volk ohne Raum* were told that the Germans were 'das reinlichste und anständigste und ehrlichste und tüchtigste und fleißigste Volk der Erde'; British perfidy, it is emphasized, was responsible for Germany's confinement and humiliation. The collusion between the British and the social democrats is repeatedly stressed, with the Jews singled out as detractors and degenerates. The book is crudely didactic and simplistic in its approach to Germany's problems; long passages of turgid exhortation predominate. Grimm continued to write on South-West Africa (*Das deutsche Südwesterbuch* (1929); *Lüderitzland* (1934)): other works which endeared him to the Nazis include *Wie ich den Engländer sehe* (1939). Grimm was not, however, a party member, and relations between him and **Goebbels** were frequently acerbic. From 1934 onwards Grimm organized the 'Lippoldsberger Dichtertreffen' to encourage 'Völkische Dichtung': Rudolf **Binding**, R. A. **Schröder**, Hans **Carossa** and E. G. **Kolbenheyer** participated. After the Second World War Grimm founded the Klosterhausverlag in Lippoldsberg. In 1950 he published *Die Erzbischofsschrift. Antwort eines Deutschen*; there appeared posthumously *Suchen-Hoffen. Aus meinem Leben 1928–1934* (1960). The *Gesamtausgabe* began to appear in 1970.

Grün, Max von der (1926–)

Von der Grün, after a period in the USA as a POW, worked in the construction industry and in the mines until 1963, when he was dismissed following revelations of inadequate safety underground in his first novel *Irrlicht und Feuer* (1963, dramatized for television, 1966). Since then he has lived as a professional writer in Dortmund, where he helped to found with the archivist Fritz Hüser the *Gruppe 61*. Its members included, until the formation in 1970 of the offshoot *Werkkreis Literatur der Arbeitswelt*, Günter **Wallraff** and Peter-Paul **Zahl**. Von der Grün is a pragmatist who has remained faithful to the initial aims of the group to provide a forum for the artistic portrayal of the industrial environment and its working inhabitants, without the documentary basis and the commitment to a political line or an operative function which informs the work of the *Werkkreis*. In the almost ignored *Männer in zweifacher Nacht* (1962) a mining accident becomes the catalyst of conflict between workers of different social backgrounds. In *Irrlicht und Feuer*, which was criticized by both employers and unions and led to a court case which von der Grün won, a miner is made redundant but fails to find his feet in a job on an assembly line. *Zwei Briefe an Pospischiel* (1968) attempts to establish a link between controlling instances in the present and in the Third Reich by focusing on the efforts of a skilled power-station worker to track down the men who caused his father's arrest in 1938; having taken time off without permission, he is sacked, a fate shared by the central character in *Stellenweise Glatteis* (1973) when he discovers a listening device has been installed at his place of work. *Flächenbrand* (1979) concerns the secret arms hoard of a neo-Nazi group, while *Späte Liebe* (1982, dramatized for television in 1979) describes the problems encountered by two widowed pensioners when they decide to marry. *Friedrich und Friederike* (1983) portrays the everyday life of two unemployed young people in a Dortmund working-class estate, and *Die Lawine* (1986) is a thriller on the mystery surrounding the death of a factory-owner who has made a will benefiting his employees. Von der Grün's short stories are collected in the volumes *Fahrtunterbrechung* (1965), *Stenogramm* (1972), *Am Tresen gehen die Lichter aus* (1972), *Etwas außerhalb der Legalität* (1980) and *Klassengespräche* (1981). He has also written numerous plays for radio and television.

Gumppenberg, Hans von (1866–1928)

Gumppenberg lived most of his life in Munich and, together with **Bierbaum** and **Wedekind**, collaborated on the satirical cabaret *Die elf Scharfrichter*, using the pseudonym Jodok; he also, as 'Professor Immanuel Tiefbohrer', published the parodies in prose *Das teutsche Dichterroß, in allen Gangarten zugeritten* (1901). Maeterlinck is parodied in the 'Mystodrama' *Der Veterinärarzt* and the naturalists in *Der Nachbar. Monodrama in einem Satz* (both 1902). Gumppenberg also translated the Swedish poet Mikael Bellman (*Bellman-Brevier* (1909)), with whom he felt an affinity. He also attempted occult dramas (*Der Messias* (1891); *Die Verdammten* (1901); *Die Einzige* (1905)). The following essays should also be noted: *Kritik des wirklich Seienden* (1892); *Grundlagen der wissenschaftlichen Philosophie*; *Philosophie und Okkultismus* (1921).

Hacks, Peter (1928–)

After studying in Munich Hacks moved to the GDR in 1955; since then he has built up a substantial *œuvre*, consisting mainly of plays, but including also poems, stories for children and essays which shed light on his own interests and methods as a dramatist collected in *Die Maßgaben der Kunst* (1977). He has developed **Brecht**'s dramatic legacy along lines which differ from those separately followed by his contemporaries Heiner **Müller** and **Volker Braun**. His early plays have historical, mythical or legendary settings, in which the traditional values embodied by heroic tales and established historical accounts are unmasked or interpreted from a Marxist point of view as the superstructure of burgeoning economic interests (*Das Volksbuch vom Herzog Ernst* (1953, première 1967), *Eröffnung des indischen Zeitalters* (1954, new version until the title *Columbus, oder: die Weltidee zu Schiffe* (1970, première 1975)).

Two plays set in the Prussia of Frederick the Great, *Die Schlacht bei Lobositz* (1955), based on Ulrich Bräker's autobiography *Der arme Mann im Toggenburg*, and *Der Müller von Sanssouci* (1957) were followed by more controversial pieces set in the early years of the GDR which show the interplay of individual interest (*Die Sorgen und die Macht*, various versions between 1959 and 1962) or individual enthusiasm (*Moritz Tassow* (1961, première 1965)) with the demands of social co-operation. The plays Hacks has written since then show a development towards 'sozialistische Klassik' which celebrates man's ability to master his fate and enjoy life now that the contradictions of pre-socialist societies have been overcome. Consequently the Brechtian model devised for the critical demonstration of man-made problems demanding a revolutionary solution is superseded by a post-revolutionary conception of drama.

Hadwiger, Victor (1878–1911)

Son of a military doctor in Prague, Hadwiger soon felt drawn to the literary cafés of that city (particularly the Café Arco) where he associated with Paul Leppin, Oskar Wiener, Gustav **Meyrink** and Max **Brod**, cultivating a bizarre and exotic style of writing. He moved to Paris, then to Berlin (1903), where he lived in extreme poverty; marriage to the grand-niece of D. F. Strauss brought some amelioration (his widow later translated Marinetti and others). Hadwiger is often regarded as a precursor of expressionism: his poem *Ich bin* (1903) prompted **Werfel** to write his *Wir sind*. Further poems were published by Anselm Ruest in 1912; the short stories were also published by him after Hadwiger's death. A novel entitled *Abraham Abt* appeared in 500 copies at the end of 1911 and consisted of a series of stories loosely strung together. These include 'Der Sarg des Riesen', 'Der Sieg des Abel' and 'Die Geschichte vom seidenen Kardinal', stories which had also appeared in *Die Aktion*. Another story, 'Des Affen Jogo Liebe und Hochzeit', was published in 1922. Hadwiger's writing is fantastic, occasionally scurrilous and often grotesque; he exemplifies the transition between Prague *fin de siècle* and certain aspects of expressionism, hence his inclusion in the anthology *Die goldene Bombe. Expressionistische Märchendichtungen und Grotesken* (1970).

Hagelstange, Rudolf (1912–84)

Hagelstange was a popular and versatile writer who remained independent of the prevailing artistic trends and groups; it is possible to place him beside **Bieler** and **Piontek** as one of the few post-war 'conservative' authors. The cycle of sonnets *Venezianisches Credo* (1945) challenges the present by declaring allegiance to the spiritual values represented by the poets of the past and cultivated in traditional forms by the poets of the inner emigration. In *Ballade vom verschütteten Leben* (1952) the survival of two soldiers after a confinement of six years in the storage bunker of a German redoubt becomes a metaphor of death and resurrection and prompts reflection on the preconditions of a new life in the post-war era.

Hagelstange offered his own versions of the material of Homer's epics in *Spielball der Götter* (1959), in which Paris tells his life-story, and *Der große Filou* (1976), which retells the adventures of Odysseus. A tolerant but condescending attitude to erotic entanglements emerges in *Venus im Mars* (1972), in which German occupying troops are shown fraternizing with local girls during the Second World War, in *Altherrensommer* (1969), in which an incurably ill writer called Thannhausen finds his Venus in the form of a Burmese girl during an Asian cruise, and in *Der General und das Kind* (1974), in which an ageing *Bundeswehr* general fights for the custody of the offspring of a late affair. *Das Haus oder Balsers Aufstieg* (1981) reflects the course of German history including the post-war division in the saga of two generations of a middle-class family.

Hagelstange's extensive travel writings cover the USA (*How do you like America?* (1957, extended as *Der schielende Löwe*, 1967), Greece (*Ägäischer Sommer* (1968) and *Das Lied der Muschel* (1958)), Rome (*Römisches Olympia* (1961)) and the Soviet Union (*Die Puppen in der Puppe* (1963)).

Halbe, Max (1865–1944)

Max Halbe's reputation rests almost entirely with the play *Jugend* (1893), a tragic 'Liebesdrama' which portrays the tender burgeoning of adolescent love and the fatal effects of religious mania and repressed sexuality in a

West Prussian setting. The play *Eisgang* (1892) showed Halbe to be an ardent disciple of Ibsen; *Der Strom* (1904), a drama of brutality and greed, uses the symbol of the river (the Vistula) and its dikes in a manner reminiscent of Theodor Storm. Halbe's more successful narrative work includes *Frau Maske* (1897), a story of village life and, later, *Die Auferstehungsnacht des Doktors Adalbert* (1929), which verges on the fantastic. The novel *Die Tat des Dietrich Stobäus* (1911) is little more than a conventional detective story enhanced by a framework structure. Halbe turned to historical novels, and also made use of mythological themes (most successfully in *Io* (1916), a tale based on a painting by Correggio). The later works include the play *Die Traumgesichte des Adam Thor* (1929) and the novel *Generalkonsul Stenzel und sein gefährliches Ich* (1931). Halbe's autobiographical writings *Scholle und Schicksal* (1933) and *Jahrhundertwende* (1935) are enlightening accounts of the literary world in Munich. The *Gesammelte Werke* appeared from 1917 to 1923 (seven vols); *Sämtliche Werke* (fourteen vols) appeared from 1945 to 1950.

Handke, Peter (1942–)

Handke burst upon the literary scene at the penultimate meeting of the *Gruppe 47* at Princeton in 1966 when he accused his colleagues of 'Beschreibungsimpotenz'. The descriptive power of Handke's own writing has been made ever more manifest since, and what began as awareness of and rebellion against social conditioning by means of linguistic and literary norms has developed to become a permanent exploration of the self through its multifarious responses to the world unhampered by abstract commitments or by the practical accommodations of everyday domestic and professional life. (Language as an instrument of consciousness by which the self relates to the world and on occasion to a dimension beyond material reality and social consensus has been an abiding theme of Austrian literature revived in the activities of the *Wiener Gruppe* and the *Forum Stadtpark* in Graz, where Handke studied law.) He began with the prose collection *Begrüßung des Aufsichtsrats* (1967) and two experimental novels *Die Hornissen* (1966), in which sections placed in discontinuous order make it impossible to make out the plot before the end, and *Der Hausierer* (1967), which plays with the formal structures and topoi of the detective story in order to make the reader aware of the artificiality of narrative conventions. *Die Angst des Tormanns beim Elfmeter* (1970) is told from the perspective of a goalkeeper who 'drops out' and commits murder. *Der kurze Brief zum langen Abschied* (1972) traces the transformation of the narrator's self after separation from his wife during a journey across the USA in which he encounters another woman, his brother and the director John Ford, while *Wunschloses Unglück* (1972) is a moving recreation of his mother's life to her suicide. In *Die Stunde der wahren Empfindung* (1975) a press attaché at the Austrian embassy in Paris, having imagined he has become a murderer, becomes progressively alienated from his work and his surroundings, yet experiences a mystical epiphany. *Falsche Bewegung* (1975) is a contrafacture of Goethe's *Wilhelm Meister* in the form of a journey across Germany by a young man with literary ambitions, while in *Die linkshändige Frau* (1976) the title-figure liberates herself from a routine marriage. *Langsame Heimkehr* (1979), in which a geologist moves from Alaska to Austria via the west coast of the USA and New York, initiates a tetralogy in which Handke cultivates a style based on a view of art as more than a registering medium; aesthetic ruminations in an elevated tone occupy much of the travel book on the Mediterranean landscape associated with the painter Cézanne *Die Lehre der Sainte Victoire* (1980); in *Kindergeschichte* (1981) Handke's relationship to his daughter during her first ten years is followed with a sensitivity which becomes the key to a new relationship to the world at large, while in the semi-dramatic *Über die Dörfer* (1981) a trivial quarrel over an inheritance in a remote village is given the archetypal dimension of Greek tragedy by means of a ceremonious style which culminates in the proclamation of the spirit of a new age by the muse-figure Nova. In *Der Chinese des Schmerzes* (1983) a teacher of classics and amateur archaeologist, having spontaneously killed a painter of swastikas on a hill overlooking Salzburg, abandons his work and crosses a threshold (a key motif) to a new life and view of his place in the world. In *Die Wiederholung* (1986) the narrator recalls a journey made twenty years before from Carinthia, Austria to Slovenia, Yugoslavia in search of his brother who had failed to return after joining the partisans; by once more crossing the frontier and the limestone landscape above Trieste he is enabled to explore and reconstitute his own self, which had been partly submerged by family circumstances and schooling. In *Die Abwesenheit. Ein Märchen* (1987), also set in Carinthia, four disparate figures, a young woman, a soldier, a gambler and an old man, break with their former way of life and undertake a quest apparently without destination in which their surroundings undergo a magical transformation. The course of Handke's prose writing places him ever more firmly in a tradition which includes the German Romantic fairy story, the self-communings of the Alpine wanderers Obermann and Amiel, the celebration of the apparently insignificant in nature by Stifter and the aesthetic transsubstantiation of phenomena by **Rilke**. It has overshadowed the experimental plays with which Handke first came to the attention of the public: *Publikumsbeschimpfung* (1966), *Weissagung, Selbstbezichtigung* (both 1961), *Hilferufe* (1967), *Kaspar* (1968), *Das Mündel will Vormund sein* (1969), *Quodlibet* (1970), *Ritt über den Bodensee* (1971) and *Die Unvernünftigen sterben aus* (1974). The most important of these mainly formalistic exercises is *Publikumsbeschimpfung*, which exposes the conventions of dramatic representation by means of radical alienation effects yet remains a highly theatrical work, and *Kaspar*, which indicates the arbitrariness of identity formation by presenting a process of linguistic drill by which the title-figure is forced to conform to certain norms. Handke's other writings include the essays *Ich bin ein Bewohner des Elfenbeinturms* (1972), the poems *Die Innenwelt der Außenwelt der Innenwelt* (1969), the poems, prose and photographs *Als das Wünschen noch geholfen hat* (1974), the diary *Das Gewicht der Welt. Ein Journal* (1977), the reflections and aphorisms *Das Ende des Flanierens* (1980), *Die Geschichte des Bleistifts* (1982), *Phantasien der Wiederholung* (1983) and *Versuch über die Müdigkeit* (1989). *Gedicht an die Dauer* (1986) is Handke's poetic formulation of his later aesthetic.

Hardekopf, Ferdinand (1876–1954)

A stenographer employed by the *Reichstag*, Hardekopf turned to writing and, between 1911 and 1916, became a contributor to Pfemfert's *Die Aktion*. When Pfemfert initiated the 'Aktionsbücher der Aeternisten' (1916–21), Hardekopf, using the pseudonym Stefan Wronski, defined the programme as being anti-bourgeois and anti-traditional, dealing with an urban setting and using a technique of simultaneity which ignored conventional logic. In 1916 Hardekopf moved to Zurich and became associated with the Dadaists, writing absurd poetry ('Aus der steilen, transparenten Nudel/Quillt ein Quantum Quitten-Quark empor . . .'). His *Lesestücke* were published in 1916, followed by *Privatgedichte* (1921). Hardekopf was also a skilled translator from the French (Cocteau, Gide, Duhamel, Malraux). A drug addict, Hardekopf was unable to settle after the First World War and lived alternately in France and Switzerland. His *Gesammelte Dichtungen* appeared in 1963.

Hardt, Ernst (pseudonym of Ernst Stöckhardt, 1876–1947)

A writer who enjoyed great popularity before the First World War, Ernst Hardt began as a journalist before writing in a neo-romantic manner with *Jugendstil* affinities. The *Novellen*, *Priester des Todes* (1898) and *Bunt ist das Leben* (1902), demonstrated Hardt's easy and accessible style: they were republished with other sketches as *Gesammelte Erzählungen* in 1919. A further *Novelle*, *An den Toren des Lebens* (1904), is regarded as his most successful. A collection of poems *Aus den Tagen des Knaben* (1904) shows the marked influence of Stefan **George**. Hardt, who became the director of the German National Theatre in Weimar, considered himself to be essentially a dramatist: early plays (*Tote Zeit* (1898), and *Der Kampf ums Rosenrote* (1903, reissued as *Der Kampf* in 1911)) are indebted to the techniques of naturalism, but it is as the author of poetic dramas that Hardt made his reputation. *Tantris der Narr* (1907) and *Gudrun* (1911) are reworkings of ancient legends plus a modern, psychological dimension; *Schirin und Gertraude* (1913) and *König Salomo* (1915) are fanciful, neo-romantic concoctions. The one-act play *Ninon de Lenclos* (1905) should also be noted. Hardt later, in the 1920s, turned his attention to broadcasting. He wrote nothing during the Nazi period and attempted to revert to his earlier form of writing as late as 1947 when he published the story *Don Hjalmar*.

Harig, Ludwig (1927–)

Harig was for twenty years a schoolteacher in the Saarland, where he was born and continues to live. He can be associated with the linguistic experiments of **Heißenbüttel** and the concrete poets, but he has reached a wider public in his prose works and radio plays thanks to his ability to offer new perspectives on familiar themes through wit and formal dexterity. His marginal geographical position places him in the small but significant group of writers whose work has encouraged and profited from Franco-German *rapprochement*; a member of the Paris *Collegium Pataphysicum*, he has been influenced by Raymond Queneau, which bears fruit in *Zustand und Veränderung* (1963). Repetition and variation, permutation and combination are the principles informing *Reise nach Bordeaux* (1965) and *im men see* (1969), as well as the later works which include the 'family novel' *Sprechstunden für die deutsch-französische Verständigung und die Mitglieder des gemeinsamen Marktes* (1971) based on the artificiality of the traditional language primer, and *Allseitige Beschreibung der Welt zur Heimkehr des Menschen in eine schönere Zukunft* (1974), in which Harig applies his method to the fundamental questions of philosophy in a playful manner embodied by the figure of Till Eulenspiegel.

Harig remains close to reality, especially in his radio plays, which include *das fußballspiel* (1966), *ein blumenstück* (1968), a montage of extracts from nursery rhymes and the diary of the commandant of Auschwitz, and *staatsbegräbnis 1* and *2* (1969 and 1975) on the funerals of Adenauer and Ulbricht. In *Rousseau. Roman vom Ursprung der Natur im Gehirn* (1978) he presents a biography in a series of scenes which combine accounts of his feelings at turning-points in his life with indications of his future influence. The 'Novelle' *Der kleine Brixius* (1980), comparable to Queneau's *Zazie dans le métro*, was followed by a late but substantial addition to the numerous works on authors' relationships to their parents which appeared in the late 1970s: *Ordnung ist das ganze Leben* (1986).

Hartlaub, Felix (1913–45, missing)

The son of the director of the Mannheim *Kunsthalle*, Hartlaub was employed at Hitler's headquarters as a historical expert with the team responsible for the official war diary from 1942 to 1945. Early stories and an attempt at drama show the influence of **Hofmannsthal** and the Bible, but he found his voice in the coolly objective diaries, 'Berliner Tagebuchblätter 1935–1939' and 'Tagebuch aus dem Krieg 1939–1945', which were published in stages in *Von unten gesehen* (1950), *Im Sperrkreis* (1955) and *Das Gesamtwerk* (1955) and which record the course of the war from the perspective of one placed at the still centre of the vortex. He disappeared during the fighting in Berlin in 1945.

Härtling, Peter (1933–)

Härtling, a prolific novelist and occasional poet, came to West Germany in 1945 via Olmütz in Czechoslovakia and Zwettl in Lower Austria. Having lost both parents, he spent thirteen years in Nürtingen, Swabia, in the care of relations, and he has since lived in Cologne, Frankfurt and Walldorf, Hessen. His family's peregrinations during and after the Second World War are conveyed in fictional form in the novels *Zwettl* (1973) and *Hubert oder Die Rückkehr nach Casablanca* (1978). Other novels trace the lives of nineteenth-century poets (Hölderlin in *Hölderlin* (1976), Lenau in *Niembsch oder Der Stillstand* (1964), Mörike in *Die dreifache Maria* (1982) and Waiblinger in *Waiblingers Augen* (1987)) in a manner which problematizes the normal biographical mode. In these and in *Das Familienfest* (1969), in which the return home of a revolutionary professor of history after 1848 prompts an attempt to relive his childhood and is juxtaposed with a gathering of his descendants in 1967, as in *Ein Abend, eine Nacht, ein Morgen* (1971), in which a Berlin lawyer withdraws from his family and his practice as he becomes more and more obsessed with the passage of time, Härtling's interest in memory, time and repetition is evident. Other novels show the transition from one way of life to another as experienced by the poet Jakobus who, having come close to a resistance group during the Third Reich, fails to adjust to the post-war situation and commits suicide (*Im Schein des Kometen* (1959)), or by a factory-owner's wife who discovers a new identity when she makes contact with the proletariat (*Eine Frau* (1974)). The memory of the father, who is unknown (*Janek* (1966)) or is rejected (*Hubert* (1978)) or whose grave is discovered (*Zwettl* (1973)), is a constant theme which receives its fullest elaboration in the autobiographical *Nachgetragene Liebe* (1980), one of the more significant of the many reappraisals of parent-child relationships which appeared between 1976 and 1982. The title of *Das Windrad* (1983) refers to an invention for the production of electricity without fossil fuel; its erection without official permission is made the excuse for its demolition by the police after it has become a rallying-point for the Green movement. *Felix Guttmann* (1985) presents a panorama of German history in the life-story of a Jewish lawyer between the years 1906 and 1977; his political apathy is contrasted with the commitment of his communist friend until he is forced into a ten-year exile in Israel.

In his play *Gilles* (1970) Härtling presents a man (the clown in Watteau's picture) whose hope that the French Revolution will enable him to realize himself after a lifetime of subservience is dashed by those who claim to act in the name of liberty. Härtling's poems have appeared in several volumes between 1953 and 1987 and in representative collections (*Ausgewählte Gedichte 1953–1979* (1979) and *Die Gedichte 1953–1987* (1989)). His Frankfurt literature lectures (*Der spanische Soldat oder Finden und Erfinden*) were given in 1984.

Hasenclever, Walter (1890–1940)

Son of a tyrannical doctor, Hasenclever studied law in Leipzig, Oxford and Lausanne before escaping the parental influence and dedicating himself to writing (in Oxford he financed the printing of his youthful play *Nirwana* by successful poker-playing). Encouraged in Leipzig by Kurt Pinthus, Ernst Rowohlt and Kurt Wolff he published in 1913 a collection of poems entitled *Der Jüngling*: Kurt Wolff also published in the same year a dramatic fragment *Das unendliche Gespräch*, a forerunner of Hasenclever's *Der Sohn*, written in 1913–14 and first performed in 1916. This play is acknowledged to be the paradigm of early expressionist drama; it is constructed formally along traditional lines (there are echoes of Goethe and **Hofmannsthal**), but the mixture of dramatic prose and blank verse reflects an intensely held vision, an emphasis upon fervour and hyperbole. The characters are not named; the Son is tyrannized by the Father, the Friend lures the young man into life, a Governess watches his revolt with trepidation. The line 'Man lebt ja nur in der Ekstase, die Wirklichkeit würde einen verlegen machen!' is quintessentially expressionistic. The Father symbolizes authority and repression: the final confrontation is one of extreme tension, but murder is pre-empted by the Father's heart attack. Hasenclever joined the army in 1914 but rapidly became disillusioned, repudiating the war and its senselessness; the poem 'Der politische Dichter' exhorts poets to become political and pacifist. In 1917 his anti-war play *Antigone* was staged (the censor, believing it to be a classical play and missing the topical allusions, passed it). The war-lord Creon apparently triumphs over Antigone, but his political power collapses and he renounces his earlier beliefs; Antigone's voice from the tomb calls for reconciliation, not vindictiveness. The play *Der Retter* (1919) carries a similar message in its portrayal of the clash between Spirit and Power. After the war Hasenclever eschewed political commitment and turned to mysticism: the fruits of this are seen in his translation and editing of Swedenborg (*Himmel, Hölle, Geisteswelt* (1925), where Swedenborg's 'Kothölle' is identified as the dock area in Marseilles). *Menschen* (1918) and *Mord* (1926) exemplify the mystical aspects of theatrical expressionism. During the 1920s Hasenclever turned to journalism, also light comedy: *Ein besserer Herr* (1926) reached

European success, also *Ehen werden im Himmel geschlossen* (1928), although the latter, with Werner Krauss as 'der liebe Gott', ran into difficulties with the church. *Napoleon greift ein* (1929) mocks fascism and the cult of the dictator. Less successful were collaborations (with Ernst **Toller**: *Bourgeois bleibt Bourgeois* (1928), and with Kurt **Tucholsky**: *Christoph Kolumbus* (1932)). Hasenclever travelled to Hollywood in 1930 to write the German version of the Greta Garbo film *Anna Christie*: although greatly admiring the actress he was unable to fulfil his contract. He went into exile in 1933, living in France, Italy and also England; the comedy *Münchhausen* (1934) was called by Tucholsky 'allerbester Hasenclever vom feinsten Jahrgang'. In London in 1937 he completed another comedy, the *Ehekomödie*, which was staged that year under the title *What should a husband do?* In 1939 his tragi-comedy *Konflikt in Assyrien* (in English *Scandal in Assyria*) was put on in the International Theatre Club in London on Sir John Gielgud's recommendation; Sir Lawrence Olivier and Vivien Leigh sought an American première (it was first seen in Germany in 1957). Hasenclever returned to France, was interned in the same camp (Les Milles) as Lion **Feuchtwanger**, and, at the news of the German advances, killed himself. The novel *Irrtum und Leidenschaft*, published posthumously in 1969, describes the restless years of exile and wandering; it is a curious mixture of autobiography and fiction, omits the author's career as writer and concentrates instead upon erotic experiences. In 1963 his lifelong friend Kurt Pinthus published *Gedichte. Dramen. Prosa*, a one-volume collection of the major works from Hasenclever's *Nachlaß*. Three volumes of *Stücke* appeared in 1990.

Hauptmann, Carl (1858–1921)

Elder brother of **Gerhart Hauptmann** and originally a scientist (obtaining a doctorate for a thesis on the development of blastemata), Carl Hauptmann turned increasingly to philosophical speculation (indebted to Haeckel) and finally to literary pursuits. He lived near his brother Gerhart in Berlin (1889–91) before moving to Schreiberau in the Riesengebirge, writing plays and stories based on the Silesian background. His early, naturalistic writing (the plays *Marianne* (1894), *Waldleute* (1896) and *Ephraims Breite* (1906)) soon gave way to more mystical leanings: *Die armseligen Besenbinder* (1913) is an attempt to emulate his brother's mystical Silesian dramas, but was unsuccessful (the critic Ihering wrote: 'Carl Hauptmann ist unplastisch. Ihm zerrinnt das Märchen in Abnormitäten und Seltsamkeiten'). The same year, however, saw Hauptmann's *Der Krieg. Ein Tedeum*, a remarkably prescient work which anticipates much expressionist drama: the visionary and grotesque elements, the clash between generations, the concept of the New Man born out of chaos and destruction, the need for *Blutrausch* and *Aufbruch*. (The third part of the play, with its Canteen Woman who follows the troops, is a forerunner of **Brecht**'s *Mutter Courage*.) Carl Hauptmann's narrative prose is largely forgotten (*Die Hütten am Hange* and *Mathilde* (1902)), although *Einhardt der Lächler* (1907), despite its over-florid description of the passage of a young man from respectability via bohemianism to artistry, deserves attention.

Hauptmann, Gerhart (1862–1946)

Gerhart Hauptmann was born in Ober-Salzbrunn, Silesia, son of an hotel-keeper. After unsuccessful attempts at studying agriculture, then sculpture, Hauptmann moved to Jena in 1882 where he attended lectures by Ernst Haeckel. In 1884 he studied in Berlin and, after his marriage to Marie Thienemann, settled in Erkner (1895), where he became associated with the so-called 'Jüngstdeutschen' of the 'Friedrichshagener Kreis' (Wilhelm Bölsche, Bruno Wille and the brothers Hart). Hauptmann joined the literary-political circle *Durch*, reading a paper on Georg Büchner, then scarcely known. His first literary work was *Promethidenloos*, an epic written in *ottava rima*, but derivative and undistinguished. The two short stories *Fasching* and *Bahnwärter Thiel* (1887–8) show, however, remarkable narrative skill, the latter particularly being regarded as a minor masterpiece, where naturalistic description fuses effortlessly with a symbolic, quasi-mystical dimension. The collection of poems *Das bunte Buch* (1888) contains alongside melancholy, neo-romantic topoi a marked social element ('Im Nachtzug'). In that year, Hauptmann spent many months with his brother **Carl** in Zurich, meeting, amongst other writers, Frank **Wedekind**. He returned to Erkner and associated with Arno **Holz** and Johannes **Schlaf**; the drama *Der Säemann* was finished in June 1889 and given (on Holz's recommendation) the title *Vor Sonnenaufgang*. The play was printed, became rapidly famous and was first performed by the *Freie Bühne* on 20 October 1889 in the *Lessing-Theater*, Berlin. The uproar was unparalleled in German theatrical history: the crass realism, the uncompromising stance of Alfred Loth, the themes of heredity and alcoholism, industrialization and degeneracy amongst the Silesian *nouveaux riches* established Hauptmann's reputation as the most talented of the young playwrights of his day. What made him adopt naturalism was not the theoretical speculation of Holz and Schlaf, nor a conscious act of will, but an intuitive awareness of his true powers, his ability to create live human characters. The play was praised by Theodor Fontane who saw Hauptmann as a successor to Henrik Ibsen. In 1890 the second play, *Das Friedensfest*, was performed in Berlin; it was based on an incident in the Wedekind household and anticipates, in the portrayal of the clash between father and son, certain expressionist concerns. Hauptmann also used details from his brother's marital difficulties in *Einsame Menschen* (1891), a play which shows certain affinities with *Rosmersholm*. The portrayal of Johannes Vockerat as a man caught between past and future, wife and companion (the 'modern woman') is particularly successful. Hauptmann's sympathy with human suffering drew him to the material of *Die Weber*, performed in 1893; it was acclaimed as a masterpiece of naturalism, but is not a play of revolution, containing, rather, an awareness of some inarticulate spiritual urge which social deprivation cannot stifle. The same year saw the performance of *Der Biberpelz*, a comedy written in Berlin dialect which contains a pointed attack on Prussian officialdom (exemplified by the narrow-minded magistrate von Wehrhahn). The character of Mutter Wolff, the shrewd washerwoman, dishonest yet kind-hearted, directly anticipates **Brecht**'s Mutter Courage (this was the only Hauptmann play that Brecht produced with the *Berliner Ensemble*). 1893 also saw the performance of *Hanneles Himmelfahrt*, a play in which the fervent visions of the dying girl reflect a mystical realm where naturalistic concerns are left far behind. Hauptmann's historical play *Florian Geyer* (1896), based on an episode from the Peasants' Revolt, met with little success; *Die versunkene Glocke* (also 1896), a 'deutsches Märchendrama', deals with the conflict between domestic life and artistry, and refers obliquely to Hauptmann's marital crises at this time. The meeting with Margarete Marschalk brought tensions within Hauptmann's marriage (the flight of his wife and children to America, his pursuit and return); in 1904 the marriage was dissolved and Hauptmann married Margarete. The building of his house in Agnetendorf, Silesia, marked the consolidation of his success as leading German author, crowned by an honorary degree at Oxford in 1904.

Hauptman was deeply aware of the ultimate loneliness of man and his dramas reflect an intuitive understanding of human frailty. *Fuhrmann Henschel* (1898) demonstrates that Hauptmann saw men not as vicious creatures, but creatures thwarted by blind impulse and cramped by social environment. *Michael Kramer* (1900) is again a description of a father-son conflict, ending with the intensely moving scene of the father standing beside the coffin of his son, gazing into an unknown and sombre future. *Rose Bernd* (1903) shows Hauptmann's ability to portray the painful oppression of a trapped, pursued girl who is dumbly aware that her struggle against an inexorable destiny is fruitless. The inability to communicate is seen in many of these plays: Hauptmann's skill at portraying the humble and the inarticulate demonstrates once more his compassion, most strikingly seen in *Die Ratten* (1911), where social criticism comes second to the description of the tragedy of the working-class woman who fights to keep an adopted child and who kills herself when it is taken away from her. Plays such as *Der arme Heinrich* (1902), *Schluck und Jau* (1904: a version of *The Taming of the Shrew*) and *Elga* (1905) were less successful, but fascinating is *Und Pippa tanzt!* (1906), a mystical 'Glashüttenmärchen', which was inspired by Hauptmann's passion for Ida Orloff, a sixteen-year-old actress. The first *Gesamtausgabe* (six volumes) appeared in the same year. 1907 was a prolific year for Hauptmann (*Die Jungfern von Bischofsberg*, *Christiane Lawrenz* and *Kaiser Karls Geisel* were written); important was the visit to Greece, a vital experience which drew Hauptmann's attention to the world of myth and Attic violence (to find expression later in the *Atriden-Tetralogie*). The *Griechischer Frühling* (1908) is an undemanding portrayal of the classical landscape. The novel *Der Narr in Christo Emanuel Quint* (1910) is a return to the Silesian world which Hauptmann knew so well, a probing account of religious fanaticism and delusion (it was his first prose work since *Der Apostel*, which treated a similar theme). Fragments from his

Nachlaß (such as *Die Wiedertäufer* and *Der Dom*) showed how much he was fascinated by this topic. On his fiftieth birthday Hauptmann received the Nobel prize for literature, and another six-volume *Gesamtausgabe* appeared. The *Festspiel in deutschen Reimen* (1913) was a surprisingly ironic treatment of the Wars of the Liberation. Another novel, *Atlantis*, had appeared in 1911 (it was filmed in the following year); the play *Gabriel Schillings Flucht*, also from 1912, is an uneven work on an overworked theme (the man torn between two women). *Peter Brauer* (1911, published 1921) recalls the earlier play *Kollege Crampton*; it was felt by many of the younger writers of the time that Hauptmann had written too much, that he was living on his earlier reputation and unable to understand modern developments in the novel and the theatre. *Der Bogen des Odysseus* (1914), a pallid play written in blank verse, seemed to convince many that Hauptmann had become a mere epigone.

Hauptmann greeted the First World War with a series of conventional war poems; he lived mostly in Berlin and Agnetendorf. *Magnus Garbe* (1915) and *Winterballade* (1916) date from this time, the latter particularly being a depiction of savagery which reflects the turmoil of the times. *Der Ketzer von Soana* (1918), his most popular prose work, is a relaxed portrayal of sexual release, yet deepened by an awareness of Dionysian powers. At the end of the war Hauptmann greeted the Weimar Republic and became its most representative spokesman: it was even suggested that he become President of Germany. His flight into myth, fantasy and exotic realms of the imagination alienated him, however, from the expressionists and other young writers of the 1920s (the 'dritter Kritiker' of *Der Bettler* by Reinhard **Sorge**, had admitted that Hauptmann was 'groß als Künstler, aber als Deuter befangen'). Hauptmann was deemed too remote from the present; his imaginative power, however, was able to bring life to the most far-flung subjects, and quintessential human situations prevail, a deep awareness of the human predicament, be the sufferings those of a servant girl or an Aztec emperor. *Indipohdi*, begun in 1913 and first performed under the title *Das Opfer* in 1922, is a powerful portrayal of pagan sun-worship; Hauptmann sought, however, to achieve in this play a synthesis between the creative activities of the heretic of Soana and the passivity and self-denial of Emanuel Quint. The dangers of Nietzschean vitalism, of pagan substitutions for Christianity, are stressed but life denial and self-deprecation are also criticized. *Veland* (1923) is an unfortunate excursion into a pseudo-Wagnerian setting; in the following year the novel *Die Insel der Großen Mutter* was completed, an ironic novel not dissimilar to *Der Zauberberg* of **Thomas Mann** in its juxtaposition of polar opposites (matriarchal and patriarchal, spirit and nature, reason and feeling). In 1925 a six-volume selection of Hauptmann's work appeared, the late realistic drama *Dorothea Angermann* was completed, together with the *Festaktus*, a work celebrating the opening of the *Deutsches Museum* in Munich. Remarkable fragments also date from this time, a *Grönlandtragödie*, more successful than *Veland* in its portrayal of Nordic darkness and terror, and also *Demeter*. Probably the most important Hauptmann work of the Weimar Republic is the verse-epic *Des großen Kampffliegers, Landfahrers, Gauklers und Magiers Till Eulenspiegel Abenteuer, Streiche, Gaukeleien, Gesichte und Träume,* published in part in the *Neue Rundschau* in 1922 and in full in 1928. The work exists on two levels, contemporary and historical-mythical, and is one of the most important contributions to the 'Narren-Renaissance' of the twentieth century: comparisons have also been made with Goethe's *Faust II*. In 1928 Hauptmann was elected to the Poetry Section of the Prussian Academy of Arts; two one-acters, under the title *Spuk*, appeared in 1929 and contain bizarre, even surrealist elements. Throughout these years Hauptmann was deeply absorbed in the problem of Hamlet and adapted the material to suit his own ends. Despite the fact that he had distanced himself from the new dramatic trends which now dominated (mainly Brechtian) he continued to immerse himself in poetic worlds which were above all concerned with human significance. Undeniable set-backs, and the production of certain works with stale, overworked situations did not prevent Hauptmann from achieving enormous acclaim by the end of the 1920s, becoming the most celebrated German writer of his age. In 1929 he bought Haus Seedorn on Hiddensee and finished his autobiographical novel *Das Buch der Leidenschaft*. In 1931 he accepted an invitation to lecture in America; before his departure he completed *Vor Sonnenuntergang*, a work which laments the decline of Goethean values and sees with foreboding the arrival of a new barbarism. In 1932 Hauptmann received an honorary doctorate of the University of Columbia, New York, and held speeches to mark the centenary of Goethe's death. He was received by the President of the USA and such writers as Sinclair Lewis and Eugene O'Neill. In Germany he received the Goethe Medallion and became honorary citizen of several cities. His seventieth birthday (15 November) was celebrated throughout Germany: Thomas Mann delivered an oration in Munich. Ten weeks later Hitler achieved power in Germany: those sinister powers which Hauptmann had hinted at in *Vor Sonnenuntergang* (Klamroth) and had portrayed in the *Dom* fragment (the shattered cathedral, and the torture-chamber) were now triumphant. The treatment of the theme of suffering in Hauptmann's last works, and the flight from the realistic to the mythical is not a symptom of waning powers but an indication of the awareness of the universal problems of human anguish; it was also prudent, after 1933, to prefer the allusive reference to the unambiguous statement.

The outward signs of acquiescence (the flying of the swastika) had not preserved Hauptmann from Nazi criticism and invective; he was attacked for his allegiance to the Jewish publisher Samuel Fischer and advised to fall silent and seek oblivion. In ever-increasing isolation and advancing age (his eightieth birthday was grudgingly noted in 1942) he refused to refrain from writing: his remarkable play *Die Finsternisse*, dating from 1937 and first published ten years later, was a moving requiem for his Jewish friend Max Pinkus, Silesian patriot and benefactor, who had died in 1934. This sombre play moves on two planes, realistic and mystical: the dead Joel is greeted by Elijah, John the Baptist and Ahasverus as he passes into a transcendental realm. *Die Finsternisse* was a play that obviously could not be performed, but Hauptmann was able to portray the horrors of the new Reich obliquely by using myth, and his greatest achievement during those dark years was the *Atriden*-cycle, an outstanding work for a writer in his eighties. The tone of sombre violence, the themes of madness and destructive frenzy which abound in these plays reach an almost unbearable intensity. The description of the evil priest Kalchas who perverts whole peoples is a striking one; most impressive is the speech of Kritolas (in Act Two of *Iphigenie in Aulis*, staged in Vienna in 1943) on the destruction of cities. *Elektra*, written in 1944, contains in the description of Agamemnon's murder (ash, bones and broken skulls) that which could be used to refer to that other place of extermination, Auschwitz, not two hundred miles east of Agnetendorf. Yet the universal horror of which this tetralogy speaks is also seen as being transient; the optimism is not platitudinous, but is the fervent conviction of the sage. Neither the suicide of Ida Orloff, nor the destruction of Dresden, which Hauptmann witnessed, could quench his resourceful and vital spirit. In 1933 he had announced: 'Meine Epoche beginnt 1870 und endigt mit dem Reichstagsbrand', yet he survived the hectic and murderous madness of the Third Reich and remained creative until the very end. On returning to his house after visiting Dresden (February 1945) he read a lament for that city on the radio; shortly after this Agnetendorf fell into the hands of the Russian army. Hauptmann was treated with respect by the Russians (he was greeted above all as the author of *Die Weber*) and his house was placed under their protection. At the end of the hostilities he was visited by Johannes R. **Becher** and pledged his support for the creation of a new, democratic Germany. His health deteriorated and he died on 6 June 1946; his body was taken, as he had requested, to Hiddensee where he is buried.

Various works, including *Der Venezianer*, *Herbert Engelmann* and *Winckelmann*, appeared posthumously in the 1950s. In the following years different editions of Hauptmann's work appeared in East and West Germany, also other unpublished material: the novel *Der neue Christophorus* (1965) and *Neue Leidenschaft*, *Das zweite Vierteljahrhundert* and *Siri* (1966–7). The first volumes of the *Centenar-Ausgabe* appeared in 1962: this edition had eleven volumes in all (by 1973). Two volumes of *Tagebücher* appeared in 1985 and 1987. Although his reputation suffered after the Second World War, and innovatory theories of drama were preferred, Hauptmann's stature is now assured and the later, more poetic, works are achieving the attention they deserve. Hauptmann's unwillingness to follow the latest trend, his healthy individualism, exuberant imagination and all-pervading humanity make him one of the great German writers of the twentieth century.

Haushofer, Albrecht (1903–45)

Albrecht Haushofer's father was Karl Haushofer, founder of the pseudo-scientific discipline of 'political geography' and close friend of Rudolf Hess. Karl Haushofer was held in esteem by the Nazis but fell from grace after Hess's flight. Albrecht was professor of political geography in Berlin; growing disenchantment with National Socialism, also support for the conspirators of the plot of 20 July 1944, led to his arrest and subsequent execution (24 April 1945) in Berlin-Moabit. In the so-called 'Roman trilogy' (*Scipio* (1934); *Sulla* (1938) and *Augustus* (1939)) Albrecht Haushofer voiced his criticism of the Third Reich (the figure of Zosias in *Sulla* is meant as a 'Kassandro'). Other works include *Makedonen* (1941) and *Chinesische Legende* (1943). His most successful literary achievement are the *Moabiter-Sonette*, found in his hands after the execution and published posthumously in 1946. These consist of eighty sonnets of varying quality which deal with guilt, transience, personal relationships and the beauty of nature. The poem 'Der Vater' expresses the awareness of Karl Haushofer's partial responsibility for the brutal irrationalism of Hitler's policies. Karl Haushofer and his wife committed suicide in 1946.

Hausmann, Manfred (1898–1986)

Hausmann was born in Kassel and studied in Göttingen; as a young man he was greatly influenced by the *Jugendbewegung*, being present at the first great assembly of the youth groups at the Hoher Meißner (1913). He served in the army in the First World War, was wounded in 1918 and returned home. At Heidelberg he studied under Friedrich Gundolf, then tried various jobs and became editor of the magazine section of the *Weserzeitung* in Bremen. He then turned to writing; the story *Holder* (1922) shows Hausmann influenced by expressionism (the protagonist being simpleton, murderer and also visionary); *Die Frühlingsfeier* of the following year eschews expressionist intensity and dislocation and is written with a lyrical delicacy more typical of its author. A collection of poems appeared in 1923 under the title *Jahreszeiten*. Hausmann achieved outstanding popularity with the picaresque novel *Lampioon küßt Mädchen und kleine Birken* (1928) which describes the adventures of a tramp: it is largely derived from Eichendorff and **Hesse** and steeped in *Wandervogelromantik*. The hero, who is also a murderer, defies social norms and exults in nature and freedom; a darker strain of pessimism is also present. The continuation, *Salut gen Himmel* (1929), is a collection of stories mostly dealing with outsiders. Hausmann, now able to live by his writing, settled in Worpswede; in 1929 he visited America and recounted his experiences in *Kleine Liebe zu Amerika* (1930), a light-hearted account of an innocent abroad. Another very popular book was *Abel mit der Mundharmonika* (1932), a story of three boys and a girl on an adventure in the North Sea (the book was filmed in 1950). The short stories *Der schwarze Tag* (1933), *Ontje Arps* (1934) and *Mond hinter Wolken* (1935) all deal with youth and comradeship. A repetitive strain in Hausmann cannot be denied, but *Demeter* (1935) and *Abschied vom Traum der Jugend* (1937) show a greater awareness of maturity, the latter particularly (Frau Fehsenfeld, after being infatuated with a young Icelander, realizes her husband's sterling qualities). In Hausmann's later work a religious element becomes discernible, although *Lilofee* (1937) is a variation on the theme of water and seduction. *Quartier bei Magelone* (1940) deals with delusion and the dangerous fascination of the past. *Der Überfall* (1944) is overtly religious in the depiction of the quest for God. Hausmann's religious thought was clearly influenced by Kierkegaard and Karl Barth, both of whom he studied in detail. The novel *Liebende leben von der Vergebung* contains little more than a series of discussions on the theme of forgiveness. *Das Hirtengespräch* (1951) is a prose portrait of the three shepherds of the nativity, as is *Das Worpsweder Hirtenspiel* (1946). *Der dunkle Reigen*, a mystery play (1951), describes the Dance of Death; *Hafenbar*, performed in 1954, tells of the power of a Salvation Army girl to convert a British sailor. Another play, *Aufruhr in der Marktkirche* (1957), commemorates the six hundredth anniversary of the foundation of the famous church in Hannover. The short story *Was dir nicht angehört* (1956) is very reminiscent of *Tonio Kröger*, both in setting and theme. Hausmann's work appeared in seven volumes, *Gesammelte Werke in Einzelbänden* between 1949 and 1956; an omnibus edition, *Fünf Romane*, appeared in 1961. A collection of plays, poems and random fiction, *Und wie Musik in der Nacht*, appeared in 1965. Hausmann was also an accomplished translator: *Liebe, Tod und Vollmondnächte* (1951) are poems from the Japanese, and *Hinter dem Perlenvorhang* (1954) from the Chinese. A further *Gesammelte Werke* began to appear in 1983.

Hein, Christoph (1944–)

After schooling in West Berlin and various jobs in the GDR, where he grew up, Hein studied philosophy in Leipzig, then worked until 1979 as literary adviser and playwright for the *Deutsches Theater* in East Berlin. His plays bear a formal and thematic resemblance to those of **Volker Braun**, especially *Schlötel* (première 1974, published 1981), in which a graduate of Leipzig University forced on to the shop-floor finds the workers apathetic when he attempts to make them socially motivated, and *Die wahre Geschichte des Ah Q* (1983), set in China, which shows intellectuals unable to find a productive role in a revolution. The temptations, hesitations, self-deceptions and failures of revolutionary leaders are the subject of *Cromwell* (1978), in which Hein points to the plot's relevance to the course of twentieth-century revolutions, and of *Lassalle fragt Herrn Herbert nach Sonja* (1981), in which the nineteenth-century workers' leader is shown as the victim of his own tendency to self-pity and quixotic romanticism as well as of others' intrigues. *Passage* (1987) is set in a French café close to the Spanish frontier during the Second World War, where six refugees wait for permission to cross.

The stories in *Einladung zum Lever Bourgeois* (1980), which appeared in the Federal Republic in 1982 under the title *Nachtfahrt und früher Morgen*, reveal hidden aspects of such famous figures as Racine and Alexander von Humboldt as they struggle against their subordinate position in the state. Hein's reputation in the West rests on his two novels *Der fremde Freund* (1982), which appeared in the Federal Republic under the title *Drachenblut*, a detached account with the aid of flashbacks of the process which leads to the resigned acceptance of a solitary state by a forty-year-old professional woman, and *Horns Ende* (1985), in which the technique of alternating narrative perspective allows five characters to retrace their relations with the museum director Horn, whose suicide prompts an agonized reappraisal of the crucial years 1953–7 in a small town in the GDR. *Der Tangospieler* and *Die Ritter der Tafelrunde* (1989) are, with hindsight, symptomatic of a growing malaise there.

Heißenbüttel, Helmut (1921–)

Probably the best-known and longest-active linguistic experimentalist in the Federal Republic, Heißenbüttel aims at creating an autonomous aesthetic realm in which conventional linguistic structures are dismantled and reassembled. He began with *Kombinationen* (1954) and *Topographien* (1956) and other short pieces later collected in *Gelegenheitsgedichte und Klappentexte* (1973). 'Texte', small-scale montages brought together in six books published between 1960 and 1967 and combined in *Das Textbuch* (1970, 1980), are marked by abstraction and formalism; elaborate collages of disparate fragments are constructed or words and phrases are constantly shuffled to produce shifting sequences devoid of punctuation and syntactic connections. These create an impression of arbitrariness, simultaneity and impersonality, in which process takes precedence over structure. Further 'Textbücher' have appeared during the 1980s, but since the late 1960s Heißenbüttel has concentrated on prose, first in a series of 'Projekte', beginning with the 'novel' *D'Alemberts Ende* (1970), which consists largely of conversations spiced with quotations from Diderot, Freud, Marx, Goethe and Ibsen between writers and media persons during two days in July 1968, and continuing with *Das Durchhauen des Kohlhaupts. Dreizehn Lehrgedichte* (1974), in which fragments of dialogue become models for the breakdown of communication. The three parts of 'Projekt Nr. 3', however, *Eichendorffs Untergang und andere Märchen* (1978), *Wenn Adolf Hitler den Krieg nicht gewonnen hätte. Historische Novellen und wahre Begebenheiten* (1979) and *Das Ende der Alternative. Einfache Geschichten* (1980), take the form of more accessible prose pieces marked by humour and an idiosyncratic relation to literary forebears which is also evident in the literary essays. These are based on an encyclopedic knowledge of the international literary avant-garde (*Über Literatur* (1966), *Briefwechsel über Literatur* (1969), *Zur Tradition der Moderne* (1972)) and of neglected curiosities of the German literary tradition (*Von fliegenden Fröschen, libidinösen Epen, vaterländischen Romanen, Sprechblasen und Ohrwürmern* (1982)).

Herburger, Günter (1932–)

Having studied in Munich and Paris, Herburger worked in various jobs abroad, lived for several years in Berlin, then from 1969 in Munich. He read from his work at meetings of the *Gruppe 47* at Sigtuna, Sweden, and at Princeton, USA. Initially associated with the new realism of the Cologne circle centred on Dieter **Wellershoff**, who edited the collection in which his first publication appeared (*Ein Tag in der Stadt. Sechs Personen variieren ein Thema* (1962)), Herburger has moved away from the objective precision in the presentation of everyday life characteristic of the French *nouveau roman*, to which the circle was indebted, towards a form of fiction in which a microscopic awareness of the surface of things is combined with fantastic projections of aspects of the present into the future, a change partly motivated by Herburger's membership of the West German Communist Party. There are numerous points of contact between his work and fiction inspired directly by the *Studentenbewegung* or the autobiographical treatments of parent-child relationships of the same period, e.g. the central figure of *Die Messe* (1969), having heard that his father might have been a concentration camp commandant, seeks confirmation of his guilt. In *Jesus in Osaka* (1970) the futuristic dystopia set in 1984 of a Swabia which has become a Japanese industrial colony is transformed into a Utopia by the appearance of a Christ figure who is made to resemble a student agitator of the late 1960s. Since the mid-1970s Herburger has been engaged in the composition of a massive fictional trilogy (*Thuja*), of which so far two volumes, the second consisting of two parts, have appeared. *Flug ins Herz* (1977) relates an attempt to prove the insignificance of genetic programming in comparison with environmental factors by forcing a kidnapped millionaire to impregnate a working woman and engineering a parallel relationship between an unskilled worker and the wife of another millionaire. In *Die Augen der Kämpfer* (1980) the children born from these liaisons turn out to be handicapped, and dystopian elements are introduced when after incidents inspired by the 1977 anti-terrorist campaign the setting shifts to Morgenthauland, an agrarian reservation between Wuppertal and the GDR marked by hunger and the rule of force, from where it is a short step to the GDR itself, where the picaresque hero of the entire trilogy finds himself at the beginning of *Die Augen der Kämpfer. Zweite Reise* (1983).

Some of Herburger's stories, collected in the volumes *Eine gleichmäßige Landschaft* (1964) and *Die Eroberung der Zitadelle* (1972), have been filmed for the cinema or television, most to the author's own scenarios (*Die Eroberung der Zitadelle* (1977), *Hauptlehrer Hofer* (1975), *Tatöwierung* (1967)). He has also written radio plays (e.g. *Exhibition oder Ein Kampf um Rom* (1971)) and children's books centred on the resourceful child-hero Birne. A selection from the six volumes of poetry which appeared between 1966 and 1983 was made in *Das Lager* (1984), to be followed by a new collection, *Kinderreich Passmoré* in 1986; in them Herburger cultivates the long, loosely structured poem advocated by Walter **Höllerer** in reaction to the prevailing hermetic and laconic trends of post-war lyric poetry.

Hermlin, Stephan (pseudonym of Rudolf Leder, 1915–)

Hermlin returned to Germany in 1945 already an established poet after service in the International Brigade during the Spanish Civil War and periods of internment in France and Switzerland. In 1947 he moved to East

Berlin, where he has remained. The *Zwölf Balladen von den großen Städten* (1945), which convey his personal struggle against fascism in traditional strophic forms, were followed by *Die Straßen der Furcht* (1947) and *Zweiundzwanzig Balladen* (1947). The elaborate imagery inspired by Romance literatures which is characteristic of these collections is absent in *Der Flug der Taube* (1952), which contains hymns to the October Revolution, Stalin and the first GDR President Wilhelm Pieck.

Hermlin's stories have appeared in different combinations in several collections and deal mainly with anti-fascist resistance during the Third Reich, e.g. the Warsaw ghetto uprising in 'Die Zeit der Gemeinsamkeit' and the activities of the Maquis in occupied France in 'Die Zeit der Einsamkeit'; the most important, *Der Leutnant Yorck von Wartenburg* (1945), brilliantly adapts the structure of Ambrose Bierce's classic 'An incident at Owl Creek Bridge' to the situation of an officer involved in the 20 July 1944 conspiracy against Hitler as he flees east after its failure. In *Abendlicht* (1979), consisting of twenty-seven prose texts musically linked, Hermlin looks back on his own life and compares himself with other exiles and victims of fascism, including his own father and brother, as well as with oppressed writers of earlier centuries. As a critic he has encouraged in the GDR a more open attitude to literary modernism, editing a *Deutsches Lesebuch* (1976) and editions of the poets Attila József, **Georg Heym** and Paul Verlaine; his translations of Eluard, Aragon, Neruda, Shakespeare, Keats, etc. can be seen in the same light. His radio play on the mad Hölderlin, *Scardanelli* (1970), has contributed to the rehabilitation of figures considered marginal to the mainstream of classicism and realism, a process in which several other GDR writers have been involved (e.g. **C. Wolf**, **Kunert**).

Herrmann-Neisse, Max (1886–1941)

Misshapen from birth, Max Herrmann-Neisse was born in Neisse, Silesia; he studied history of literature and art in Munich and Breslau, where his love of the theatre, particularly cabaret, was encouraged. He returned to Neisse without qualifications and worked as a theatre critic on a provincial newspaper. His years as a student and his love-hate relationship with Neisse are described in his novel *Cajetan Schaltermann* (1920), which finishes with the grotesque poem 'Es taumelt in verborgenen Flüsterecken' and its culmination: 'Die Stadt schwillt wie ein Stinkpilz auf und platzt'. It is primarily for his poetry that Herrmann-Neisse is remembered: collections include *Buch Franziska* (1911), *Sie und die Stadt* (1914), *Empörung, Andacht und Ewigkeit* (1918) and *Verbannung* (1919). The early verse contains stereotype neo-romantic images; expressionistic elements are found in the later anthologies, both as regards form and content. Herrmann-Neisse moved to Berlin where he associated with Franz Pfemfert, writing for *Die Aktion*; he also wrote reviews for C. F. W. Behl's journal *Kritiker*. In 1919 his short play *Albine und Aujust* was performed in Berlin; it resembles **Wedekind** and also anticipates the theatre of the absurd (the author climbed on to the stage and spoke of his 'Kainszeichen auf dem Rücken'). Ludwig Meidner and Georg Grosz both sketched him. He felt a close affinity with expressionism, and similarities are noted between his poetry and that of **Blass** and **Lichtenstein**; he insisted however (to Paul **Zech**) that '*Ich* habe kein Programm und schwöre auf keine Richtung'. He fled Germany in 1933 and lived in exile in London until his death in 1941. He is buried in Marylebone cemetery. A collection of his poetry, *Lied der Einsamkeit. Gedichte 1914–1941*, appeared in 1961; a further selection, *Ich gehe wie ich kam*, in 1979.

Herzfelde, Wieland (pseudonym of Wieland Herzfeld, 1896–1989)

Son of the socialist poet, dramatist and prose-writer Franz Herzfeld, who wrote under the name of Franz Held, Wieland Herzfeld (later calling himself Herzfelde) and his brother Helmut, who in 1916 changed his name to John Heartfield in protest against the anti-British hate campaign, were abandoned by their parents in a mountain hut near Salzburg, taken in by the village *Bürgermeister*, settled in Wiesbaden and from there moved to Berlin. Bitterly opposed to the war, the brothers collaborated with Georg Grosz in satirical attacks against the established order. Wieland Herzfelde bought the rights to a defunct school magazine *Neue Jugend* in 1916; in the following year it was issued by Malik-Verlag (the name was borrowed from the story *Malik* by Else **Lasker-Schüler**) and became famous for publishing the work of Grosz and the writing of many left-wing novelists for whom Heartfield designed the book-jackets: his photomontage technique became a formidable weapon in his hands. Wieland Herzfelde also edited the avant-garde journals *Jedermann sein eigener Fußball*, of which only one number appeared (15 February 1919), *Die Pleite*, and also the portfolios of Georg Grosz's lithographs. Wieland Herzfelde also participated in the antics of the Berlin Dadaists. During the Third Reich the brothers lived in exile: Wieland fled to America in 1939 and Heartfield lived in London from 1939 to 1950. Wieland's poems and stories were published later under the title *Unterwegs. Blätter aus fünfzig Jahren* (1961); this collection contains the autobiography *Immergrün. Merkwürdige Erlebnisse und Erfahrungen eines fröhlichen Waisenknaben*. After the Second World War the brothers returned to Germany and settled in East Berlin. Wieland Herzfelde was also active as an editor, particularly of the work of Tolstoi.

Hesse, Hermann (1877–1962)

Born in Calw, Württemberg, of pietist parents (his father had been a missionary in India), Hesse lived as a child partly in Switzerland, partly in Germany; it was intended that he should study theology in Kloster

Maulbronn. After six months at that establishment he fled (1892), studied desultorily at other schools, then became briefly an apprentice in a tower-clock factory before working in a bookshop in Tübingen (1895–8). Having failed to matriculate he felt alienated from erstwhile colleagues who were studying at the university; he turned to writing and published, at his own expense, a volume of poems entitled *Romantische Lieder* (1898). These are mostly derivative and use many overworked, neo-romantic topoi (the first poem, 'An die Sehnsucht', explains: 'Überm Ufer meiner kranken/Seele liegt mein Heimwehland'). In the following year nine prose sketches under the title *Eine Stunde hinter Mitternacht* appeared, the title deriving from one of the *Romantische Lieder*, and Hesse described them as being 'eine kleine, wahre Dichtung, ein Stück Seelengeschichte'. The best known is probably *Inseltraum*; the influence of Maeterlinck, also Novalis, is undeniable. The *Hinterlassene Schriften und Gedichte von Hermann Lauscher*, supposedly edited by Hermann Hesse, appeared in 1901; the 1907 edition abandoned the pseudonymous pretence. Hesse claimed that he was editing the writing 'eines modernen Ästheten und Sonderlings': pretentious attitudinizing prevails as Lauscher agonizes over the inability of writers to capture genuine feeling. With *Peter Camenzind* (1904), Hesse's first successful work, the natural world is extolled and aestheticism rejected out of hand (in the words of Hugo **Ball**, 'War *Lauscher* das Echo bibliophiler Studien, so ist *Camenzind* der Schritt ins Leben, in eine andere, schwere Natur'). Camenzind, a gauche, inhibited misfit, dislikes academic study, rejects contemporary literature and philosophy, takes to drink and only finds solace in love or nature; he finds true culture in Italy and fulfilment, albeit temporary, in caring for a cripple. Camenzind becomes a 'poet' (according to Hesse in a letter of 1907) because he leaves society and turns to nature. The book achieved immediate success; Hesse was able to marry and settle at Gaienhofen on Lake Constance, living now as a fully-fledged writer and contributor to various journals. The next novel, *Unterm Rad* (1906) deals with Hesse's own experiences at Maulbronn and the abortive attempt to become a clockmaker. (The essays 'Die Kunst des Müssiggangs' and 'Über das Reisen', both of 1904, adumbrate the book's main theme: rejection of intellectualism and academic achievement.) The novel provided a further variation on a popular theme, that of the sensitive youth crushed by the school system. Hans Giebenrath is unable to cope and, after leaving school, finds no place in the world; his death is in all probability suicide. *Unterm Rad* is not, however, simply an attack on a particular school and its syllabus, but is meant to be an indictment of arid, brutal pedagogy and the autocratic structure of Wilhelmine Germany: only the representative of rural good sense escapes the general anathema. After settling at Gaienhofen Hesse published various prose pieces ('Septembermorgen am Bodensee', etc.); two collections of stories entitled *Diesseits* and *Nachbarn* appeared in 1907 and 1908 respectively. A novel-fragment *Berthold* also dates from this time, and *Umwege*, a further collection of stories, in 1912. The next major work after *Unterm Rad* was the artist-novel *Gertrud* (1910), a somewhat trite variation on the theme of art versus life. The portrayal of Gertrud is unconvincing, although the characterization of Kuhn, the crippled musician, and Muoth, the opera-singer, is more successful. The former finds the formal study of music inhibiting and extols intuition above all; the latter enjoys the acclaim of the world yet also believes that it is worth nothing. The book had a mixed reception: Hesse's artistic and intellectual position at this time was confused, and tensions within his marriage became increasingly apparent. He travelled widely, visited India in 1911, published an account *Aus Indien* two years later. *Rosshalde* was written during 1912 and 1913 in Gaienhofen and Berne, where Hesse had moved in 1912 without his family. The book is concerned above all with the problem of an artist's marriage: autobiographical allusions are unmistakable. A sharpness of writing separates *Rosshalde* from the novels that preceded it: most moving (and clinically precise) is the account of the death of the young boy Pierre of cerebral meningitis. Divorce and flight are all that remain for the protagonist.

The outbreak of the First World War found Hesse in a depressed and unstable condition. Like many other writers he accepted the war as a cleansing process. Although a convinced opponent of nationalism, and proud of being totally unpolitical (he had boasted to a friend in 1903 that he had never read a newspaper), he was deeply committed to the German cause and immediately placed himself at the disposal of the German consulate in Berne after being pronounced unfit (because of his eyesight) for military service. He founded the *Interniertenzeitung* and provided articles for consumption by Swiss internees. As the war continued Hesse became increasingly dispirited; the essay 'O Freunde, nicht diese Töne!' (published 13 November 1914), which appealed for humanity, brought forth Romain Rolland's enthusiastic response. The story *Knulp* (1915) is a throw-back to Hesse's apolitical stance prior to 1914, a lyrical evocation of the German landscape and a portrayal of the eponymous outsider. Hesse's father died in 1916 and he travelled to Germany for the funeral: he wrote later of the abundance of hatred and bitterness he found there, and longed for a 'späteres Neuanknüpfen der Beziehungen zwischen den Völkern'. He was attacked in the German press for his alleged 'Drückerbergerei und schlaue Feigheit'. His wife's mental condition deteriorated and his son Martin suffered a severe illness. It was at this low point in his life that Hesse met Dr J. B. Lang, a pupil of C. G. Jung and between 1916 and 1917 he underwent seventy-two psychoanalytic sessions in Lucerne. The novel *Demian. Die Geschichte von Emil Sinclairs Jugend* is a direct result of these experiences (published 1919): Jung's depth psychology provided Hesse with fascinating insights into the world of archetypal symbols which would supersede the earlier, overworked preoccupations. The novel may be seen as a *Bildungsroman*, the development of a young man under the guidance of his mentor Demian. Sinclair must 'know himself' and penetrate his innermost being, transcending conventional morality: a triadic process is suggested, 'unconscious harmony', 'disharmony' and finally a 'conscious harmony'. (Later, in 1932, Hesse will write on this again in *Ein Stückchen Theologie*, which describes the desirability of attaining the Third Kingdom of *Geist*, a state beyond ethics and law, a higher irresponsibility.) A plethora of symbols (mostly derived from Jung) abounds: bird, egg, Frau Eva and Abraxas (the deity beyond good and evil); the sultry storm-clouds portend the violence of war about to be unleashed. It would seem that, after turmoil and psychic disturbance, Sinclair attains a new health, an ability to reunite opposites; *Demian* makes a muddled impression on the reader, with its pseudo-psychological treatment of mystical situations. Hesse's stance as popularizer, as purveyor of easily assimilated philosophical clichés is seen in the *Brüder Karamazov* essay of 1919, which speaks of decline and also a new psychic orientation. *Zarathustras Wiederkehr. Ein Wort an die deutsche Jugend* (also 1919) uses similar terms to express the hope that new life would emerge from the destruction of the past: a certain looseness in Hesse's thought is apparent, a rhetorical pseudo-philosophy deriving from Nietzsche, Jung, Dostoevsky and oriental mysticism.

In 1919 Hesse moved to Montagnola in the Ticino; in the following year three *Novellen* were published under the title *Klingsors letzter Sommer* (one bears this title, the others are called *Kinderseele* and *Klein und Wagner*). The three stories are concerned with dissolution; two contrast it with duty, whereas the main story treats it in relation to an artist's life. *Siddhartha, eine indische Dichtung* was published in 1922 and included with the last three named *Novellen*, in the collection *Weg nach Innen* (1931); it recounts the journey of self-exploration of the Brahmin Siddhartha, the attainment of wisdom and a Buddha-like serenity. Hesse's friendship with Hugo Ball dates from this time; he became a Swiss citizen and, in 1923, married Ruth Wenger. His most famous novel, *Der Steppenwolf*, was published in 1927; this and *Siddhartha* became cult books among the disaffected students of the 1960s. The fifty-year-old protagonist, whose initials are Hesse's own, is an outsider who despises, yet also admires, bourgeois normality and order. He insists (erroneously) on dividing the world between the realms of 'Mensch' and of 'Wolf' and oscillates to no purpose between the two. A booklet, the 'Tractat vom Steppenwolf' (a work 'Nur für Verrückte', as is a Magic Theatre whose entrance he seeks) insists on the crudeness of this polarity; the protagonist must learn that the psyche is composed of a myriad sections, and that to rail against the jejune and the insipid aspects of reality is unrewarding. A bizarre experience in the Magic Theatre (i.e. the unconscious), encouraged by drugs, leads him to transcend his former tensions as he realizes that the immortals, Mozart among them, have the gift of laughter's serene detachment. The book owes something to Hesse's friendship with Hugo Ball (the surrealist episodes), also to depth psychology. It is a book that owes its appeal to the pseudo-profundities that it attempts to express, promising 'ecstasy and transcendence on the easy-payment plan' (G. Steiner); Colin Wilson would later, in the 1950s, bring its attention to an undiscriminating readership.

Hesse became a member of the Prussian *Dichter-Akademie* in 1926, but remained a member for only one year. In 1930 he published *Narziß und Goldmund*, a portrayal of the conflicting claims of the *vita activa* and the *vita contemplativa* in a highly romanticized medieval world; its mawkish sentimentality confirms the suspicion that Hesse was unable to shake off the elegiac *Schwärmerei* of his youth. In 1932 he published *Morgenlandfahrt*, an expression of the desire for spiritual idealism and communion in the face of a threatening Europe. In the 1930s Hesse turned his attention increasingly to poetry; after his third marriage (to Ninon Dolbin) he lived outside Montagnola and increasingly cultivated the role of sage. The major enterprise of the 1930s, a book not published until 1943, is *Das*

Glasperlenspiel. In this novel the year 2400 is posited and the life of Josef Knecht, erstwhile musical prodigy and *Magister Ludi*, is described. An utopian realm of pure idealism is encouraged, the game of the title being an intellectual game with all the contents and values of human culture. Knecht, however, questions the aridity of such self-sufficient idealism, feeling that the restless flux of the world, with its disorder and confusion, is richer than the realm of Castalia in which the glass bead game is enacted. He satisfies an emotional as well as an intellectual need by leaving Castalia to become tutor to the son of an old friend. A few days after leaving the order he dies after plunging after the boy into an icy lake. The death is ambiguous: is it a sacrificial act or an admonition not to leave the static serenity of Castalia? Hesse's study of Eastern religions may have influenced him in his emphasis on the lack of importance of the individual; certain poems by 'Knecht', appended at the end of the book, insist on flux and indeterminacy.

After the war Hesse received many honours, chief among them being the Nobel prize for literature (1946). *Späte Prosa* appeared in 1951, and *Letzte Gedichte* in 1960. The *Gesammelte Werke in Einzelausgaben* (twenty-two vols) appeared between 1956 and 1967; the *Gesammelte Schriften* (seven vols) in 1957. After his elevation to the cult hero of the 'Beat' generation his work was in great demand: a *Werkausgabe* (twelve vols) was printed in 1970 and again in 1975. Two volumes of *Politische Schriften* appeared in 1981.

Heym, Georg (1887–1912)

Acknowledged to be one of the most talented among the early expressionist poets, Georg Heym was born in Hirschberg, Silesia; his father was a lawyer. Heym embarked on studies for a legal career in Würzburg, but soon took up writing; a longing for violence and upheaval characterized his work from its beginnings. A diary entry of 6 July 1910 expresses a longing for war ('Oder sei es auch nur, daß man einen Krieg begänne, er kann ungerecht sein. Dieser Frieden ist so faul ölig und schmierig . . .'). Attempts at historical drama, modelled on Grabbe, were unsuccessful; important was the meeting in Berlin with Kurt **Hiller** and the association with the *Neuer Club*. Poems by Heym appeared in *Der Demokrat* and *Die Aktion* (1910–11); Ernst Rowohlt requested more and published Heym's first collection, *Der ewige Tag*, in 1911. Poems such as 'Der Gott der Stadt' and 'Die Dämonen der Städte' portray the grotesque horror of cities (Berlin) and contain sombre presentiments of doom; the tension between conventional structure (quatrain) and apocalyptic vision is singularly impressive. Heym read his poems in the *Neuer Club* in a staccato, withdrawn manner; Kurt Hiller wrote of him thus (in *Pan*, 1911): 'Georg Heym ist der wuchtigste, riesenhafteste; der dämonischste, zyklopischste; ein Platzendes, Hinhauer unter den Dichtern dieser Tage . . .'. On 16 January 1912 Heym was drowned in the Havel Lake near Berlin; it is claimed that he attempted to save his friend Ernst Balcke from suicide. The second collection of poems, *Umbra Vitae*, appeared posthumously later that year, despite the objections of Heym's father. It includes the famous poem 'Der Krieg', which is his best known ('Aufgestanden ist er, welcher lange schlief . . .'). A sense of dread is combined in this poem with feelings of awe; it also exemplifies that expressionist tendency to see through the surface of things to behold a mythical, archetypal dimension. Other poems ('Deine Wimpern, die langen . . .') are tender love lyrics inspired by Hildegard Krohn. A collection of *Novellen* and sketches, *Der Dieb*, appeared in 1913; most famous is 'Die Sektion', where a clinical description of an autopsy is transfigured by poetry and vision. E. L. Kirchner provided forty-seven lithographs for an edition of *Umbra Vitae* in 1924. The *Dichtungen und Schriften* (vols 1–3) appeared from 1960 to 1964; vol. 6 (*Dokumente zu Leben und Werk*) appeared in 1968, *Gedichte 1910–1912* in 1990.

Heym, Stefan (originally Flieg, Helmut) (1913–)

Born Helmut Flieg the son of a Jewish businessman, Heym adopted his present name in 1942 after several years in the USA, where he had been editor of a German-language newspaper in New York. He served as an officer in the psychological warfare section of the US army and took part in the Normandy invasion of 1944 before returning to journalism with the *Neue Zeitung* in Munich. Growing dissatisfaction with American conduct of the Cold War led him to abandon this work and move to the GDR in 1953, where he has remained, having over the years maintained a marked degree of independence from official cultural policy, sometimes at some personal cost. Many of his novels were written and first published in English, including *Hostages* (1942), which appeared as *Der Fall Glasenapp* in the GDR in 1958, in the Federal Republic in 1976, a hostage drama set in Nazi-occupied Prague; *The Crusaders* (1948), which appeared as *Kreuzfahrer von heute* in the GDR in 1950, and as *Bitterer Lorbeer* in the Federal Republic in the same year, a critique of American war aims arising from the gradual awareness on the part of an American professor of German of the contradictions between proclaimed democratic ideals and the deficiencies of the capitalist system; *The Eyes of Reason* (1951) (*Die Augen der Vernunft* (1955)), in which the differing paths taken by three brothers of a Czech family in the years up to the communist *coup* of 1948 allow Heym's commitment to the consolidation of the new system in Eastern Europe to emerge; and *Goldsborough* (1953), an account of a miners' strike in 1950 in the USA. In the 1960s Heym turned to the nineteenth century as the prehistory of the revolutionary upheavals of his own time and offered in *Die Papiere des Andreas Lenz* (1963), which appeared in the Federal Republic as *Lenz oder Die Freiheit* in 1965, a Marxist account of the Baden uprising in 1848–9 in which Engels took part, and in *Lassalle* (1969 in the Federal Republic, 1974 in the GDR), a portrait, warts and all, of the president of the first German workers' organization. The 1970s saw the publication only in the Federal Republic of Heym's two most controversial novels: *5 Tage im Juni* (1974), in which the events of 17 June 1953 are observed from the point of view of a union official, a working woman and a stripper, challenging the authoritative GDR view of the uprising, while *Collin* (1979) combines a retrospective examination of GDR history with portraits of élite functionaries whom the title-figure encounters during a hospital stay. Heym masks his critique of official attempts to rewrite history in the twentieth century by turning to the Old Testament for *Der König David Bericht* (1972), in which Ethan, poet and historian at the court of Solomon, having cunningly introduced unsavoury facts about his predecessor David in what is supposed to be a bowdlerized version of his life commissioned for propaganda purposes, is tried and sentenced to future silence. *Ahasver* (1981) is undoubtedly Heym's most complex and ambitious work; by means of its three levels of narrative, belonging to the twentieth century, the sixteenth century and timeless myth, Heym is able to demonstrate the historical dialectic of reaction and revolution represented in myth by Lucifer and Ahasver and looks forward to a Utopia in which compassion (Christ) and struggle for change (Ahasver) can be allied. *Schwarzenberg* (1984) is based on authentic accounts of the brief survival of a small area in southern Saxony outside the power blocks that were to divide Germany after the end of the Third Reich. Heym has also produced several volumes of stories (*Die Kannibalen und andere Erzählungen* (1953), *Schatten und Licht* (1960), *Die richtige Einstellung und andere Erzählungen* (1977)) and an autobiography (*Nachruf* (1988)). In *Einmischung. Gespräche, Reden, Essays 1982–1989* (1990) he expresses disappointment at the rush to capitalism at the opening of the Berlin Wall.

Heynicke, Kurt (1891–1985)

Born in Silesia, Heynicke described himself as 'Arbeiterkind, Volksschüler, Bureaumensch, Kaufmann'. His first poems were published by Herwarth **Walden** in the *Sturm*, although Heynicke's association with the other contributors was never close. He fought on the French and Russian fronts during the First World War. His first collection of poems, *Rings fallen Sterne*, appeared in 1917: the themes are generally those of loneliness and striving ('Nach Strindbergs Ostern' and 'Erhebung'). Otiose abstractions prevail in *Gottes Geigen, Gedichte* (1918); *Das namenlose Angesicht* (1919) is much indebted to **Werfel**, particularly 'Psalm'. The poem 'Volk' included in *Menschheitsdämmerung* ('Mein Volk, blühe ewig, Volk . . ./einst werden alle Dinge knien/vor dir . . .') anticipates Heynicke's later contributions to the literature of the Third Reich. During the Weimar Republic Heynicke worked as *Dramaturg* for theatres in Düsseldorf and Berlin; he also worked for the UFA film studios. A series of somewhat trivial novels and plays dates from this time. In 1933 Heynicke wrote his first 'Thing-Spiel' (festival cultic play) *Neurode*, a 'Play of German Work' dealing with the creation of a work community run on Nazi lines in the Silesian town of that name. The second, *Der Weg ins Reich* (1935) deals in religiose, mystical terms with the 'Heimkehrer' who persuades 'Die Opfernde' to surrender land to the community. Heynicke lived in obscurity in the Black Forest throughout the Second World War; *Ausgewählte Gedichte* appeared in 1952. He also turned to *Hörspiele* and plays for television. *Das lyrische Werk* (three vols) appeared in 1975.

Hildesheimer, Wolfgang (1916–)

Hildesheimer was partly educated in Britain before emigrating with his parents in 1933 from Germany to Palestine. After 1936 his exile odyssey continued via Salzburg and London back to Palestine in the uniform of the British army. After acting as an interpreter at the Nuremberg trials he settled as a painter in Bavaria, then moved to Switzerland in 1957, having begun to write in 1950. Although a member of the *Gruppe 47* Hildesheimer remained apart from prevailing trends in the Federal Republic, preferring to cultivate a refined, even precious style geared to the satirical exposure of the absurdities which arise in an over-sophisticated ambience, for which there is hardly any parallel in German literature (*Lieblose Legenden* (1952, second version 1962), *Paradies der falschen Vögel* (1953)). His dramas and radio plays, which include *Der Drachenthron* (1955, second version as *Die Eroberung der Prinzessin Turandot* (1961)), *Das Opfer Helena* (1959), *Spiele, in denen es dunkel wird* (1958), *Die Verspätung* (1961), *Nachtstück* (1963) and *Mary Stuart* (1971), are more radical treatments of human reactions to an existential void and along with the early plays of **Grass** and **Peter Weiss** come closer than any other German works to the theatre of the absurd as exemplified by Beckett and Ionesco, establishing a trend which resurfaced in a new form in the plays of **Bernhard**. The monologue form is the chief characteristic of the prose and drama of the 1960s (*Vergebliche Aufzeichnungen* (1963), *Tynset* (1965), which elaborates the situation presented in *Nachtstück*, *Zeiten in Cornwall* (1971) and *Masante* (1973), in which the narrator's standpoint is a bar on the edge of the desert). An acute psychological study of *Mozart* (1977) was followed by *Marbot* (1981), the biography of a fictional English aristocrat whose incestuous relationship with his mother is subtly linked to the psychological aesthetic he develops in meetings with real artists and philosophers of the Romantic period before committing suicide. In 1983 Hildesheimer declared his intention to abandon writing in the face of the uncontrollable progress of science and industry towards catastrophe; only a few essays and translations have appeared since.

Hille, Peter (1854–1904)

Peter Hille is known primarily as an arch-Bohemian and vagabond; Else **Lasker-Schüler** in her *Peter Hille Buch* (1906) propagated the legend. Hille studied briefly in Leipzig (1887), then attempted journalism and finally turned to writing; he lived in the slums of Whitechapel, worked sporadically in the British Museum and visited Swinburne (with a recommendation from

Victor Hugo). He published three essays on literary topics in the *Deutsche Monatsblätter* in 1878 and in 1885 edited his own journal *Die Völkermuse: ein kritisches Schneidemühl*, which only survived two numbers but which also brought forth the enthusiastic praise of Detlev von Liliencron. A novel, *Die Sozialisten*, appeared in 1886 and consisted mainly of descriptions of the author's stay in London and Amsterdam; three other novels followed (*Cleopatra* (1902); *Semiramis* (1902); *Die Hassenburg* (1905)). Hille also attempted to write drama: *Des Platonikers Sohn* (1896) deals with the conflict between father and son, while *Myrddin und Vivian*, which remained unfinished, adapts one of the Arthurian legends. Hille was rarely successful in sustaining a narrative thread and was not at ease in conventional drama, preferring sketch, impression and aphorism (he was famous for the sack which he carried constantly and which contained scraps of paper on which were written his notes and jottings). He was more successful as a lyric poet and frequently used the ode form. Another novel, *Das Mysterium Jesu*, was published posthumously. Hille, impoverished, frequently slept in the open, often in the Tiergarten: he appeared as the homeless poet Peter Hullenkamp in Gerhart **Hauptmann**'s *Der Narr in Christo Emanuel Quint*, also in works by **Bierbaum**, **Löns**, Paul **Ernst** and Wilhelm **Schäfer**. The brothers Hart, who had helped him earlier in Bremen, introduced him to the 'Neue Gemeinschaft', where he met Gustav Landauer and Erich **Mühsam**. He collapsed on a railway station in Berlin and died in hospital. His *Gesammelte Werke* (ed. by the brothers Hart), in four volumes, appeared in 1904. A painting of Peter Hille by Lovis Corinth dates from 1902. *Gesammelte Werke* (6 volumes) appeared from 1984.

Hiller, Kurt (1885–1973)

Kurt Hiller was one of the leading advocates of an alliance between anti-militarist intellectuals in Germany before the First World War and the Weimar Republic. Before the war he helped to found the *Neuer Club* (1908) with its 'Neopathetisches Cabaret' (1910) where the young writers read from their works (Hiller provided the poems 'der Eth' and 'Elegien'); a further cabaret, 'Gnu', also dates from this time, where Hiller read from the works of Nietzsche, Ernst **Blass** and others. 'Nacht-Schluß bei Bols' shows Hiller's expertise at evoking the sleazy and the flippant. In 1912 he edited the anthology *Der Kondor* which displayed primarily the work of those Berlin poets with whom Hiller had been in contact. During the war Hiller's political activism became increasingly apparent and he gathered a circle together to contribute to *Das Ziel* (1915), a pacifist journal consisting of 'Aufrufe zu tätigem Geist'. An avowed homosexual, Hiller also campaigned for permissiveness and tolerance; he hoped for a Weimar Germany ruled by 'Platonic Guardians'. In 1925 he published *Verwirklichung des Geistes im Staat. Beiträge zu einem System des logokratischen Aktivismus*, where his concept of 'Logokratie' is propounded in a portentous and over-idealistic manner. Being Jewish, homosexual and an anarcho-socialist, Hiller was an obvious target for attack from the right. After the Second World War he published, in 1969, *Leben gegen die Zeit*, a work in two parts, *Logos*, dealing with his political career, and *Eros*, a detailed account of his sexual experiences. Of interest are also *Geistige Grundlagen eines schöpferischen Deutschlands der Zukunft*, a speech made in Hamburg in 1947, *Köpfe und Tröpfe. Profile aus einem Vierteljahrhundert* (1950) and *Der Aufbruch zum Paradies. Ein Tagebuch* (1952).

Hochhuth, Rolf (1931-)

Hochhuth's first play *Der Stellvertreter*, directed at its première in 1963 by Erwin Piscator, who had developed his own form of political theatre during the 1920s, made its author internationally famous and marks a turning-point in the history of post-war German drama. Initiating a documentary phase which lasted into the 1970s, it had an impact which must be attributed not only to its theme, the failure of Pope Pius XII to publicly condemn the Holocaust or to appeal to the German leadership to halt the excesses of anti-Semitism, but to the rhetorical power and conviction with which it is handled. Conservative in form, it owes a debt to the classicism of Lessing and Schiller which is more significant than its documentary foundation, and Hochhuth has since held consistently to the formula of the *pièce à thèse* which combines a discursive treatment of burning issues of the day with sensational effects produced when the abstract commitments of larger-than-life characters are transformed into action. *Der Stellvertreter* was followed by *Soldaten. Nekrolog auf Genf* (1967), in which the question of responsibility for the death of the Polish general and prime minister in exile Sikorski is linked to the moral and strategic arguments for and against the bombing of civilian targets. *Guerillas* (1970), one of Hochhuth's least convincing plays, concerns the eventually unrealized plan devised by a radical American senator to effect a redistribution of wealth in the USA by means of a *coup d'état*. The 'comedy' *Die Hebamme* (1971, second version 1973), resembles Heinrich **Böll**'s *Ende einer Dienstfahrt* in its presentation of the ultimately successful campaign waged by a resolute old nurse for the transfer of homeless persons from a dilapidated camp to new accommodation intended for the *Bundeswehr*. In *Lysistrate und die NATO* (1974) Hochhuth updates the theme of Aristophanes's comedy; in withholding conjugal rights the women successfully challenge the plan of their husbands to sell the land necessary for the establishment of a naval base on a Greek island shortly before the colonels' *coup* in 1967. After *Tod eines Jägers* (1976), a monologue in which Ernest Hemingway takes stock of his writing career before committing suicide, Hochhuth resumed his role of counsel for the prosecution by bringing to public attention the harsh decisions made by the Prime Minister of Baden-Württemberg Filbinger when he was a military judge at the end of the Third Reich and then modelling on him the politician who appears in the play *Juristen* (1979) as the architect of the

'Radikalenerlaß' (law excluding political radicals from employment in government and public service) and who is exposed as a war criminal by a medical student threatened by it. *Ärztinnen* (1980) attacks corruption in the medical profession and the pharmaceutical industry, and *Judith* (1984) supplies several variations of the Old Testament story of Judith and Holofernes culminating in the successful assassination of the President of the USA with the poisonous chemical which would have ensured a further escalation in the arms race. In *Unbefleckte Empfängnis* (1988) Hochhuth offers a spirited defence of surrogate motherhood in the form of an adaptation of the chalk circle legend which had formed the basis of plays by **Klabund** and **Brecht**.

For all his faults (characters who are rarely more than the mouthpieces of ideas, melodramatic effects, speeches swamped by documentation, the mythical overtones present in the idealization of women as procreators and martyrs) Hochhuth demands to be taken seriously, especially in the commentaries of Shavian dimensions added to the plays and the essays devoted to his philosophy of history. He asserts the absolute moral claim on the individual, even in conditions which render a moral stand futile and self-destructive, as embodied in the figure of Antigone, two of whose modern avatars appear in Hochhuth's prose works: 'Die Berliner Antigone' (1966, dramatized by Leopold Ahlsen for television in 1968) and *Eine Liebe in Deutschland* (1978) and bear witness to his conclusion, 'daß der einzelne heute wie immer *sein* Leid, *sein* Sterben ertragen muß, gerade auch dann, wenn er keine Wahl hat und keine Waffe, . . .'

Hochwälder, Fritz (1911–86)

Hochwälder, born in Vienna, is a dramatist who eschews modernism and bases his work firmly on the classical tradition. Early plays (*Jehr* (1932); *Liebe in Florenze* (1936); *Esther* (1940)) met with little success, but fame came with *Das heilige Experiment* (1943). This is a drama of ideas, without female characters, and is set in eighteenth-century South America. The clash between conflicting claims (the Jesuit state and the power of Spain) is worked out with logical intensity: a realm of love and justice has no place in a world dominated by politics. *Hotel du commerce* (1940) is based on Maupassant's story *Boule de suif* and is a portrayal of hypocrisy and complacency. *Meier Helmbrecht* (1946) is a variation on the theme of the generation gap; *Donadieu* (1953) is based on Conrad Ferdinand Meyer's *Die Füße im Feuer* and deals with religious strife and vengeance. *Der Flüchtling* (1945) has a more modern setting and has as its theme the problems of responsibility and humanity. A popular play is *Der öffentliche Ankläger* (1948); set during the French Revolution it touches again on guilt and involvement ('Ich habe immer nur getan, was man von mir verlangte'). *Der Unschuldige* (1949) is a comic variation on this theme; *Die Herberge* (1956) deals with the curse of money. *Donnerstag*, first performed at the Salzburg Festival of 1959, is called 'ein modernes Mysterienspiel'. Other plays include

Schicksalskomödie (1960) and *1003* (1964). Hochwälder's plays are generally simplistic, dealing with straightforward moral issues; a certain predictability cannot be denied. *Dramen* (vol. 1) appeared in 1959, with vol. 2 in 1964; a selection, *Dramen*, appeared in 1968; *Dramen* (two vols) were published in 1975. Hochwälder moved to Switzerland after the *Anschluß* and lived there until his death.

Hoddis, Jakob van (pseudonym of Hans Davidsohn, 1887–probably 1942)

Jakob van Hoddis studied in Berlin and Munich; in Berlin he met Kurt **Hiller** and, in the years 1909–11, helped to found the *Neuer Club* and the 'Neopathetisches Cabaret'. It was here that he read his poem 'Weltende', which was published on 11 January 1911 in Franz Pfemfert's Berlin weekly *Der Demokrat*, a poem held by many to be the overture to German expressionism (**J. R.** Becher described the electrifying effect of the poem in *Ein Mensch unserer Zeit*, and in the sequel to his novel *Der Abschied* Becher calls van Hoddis the founder of the Neopathetic School and 'Weltende' the 'Marseillaise der expressionistischen Revolution'). Other poems were published in the *Sturm* and the *Aktion* in 1912. In the same year the first signs of mental instability became apparent; in November 1912 he was forced to enter a mental home in Berlin-Nikolasee (Franz Pfemfert objected in the *Aktion*). Van Hoddis leapt from a window and escaped in December, and spent the following year in Paris, Munich and Berlin. On 25 April 1914 he read his poems for the last time to a gathering of authors who had contributed to the *Aktion*. Schizophrenia was diagnosed shortly afterwards; van Hoddis was treated in various clinics. In 1918 his only collection of poems, *Weltende*, appeared, containing sixteen from the *Aktion*: mostly quatrains, they attempted, by a collage effect, a concatenation of bizarre and disparate images, to express a disturbing sense of fragmentation and malaise (good examples are 'Aurora' and 'Kinematograph'). After 1933 van Hoddis was interned in the only Jewish mental home left in Germany (Bendorf-Sayn, near Coblenz); on 30 April 1942 he was deported as 'Number 8' with other inmates; none returned. The *Gesamtausgabe* appeared in 1958.

Hofmann, Gert (1932–)

After studying in Leipzig and Freiburg, Hofmann taught at various foreign universities, including from 1971 to 1980 Ljubljana, the setting of the novel *Die Fistelstimme* (1980). In 1981 he became a professional writer and moved to Munich. He began with radio plays, which include *Leute in Violette* (1961) on the fate of a Jewish couple in the Third Reich, *Verluste* (1972) in which a woman leaves her husband when she becomes aware of how he has made language an instrument of subjection, and *Die Überflutung* (1979), the monologue of a man who attempts to rid himself of the memory of how Nazis flooded a Berlin underground railway tunnel in which hundreds of children were taking shelter.

The protagonists of Hofmann's novels and stories usually suffer from an oblique or disturbed relation to reality; their problems are often conveyed by a highly complex narrative technique in which direct and indirect speech, present and imperfect tense, first and third person alternate and narrators draw on documents and reports of others. These features are present also in the work of the Austrians Thomas **Bernhard** and **Gerhard Roth**, although the impaired perceptions of Hofmann's figures can be attributed to various factors: historical (*Die Denunziation* (1979)), psychological (*Die Fistelstimme* (1980), *Auf dem Turm* (1982)), ideological (*Unsere Eroberung* (1984), *Veilchenfeld* (1986)) or physical (*Gespräch über Balzacs Pferd* (1981), *Der Blindensturz* (1985)).

Hofmannsthal, Hugo von (1874–1929)

Born in Vienna of part Austrian-Jewish, part Italian extraction, Hofmannsthal astonished his contemporaries at an early age by his precocity and his remarkably mature awareness of the European cultural tradition. As a schoolboy he published verses of flawless perfection (under various pseudonyms); at university he started by studying law, then changed to Romance philology and gained his doctorate with a thesis on the Pleïades. The titles of his first lyrical dramas (*Gestern* (1891); *Der Tod des Tizian* (1892); *Der Tor und der Tod* (1893)) betray an obsession with beauty, death and transience; heir to French symbolism and Viennese neo-romanticism, Hofmannsthal, in his early writing, cultivated an exquisite sensibility and dwelt on the mysterious beauty inherent in existence. Other lyrical plays include *Der weiße Fächer* and *Die Frau im Fenster* (1897), *Die Hochzeit der Sobeide* (1899) and *Der Kaiser und die Hexe* (1900): the influence of Maeterlinck is apparent. Hofmannsthal was an *habitué* of the Cafe Griensteidl together with **Schnitzler** and **Beer-Hofmann**; he was approached there towards the end of 1891 by Stefan **George**, who admired his poetry and invited him to contribute to the forthcoming *Blätter für die Kunst*. Hofmannsthal, in the poem 'Der Prophet', expresses the dangerous nature of George's emphasis on aestheticism, and also its sterility. The short story *Das Märchen der 672. Nacht* (1894) likewise stresses the emptiness of a life devoted to aesthetic sensations; the squalid death of the 'Kaufmannssohn' seems a fitting punishment. Hofmannsthal's *Ausgewählte Gedichte* appeared in 1903; a year before he published the essay *Ein Brief* written in the form of a letter purporting to be from Philipp, Lord Chandos, to Francis Bacon. Using a historical mask, Hofmannsthal explains that he felt separated from his earlier works which had been written so effortlessly and had been highly praised; he had lost the sense of magic harmony (called elsewhere 'Präexistenz') and also his trust in the power of language, feeling unable to communicate with others. The poet who had hitherto used language with grace and ease now expresses his reservations and inhibitions; the *Brief* is an important document in any discussion of the 'Sprachkrise' which affected many writers, particularly Austrian, at the beginning of the century.

Hofmannsthal turned to themes of violence and obsession in his 'Greek' plays (*Elektra* (1904), and *Ödipus und die Sphinx* (1906)): anticipations of expressionist excess may be traced here. (The short story *Reitergeschichte* of 1899 had also portrayed brutality and violent death.) *Gesammelte Gedichte* appeared in 1907: it is, however, the realization of his indebtedness to a long cultural tradition that gave Hofmannsthal a new direction in his writing; the flirtation with Dionysian atavism was alien to him. The medieval mystery-play *Jedermann* provided him with suitable material, and his version (1911) became the nucleus of the Salzburg Festivals; it was Max Reinhardt who staged it before Salzburg Cathedral, using the square as an auditorium. (Later, in 1923, the *Salzburger Großes Welttheater*, an adaptation of Calderon, would be performed before the high altar of the Collegiate Church.) Most fruitful was the collaboration with Richard Strauss (who had earlier used *Elektra* as a libretto) and, in the same year, 1911, the first performance of *Der Rosenkavalier* took place. Hofmannsthal devoted himself increasingly to the furtherance of the Austrian dramatic and operatic tradition, establishing via the music of Strauss a means to reach as wide an audience as possible. The collaboration with Strauss was highly successful, although the relationship between the two artists was not always free of dissension. *Ariadne auf Naxos* followed in 1916, a work meant to be in the spirit of Molière's *Le bourgeois gentilhomme*; *Die Frau ohne Schatten* (1919), intended as a *Volksstück*, became a profound and moving portrayal of loss, trial and purification in the manner of *Die Zauberflöte*; *Die ägyptische Helena* (1928) is a 'mythologische Oper', which none the less deals with marriage and its problems in a modern manner.

The collapse of Austria-Hungary in 1918 was a profound shock to Hofmannsthal, who nevertheless sought to reassert cultural and spiritual values and to extol the great figures of Austrian literature in the face of a threatening world. Those works were greeted above all by Hofmannsthal which, in their irony and refinement, seemed to be quintessentially Austrian rather than German; the tendency towards humourless excess which he observes in German culture became increasingly distasteful to him. His *Der Schwierige* (1921) portrays upper-class Viennese society at its finest, with its memorable representative Hans-Karl Bühl: the humour, often wry, urbane, and never forced, circumvents or disposes with the darker problems of the age. *Der Unbestechliche* (1923) takes place in a similar milieu. The truly civilized values, Hofmannsthal sees, are those of tolerance, of respect for the elusive nature of truth, and the refusal to pass a heavy-handed judgement. But despite the statement of humane values in these plays, weariness and resignation characterize much of Hofmannsthal's work in its later stages: the correspondence with C. J. **Burckhardt** is full of disillusionment and foreboding when the European situation is considered. The play *Der Turm* (1928) is Hofmannsthal's most profound statement concerning the nihilistic forces of his time, and the second version particularly, without the intoxicated language of the first, is a work of undeniable power. The tower represents that state of enchanted inwardness, that aesthetic condition of 'Präexistenz' which Hofmannsthal criticizes for its lack of ethical core. The hero, Sigismund, emerges, but is destroyed, yet not before the appearance of a 'Kinderkönig' who symbolizes the ultimate regeneration of man. (The second version eschews this facile ending, however, and is a much tauter, more dramatic piece of writing.)

Two years before his death Hofmannsthal asserted in his Munich address 'Das Schrifttum als geistiger Raum der Nation' his faith in the triumph of civilized values and his hope for a 'conservative revolution', a transformation of German life away from the irrational and the musical towards order, lucidity and tolerance. (The fragmentary novel *Andreas oder die Vereinigten*, published posthumously in 1930, was called by Jakob **Wassermann** an Austrian *Wilhelm Meister*: responsibility and maturity were to have been the goals to which the hero strives.) Serenity was not, however, to be achieved by Hofmannsthal, and the realization that his life was moving away from order into fragmentation and turmoil undermined his hope for the future. The eldest of his sons committed suicide on 13 July 1929, and Hofmannsthal died of a heart attack two days later.

Hofmannsthal's work as essayist and anthologist should also be noted; his correspondence was considerable, and published letters include those addressed to famous contemporaries as well as lesser-known figures. The *Gesammelte Werke* (six vols) appeared in 1924; the *Gesammelte Werke in Einzelausgaben* (fifteen vols) came out between 1945 and 1959 (the *Aufzeichnungen*, including the *Ad me ipsum* essay, appeared that year). The definitive, authoritative edition, the *Sämtliche Werke*, started to appear in 1975; a *Gesammelte Werke* (ten vols) followed in 1979 and 1980.

Holitscher, Arthur (1869–1941)

Holitscher was born in Budapest, son of a Jewish businessman. He turned from banking to literature and published his first book, *Leidende Menschen*, in 1893: the influence of Knut Hamsun is apparent. He moved to Paris, had contact with anarchist circles and published a novel, *Weiße Liebe*, with Albert Langen in Munich. In 1896 he settled in that city as a publisher's reader and contributed to the satirical *Simplicissimus*. His most famous novel, *Der vergiftete Brunnen*, appeared in Munich in 1900: **Thomas Mann** recommended it (Mann would later use Holitscher as the model for Detlev Spinell in *Tristan*). *Der vergiftete Brunnen* is one of the best examples of German decadent literature; a further *Novelle, Von der Wollust und dem Tode*, portrays a grotesque 'Liebestod'. In 1907 Holitscher moved to Berlin where he worked as a reader for Ernst Cassirer. A journey to America resulted in *Amerika heute und morgen* (1912); after the First World War Holitscher published *Drei Monate in Sowjetrußland* (1921). Sympathy with the Soviet Union became manifest in his writing and his life: he was active in the *Bund für proletarische Kultur*, in which he worked with Franz **Jung** and Ludwig **Rubiner**. *Das unruhige Asien* followed in 1926. Holitscher described his disenchantment with Bohemian attitudes and the growth of his political awareness in *Lebensgeschichte eines Rebellen*, published in two volumes (1924, 1928). He was in Paris in January 1933 and moved first to Ascona, then to Geneva. He died in 1941; Robert **Musil** spoke at his grave.

Höllerer, Walter (1922–)

Like Hans Werner **Richter**, Peter **Huchel** and Stephan **Hermlin** Höllerer has combined the roles of creative writer and patron/impresario of letters; consequently his writing has been overshadowed by his activities as founder and organizer of the *Literarisches Colloquium* in Berlin, as co-editor of *Akzente* from 1954 to 1967, of *Sprache im technischen Zeitalter* from 1961 and of numerous anthologies, especially *Transit* (1956), as professor at the Berlin *Technische Hochschule* and as critic.

The openness to international modernist trends Höllerer advocated as editor is demonstrated in the poems collected in *Gedichte 1942–1982* (1982). In the 'Thesen zum langen Gedicht', which led to a lengthy debate, and in his later poems he contributed to the loose forms and everyday themes which prevailed in the German poetry of the 1970s. His fragmentary novel *Die Elephantenuhr* (1973, shortened version 1975) concerns the efforts of a museum employee to set up an exhibition on the subject of semiology; unable to realize his ideal of a museum in which the constant metamorphoses of life find expression he blows up the building and the Schiller monument in front of it.

Holz, Arno (1863–1929)

Holz is associated first and foremost with German naturalism: his essay *Die Kunst: ihr Wesen und ihre Gesetze* formulated the theory of 'konsequenter Naturalismus' which attempted, in its radicalism (art equals nature minus 'x', where 'x' represents the deficiency in the writer's imitative skills) to go beyond Zola. Holz collaborated with Johannes **Schlaf** in the writing of the *Novelle Papa Hamlet* (1889), a bleak 'slice of life' which, although in narrative prose, verges on the transcript of a radio play. A Scandinavian pseudonym was used ('Bjarne P. Holmsen'), such being the influence of Northern writers at this time. *Die Familie Selicke* (1889, again by Holz and Schlaf) is a grim evocation of life in the Berlin slums: 'Sekundenstil' ('second-by-second technique') is used throughout. As well as writing prose and drama, Holz also attempted poetry, contributing to the journals *Pan* and *Die Jugend*: his first publications had been in verse, the 'Liedersammlung' *Klinginsherz* (1883); in the *Buch der Zeit* (1886) he had insisted upon the rejection of stale, pseudo-romantic imagery, and in the *Revolution der Lyrik* he expounded upon the need to seek an inner rhythm in poetry which was born directly from the subject-matter. Holz insisted upon a new arrangement in the printing of poems, his 'Mittelachsenverse': these 'central axis verses' are built around the axis to give emphasis and clarity of design. In 1893 he published the first version of his *Phantasus*, using this form; a hundred poems are spun from the brain of the poet in his solitude: reality and fantasy, stylized idylls and *Jugendstil* situations are invoked. 'Phantasus' is the poet's imagination which is able to embrace all aspects of reality. Holz included a 'laurel wreath' for himself ('Dem einsamen Bahnbrecher, dem genialen Pfadfinder, dem großen Erneuerer und Wiedererwecker unserer Literatur'). Subsequent editions of the work would swell to grotesque proportions (336 pages in 1916, 1,345 in the 1925 version and, later, material from the *Nachlaß* made it reach 1,584 pages).

Holz sought to create an ultimate poetic work and also to achieve, in an enormous cycle of plays, the consummate dramatic *œuvre*. Twenty-five were planned, to be entitled *Berlin. Das Ende einer Zeit*; three were completed, the comedy *Sozialaristokraten* (1890) and the two tragedies *Sonnenfinsternis* (1908) and *Ignorabimus* (1913). Holz's growing megalomania is seen in the claim that he had written the greatest comedy and also the greatest tragedies in German literature. *Sozialaristokraten* is a thinly veiled attack on Bruno Wille (who had coined the term used by Holz as a title); Holz portrayed himself as the poet Hahn, victim of unscrupulous literati, and John Henry **Mackay** and Stanislaw **Przybyszewski** are also depicted. (The play has also been described as showing 'die erste Phase in jenem ideologischen und politischen Verlumpungsprozeß, den das deutsche Kleinbürgertum im Zeitalter des Imperialismus durchgemacht hat'.) *Sonnenfinsternis*, a play of some 300 pages, deals with the clash between art and life; Holz's erstwhile colleague Johannes **Schlaf** is viciously attacked (Musmann is portrayed as an embittered crank, shabby and moth-eaten). The title refers to a painting by the hero Hollrieder (i.e. Holz) which is destroyed by Musmann out of envy. *Ignorabimus*, another gigantic play (450 pages) deals with occult phenomena: Holz appears as the scientist Dorninger who is increasingly drawn to mysticism (the Berlin physicist Emil du Bois-Reymond stands as model for the father-in-law). Alongside these plays Holz wrote, with Oskar Jerschke, five pot-boilers (*Frei!* (1907), *Gaudeamus!* (1909), *Heimkehr* (1903), *Traumulus* (1905) and *Büxl* (1911)).

Holz's irritability and tendency to hyperbole led to an increasing isolation. He did, however, achieve popularity with *Dafnis. Freß- Sauff- und Venuslieder* (1903), a mock *carpe diem* in the baroque style; twenty thousand copies were sold in one year. Another monstrous inflation, *Die Blechschmiede* followed (the first section had appeared in *Die Insel* in 1900): it purports to take place in the poet's pineal gland and is described by Holz as a 'grandioses, apotheoses, naturalistisch-symbolistisch-pointillistisch-expressionistisches, dionysisch-apollinisches, venusinisches Pandivinum, Pandemonium und Panmysterium'. The work suffers from the elephantiasis that afflicted *Phantasus*; it is a hybrid in five acts with four interludes, plus narrative and lyrical episodes; the absurd play with rhymes anticipates the more grotesque forms of expressionism. Holz published his own work as *Werke* (ten vols) in 1924, also as a *Monumentalausgabe* (twelve vols) in 1926. *Werke* (seven vols) appeared from 1961 to 1964.

Horváth, Ödön von (1901–38)

Horváth was born in Fiume of Hungarian parents; his father, a diplomat, travelled extensively. (Horváth later wrote: 'Ich habe keine Heimat und leide natürlich nicht darunter, sondern freue mich meiner Heimatlosigkeit, denn sie befreit mich von einer unnötigen Sentimentalität'). After a restless childhood he studied in Vienna and moved (in 1919) to Munich, where his first work was published, *Das Buch der Tänze*, a collection of impressionistic, pseudo-oriental poems; he later rejected them and wished all copies to be destroyed. He turned to writing plays in 1923, also prose poems; in 1924 he moved to Berlin, preferring the city to his parents' country house in Murnau. His first successful play, *Révolte auf Côte 3018*, later rewritten and called *Die Bergbahn*, was written here (1927–9): it deals with an accident caused during the building of the cable-railway to the Zugspitze and criticizes social injustice. The next play, *Sladek oder Die schwarze Armee*, later called *Sladek der schwarze Reichswehrmann* (1930), describes the death of a young girl at the hands of a paramilitary right-wing group who fear that she may betray them: her lover, Sladek, a member of the group, is powerless to help her. The play uses a court scene, a device used successfully by both Horváth and **Brecht**, who knew his work intimately, having obtained copies of even the unpublished plays. Here, as elsewhere, Horváth reserves his sympathy for the women characters while ferociously attacking the blindness of men when involved with political ideologies. Horváth was offered a contract by Ullstein which allowed him to write in whatever form he pleased; the novel *Der ewige Spießer* (1930) is a result of this. It is the plays written at this time, however, which demonstrate his true mastery, *Geschichten aus dem Wienerwald* (1931), *Italienische Nacht* (1931) and *Kasimir und Karoline* (1932). Horváth revived the so-called *Volksstück*, a play portraying the life of the ordinary people, characterized by a loose, episodic structure where the banal, humorous and the grotesque are juxtaposed (he clarified his meaning of the term in a Bavarian radio interview in April 1932). *Italienische Nacht* shows how political jargon ousts true communication; *Geschichten aus dem Wienerwald*, not overtly political, shows the girl Marianne as a victim of male aggression and stupidity. In 1931 Horváth was awarded the Kleist prize on the recommendation of Carl **Zuckmayer**; with this and the performance of *Geschichten aus dem Wienerwald* in Berlin Horváth's fame was assured, despite bitter attacks from the right-wing press. *Glaube Liebe Hoffnung* (1932), another *Volksstück*, again shows the women as victims in a ruthless battle between individual and society. Horváth also excelled at exposing the contradictions between words and motives, the linguistic masks the characters so fervently adopt. The deceptively simple urban idiom he uses frequently belies the seriousness of his quest. In 1933 this play was banned and Horváth moved back to Vienna; *Die Unbekannte aus der Seine* leaves the realm of politics for a more mystical dimension (woman, water and astrology). The two plays *Don Juan kommt aus dem Krieg* (1937) and *Figaro läßt sich scheiden* (also 1937) are mediocre updatings of traditional stories. In 1936 Horváth became a true exile and in 1938 he moved to Paris. Two short novels date from this time, *Jugend ohne Gott* and *Ein Kind unserer Zeit* (both 1938), the former dealing with compromise and brutalization during the Nazi period, the latter with disillusionment on the part of one who initially supported the regime. It was whilst Horváth was about to visit Robert Siodmak to discuss the filming of *Jugend ohne Gott* that he was struck and killed by a falling branch on the Champs Elysées during a thunderstorm (on 1 June 1938). The funeral oration was given by Carl Zuckmayer. Interest in Horváth's work grew in the late 1960s, and in 1972 a *Gesammelte Werke* appeared (in eight vols). Horváth is now regarded as one of the more important German playwrights of the 1930s, with *Geschichten aus dem Wienerwald* as a minor modern classic. The *Gesammelte Werke (Große kommentierte Werkausgabe*, 15 vols) appeared in 1983.

Huch, Friedrich (1873–1913)

A cousin of **Ricarda Huch**, Friedrich Huch studied in Munich, Berlin and Paris and subsequently became tutor to a family on a Polish estate. He made his reputation as a writer of sensitive novels which deal with the problems of adolescence (*Peter Michel* (1901); *Geschwister* (1903) and above all *Mao* (1907)). *Pitt und Fox. Die Liebeswege der Brüder Sintrup* (1909) is a skilful portrayal of emotional entanglements (Pitt is the nickname for Philipp; the protagonist's brother is whimsically called Fox). *Enzio. Ein musikalischer Roman* (1911) deals at length with Wagner and his influence ('Wagner ist ein Magiker, ein Zauberer'); Wagner parodies are found in *Tristan und Isolde, Lohengrin und Der fliegende Holländer* of the same year (the Flying Dutchman is seen as a blasé decadent). Thomas **Mann**, in the funeral oration for Friedrich Huch, explained: 'Seit Herman Bangs Tode hat der moderne Roman keinen so schweren Verlust erfahren, wie durch das Abscheiden Friedrich Huchs'. The *Gesammelte Werke* (four vols) appeared in 1925; *Romane der Jugend* in 1934.

Huch, Ricarda (1864–1947)

Ricarda Huch was the daughter of an old and cultured patrician family in Brunswick; as her father's interests lay more in the study of literature and history rather than in trade the firm became bankrupt. She studied history at Zurich from 1888 to 1891 (women being refused entry to German universities) and worked for five years as a secretary in the Central Library. She published her first novel, *Erinnerungen von Ludolf Ursleu dem Jüngeren*, an account of the decline of a Hanseatic merchant family based closely on her own, in 1893. In 1898 she settled in Vienna from where, after her marriage, she moved to Trieste, a city whose slums she described in her second novel *Aus der Triumphgasse* (1902). In the following year she published *Vita somnium breve*, republished as *Michael Unger*, a novel which reverts, not entirely successfully, to the theme of her first. Between 1900 and

1907 she lived in Munich, where she devoted herself to literary and historical studies. She became famous for her two books on Romanticism (*Blütezeit der Romantik* (1899) and *Ausbreitung und Verfall der Romantik* (1902)) and for her studies of nineteenth-century Italy (*Merkwürdige Menschen und Schicksale aus dem Zeitalter des Risorgimento* (1908); *Die Geschichten von Garibaldi* (1906–7); *Das Leben des Grafen Federigo Confalonieri* (1910)). Between 1912 and 1914 she published, in three volumes, an account of the Thirty Years War (*Der große Krieg in Deutschland*, renamed *Der dreißigjährige Krieg* in 1937). Her second marriage was to her Brunswick cousin Richard; after it had failed she continued to live in Munich, but moved to Berlin in 1927. Interest in modern Russian history led to the Novelle *Der letzte Sommer* (1910), and also *Michael Bakunin und die Anarchie* (1923). Later writing turns away from historical biography to themes of a religious nature (*Luthers Glaube* (1916); *Der Sinn der Heiligen Schrift* (1919); *Entpersönlichung* (1921)). In 1931 she received the Goethe prize from the city of Frankfurt; she became a member of the Prussian Academy of Arts and Sciences, but left after the Nazi seizure of power. From 1936 to 1946 she lived in Jena, victim of constant harassment during the Third Reich. She intended to write the history of the German resistance to Hitler, but completed only *Die Akten der Münchner Studenten gegen Hitler*, which was published posthumously in 1948. **Thomas Mann** called her 'die erste Frau Deutschlands, ja wahrscheinlich Europas'. Her *Gesammelte Werke* (ten vols) appeared from 1966 to 1974.

Huchel, Peter (1903–81)

After a period as a POW in the Soviet Union Huchel returned to radio, in which he had been employed before 1938. In 1949 he became editor of the GDR's most important literary magazine *Sinn und Form*, but in 1962 he was deprived of his post because of his open policy towards ideologically alien writing and placed under supervision at his home. He was eventually allowed to move to the Federal Republic, where he remained until his death.

After the early collection *Der Knabenteich* (1933) was withdrawn Huchel's poems appeared in *Die Kolonne* and *Das innere Reich*, outlets for writers of the 'inner emigration', but these were assembled only after the Second World War in the collections *Gedichte* (1948) and *Die Sternenreuse* (1967). *Chausseen, Chausseen* (1963) contains the poems of the early post-war years, *Gezählte Tage* (1972) and *Die neunte Stunde* (1971) are, as their titles suggest, poems of old age. Huchel wrote landscape poems which evoke memories of his childhood in the Mark Brandenburg, war poems ('Dezember 1942', 'Der Rückzug') and poems with a Mediterranean setting. Later he resorted increasingly to motifs from literature (especially Shakespeare) and myth in order to come to terms with his own isolation and ageing. In all his work concentration is achieved without the sacrifice of precision and comprehensibility, usually in varied forms of free verse in which a few basic images (night, light, twilight, snow) recur in changing combinations and contexts.

Huelsenbeck, Richard (1892–1974)

A student of medicine in Munich, Huelsenbeck met Hugo **Ball** in the Café Stephanie and collaborated with him (1913) on the expressionist journal *Revolution*. In 1914 the two men were in Berlin and became deeply involved with the expressionists in that city. An 'Expressionistenabend' (12 May 1915) included readings by Huelsenbeck of his so-called 'Negergedichte'; *Phantastische Gebete*, with illustrations by Hans **Arp**, appeared in 1916 (this collection includes such 'selige Rhythmen' as 'Straßenbahn héhé Deine Feuerzange' and 'Die Köpfe der Pferde'). In 1916 Huelsenbeck followed Ball to Zurich and was one of the founder members of the Dada movement in the Café Voltaire; he returned to Berlin and, with Raoul Hausmann and Walter **Mehring**, founded Berlin Dada. From that time date the *Novellen*, *Azteken oder die Knallbude* and *Verwandlungen* (1918), also *En avant Dada* and *Die dadaistische Bewegung* (in *Die neue Rundschau* (1920)). The experimental film-maker Hans Richter called Huelsenbeck (in his *Dada-Profile* (1961)) 'Doktor der Medizin, Schiffsarzt, Journalist, Schriftsteller, Dichter . . . einer der Väter Dadas in Zürich und der Urvater Dada in Berlin'.. Huelsenbeck travelled widely and settled in New York in 1936, where he worked as a psychiatrist. His later, more conventional novels include *Doktor Billig am Ende* (1921), *China frißt Menschen* (1930) and *Der Traum vom großen Glück* (1933). The *New Yorker Kantaten* appeared in 1952 and his autobiography *Mit Witz, Licht und Grütze* in 1967. The *Phantastische Gebete* were republished in 1960 and 1988, the *Auto-biographische Reise bis ans Ende der Freiheit* in 1984.

J

Jahnn, Hans Henny (1894–1959)

Born near Hamburg into a family of organ-builders and ship's carpenters, Jahnn began writing plays whilst still at school; a convinced pacifist, he spent the years 1915–18 in Norway with his friend Gottlieb Harms. On his return he published two plays, *Pastor Ephraim Magnus* (1919) and *Die Krönung Richards III* (1921), depictions of violent sexual tensions which share some of the preoccupations of expressionism. In 1920 Jahnn founded the *Glaubensgemeinde Ugrino*, a 'Religionsgemeinschaft' which met in a Hamburg suburb: it lasted until 1925 (attempts were made after the Second World War to resurrect it). The 'Abteilung-Verlag' of the society published the next play, *Der Arzt. Sein Weib. Sein Sohn* (1922), also Jahnn's writing on organ-building; renamed 'Ugrino-Verlag' it would later publish the work of early North German musicians (also Gesualdo and Mozart). Other plays by Jahnn included *Der gestohlene Gott* (1924), *Medea* (1926), *Neuer Lübecker Totentanz* and *Straßenecke* (both 1931). Jahnn showed himself to be obsessed by the vagaries of sexual appetites; perversion and also a longing for harmony exist side by side.

It is, however, as a novelist that Jahnn achieved European recognition (Walter Muschg called him 'den größten deutschen Prosaisten unserer Zeit'). In 1929 he published the experimental novel *Perrudja*: the elemental force and vitality of the nature descriptions, particularly of the Norwegian mountains, is unparalleled in German literature, as is the ability to communicate the essence and the consciousness of the animal world. The cascade of nouns, the parataxis and the merging of fact and vision are very much of the expressionist mould. (That Jahnn should have been an admirer of the Welsh novelist John Cowper Powys is illuminating.) Jahnn also, at this time, worked to restore the Arp-Schnitger organ of the Jacobi-Kirche in Hamburg; he built and repaired over a hundred others. In 1934 he moved with his family to the Danish island of Bornholm, where he bought a farm, Hof Bondegaard, and turned his attention to stud-farming and the investigation of the hormones of mares. During the occupation of Denmark he lived in a remote house in the north of the island, sheltering a Hungarian Jewess. These are the years in which he worked at his vast trilogy *Fluß ohne Ufer*: part one, *Das Holzschiff*, appeared in 1949; part two, *Die Niederschrift des Gustav Anias Horn* (in two volumes) appeared from 1949 to 1950; part three, *Epilog* (a fragment) was published posthumously in 1961. The trilogy is unique in world literature in its fusion of the biological and the musical, the elemental and the symbolic: an enormous 'shoreless river of life' carries the protagonist into manifold experiences. A cosmic love for all natural things is conveyed in epic prose which transcends the conventional novel form: long digressions on music are given (including extracts from the work of Samuel Scheidt and Vincent Lübeck), and quotations from Klopstock emphasize the vastness of the concept. Jahnn's work is essentially life-enhancing in its almost pagan openness to nature and to love in all its manifestations (particularly moving is the account of the love of the protagonist for his friend Alfred Tutein and his mare Ilok).

Jahnn returned to Hamburg in 1950 (his property had been confiscated by the Danes), and turned his attention to the theatre again with a group of plays: *Armut, Reichtum, Mensch und Tier* (1948), *Thomas Chatterton* (1950), *Spur des dunklen Engels* (with music by Yngve Jan Trede, 1952) and *Die Trümmer des Gewissens* (published posthumously in 1961 as *Der staubige Regenbogen*). The short novel *Die Nacht aus Blei* appeared in 1956; it was planned as part of a longer work, *Jeden ereilt es*, which remained unfinished, and is unusual in Jahnn in that it resembles the nightmare world of Franz **Kafka**. Jahnn spent the last years of his life campaigning vigorously against atomic warfare, and published several articles on this topic. He became president of the *Hamburger Akademie der Freien Künste* and intended visiting North Wales to present the Academy's medal to John Cowper Powys in 1957, but ill health prevented this. His reputation as a novelist is assured, although the vastness of his work makes it difficult of access. The *Werke und Tagebücher in 7 Bänden* appeared in 1974: an 11 volume *Werke* (Hamburger Ausgabe) started to appear in 1985.

Jakobs, Karl-Heinz (1929–)

Jakobs studied at the Johannes R. Becher Institute of Literature in 1956 and became a journalist and writer in 1958. He moved to the Federal Republic in 1981. He began by following the 'Bitterfelder Weg' and his early novels took their themes from contemporary industrial development in the GDR. Here already, however, there was an implicit challenge to party norms in his treatment of private conflicts emerging during the construction of a socialist society and his manner of focusing on the role of the intellectual in this process. *Beschreibung eines Sommers* (1961) is an 'Ankunftsroman' (cf. **C. Wolf**, *Der geteilte Himmel* and **Reimann**, *Ankunft im Alltag*) which is neither simplistic nor predictable in its presentation of the conflicting views on sexual morality of protagonist and party. In *Eine Pyramide für mich* (1971), in which a scientist returns to the place of his first employment and takes stock of his former self, and in *Die Interviewer* (1973), in which the professional and domestic difficulties of an expert who is not a positive hero lead to no clear solution, Jakobs turned to the level of administrators, managers and technicians. After some critical science fiction ('Köthen', 'Hinein ins neue Jahrtausend' and 'Quedlinburg' in *Fata Morgana* (1977)) he signalled his nonconformity by allowing his protagonist to protest against the Warsaw Pact invasion of Czechoslovakia in *Wilhelmsburg* (1979), a more radical version of *Die Interviewer*, and after leaving the GDR offered an uncoded account of the intrigues and manœuvrings surrounding the expatriation of Wolf **Biermann** in *Das endlose Jahr* (1983).

Jandl, Ernst (1925–)

After studying in Vienna Jandl became a secondary school-teacher of English. Having been influenced by the *Wiener Gruppe*, he began in the 1950s a close friendship and working relationship with Friederike **Mayröcker**, which led to the joint composition of experimental radio plays, for one of which, *Fünf Mann Menschen*, they received the prestigious *Hörspielpreis der Kriegsblinden* in 1968. Drawing on the innovations of the Dadaists, the *Wiener Gruppe* and the concrete poets, he has developed his own characteristic form of sound poem, which achieves its full impact only in performance or recordings, as well as a wide variety of other games with linguistic material, based on simple procedures such as the omission, addition and transposition of sounds, syllables and words, including English, marked by wit and, in *Selbstporträt des Schachspielers als trinkende Uhr* (1983), melancholy. Other collections include *Laut und Luise* (1966), *der künstliche baum* (1970), *dingfest* (1973), *serienfuss* (1974), *die bearbeitung der mütze* (1978) and *der gelbe hund* (1980). In the four talks *die schöne kunst des schreibens* (1976) and the Frankfurt literature lectures *Das Öffnen und Schließen des Mundes* (1985) he makes illuminating comments on his own work. The *Gesammelte Werke* appeared in four volumes in 1985.

Jelinek, Elfriede (1946–)

Jelinek trained as an organist and pianist, then studied art history and drama at the University of Vienna. She is firmly rooted in the Austrian tradition of social criticism via a critique of language (**Kraus**, **Horváth**, *Wiener Gruppe*), to which she adds a combative feminism and a radical subjectivity. *wir sind lockvögel baby!* (1970), a montage of motifs drawn from pop culture and *Michael. Ein Jugendbuch für die Infantilgesellschaft* (1972) criticize the mass media. *Die Liebhaberinnen* (1975) shows the effects of marriage on the lives of two women; here Jelinek is revealed as a Marxist feminist, aiming to transform a male-dominated and class-divided society. *Die Ausgesperrten* (1980) traces the origins of European urban terrorism by exposing the social and psychological disorientation of a group of young people in the Vienna of the 1950s. *Die Klavierspielerin* (1983) reveals the failure of a pianist to climb to the heights of her profession or to establish a satisfying stable relationship with a man. *Oh Wildnis, oh Schutz vor ihr* (1985) belongs to the genre of anti-*Heimatroman* common in recent Austrian literature.

Jelinek's first play *Was geschah, nachdem Nora ihren Mann verlassen hatte oder Stützen der Gesellschaft* (1979), which combines motifs from Ibsen's *The Doll's House* and *Pillars of Society*, relates what happened to Nora after she broke with her family; having found work in a factory, she becomes a pawn in her employer's plan to ruin her husband, to whom she is forced to return. *Clara S.* (1982), by devising a relationship between Clara Schumann and Gabriele d'Annunzio, indicates that high culture provides no insurance against the exploitation of women. *Burgtheater* (1985), which adapts the

Austrian dramatic form of *Posse mit Gesang* (musical farce) to a plot involving a family of actors during the Third Reich, satirizes the star cult, and *Krankheit oder Moderne Frauen* (1987), a musical phantasmagoria, adds a mythical dimension to the feminist critique by introducing women as revenging vampires.

Jens, Walter (1923–)

Jens has combined an academic career at the University of Tübingen (from 1956 as professor of Classical Philology, from 1962 as professor of Rhetoric) with work as a novelist, author of plays for radio and television, translator and critic of literature (in essays and at meetings of *Gruppe 47*) and of television (as Momus in the newspaper *Die Zeit*). The novels, all of which belong to the first phase of Jens's activities, consist of *Nein. Die Welt der Angeklagten* (1950), a dystopia similar to Orwell's *1984* in its focus on one character confronting a totalitarian system, *Der Blinde* (1951), in which the title-figure learns to come to terms with blindness and at the same time to 'see' the past errors in his relations to others, *Vergessene Gesichter* (1952) which portrays actors in a French old people's home, *Der Mann, der nicht alt werden wollte* (1955) which, by means of a complex set of encapsulated narratives, reconstructs the life of a novelist who has committed suicide, *Das Testament des Odysseus* (1957) a demythologization of the wanderer who refuses to permit his violent reinstatement as king of Ithaca, and *Herr Meister. Dialog über den Roman* (1963), an exchange of letters between an author and an academic critic on the project for a novel on the title-figure whose metamorphoses render him elusive and thus ensure that the novel remains unwritten. Most of Jens's other writings relate to three themes and disciplines: the Third Reich in the prison story *Das weiße Taschentuch* (1947, 1988), a typical example of 'Trümmerliteratur', the radio plays *Der Besuch des Fremden* (1952), *Ahasver* (1956) and *Der Telefonist* (1957); classical literature and the ancient world in the diary of a journey through Greece *Die Götter sind sterblich* (1959), the literary criticism *Hofmannsthal und die Griechen* (1955), *Zur Antike* (1978), translations of Sophocles and Aeschylus and adaptations of Euripides' *The Trojan Women* (*Der Untergang* (1983)) and of Aristophanes' *Lysistrata* (*Die Friedensfrau* (1985)), the radio plays *Die Verschwörung* (1969) on Julius Caesar and *Der tödliche Schlag* (1974) on Odysseus and Philoctetes; theology in the lectures given with Hans Küng in *Dichtung und Religion* (1985), the translation of St Matthew's gospel *Am Anfang der Stall – am Ende der Galgen* (1972) and the tract within a fictional framework *Der Fall Judas* (1975) which may be compared in some respects with *Ahasver* by **Stefan Heym**. Jens has traced a neglected tradition of German oratory in *Von deutscher Rede* (1969) to which he shows himself to be a worthy successor in the essays and speeches assembled in *Republikanische Reden* (1976), *Ort der Handlung ist*

Deutschland (1981) and *Kanzel und Katheder* (1984). He is also the author of a history of Tübingen university *Eine deutsche Universität – 500 Jahre Tübinger Gelehrtenrepublik* (1977).

Johnson, Uwe (1934–84)

After school in Güstrow, Mecklenburg, Johnson studied German and English literature at Rostock and Leipzig universities. In 1953 he failed to secure publication of his first novel *Ingrid Babendererde*, which eventually appeared posthumously in 1985. When his second novel *Mutmaßungen über Jakob* was published in 1959 in the Federal Republic, he moved to West Berlin and made contact with *Gruppe 47*. Apart from stays in Rome in 1962 and in New York in 1961 and from 1966 to 1968 he remained in Berlin until 1974. He then transferred to Sheerness on the Isle of Sheppey, where he died ten years later.

He resisted the label 'Dichter der beiden Deutschland' devised by critics struck by his detached treatment of characters from both East and West and his evident concern not to allow his plots to become vehicles for the endorsement of either system. For him divided Germany was in the first place a model for a complex reality and its reflection in separate consciousnesses and a testing ground for a narrative technique which focuses on a situation from various directions and thus renders it gradually less opaque (*Mutmaßungen*) or ensures that it is seen without ideological blinkers (*Das dritte Buch über Achim* (1961)). Johnson's radical approach to the presentation of conflicting and interacting points of view can also be related to the abandonment of authorial authority which is a feature of literary modernism and to a humane concern with the survival of individual identity.

Mutmaßungen reconstructs the events leading to the mysterious death of the title-figure and introduces a tightly knit constellation of characters: a technical expert in the GDR railways (Jakob), his girlfriend who has moved to the Federal Republic, a dissident intellectual, a secret service official, and others, who offer disparate views. *Das dritte Buch über Achim* is also concerned with the quest for the truth about its title-figure, a GDR cycling champion whose status as national hero has already been enshrined in two officially approved biographies. Karsch, the journalist from the West commissioned to write a third biography, proves unable to disentangle Achim's true identity from his image and abandons the project. Thus in this novel the difficulties, subjective and objective, encountered by the author figure form a second narrative strand which, merely implicit in *Mutmaßungen*, looks forward to such self-reflexive narrative experiments as **Christa Wolf**'s *Nachdenken über Christa T.* and *Kindheitsmuster*. Johnson's third novel *Zwei Ansichten* (1965) prompts a thematic comparison with another work by Wolf, *Der geteilte Himmel* 1963, as both show how an attachment between an East Berlin girl and a West German is affected by the construction of the Berlin Wall in 1961. In the *magnum opus* in four volumes *Jahrestage* (1970, 1971, 1973, 1983) Johnson devises several distinct narrative strands within the framework of a minute day by day account of the personal and professional life of Gesine Cresspahl as a bank employee during a whole year beginning on 21 August 1967. These strands include lengthy quotations from the *New York Times*, memories of childhood in Mecklenburg contrasted with the growing pains and school experiences of Gesine's daughter Marie, and the story of the difficult adjustment made by Gesine's father Heinrich during his emigration from the Third Reich to Britain, where he settles and establishes himself as a carpenter in Richmond-on-Thames. The subtlety with which these strands are linked and associated provides an illumination of present and past which relates Johnson's work to that of Proust.

'Berliner Stadtbahn', in *Berliner Sachen* (1975), encapsulates Johnson's approach to a reality complicated by political divisions; other short prose pieces, some related to the novels, are to be found in *Karsch und andere Prosa* (1964). *Begleitumstände* (1980) contains his Frankfurt literature lectures.

Johst, Hanns (1890–1978)

Johst studied medicine in Leipzig and trained as a male nurse before turning to philosophy and art history in the universities of Munich, Vienna and Berlin. His first play was the anti-war drama *Die Stunde der Sterbenden* (1914), which brought him the sympathetic interest of Franz Pfemfert. Other plays include *Stroh* and *Der Ausländer*, but Johst, attracted by expressionism, achieved fame through *Der junge Mensch. Ein ekstatisches Szenarium* in 1916 (its hero proclaims: 'Es ist eine rasende Wollust, jung sein und um die Verzückung des Todes wissen') and also *Der Einsame. Ein Menschenuntergang* of 1917 (**Brecht** would later, with his first play *Baal*, attempt to supersede this play). Johst rapidly distanced himself from the left-wing, internationalist aspects of expressionism and turned more and more to the right. Other plays of the 1920s include *Der König, Propheten* (1923), *Wechsler und Händler, Die fröhliche Stadt* (1925) and *Thomas Paine* (1927): the latter particularly demonstrates pre-fascist tendencies. Johst was made president of the Nazi *Kampfbund für deutsche Kultur* in 1929; his play *Schlageter* (1933) was dedicated to Adolf Hitler 'in liebender Verehrung und unwandelbarer Treue' and performed on the Führer's fiftieth birthday. It became a national sensation and is now remembered for its one line 'Wenn ich das Wort Kultur höre, entsichere ich meinen Browning'. Johst also attempted prose (*Mutter ohne Tod* (1933) and poetry (*Lieder der Sehnsucht* (1924)). In 1935 he became president of the *Reichsschrifttumskammer*, and later achieved the rank of *SS Gruppenführer*. After the war he was categorized as a major offender, was given three-and-a-half years in a labour camp, and forbidden to write. Of his work, only *Die Stunde der Sterbenden* remains in print (*Einakter und kleine Dramen des Expressionismus*, Reclam).

Jonke, Gert Friedrich (1946–)

Jonke studied music and German literature in Vienna, where he also had contact with the Film and Television Academy. He began with *Geometrischer Heimatroman* (1969), which challenges the sub-genre of the 'homeland novel' which had become a staple of commercially produced fiction in Austria by underlining its artificiality and conformity to pre-established patterns. Parodistic exaggeration of both experimental literary techniques and bureaucratic jargon produces an uncanny amalgam of humour and social criticism. Jonke has since extended his experimental approach in the direction of an extreme dissolution of reality based on scepticism regarding the possibility of presenting it in words. The result in *Schule der Geläufigkeit* (the title of Czerny's piano exercises) (1977) is an unsettling mixture of subjective fantasy indebted to the German Romantics and a strict logic which approaches a mathematical ideal and finds expression in musical forms. *Der ferne Klang* (1979) goes far beyond the experimentalism of Jonke's Austrian colleagues, who maintain a relation to the reality they aim to subvert, if only by the unorthodox combination of linguistic tropes and formulae. Instead Jonke dismisses the effort to relate to any recognizable world, as the distant tone of the title swamps the categories – space, time, logic, individual identity – by which reality is perceived and conveyed in art. Other works include *Glashausbesichtigung* (1970), *Die Vermehrung der Leuchttürme* (1971), *Die erste Reise zum unerforschten Grund des stillen Horizonts* (1980) and *Erwachen zum großen Schlafkrieg* (1982).

Jung, Franz (1888–1963)

Franz Jung studied law and economics at Jena, Berlin and Munich, worked as a journalist and, in Munich (Café Stephanie), came into contact with Karl **Otten**, Erich **Mühsam** and Leonhard **Frank**, also the psychologist Otto Gross. In 1912 he published *Das Trottelbuch*, which consisted of three *Novellen* dealing with the tragic lack of communication between man and woman. He turned his attention increasingly to politics and, in Berlin, became a member of the circle around Franz Pfemfert. On 2 August 1914, he wrote to the Kaiser demanding acceptance as a soldier; this patriotic gesture concealed a desire to incite insurrection at the front. Jung was wounded and later imprisoned as a deserter. He had, by this time, published *Kameraden . . !* (1913), *Sophie. Der Kreuzweg der Demut* (1915), *Opferung* (1916) and *Der Sprung aus der Welt* (1918), novels encouraged by Pfemfert. After the war Franz Jung associated with the Berlin Dadaists and became a committed communist. Various agitprop dramas (e.g. *Die Kanaker* (1921) and *Wie lange noch?* (1921)) were published by Wieland **Herzfelde** in the Malik-Verlag. In 1921 the 'Aktionsbibliothek' published *Joe Frank illustriert die Welt*. *Die Rote Woche*, a novel with nine illustrations by Georg Grosz, appeared the same year. The Malik-Verlag's 'Rote Romanserie' also published the novels *Arbeitsfriede* (1922) and *Die Eroberung der*

Maschinen (1923). Franz Jung worked in Soviet Russia as an official of the *Internationale Arbeiterhilfe*, an organization attempting to ameliorate hunger and suffering; the novel *Die Geschichte einer Fabrik* (1924) describes his experiences as the head of a match factory near Novgorod. Growing disillusionment with conditions in the Soviet Union caused him to return to Germany; descriptions of his experiences in Russia are found in *Hunger an der Wolga* and *An die Arbeitsfront nach Sowjetrußland* (1922). After 1933 Jung lived in Vienna and wrote for various journals; in 1944 he was arrested in Budapest, but later escaped. His adventures are described in the autobiography *Der Weg nach unten*, which appeared in 1961. After the Second World War he went to America, and returned in 1960. Georg Grosz wrote of him: 'Er war einer der intelligentesten Menschen, die ich je getroffen habe, aber auch einer der unglücklichsten.' Franz Jung's *Werke in Einzelausgaben* were published from 1981.

Jünger, Ernst (1895–)

Ernst Jünger was the son of a wealthy chemist who later owned a pharmaceutical factory in Hanover; he broke away from his home background and, not yet 18, joined the French Foreign Legion, from where he was forcibly brought back (these adventures would be subsequently described in *Afrikanische Spiele* (1936)). At the outbreak of the First World War he volunteered, served as an officer throughout, was frequently wounded and received the highest Prussian award for bravery ('Pour le mérite'). His war book (*In Stahlgewittern* (1920)) is subtitled 'Aus dem Tagebuch eines Stoßtruppführers': it is a vivid account of life in the trenches and dispassionately depicts the suffering and the heroism. It was praised by André Gide as one of the finest pieces of writing to have come out of the war, although its objectivity and refusal to denounce militarism alienated its author from those of a pacifist bent. Jünger remained in the army until 1923, finding its discipline and camaraderie satisfying; his essays *Der Kampf als inneres Erlebnis* (1922), *Das Wäldchen 125* and *Feuer und Blut* (1925) showed that war was his element, and the fusion of steely description with mystical fanaticism came to characterize his writing. A proto-fascist tendency is undeniable, although Jünger's fastidiousness precluded an unambiguous commitment. After studying zoology, geology and botany (1923–5) he returned to essay writing: *Das abenteuerliche Herz* (1929) expressed a half-romantic, half-technocratic *Weltanschauung*; de-anthropomorphizing techniques exist side by side with abstract ideas concerning totalitarian mass movements. Jünger was close to **Goebbels**, but also flirted with the idea of 'Prussian communism'. He envisaged a worker-state where military values held absolute sway: total mobilization in the interest of the state is recommended in *Die totale Mobilmachung* of 1931, and *Der Arbeiter. Herrschaft und Gestalt* of the following year. *Blätter und Steine* (1934) seeks symmetry and objectivity in the natural world.

Jünger was offered a seat in the *Reichstag* by the Nazis in 1933 but he did not accept (a letter of 16 November 1933 explains his reasons); he also refused to contribute to the *Völkischer Beobachter*. The ignorance of the Nazi leadership offended him, although the vitalism and amorality of fascism he found appealing. Essays from this time include *Lob der Vokale* (1934) and *Geheimnisse der Sprache* (1939). The most important work of the 1930s is *Auf den Marmorklippen* (1939), an allegorical meditation on power and resistance. The theme was manifestly dangerous at the time but the remoteness and intellectual abstraction of the author's discussion prevent the book from being subversive. (Printing was, however, stopped in 1940 after the sale of 3,500 copies.) Jünger rejoined the army (a form of 'aristocratic inner emigration') and served on the staff of the German Military Command in Paris. He was discharged in October 1944 for unsatisfactory military conduct; his son was killed in the following month. An indictment of the system of totalitarianism which Jünger had earlier half-welcomed, but which he now saw bent on world destruction, *Der Friede*, was clandestinely circulated during the last months of the war. The war diaries were published under the title *Strahlungen* in 1949: a neutral stance is adopted in an attempt to give an objective account of his experiences. Disdain for the Nazi mentality is apparent, although humanity is conspicuously lacking. *Heliopolis* appeared in the same year: the clarity of the landscape descriptions is admirable, but imaginative empathy is again underdeveloped. Jünger has continued to publish essays and travel accounts throughout the last thirty years and to cultivate an aesthetic, detached and impersonal style. His recent work includes the novels and stories *Besuch auf Godenholm* (1952), *Gläserne Bienen* (1957), *Die Zwille* (1973), *Eumeswil* (1977), *Aladins Problem* (1983) and *Eine gefährliche Begegnung* (1985). *Werke* (in ten vols) appeared from 1960 to 1965; *Sämtliche Werke* (eighteen vols) appeared from 1978 to 1983.

Jünger, Friedrich Georg (1898–1977)

Ernst Jünger's young brother Friedrich Georg followed a similar career. He wrote poetry in a classical, conventional manner (favouring the 'Spruchdichtung' of late Goethe), also speculative essays. The autobiography *Spiel der Jahre* was published in 1958; *Gesammelte Erzählungen* appeared in 1967, and a volume of poetry, *Es pocht an der Tür*, in 1968. The most well known of his poems is 'Scharlachfarbener Mohn, ich sehe dich gern auf den Gräbern', which rejects 'das kindische Lied ruhmloser Trunkenheit', that is, the intoxicated fanaticism of National Socialism. It was circulated secretly in 1935.

K

Kafka, Franz (1883–1924)

Kafka was born in Prague of prosperous Jewish parents; the sense of alienation which is characteristic of his work derives from the position of the Jewish intellectual of that time, neither fully emancipated nor assimilated, and from the situation of the German-speaking Jewish writer in Prague who, as a Jew, was not accepted by the German community and who, as German speaker, was remote from the Czechs. Kafka's father, a self-made businessman, insisted on German schools and the German University for his son; later, Kafka would seek to master the Czech language and also, having been brought up as a non-orthodox, Western Jew, would take a deep interest in Jewish customs and literature. At university he studied law, yet was also drawn to the literary circles of his city; the convolutions and excrescences of much Prague German writing he did not find congenial and, as early as 1902, he spoke of his attempt to write in a language 'ohne Schnörkel und Schleier und Warzen': a cool, sober and elegant prose style would be very much his own. Through Max **Brod** he made contact with the literati of the Café Arco; his first publications were eight small vignettes under the title *Betrachtungen* which appeared in 1908 in the journal *Hyperion*. With extreme reluctance Kafka let these impressionistic sketches be published in book form: his increasing fastidiousness and high literary standards prevented the rush into print of so many young writers. Early attempts at writing at this time include *Beschreibung eines Kampfes* (1904–5) and *Hochzeitsvorbereitungen auf dem Lande*, a projected novel.

In 1908 Kafka joined the *Arbeiter-Unfall-Versicherungs-Anstalt*, an insurance office; he remained there until 1922, a conscientious and respected official. The problems of marriage and integration concerned him deeply; his father's tyrannical presence seemed to overshadow his own emotional life, and feelings of inadequacy became dominant. In 1912 he met a Jewish girl from Berlin, Felice Bauer, at Max Brod's house, and his literary breakthrough stems from this meeting: the short story *Das Urteil*, written some six weeks later, was the direct result. It may be seen as an expression of the awareness of the conflicting claims of domesticity, artistry and the father-figure: the protagonist is sent to his death, and both friend (writer) and father triumph. Although desirous of marriage, Kafka felt that his writing was more important; isolation brought strength as well as anguish. His life from 1912 to 1917 would be dominated by Felice Bauer, and the subsequent disengagement from her would not prove easy. From the end of 1912 he worked on a novel to be called *Der Verschollene* (this would be published posthumously in 1927 as *Amerika*), but sensed that the longer forms of prose fiction were not conducive to him. (The first chapter, *Der Heizer*, was published in 1913; Kafka also announced the forthcoming story

Die Verwandlung at this time and suggested that *Das Urteil*, *Die Verwandlung* and *Der Heizer* could be published together under the title of *Die Söhne*.) *Amerika* is an uneven work; the laboured allegory of the 'Oklahoma Nature Theatre' is of inferior quality, although the portrayal (in the chapter 'Hotel Occident') of unemployment and poverty, written in an entirely realistic fashion, shows Kafka's skill at portraying the suffering of New York's social outcasts. *Die Verwandlung* (published in 1915) is an acknowledged masterpiece of precision, lucidity and grotesque implication. The lack of commensuration between situation and response gives rise to humour, although the story is one of degradation. The portrayal of the life of the insect-protagonist demonstrates the stunting influence of the claims of the family and of professional life. The metaphor is taken literally: the beetle 'Samsa' represents the essential nature of the protagonist. The father-son relationship is much to the fore; Kafka also sees the jostling for power within a family which takes place beneath the apparently altruistic stance (the relationship between brother and sister). The selfishness of the family, but also Samsa's docility and submission, are the cause of the catastrophe.

The outbreak of the war in 1914 passed practically unnoticed by Kafka who was, as a writer, concerned above all with the possibility of objectifying his inner preoccupations into satisfactory images. The story *In der Strafkolonie* (1916) could be seen as an oblique reference to the war machine, but deeper issues (self-immolation, the need for punishment) are also present. The novel *Der Prozeß* dates from this time (it was published posthumously by Max Brod in 1925); unfinished, unpolished, and with its undeniable *longueurs*, it deals in an almost surrealist manner with guilt and punishment; the protagonist ('Josef K.') is, it seems, 'arrested' by those aspects of his psyche which insist upon demonstrating to him his human failings. The novel may well have been caused by the first disengagement (there were two) from Felice Bauer; the description of the legal confusion may derive from Charles Dickens, a writer whom Kafka admired. Josef K. may also be seen as a modern Everyman, culpable in his selfishness, his arrogance *vis-à-vis* women, and his ambition; wider, metaphysical issues are hinted at, but one-sided interpretations of this book (whether they be Jewish, Christian, existentialist, Freudian or Marxist) do damage to its elusive nature. The nucleus of the work is the exemplary parable *Vor dem Gesetz*. Kafka thought long on the problems of sin and evil at this time; the story *Ein Landarzt* (1920) deals with the inability of physician and priest to heal and bring comfort, and the collection of aphorisms *Betrachtungen über Sünde, Leid, Hoffnung und den wahren Weg* (1953) contains many trenchant and profound *aperçus*.

At the end of 1917 tuberculosis of the lung was confirmed and the relationship with Felice Bauer was finally terminated. A brief, abortive engagement to Julie Wohryzek inspired the writing of the remarkable *Brief an den Vater* (1919), an attempt to exorcize a daunting presence, but also a letter (never delivered) which also expresses admiration, even love. The letters to Milena Jesenká, his Czech translator, contain his main preoccupations at this time, but a certain posturing, never found in the works of fiction, is apparent. Kafka's health deteriorated at the end of the war during the subsequent privations, but the early 1920s saw some of his finest stories, including *Ein Hungerkünstler* and *Forschungen eines Hundes*. The novel *Das Schloß* (1922, published posthumously in 1926) is a flawed work, a portrayal of obsession and quest. The symbolism is elusive, but the castle may be seen as a representation of the protagonist's self, the fascination being deleterious rather than helpful. (A dramatization of the novel was made by Max Brod in 1953.) Kafka's mastery is seen above all in the short story, where a pellucid and fastidious style, occasionally ironic, hints at a possibly symbolic extension. The last stories, *Der Bau* and *Josefine die Sängerin*, are concerned again with solipsism and integration. Ill health forced Kafka to retire in 1922; he worked at his writing until his death in a sanatorium near Vienna in 1924. He was nursed in his last months by Dora Dymant, daughter of an orthodox Polish rabbi. He insisted that his unpublished work be destroyed, yet Max Brod, his executor, felt unable to accede to this wish. As well as being responsible for the publication of the novels, Max Brod also edited a selection of short fiction, *Beim Bau der chinesischen Mauer*, in 1931.

Kafka is acknowledged as one of the greatest German prose writers of the twentieth century. Writing at the time of expressionism, he chose to keep his distance from his contemporaries, eschewing hyperbole and rodomontade. His individualism is extreme, yet, paradoxically, he seems to speak for many, particularly for those who suffer from alienation from community or family. He speculated upon religious topics, but remained the intellectual, a sophisticated thinker, trained in legal and exegetical practice. He should be regarded above all as a literary craftsman, not as guide or prophet. His influence has been considerable, although his voice is unique. The edition of the 1950s enhanced his reputation enormously, but Auden's claim that he shares equal stature with Shakespeare and Dante as spokesman of modern man is manifestly excessive. The increasing popularization of his work has brought many eccentric appraisals, but his stature is uncontroversial.

In 1961 the bulk of Kafka's literary remains was deposited in the Bodleian Library, Oxford, on the instruction of Kafka's niece; they had been in Zurich since the Suez crisis of 1956. Apart from the publications already mentioned, the following editions should be noted: *Gesammelte Schriften* in six volumes (I–IV Berlin, 1935; V Prague, 1935; VI Prague, 1937); a second edition (New York, 1946); a third edition in eight volumes (Frankfurt, 1946–58, including *Tagebücher* (1951)), *Briefe an Milena* (1952), *Hochzeitsvorbereitungen auf dem Lande und andere Prosa aus dem Nachlaß* (1953) and the *Briefe* (1958). The *Briefe an Felice* were published in 1967; the *Briefe an Ottla* in 1974. The *Kritische Ausgabe der Schriften, Tagebücher und Briefe* is in progress: *Das Schloß* (two vols) appeared in 1982, *Der Verschollene* (two vols) in 1983, *Tagebücher* in 1989 and *Der Prozeß* in 1990.

Kaiser, Georg (1878–1945)

Georg Kaiser, the most prolific and representative of the German expressionist dramatists, worked briefly as a bookseller in Magdeburg before spending the years 1898–1901 in the Argentine. He returned home after a severe illness and spent four months in a sanatorium near Berlin, where he made contact with some of the members of the circle around Stefan **George**. He had begun writing plays at an early age, but regarded his career as a writer to have begun with *Rektor Kleist* in 1905. *Die jüdische Witwe* (published in 1911) is a variation on the biblical story; *König Hahnrei* (1913) is a Wagner parody. Kaiser's early work is indebted to the fashionable Freudian preoccupations of the times; the theme of the clash between body and mind also anticipates certain later concerns. Kaiser's devotion to his literary work became almost monomaniacal, and his concentration on the theme of regeneration became all-consuming. The play which brought him fame was *Die Bürger von Calais*, written in 1913 and performed four years later; Kaiser, from this play onwards, would become increasingly identified with the expressionist tendency to concentrate on pure essences, on absolute vision, and would become the most prominent among the new playwrights. The anti-war theme of this play also illustrates the expressionist emphasis on idealism and the realization of the highest human potential; although a hectic, even febrile quality cannot be denied in many of Kaiser's plays his insistence upon human perfectibility (expressed most forcibly in the essay *Vision und Figur* of 1918) may be seen as a salutary antidote to Wilhelmine warmongering. The concept of the New Man emerges at this time, a vision of hope and ecstasy, messianic and fervent. *Von morgens bis mitternachts* (written in 1912) was performed in 1917 and became his best-known play; this staccato *Stationendrama* eschews naturalistic plausibility and psychological characterization and insists upon a reduction to types to let the essential idea be revealed.

Kaiser was living at this time in Munich in great poverty, although he subscribed to a memorial to the murdered socialist writer Gustav Landauer (1919); he was also imprisoned for the misappropriation of property, insisting at the trial that a writer's mission transcended conventional morality. International acclaim came with the so-called *Gas* trilogy (*Die Koralle*, *Gas I* and *Gas II* (1917–20)), where the clash between the ideal and the real is worked out with intense passion; the apocalyptic ending is, however, a sombre vision of destruction. The purifying power of love becomes the theme of other plays at this time, also the theme of a quest, often with religious overtones. Kaiser became, from 1920 to 1933, the most frequently performed playwright on the German stage, although a mechanical, predictable quality is apparent in many of his works. Of the more memorable plays, *Hölle Weg Erde* (1919), *Der gerettete Alkibiades* (1920), *Gats* (1925) and *Zweimal Oliver* (1926) should be mentioned; Kaiser's enormous output (some fifty plays, as well as poetry and two novels) meant that repetitiveness and a certain tedium became inevitable. The *Gesammelte Werke* (three vols) appeared between 1928 and 1931.

The performance of *Silbersee* in 1933 (music by Kurt Weill) prompted a Nazi demonstration; Kaiser, whose themes included self-sacrifice, ecstatic awareness of humanity and regeneration beyond national self-interest, was expelled from the Prussian Academy of Arts and forbidden to write. The period of 'inner emigration' also saw the writing of several plays dealing with purification and idealism. Kaiser emigrated to Switzerland in 1938 and was befriended by the playwright Cäsar von **Arx**. The more successful plays include *Rosamunde Floris* (1936), *Der Soldat Tanaka* (1941) and *Das Floß der Medusa* (1942). Kaiser's reputation suffered after his death, but the interest in expressionism in the 1960s brought his name once more to the fore. *Stücke, Erzählungen, Aufsätze, Gedichte* was published in 1966; *Werke* (six vols) from 1970 to 1971.

Kant, Hermann (1926–)

Kant's experiences as a young army recruit at the end of the war and as a POW in Poland from 1945 to 1949 were eventually to form the background of his novel *Der Aufenthalt* (1977). From 1949 to 1952 he was a student and teacher in the Faculty for Workers and Peasants at the University of Greifswald (see *Die Aula*), then moved to Berlin, where he taught at the Humboldt University and worked as a journalist, becoming a free-lance writer in 1962. From 1978 to 1989 he was president of the GDR Writers' Union in succession to Anna **Seghers** and thus occupied a key position in his country's cultural life.

Kant has succeeded in basing sophisticated and inventive narratives spiced with humour and satire on his personal experiences as a soldier, student and journalist, without departing from a fundamental commitment to socialist realism. In *Die Aula* (1965) the invitation to address the closing ceremony of a Faculty for Workers and Peasants prompts the central figure to review his life as a student there in the 1950s, especially his friendships, one of which he attempts to renew on a visit to Hamburg. *Das Impressum* (1972) adopts the same structure, as a man due to become a minister looks back on a career in journalism from errand-boy to chief editor of an illustrated magazine. *Der Aufenthalt* (1977) focuses on a young soldier captured in Poland in 1944 who during work in Warsaw with other POWs is falsely accused of murder and passes from solitary confinement to incarceration with a group of hardened Nazis. When his innocence is proved he decides to remain and help in reconstruction, having realized that although not guilty of a specific crime he has become involved in a murderous system. Kant's short stories have appeared in the volumes *Ein bißchen Südsee* (1962), *Eine Übertretung* (1975), *Der dritte Nagel* (1981), *Bronzezeit* (1986) and *Die Summe* (1987) and essays written between 1957 and 1980 in *Zu den Unterlagen* (1981).

Kasack, Hermann (1896–1966)

Although he began as an expressionist with the poems *Der Mensch* (1918) Kasack is remembered today almost exclusively for the novel *Die Stadt hinter dem Strom* (1947), which belongs to a small group of dystopias (including also Ernst **Jünger**'s *Auf den Marmorklippen* (1939), **Nossack**'s

Nach dem letzten Aufstand (1961) and **Schnurre**'s *Das Los unserer Stadt* (1959)) which, although undoubtedly inspired by the Second World War and its aftermath, approach their theme – the deadening effect of totalitarian rule – by translating contemporary events into an allegorical code. Kasack's protagonist, an archivist given the task of composing a history of the city of the title, finds himself in a landscape of ruins populated by the dead, including his father and the woman who had loved him. After visiting the city's archive and two factories and witnessing a suppressed rebellion he becomes convinced of the futility of human striving; when however he is granted insight into the moral legacy of the wise men of the past he decides to return to the living world and proclaim to his fellow men their individual responsibility for its state. The novel marks the transition from the advocacy of a higher spiritual reality which is a feature of the 'inner emigration' to the preoccupation with existentialism of the first post-war years. A similar allegorizing tendency is present in the satirical novel *Das große Netz* (1952) and the story *Fälschungen* (1953).

Kaschnitz, Marie Luise (1901–74)

Kaschnitz belongs with **Eich**, **Huchel** and **Weyrauch** to the 'lost generation' of writers who began their careers during the Third Reich, but found their voice only later. Although her first collection of poems, *Gedichte* (1947), assembling the work of the two preceding decades, barely reflects the post-war situation, the following volumes, *Totentanz und Gedichte zur Zeit* (1947) (including a play which confronts a pair of lovers with the war dead), *Rückkehr nach Frankfurt* (1947) and *Zukunftsmusik* (1950) are marked by contemporary upheavals. *Ewige Stadt* (1952) celebrates Rome, where she had lived from 1925 to 1932 after marrying the archaeologist Guido von Kaschnitz-Weinberg and to which she returned with him in 1955. *Neue Gedichte* (1957) contains the religious cycle 'Tutzinger Gedichtkreis' and a poem inspired by the destruction of Hiroshima, *Dein Schweigen – meine Stimme* (1965), mourns her husband's death, *Ein Wort weiter* (1965) considers the prospect of her own death and contains the cycle 'Zoon Politikon', prompted by the trial of Auschwitz guards (1963–5), *Kein Zauberspruch* (1972) combines laconic poems of the years 1962 to 1970 with longer poems written between 1970 and 1972. Kaschnitz was able throughout to adapt a wide variety of forms to convey personal experiences in timeless existential terms with reference to nature, art and political events.

Her prose writings begin with two novels *Liebe beginnt* (1933), a psychologically acute examination of the differing attitudes of man and wife to their marriage and *Elissa* (1937), inspired by the fate of Dido, but she is now mainly remembered for the short stories of the volumes *Das dicke Kind und andere Erzählungen* (1951), *Lange Schatten* (1960) and *Ferngespräche*

(1966), in which she reveals the presence of mysterious forces in what appear to be everyday situations, and the longer autobiographical pieces *Wohin denn ich* (1963) and *Das Haus der Kindheit* (1956), to which *Beschreibung eines Dorfes* (1966), on the village where her family had its roots, can also be related, together with the diaries *Engelsbrücke* (1954) on Rome, and *Tage, Tage, Jahre* (1968) and the short prose pieces *Steht noch dahin* (1970) and *Orte* (1973). She also wrote numerous plays for radio collected in *Hörspiele* (1962) and *Gespräche im All* (1972). Her complete works, *Werke* in seven volumes, appeared from 1981.

Kästner, Erich (1899–1974)

Of impoverished parents, Erich Kästner attended the *Lehrerseminar* in Dresden before being conscripted (1917) into an infantry regiment; the harsh discipline which he experienced caused a life-long dislike of militarism. After 1918 he studied at Leipzig university; in the 1920s he worked as a bookkeeper and journalist, writing for *Die Weltbühne* and associating with **Tucholsky** and **Stefan Zweig**. A collection of poems (*Herz auf Taille*) appeared in 1928; the following year saw the publication of Kästner's most popular book *Emil und die Detektive*, which brought international recognition. The same year saw the anthology *Lärm im Spiegel*. Kästner moved to Berlin, became involved in the film world and, in 1931, was elected to the membership of the German PEN club. The satirical novel *Fabian. Die Geschichte eines Moralisten* appeared that year, to be followed by the children's book *Das fliegende Klassenzimmer* in 1933. With the Nazi seizure of power Kästner, surprisingly, returned to Germany from Zurich: he remained there throughout the Nazi period and the Second World War. His left-wing attitudes meant that his books were burned in May 1933 but he was permitted to publish abroad. He was asked to move to Switzerland to found a journal attacking emigrants, but refused. In 1934 *Emil und die drei Zwillinge* and *Drei Männer im Schnee* appeared, to be followed by *Die verschwundene Miniatur* (1935) and a collection of poetry *Dr. Erich Kästners lyrische Hausapotheke* (1936). Film rights for two of his novels were acquired by Metro-Goldwyn-Mayer and Kästner, in 1942, wrote a script for the film *Münchhausen*. A ban was imposed on his writing for the next three years. After the war he became a co-founder of the cabaret *Die Schaubude*; he also edited the magazine section of the *Neue Zeitung* and founded *Pinguin*, a magazine for young people. *Bei Durchsicht meiner Bücher*, a collection of poems, appeared in 1946; *Der tägliche Kram* in 1948. Another book for children, *Das doppelte Lottchen*, was filmed in 1950. The later works include *Die kleine Freiheit* (1952) and *Als ich ein kleiner Junge war* (1957). A satirical comedy *Die Schule der Diktatoren* appeared in the same year. *Der kleine Mann und die kleine Miß* was published in 1966. It is as a writer for children that Kästner is best known, but the satirical elements are also noteworthy. *Gesammelte Schriften* (seven vols) appeared in 1959; the *Gesammelte Schriften für Erwachsene* (eight vols) in 1969.

Kellermann, Bernhard (1879–1951)

Kellermann was both journalist and novelist: his first novel, *Yester und Li. Die Geschichte einer Sehnsucht* (1904) deals in an overtly sentimental manner with unrequited love; the second, *Ingeborg* (1906) is another love story which, although less mawkish, is memorable for its landscape descriptions. *Der Tor* (1909) is a tragic account of failure and death; *Das Meer* (1910) excels at descriptions of the Breton coast. Kellermann's most successful novel is *Der Tunnel* (1913), a powerful account of the building of a tunnel beneath the Atlantic linking America with Spain: the scenes of catastrophe are well handled and the crowd scenes, together with the portrayal of the charismatic leader, brought forth the enthusiastic praise of Adolf Hitler. Kellermann served as a war correspondent from 1914 to 1918 and later published an account of his experiences; the novel *Der neunte November* (1920) is overtly anti-militaristic (it was publicly burned in 1933). Although a patriot, Kellermann was unable to support the Nazi regime; after the Second World War he settled in East Berlin and founded the 'Kulturbund zur demokratischen Erneuerung Deutschlands'. The later novels are generally undistinguished, and a play, *Die Wiedertäufer von Münster* (1925), met with little success. *Ausgewählte Werke* (six vols) appeared from 1958 to 1960.

Kempowski, Walter (1929–)

Kempowski grew up in Rostock as a member of a shipbuilding family. In 1948 he was arrested, accused of espionage and sentenced to twenty-five years hard labour; having been amnestied he moved to the West in 1956, where he studied in Göttingen and became a schoolteacher. Since 1969 he has written a series of novels which together chronicle the history of his family in relation to the economic development of his home town and the history of Germany as a whole. The novels form the following historical sequence, which does not correspond with the order of publication: *Aus großer Zeit* (1978) on the years 1900 to 1918, *Schöne Aussicht* (1981) on 1920–38, *Tadellöser & Wolff* (1971) on 1939–45, *Uns geht's ja noch gold* (1972) on 1945–48, *Ein Kapitel für sich* (1975) on 1948–56 and *Herzlich willkommen* (1984) on 1956–7. Kempowski's microscopic approach to events gives the appearance of an arbitrary series of anecdotes, but the technique of free association adopted in order to conjure memories ensures that no biased retrospective interpretation is allowed to take precedence over the stuff of life. The family epic was preceded by *Im Block. Ein Haftbericht* (1969), an autobiographical account of his imprisonment, and followed by

Hundstage (1988), a new departure in the form of a novel in which an author finds himself accused of sexual assault, proves his innocence but remains the victim of local suspicion.

Keyserling, Eduard Graf von (1855–1918)

Graf Keyserling studied at Dorpat University and moved from his home in Latvia to Vienna and later to Berlin. In his novels and *Novellen* he excels at portraying the lives and *mores* of the minor Baltic nobility which he knew so well. A sensitive and impressionistic author, Graf Keyserling wrote in the manner of Fontane, although his diffidence led to a devotion to the country gentry which lacks Fontane's critical eye. The novels *Beate und Mareile* (1903), *Dumala* (1907), *Wellen* (1908), *Abendliche Häuser* (1914), *Fürstinnen* (1917) and *Feiertagskinder* (1919) deal mostly with the social norms and the restrictions imposed upon personal development; a changing world is hinted at. Collections of *Novellen* include *Schwüle Tage* (1906), *Bunte Herzen* (1908) and *Im stillen Wald* (1918). The story 'Am Südhang' (1916) is probably his best, demonstrating a tight narrative control and a cunning unmasking of evasions and self-deception. Graf Keyserling went blind in 1907. He also attempted drama (*Frühlingsopfer* (1899); *Dummer Hans* (1901)) which enjoyed popular acclaim. An enlightening essay is 'Zur Psychologie des Komforts' which is a panegyric for the country house as a retreat from the threatening claims of modernity. The *Gesammelte Erzählungen* (four vols) appeared in 1922, and the *Gesammelte Werke* from 1956. He is the cousin of the philosopher Graf Hermann Keyserling (1880–1946).

Kipphardt, Heinar (1922–82)

Born in Silesia, Kipphardt served in the army during the Second World War, at the end of which his family was forced to move West. After studying medicine in Düsseldorf he settled in East Berlin, where he worked as a psychiatric specialist in the main hospital and from 1950 to 1959 as artistic adviser at the *Deutsches Theater*. At this time he began writing plays, some of which were performed, but ideological pressures induced him to move back to the West in 1959 where his reputation was secured by the performance of *Der Hund des Generals* (1962), the first of a series of plays which, with equivalent works by Rolf **Hochhuth** and **Peter Weiss**, are the most significant to emerge from the West German theatre's documentary phase. The plays which precede these are farcical satires directed against confidence tricksters in the West (*Der Aufstieg des Alois Piontek* (1956)) and the East (*Die Stühle des Herrn Szmil* (1961)) or official cultural policy in the GDR (*Shakespeare dringend gesucht* (1954)). The trial form, first applied in *Der Hund des Generals*, the investigation of a Second World War general who sent sixty men to certain death in revenge on a soldier who accidentally shot his dog, is made a means of exploring questions of conscience in Kipphardt's best-known documentary play *In der Sache J. Robert Oppenheimer* (1964), in which the title-figure is accused of having delayed the development of the hydrogen bomb. *Die Geschichte von Joel Brand* (1965) on the failure of the deal initiated between Adolf Eichmann and the title-figure for the supply of lorries by the Allies in exchange for the liberation of the Hungarian Jews led to a fascination with the notorious organizer of the Holocaust which bore fruit in the last play *Bruder Eichmann* (1982), a controversial reconstruction of the title-figure's self-justification, based on a hearing conducted by an Israeli officer and interrupted by scenes intended to demonstrate that his case, far from being unique, is both typical of his time and relevant to the present. Kipphardt's work in psychiatry undoubtedly inspired the 'März' complex consisting of the film *Leben des schizophrenen Dichters Alexander März* (1975), the novel *März* (1976), the 'März-Gedichte' in the collection of poems *Angelsbrucker Notizen* (1977) and the play *März, ein Künstlerleben* (1981), in which the title-figure, diagnosed as a paranoid schizophrenic, sinks into apathy until treated by a young unorthodox doctor who encourages him to write, flees the hospital with a female fellow-patient and commits suicide after their return. This multimedia treatment of a single theme (cf. the Merz saga of Tankred **Dorst**) also has documentary features, being based on the authentic case of Ernst Herbeck or Herbrich, whose *Alexanders poetische Texte* appeared in 1977. Kipphardt's other works include the stories set in the Third Reich *Die Ganovenfresse* (1964) and *Der Mann des Tages* (1977) and *Traumprotokolle* (1981), a record of his dreams between 1978 and 1981. *Gesammelte Werke* appeared in 1990.

Kirsch, Rainer (1934–)

Having been forced to end history and philosophy studies prematurely, Kirsch worked in various jobs before joining the Johannes R. Becher Institute of Literature in Leipzig, the only university school of creative writing in Germany, in 1963. Married from 1960 to 1966 to **Sarah Kirsch**, his first publications were collaborations with her (the poems *Gespräch mit dem Saurier* (1965), the reportages *Berlin – Sonnenseite* (1964) and the radio plays in *Die betrunkene Sonne – Der Stärkste* (1963)). His poems, which have appeared in *Ausflug machen* (1980) and the West German selection from his work in several genres *Auszog das Fürchten zu lernen* (1978), convey usually in strict conventional forms a critical view of aspects of GDR reality, especially the inflexibility and complacency of the older generation. His play *Heinrich Schlaghands Höllenfahrt*, published in 1973 and again in the above selection but unperformed, is a variation of the Faust legend which, set in a housing construction project in the GDR, opposes the individual aspirations of its leader to the inefficiency of the system and the control exercised over private life by the party, thus representing a more radical version of problems treated in **Hacks**'s *Moritz Tassow*, **Lange**'s

Marski and **Braun**'s *Die Kipper*. Kirsch has also translated the major Russian poets of the interwar years, produced a series of portraits of eminent GDR scientists and academics, *Kopien nach Originalen* (1974), and written stories which convey their point through the adaptation of fairy-tale motifs and other forms of fantasy ('Erste Niederschrift', 'Die Rettung des Saragossameeres', the collection *Sauna oder Die fernherwirkende Trübung* (1985)).

Kirsch, Sarah (originally Ingrid Bernstein, 1935–)

Sarah Kirsch, whose original name was Ingrid Bernstein, studied under the poet Georg **Maurer** at the *Literaturinstitut* in Leipzig and wrote her first works in collaboration with her then husband **Rainer**. After protesting with many other GDR writers of her own generation against the expatriation of Wolf **Biermann** she was allowed to move to West Berlin in 1977 and now lives in rural Schleswig-Holstein. Although she has developed a distinct tone, identified by Peter **Hacks** in a review as the 'Sarah-sound' and emerging from her cultivation of *enjambement* and sparing use of punctuation, her work is best seen in relation to the tradition of German nature poetry originating with the Romantics and continuing via **Trakl**, **Huchel** and **Bobrowski** through to **Bachmann**. She has written poems of sympathetic identification with Petrarch, Chamisso, Annette von Droste-Hülshoff and, in the 'Wiepersdorf' cycle, Bettina von Arnim. The identifiable landscapes of her verse include the GDR countryside (*Land-aufenthalt* (1967), *Zaubersprüche* (1973), *Rückenwind* (1976)), Italy (*Drachensteigen* (1979)), Provence (the prose poems of the intimate diary *La Pagerie* (1980)), USA (*Erdreich* (1982)) and Schleswig-Holstein (*Erdreich* and *Katzenleben* (1984)). The other major themes, love and separation, are present throughout, finding most uninhibited expression in *Zaubersprüche*. Water – streams, lakes, the sea – plays an important role and can be related to her preoccupation with metamorphosis and her predilection for flowing verse forms. Two selections appeared in 1985: *Hundert Gedichte*, drawn from the four collections of 1967–79, and *Landwege* containing poems from the years 1980–5.

Kisch, Egon Erwin (1885–1948)

Born in Prague, Kisch became a close observer of the literary life of that city ('Es werfelt und brodelt, es kafkat und kischt' was his flippant comment). He excelled above all at journalism, but also wrote novels (*Der Mädchenhirt* (1914), a portrayal of bars, prostitutes and night-life, also *Die Abenteuer in Prag* (1921)) and plays (*Die gestohlene Stadt* (1921), and *Die Himmelfahrt des Galgentoni* (1922)). It is his essays in *Der rasende Reporter* (1925) which made him famous, and he was henceforth to be known by this designation.

Of marked left-wing tendencies, Kisch was arrested by the Nazis but later released; he later emigrated and contributed to the anti-Nazi journals in exile. He wrote for the Spanish number of *Der deutsche Schriftsteller* (July 1937) and also published *Soldaten am Meeresstrand. Eine Reportage* in Valencia (1936). His best-known story from this time is 'Die Kuh', printed in *Das Wort* (April 1938). Kisch returned to Prague after the war; a collection of essays *Nichts ist erregender als die Wahrheit. Reportagen aus vier Jahrzehnten* (two vols) appeared in 1979; the *Gesammelte Werke* (eight vols) started to appear from 1960 onwards.

Klabund (pseudonym, a conflation of 'Klabautermann' and 'Vagabund', of Alfred Henschke, 1890–1928)

Klabund began as a lyric poet, encouraged by Alfred Kerr and contributing to the periodical *Pan*; his first collection *Morgenrot! Klabund! Die Tage dämmern!* (1913) was a sensational mixture of the romantic, the burlesque and the grotesque which recalled Heine. In 1914 Klabund enlisted but was found to be consumptive. His patriotic 'Lied der Freiwilligen' was very popular, but growing disenchantment with the war led to the writing of an open letter to the Kaiser (May 1917) and further pacifist statements. Klabund met **Wedekind** and **Brecht** in Munich; he and Brecht became close friends. He married Carola Neher after the death of his first wife Irene; Carola Neher played the part of Polly in the film version of the *Dreigroschenoper*. Klabund achieved fame with his adaptations of oriental poetry (some eleven volumes were published between 1915 and 1930); in the 1920s he was known, however, above all for the popular novels *Bracke* (1918: an account of a vagabond reminiscent of Till Eulenspiegel), *Pjotr* (1923), *Borgia* (1928) and the stories *Kunterbuntergang des Abendlandes* (1922). Of his plays *XYZ* (1928) deserves mention; most well-known is *Der Kreidekreis* (1925), which formed the basis of Brecht's play. Klabund's virtuosity and facility of writing led to an occasional slickness; Ernst **Lissauer** commented that the work was 'unausgearbeitet'. The *Gesammelte Werke* (six vols) appeared in 1930 and were banned by the Nazis. A selection *Der himmlische Vagabund* appeared in 1968. Gottfried **Benn** wrote a moving *Totenrede für Klabund* at his death (1928); *Briefe an einen Freund* was published in 1963.

Klemm, Wilhelm (1881–1968)

Klemm's career and writing show similarities to those of Gottfried **Benn**; both men were doctors, both served in that capacity in the First World War, both professed a lack of interest in politics and both were drawn to nihilism and irrationalism, retreating into dreams, exotic climes and submission to the doctrine of fatalism. Klemm served throughout the war; he had published poems before 1914 (in *Simplicissimus* and *Die Jugend*) but it was with the publication of *Gloria. Kriegsgedichte aus dem Feld* (1915) that he made his reputation as a poet. Outstanding is 'Schlacht an der Marne', included by Kurt Pinthus in the anthology *Menschheitsdämmerung* (where there are, in all, some nineteen poems by Klemm). These war poems are detailed and tangible, with many powerful and striking images. The collections *Verse und Bilder* (1916) and *Aufforderung* (1917) were less successful, with titles such as 'Weltflucht' and 'Magische Flucht'; other collections are entitled *Ergriffenheit* (1919), *Entfaltung* (1919), *Traumschutt* (1920) and *Verzauberte Spiele* (1921). *Die Satanspuppe* (1922; the pseudonym Felix Brazil is used) deals with themes of violence and cruelty ('O du großartiges Wort: primitiv! primitiv!'). Klemm fell silent after 1922 and devoted himself to publishing (his first wife was the daughter of the publisher Alfred Kröner). Although his flirtation with atavism and nihilism might have appealed to the Nazis he was expelled from the *Reichsschrifttumskammer* in 1937. His publishing houses were destroyed by bombing in 1943; two sons were killed in the same year. *Aufforderung* was published in a new edition in 1961 (with an introduction by Kurt Pinthus). A collection, *Geflammte Ränder*, appeared in 1964. *Ich lag in fremder Stube. Gesammelte Gedichte* was published in 1981.

Klepper, Jochen (1903–42)

The son of a Protestant pastor, Klepper committed suicide with his Jewish wife in 1942 when she was due to be deported to a concentration camp. The informing spirit of his one major work *Der Vater* (1937), which traces the life of Friedrich Wilhelm I King of Prussia from 1713 to 1740, is a Christianity absent from the cultivation of the Prussian ethos and the adulation of the Prussian monarchy and military establishment characteristic of conservative and nationalist writers active between the mid-nineteenth century and the end of the Third Reich. Klepper also wrote a lighter novel *Der Kahn der fröhlichen Leute* (1933) and the first chapter, *Die Flucht der Katharine von Bora* (1951), of a planned novel on Luther *Das ewige Haus*, poems collected in *Ziel der Zeit* (1962) and the diaries *Unter dem Schatten deiner Flügel* (1956) and *Überwindung* (1958).

Kluge, Alexander (1932–)

Kluge qualified as a lawyer in 1956 and has played a key role as writer, director and producer in the development of the New German Cinema from its inception in 1962, when he helped to compose the Oberhausen manifesto. His published writings are often cinematic in style even when they are not conceived as scenarios; some contain material later expanded in the other medium (such as the story 'Anita G.' in *Lebensläufe*, the nucleus of *Abschied von gestern* (1966), with which his film career began). The stories collected in the volumes *Lebensläufe* (1962, extended 1974), *Lernprozesse mit tödlichem Ausgang* (1973) and *Neue Geschichten. Hefte 1– 8. 'Unheimlichkeit der Zeit'* (1977) are written in a style marked by laconic elliptical formulations which recall the legal or civil service report, yet the reader becomes aware between the lines of the frustration and homelessness which lead his subjects to make desperate attempts to conform or to drift into crime or other forms of antisocial behaviour. The course of an entire life is compressed into the space normally devoted to a news item or a *fait divers* and is made the starting-point for the illumination of a situation of exemplary social relevance. In *Schlachtbeschreibung* (1964, followed by a later version entitled *Der Untergang der sechsten Armee* (1969)), by juxtaposing anecdotal material concerning the suffering and death of individual soldiers with information from varied documentary sources (propaganda, strategic planning conferences, letters, eyewitness accounts of particular engagements, information on weather conditions and provision of food and ammunition, etc.) in a day-by-day record of the battle of Stalingrad, Kluge aims at a record more complete than in the official history, yet does not deny the presence of a fictional element. Here as in his films, especially those such as *Die Patriotin* (1979) which deal with German history, he is also concerned with the irrationalism of national myths.

Koeppen, Wolfgang (1906–)

Koeppen spent his early years in East Prussia, went to sea, took various odd jobs, then studied at several universities. After a brief spell as cultural editor of a Berlin newspaper he wrote two novels, *Eine unglückliche Liebe* (1934), on a young man's relationship to a variety performer, and *Die Mauer schwankt* (1935), which was republished in 1939 under the title *Die Pflicht*, on the undermining of accepted certainties experienced by an architect imbued with the Prussian ethos when he meets a young Slav revolutionary. Although Koeppen wrote his second novel in the Netherlands, he did not remain in exile, and although he made no concessions to the Nazi cultural programme, he cannot be associated with the 'inner emigration' of already established writers (**Klepper**, **Langgässer**, **Wiechert**, **Reinhold Schneider**), many of whom adopted a clear Christian stance. He belongs rather with those of his generation (**Eich**, **Huchel**, **Andersch**), whose initial careers suffered inevitable disorientation during the Third Reich, but who went on to find themselves in the early post-war years. Koeppen's early novels can be read as anti-Nazi, but proved acceptable on publication because the criticism present in them is made in the context of the Weimar Republic by characters who cannot be clearly identified as the author's mouthpiece.

Koeppen's high reputation is based almost entirely on three novels which appeared at short intervals in the early 1950s. In *Tauben im Gras* (1951) he uses the montage technique to juxtapose the inner monologues of a number of Germans and Americans during a single day in 1949 in Munich who share a deep insecurity. *Das Treibhaus* (1953) focuses on a Socialist member of the

Bonn parliament and former exile who commits suicide in disappointment with the drift to rearmament in the Federal Republic in 1953. *Der Tod in Rom* (1954) concerns the difference between the generations in two families; while the older characters, represented by a former SS general, his wife and his brother-in-law, now a mayor in West Germany, is incorrigible and unrepentant, the younger, represented by their respective sons, a Catholic priest and an avant-garde composer, is impotent and resigned. Koeppen's other writings include the travel books *Nach Rußland und anderswohin* (1958), *Amerikafahrt* (1959) and *Reisen nach Frankreich* (1961), the collection of assorted prose *Romanisches Café* (1972), the literary essays *Die elenden Skribenten* (1981) and the highly praised and best-selling semi-autobiographical work *Jugend* (1976). *Gesammelte Werke in sechs Bänden* appeared in 1986.

Kokoschka, Oskar (1886–1980)

One of the greatest expressionist painters, Kokoschka also wrote stories, essays and above all plays, some of which are of outstanding merit. A lyrical monologue *Die träumenden Knaben* (1907), dedicated to Klimt, is a typical piece of Viennese *Sezession*; *Mörder Hoffnung der Frauen*, of the same year, is a violent portrayal of the battle between the sexes. Also of 1907 is *Sphinx und Strohmann*, a *curiosum* which anticipates the theatre of Dada (*Hiob*, published ten years later, is an extended version of this play). *Der brennende Dornbusch* dates from 1911. Kokoschka was initially encouraged by Herwarth **Walden** and *Der Sturm* benefited greatly from Kokoschka's graphic work (illustrations to *Mörder Hoffnung der Frauen* appeared on the front page in 1910). The famous painting *Die Windsbraut* (1914) was greatly admired by Georg **Trakl**. Kokoschka was badly wounded in 1915 on the Eastern Front; from 1917 to 1924 he lived in Dresden where he became professor at the Academy of Art. His literary activity was at its peak during this period; he completed *Hiob* as well as *Orpheus und Eurydike* (1919) here. Hindemith and Křenek used his plays as libretti. From 1931 to 1934 Kokoschka lived in Vienna, and from there moved to Prague and London. In 1943 he became president of the Free German League of Culture. In 1947 he took up British nationality; he moved to Switzerland in 1954. A collection of stories *Spur im Treibsand* appeared in 1956; in the same year *Oskar Kokoschkas Schriften 1907–1955* were published. *Mein Leben* appeared in 1971 and *Das schriftliche Werk* (four vols) from 1973 to 1976. Four volumes of *Briefe* appeared 1984–8.

Kolb, Annette (1870–1967)

Daughter of a German architect and a French pianist, Annette Kolb is best known for her novels *Das Exemplar* (1913), set in London high society, *Die Last* (1918), *Daphne Herbst* (1920) and *Die Schaukel* (1934). Excluding *Die*

Last, these were reprinted in 1968 (*Das Exemplar* had also appeared as one of the 'Forum Bücher' in Amsterdam in 1939). Annette Kolb regarded herself primarily as a European and was averse to any form of nationalism; she spent the First World War in Switzerland and the Second in America, where she contributed to *Maß und Wert*, the journal for exiled writers edited by **Thomas Mann**. Her numerous essays demonstrate her enlightened and tolerant attitudes; *Memento* (1960) contains her reminiscences, as does *1907–1964 – Zeitbilder* (1964). *Die Schaukel* also contained autobiographical elements (the depiction of the children of opposing Munich families who were neighbours, the tensions and the resolution). She received the Goethe prize in 1955 and other distinctions at the end of her long life.

Kolbenheyer, Erwin Guido (1878–1962)

Born in Budapest, Kolbenheyer spent his formative years in Karlsbad before studying philosophy, psychology and zoology in Vienna. A conviction concerning the apparent superiority of the Sudeten Germans over their Slav neighbours informed much of his thinking; the German language he extolled as a metaphysical force which held together the ramshackle Austro-Hungarian Empire. Possessing an obvious flair for historical evocation he turned to writing novels: *Amor dei* (1908) is an attempt to convey the 'Parakosmos der spinozistischen Zeit'; *Meister Joachim Pasewang* (1910), in which Jakob Boehme appears, praises the fervent force of German mysticism. Kolbenheyer's most renowned work is the Paracelsus trilogy (*Die Kindheit des Paracelsus* (1917); *Das Gestirn des Paracelsus* (1922) and *Das dritte Reich des Paracelsus* (1926)). These books were written in a pseudo-archaic stryle and contrast the glowing mysticism of the hero with the arid rationalism of his contemporaries; the evocation of Strasburg cathedral is a memorable purple passage. *Das gelobte Herz* (1938) is a portrayal of the fourteenth-century nun Margareta Ebner. Kolbenheyer strove to elucidate his philosophical position in *Die Bauhütte. Elemente der Metaphysik der Gegenwart* (1925) and *Bauhüttenphilosophie* (1942): the primeval substance of life is traced. The superiority of the Germanic race is stressed and its inevitable mastery over all others is posited. Kolbenheyer also attempted plays: *Giordano Bruno* (1903), *Gregor und Heinrich* (1934) and the tetralogy *Götter und Menschen* (1944). Verse includes *Lyrisches Brevier* (1929) and *Vox humana* (1940). Kolbenheyer welcomed the Nazis in 1933 and defended the burning of the books. His support of Hitler was unshakeable: he accepted the presidency of the Sudeten German Cultural Society, yet also assisted colleagues who had not been tolerated under the Third Reich (he was able to bring about the release of Karl **Bröger** from Dachau). After 1945 he was forbidden to write for five years; his autobiographical work *Sebastian Karst über sein Leben und seine Zeit* (1957–8) is a convoluted attempt at self-exculpation. *Gesammelte Werke* (eight vols) appeared from 1939 to 1941; the *Gesamtausgabe der Werke letzter*

Hand (fourteen vols) began to appear in 1957. *Der dichterische Nachlaß* was published in 1973.

Kolbenhoff, Walter (pseudonym after 1933 of Walter Hoffmann, 1908–)

After periods as a vagabond in three continents and as a communist journalist in Berlin Kolbenhoff moved to Denmark in 1933, where he found employment in radio and wrote under a pseudonym. Forced into the army after the German occupation of 1940 he became an American POW in 1944. Having got to know fellow-prisoners **Andersch** and **Richter** in the USA he contributed to the magazine they edited *Der Ruf* and was a co-founder (with Richter) of *Gruppe 47*. His first novel, *Untermenschen* (1933), is a case-study of the isolation and political apathy of the underclass towards the end of the Weimar Republic as embodied by the narrator, overshadowed by the two novels by which he is now mainly remembered, *Von unserem Fleisch und Blut* (1946), in which a seventeen-year-old member of the Werewolf organization, his loyalty to the Führer unimpaired, spends a night running amok in a devastated city already occupied by the Americans, and *Heimkehr in die Fremde* (1949), in which a motley group of men and women find different ways of coming to terms with the material shortages and spiritual vacuum of the hunger years; both are quintessential 'Trümmer-literatur'. After *Die Kopfjäger* (1960), a thriller, Kolbenhoff returned to social realism with *Das Wochenende* (1970), which makes election day on what is otherwise a typical weekend in the lives of two working-class youths the occasion for the confrontation of their political apathy and the combative socialism represented by the grandfather of one of them and by a student drop-out. *Schellingstraße 48* (1984) is an autobiographical account of Kolbenhoff's involvement in the literary life of the first post-war years.

Kolmar, Gertrud (pseudonym of Gertrud Chodziesner, 1894–1943)

A Berlin Jewess, Gertrud Kolmar published two collections of poetry in her lifetime, *Preußische Wappen* (1934), a cycle on the coats of arms of Prussian towns, and *Die Frau und die Tiere* (1938). After her death (she was murdered in a Nazi extermination camp) her most memorable collection, *Welten*, appeared (1947). The collected poems were published as *Das lyrische Werk* (1955; enlarged edition 1960), and their impact was such that she was acknowledged as one of the greatest of Germany's women poets, demonstrating a remarkable range of style (*Volkslied*, sonnet, free verse) and a unique sensitivity and strength of expression. Valid comparisons have been made between her work and that of Annette von Droste-Hülshoff and also Emily Dickinson. A selection of her work, *Tag- und Tierträume*, appeared in 1963; a story, *Eine Mutter*, in 1965: they are passionate, sensuous and highly structured. The main themes are those of unrequited love and the unfulfilled desire to be a mother. *Frühe Gedichte* appeared in 1980; a selection (*Gedichte*) was published in 1983.

Kornfeld, Paul (1889–1942)

Born in Prague, Kornfeld worked as *Dramaturg* in Frankfurt, Darmstadt and Berlin. He insisted upon the ecstatic, religious elements within expressionism: his essay 'Der beseelte und der psychologische Mensch, Kunst, Theater und anderes' (1918) called for vision and transcendence, for essential fervour ('Ja, alle Wirklichkeit ist nur Irrtum, da ja die Beseeltheit die Wahrheit ist'). He achieved fame with his exemplary expressionist play *Die Verführung* (1916): the ecstatic hero, Bitterling, murders the bourgeois Joseph simply because the latter represents undistinguished normality. (Notes to the actors explain: 'Der Schauspieler abstrahiere also von den Attributen der Realität und sei nichts als Vertreter des Gedankens'.) *Himmel und Hölle* (1919) is a form of mystery play, in which the protagonist is tossed between good and evil. Kornfeld also wrote comedies (*Der ewige Traum* (1922); *Palme oder der Gekränkte* (1924); *Kilian* (1926)) which were not successful in their attempt to use urbane social criticism. Kornfeld's novel *Blanche oder das Atelier im Garten* (published posthumously in 1957) has little action; it would seem that Kornfeld could only succeed in the depiction of rhapsodic states. He was murdered in the concentration camp at Lodz. *Paul Kornfeld. Revolution mit Flötenmusik und andere kritische Prosa* was published in 1977.

Kramer, Theodor (1897–1958)

Son of a country doctor from Lower Austria, Theodor Kramer was called up in 1916, badly wounded on the Eastern Front but continued to serve as an officer until the end of the war. He commenced the study of law in Vienna in 1919 but did not find it congenial; he worked in a bookshop and started to write. His first volume of poems, *Die Gaunerzinke* appeared in 1929 and was praised by Ernst **Lissauer** and Georg von der **Vring**. Further collections include *Kalendarium* (1930), *Wir lagen in Wolhynien im Morast* (1931) and *Mit der Ziehharmonika* (1936); the verse is generally conventional in form, with occasional echoes of **Trakl** in the content. Being partly Jewish, Kramer emigrated to England in 1939; in 1940 he was interned on the Isle of Man. The collection *Verbannt aus Österreich* appeared in London in 1943 (reprinted 1983). Kramer worked as a librarian in Guildford Technical College for most of the war and until 1957; during that time he published *Wien 1938 – Die grünen Kader* (1946), *Die untere Schenke* (1946) and *Vom schwarzen Wein* (1956). The return to Austria in 1957 did not bring happiness to Kramer who was unable to adapt to modern conditions. He died of a stroke on 3 April 1958, shortly before he was to receive the 'Preis der Stadt Wien für Literatur'. His *Gesammelte Gedichte* were published in 1983.

Kraus, Karl (1874–1936)

Kraus was born of Jewish parents in the small Bohemian town of Gitschin: the family moved to Vienna when he was 3 years old. Still at school, he published reviews in the *Wiener-Literatur-Zeitung*; in 1892 he entered Vienna University to study law, but he soon turned his attention to acting, also to satire. In 1896 the essay *Die demolirte Literatur* appeared in the *Wiener Rundschau*: it is a brilliant and often scurrilous attack on the *habitués* of the Café Griensteidl (including Hermann **Bahr**) and their literary pretensions. In the spring of 1899 the first number of Kraus's journal *Die Fackel* appeared: this would be published until February 1936 (with only occasional interruptions), edited by Kraus who, towards the end, was the sole contributor. Kraus assumed, over the years, the stance of moralist, the man incensed by hypocrisy and mendacity: the abuse of language incensed him above all, for language, he believed, defined the speaker, and slovenly or inflated language betrayed an inner corruption. The press above all bore the brunt of his attack, also politicians, whose phrases Kraus analysed as concealing the lack of integrity. Kraus was also a fearless defender of the avant-garde: he arranged the first performance in Vienna of *Die Büchse der Pandora* by **Wedekind** in 1905, and played the part of Kungu Poti. The collection of essays *Sittlichkeit und Kriminalität* (1908) showed Kraus to be a champion of penal reform: sanctimonious hypocrisy was his target here. The aphorisms *Sprüche und Widersprüche* appeared in the following year. In 1910 Kraus gave several readings from his works in Berlin, where he befriended Else **Lasker-Schüler**; later (1911) he became associated with the *Brenner-Kreis* and met and greatly admired the poet Georg **Trakl**. Kraus sensed that not only Austria-Hungary, but Europe at large had lost all sense of moral direction and was bent on destruction: the specious glitter of Vienna concealed a total bankruptcy of values. The outbreak of the First World War called forth an almost Messianic tirade from Kraus, a violent hostility which resulted in the frequent confiscation of the *Fackel* and the loathing of patriotic circles. Throughout the war Kraus worked at an enormous apocalyptic indictment, *Die letzten Tage der Menschheit*, published in part in the *Fackel* in 1918; he added to it and revised it until the final version of 1922. Kraus explained: 'Die Aufführung des Dramas, dessen Umfang nach irdischem Zeitmaß etwa zehn Abende umfassen würde, ist einem Marstheater zugedacht. Theatergänger dieser Welt vermöchten ihm nicht standzuhalten. Denn er ist Blut von ihrem Blute . . . .'. Using original documents, speeches of politicians and generals, combined with the chit-chat of Viennese coffee-houses, Kraus shows that language, and thereby thought, have been so corrupted and vulgarized that the catastrophe had been inevitable. 'Der Nörgler' comments on the stupidity and bestiality of those around him; factual reporting is juxtaposed with comment and, finally, a visionary element (the voice of God, using words attributed to the Kaiser, explains: 'Ich habe es nicht gewollt'). Other satirical plays followed in the 1920s, but more successful were the collection of essays *Untergang der Welt durch schwarze Magie* (1922) and *Literatur und Lüge* (1929). Kraus read from his works in several European cities at this time; he was famous for his advocacy of Offenbach and for his readings of Goethe, Nestroy and Shakespeare (in 1930 he adapted *Timon of Athens* for Austrian radio and read the title-role). Kraus, convinced of the banality of evil, refrained from a full condemnation of Hitler in 1933 ('Mir fällt zu Hitler nichts ein'): this came later, and was only published in 1952 as *Die dritte Walpurgisnacht*. Kraus has been hailed as the greatest satirist since Swift, a moralist whose excoriations were meant to reveal the truth and the light; dissenting voices (Walther Benjamin) detected a self-indulgence, even a hysteria, behind the polemic. The poems are surprisingly tender and contain much lyrical beauty. *Werke in Einzelausgaben* appeared from 1952; *Werke* (fourteen vols) between 1956 and 1970. The complete *Fackel* was reprinted in 1968. An *Auswahl aus dem Werk* (three vols) was published in 1971. *Frühe Schriften* (1892–1900) appeared in 1979, an eight volume *Werke* in 1986.

Kreuder, Ernst (1903–72)

Kreuder's work after 1945, although it differs from the adventure and love-stories he wrote during the Third Reich, has little in common with the 'Trümmerliteratur' of a younger generation and the political engagement of writers who came to the fore in the 1960s. All his works represent forms of a challenge in the name of the imagination to machine civilization; they thus become the vehicle for views which can be traced back via Hermann **Hesse** to the Romantics, to whom Kreuder also owes a stylistic debt. Secret societies (in *Gesellschaft vom Dachboden* (1946), the first German novel of the post-war period to become known abroad, and *Agimos oder die Weltgeschichte* (1959)) or an anarchist sect (in *Die Unauffindbaren* (1948), his principal work) or a sanatorium (*Herein ohne anzuklopfen* (1954) and *Der Mann im Bahnwärterhaus* (1973)) become refuges from the pressures of a mundane reality which allows no scope for fantasy and self-realization. Other works include the stories *Schwebender Weg. Geschichte durchs Fenster* (1947) and *Spur unterm Wasser* (1963) and the 'Unroman' *Hörensagen* (1969).

Kroetz, Franz Xaver (1946–)

Of lower-middle-class background and originally an actor, Kroetz has succeeded in reviving the *Volksstück* in the tradition of **Horváth** and **Fleißer** along with Martin **Sperr** and Rainer Werner **Fassbinder** by focusing on the problems of the contemporary skilled and unskilled working class and peasantry in Bavaria in a manner which is neither patronizing nor lacking in awareness of the individual limitations, indeed self-destructive capacity of his subjects. The resonance of his numerous plays made him for a time the most performed playwright in Germany. Any summary of his plots is likely to lead to the assumption that they are black farces; however, Kroetz is more often than not activated by a deep compassion for his characters which renders convincing his claim that he is 'ein christlicher Autor'. Although some of his figures occupy a marginal position in society and adopt attitudes which are more characteristic of pre-war provincial class-consciousness than a modern industrial society and although his occasional departures from realism lead to grotesque exaggeration of their predicament, he also demands to be taken seriously as a social critic, not only in the brief agitprop phase (*Globales Interesse* (1972), *Münchner Kindl* (1973)) which coincided with his membership of the German Communist Party from 1972 to 1980. Kroetz's awareness of his dramatic predecessors is reflected in his adaptations of plays by the nineteenth-century dramatist Friedrich Hebbel (*Maria Magdalene* (1972), *Agnes Bernauer* (1977)) and of *Hinkemann* by Ernst **Toller** (*Der Nusser* (1986)).

In the early plays the protagonists are driven by the frustration and impotence which arise from social rejection, inarticulacy or mental and physical handicap to commit murder, infanticide, suicide, or to plan abortions which if undertaken are botched (*Wildwechsel, Heimarbeit, Hartnäckig, Stallerhof, Geisterbahn, Michis Blut* (all 1971) and *Wunschkonzert* (1973)). After a play accompanied by songs in **Brecht**'s style set in an Austrian prison (*Dolomitenstadt Lienz* (1972)) came two plays (*Oberösterreich* (1972) and *Das Nest* (1975)) in which working-class couples come to terms in different ways and with different consequences with the desire for a family in the face of powerful inducements to fulfil the dream of material prosperity. With the *Volksstücke Der stramme Max* and *Mensch Meier* (both 1978) Kroetz turns to the theme of unemployment, which is then treated in further variations in *Nicht Fisch, nicht Fleisch* (1981), in which it is examined in the context of the introduction of new technology into printing, *Furcht und Hoffnung der BRD* (1984), an episodic series of scenes of everyday life in Germany partly modelled on Brecht's *Furcht und Elend des Dritten Reiches*, *Heimat* (1987, written 1975), in which a child, rejected by her mother, lives with her unemployed grandfather, and *Bauern sterben* (1985), in which brother and sister flee the family farm for the city, where, unable to find work, the former survives as a blood donor, the latter as a prostitute, while in *Der Weihnachtstod* (1986) a Turkish *Gastarbeiter* couple corresponding to Mary and Joseph seek accommodation in the home of an unemployed accountant.

Kroetz's prose works consist of *Chiemgauer Geschichten* (1977), based on taped interviews with inhabitants of a rural neighbourhood in Upper Bavaria, *Weitere Aussichten* (1976), essays and a report on agriculture in the GDR 'Sozialismus auf dem Lande' (1976), together with four radio plays and two film scenarios, *Der Mondscheinknecht* (in two parts, 1981 and 1983), in which the themes of *Hartnäckig* and *Nicht Fisch, nicht Fleisch* are combined in the story of a handicapped man forced to live in a hostel, whose job as a typesetter is under threat from new technology, and two travel diaries, *Nicaragua Tagebuch* (1986) and *Mein Olympia Tagebuch* (1988) on Korea.

Krolow, Karl (1915–)

Krolow has built up a substantial lyrical *œuvre* which includes nature poetry influenced by **Loerke** and **Lehmann** and poems which adapt in a subdued manner modernist techniques (e.g. imagery drawn from surrealism) to German formal traditions as exemplified by the elegiac, pastoral and idyllic verse characteristic of the eighteenth and nineteenth centuries. His numerous collections are brought together in three volumes of *Gesammelte Werke* (1965, 1975, 1985). He has translated extensively from Spanish and French and offered reflections on poetry in the essays *Schattengefecht* (1964), *Das Problem des langen und kurzen Gedichts* (1966) and *Unter uns Lesern* (1967) and in the Frankfurt lectures *Aspekte zeitgenössischer deutscher Lyrik* (1961). His prose fiction consists of muted studies of love (*Das andere Leben* (1979)), depression (*Im Gehen* (1981)), introversion (*Melanie* (1983)) and the autobiographical *Nacht-Leben oder Geschonte Kindheit* (1985).

Kubin, Alfred (1877–1959)

Son of an Austrian army officer, Kubin served briefly in the army until a nervous breakdown necessitated his release. He studied art in Munich and became a graphic artist and book illustrator: his style is visionary and frequently grotesque. In 1909 he published his novel *Die andere Seite*, using illustrations originally intended for *Der Golem* by Gustav **Meyrink**; Meyrink's *impasse* encouraged Kubin to write his own narrative. He was a close friend of **Mynona**, who dedicated his 'Unroman' *Die Bank der Spötter* to him. *Aus meinem Leben* is an autobiography which Kubin prefixed to the first edition of *Die andere Seite* and was reprinted in 1977. He is particularly renowned for his illustrations of Hoffmann and Edgar Allan Poe. His autobiographical prose is also of interest (*Vom Schreibtisch eines Zeichners* (1939), *Aus meiner Werkstatt* (1973) and *Aus meinen Leben* (1974)).

Kühn, Dieter (1935–)

Since 1970 Kühn has produced a series of novels on historical personalities and themes in which awareness of the past as cultivated by the historian and the writer of fiction is a major preoccupation. The influence of Robert **Musil**'s *Der Mann ohne Eigenschaften*, on which he wrote a dissertation published in 1965, is evident in his view of character as a complex of possibilities, latent and realized, which is applied to Napoleon in *N* (1970), a biography which sketches alternative projections, and to a schoolteacher in *Ausflüge im Fesselballon* (1971), whose life from the Second World War to the mid-1960s is accompanied by similar hypothetical variations. The three stories of *Siam-Siam* (1972, second version 1974) are variations on the theme of the fated pair or change of identity. In *Die Präsidentin* (1973), on the stock exchange speculator Marthe Hanau, more a study of fraud than a biography, a self-conscious narrator makes his readers aware of the difficulties inherent in reconstructing a life, even when there is no lack of documents and specialized literature. The difference between image and reality is the guiding theme of the works which follow, although their subjects vary between the exploitation for purposes of political propaganda of a visit by four Indian chiefs to London in 1710 (*Festspiel für Rothäute* (1974)), an analysis of factors in the making of a 'star' biography in *Josephine. Aus der öffentlichen Biografie der Josephine Baker* (1976), public relations activities in multinational oil concerns at the time of the 1973 oil crisis in *Und der Sultan von Oman* (1979), the demythologization of royalty in *Der wilde Gesang der Kaiserin Elisabeth* (1982). The discovery in the course of psychotherapy of a true self hitherto suppressed by the need to conform to private and professional roles is the related theme of *Die Kammer des schwarzen Lichts* (1984).

Kühn's major achievement in reconstructing the lives of the medieval poets Oswald von Wolkenstein (*Ich Wolkenstein* (1977), including translations of his songs), Wolfram von Eschenbach (*Der Parzival des Wolfram von Eschenbach* (1977) in two volumes, the second a translation of most of his most important epic) and Neidhart von Reuenthal (two versions of a biography *Herr Neidhardt* (1981) and *Neidhart aus dem Reuental* (1988)) results from a judicious amalgam of the methods applied in Kühn's fiction.

Kunert, Günter (1929–)

After Kunert's partly Jewish descent had excluded him from secondary education but saved him from military service he studied applied art in Berlin from 1946. His first poems appeared in the satirical magazine *Ulenspiegel* in 1948, his first collection *Wegschilder und Mauerinschriften* in 1950, to be followed at regular intervals by further volumes. He has also written film scenarios, plays for radio and television, the novel *Im Namen der Hüte* (1967), the picaresque adventures of a simple man who comes into possession of a hat which endows its wearer with clairvoyant powers, travel writings which include *Der andere Planet* (1974) on the USA and *Ein englisches Tagebuch* (1978), literary essays *Warum schreiben?* (1976), the Frankfurt literature lectures *Vor der Sintflut. Das Gedicht als Arche Noah* (1985), short stories collected in *Die Beerdigung findet in aller Stille statt* (1968) and *Zurück ins Paradies* (1984), the longer story *Gast aus England* (1973) and a large number of short prose pieces which include aphorisms, reflections, anecdotes, portraits, grotesque fables, descriptions of places, etc., which have appeared in overlapping collections: *Betonformen, Ortsangaben* (1969), *Tagträume in Berlin und andernorts* (1972), *Die geheime Bibliothek* (1973), *Der Mittelpunkt der Erde* (1975), *Verspätete Monologe* (1981) and *Diesseits des Erinnerns* (1982).

Kunert's move to the Federal Republic in 1979 after he had supported the protest against the expatriation of **Biermann** in 1976 marks a turning-point in his career but has not led to any marked change in style or theme. There has been a steady development in his work from commitment under the influence and patronage of **Becher** and **Brecht** to socialism in the GDR, accompanied by warnings against the revival of Nazism and the suppression of its memory, to a pessimism in the face of phenomena not confined to the GDR culminating in loss of faith in progress and fear of nuclear catastrophe, ecological disaster and society under total bureaucratic control. Kunert's predilection for paradox shows itself in his intellectual approach to the structuring of his material, his mastery of grotesque and uncanny effects and his manner of magnifying and distorting observations, experiences and fantasies and placing them in a context which reveals their relation to man's social and existential situation.

Kunze, Reiner (1933–)

The course of Kunze's life and career before his move to the Federal Republic in 1977 reflects the opportunities and restrictions which mark the development of literature in the GDR during the 1950s, 1960s and 1970s. Born the son of a miner in southern Saxony, he studied in Leipzig from 1951 to 1955. His first publications were naïvely optimistic and affirmative in the spirit of socialist realism, but he soon found his own voice after contact with contemporary Czech poets, whose work he has translated, and marriage to a Czech. In the laconic verse of *widmungen* (1963), *sensible wege* (1969) and *zimmerlautstärke* (1972) and in the prose texts of *Die wunderbaren Jahre* (1976) Kunze broke most of the taboos prevalent in the Eastern Bloc, while claiming – initially at least – that the GDR was a country 'das ich wieder und wieder wählen würde'. The objects of his criticism include the occupation of Czechoslovakia by Warsaw Pact troops in 1968, the fate of Solzhenitsyn in the Soviet Union, ideological indoctrination and military training in schools, censorship, regulations and controls, invasion of privacy and restrictions on the free development of the individual, thinking in terms of black and white, but his style is neither aggressive nor declamatory. His poems combine argument and vivid imagery in order to convey in concentrated form experience which is both individual and typical. His recent collections *auf eigene hoffnung* (1981) and *eines jeden einziges leben* (1986) contain landscape poems inspired by journeys abroad, including to Scotland. The early collections are brought together in *gespräch mit der amsel* (1984).

L

Lange, Hartmut (1937–)

After writing his first play *Senftenberger Erzählungen* (1967), a conventional piece of socialist realism with an industrial setting, Lange worked in the *Deutsches Theater* in East Berlin from 1961. His next play *Marski*, completed in 1963 and performed in 1966, is a variation on the theme of the master-servant relationship treated by **Brecht** in *Herr Puntila und sein Knecht Matti*. The historical analogy of Stalin's dispossession of the big farmers, hinted at here, was made more specific in the following plays *Hundsprozeß* and *Stalin als Herakles*, published together with an interlude under the title *Herakles* in 1968, which approach the Stalin system from different points of view. Lange had meanwhile moved to the West in 1965, but he remained for a time a Marxist in his approach to his principal theme (the position of the artist-intellectual in society), while at the same time taking the opportunity to write on subjects taboo in the East. After a successfully realized free adaptation in dramatic form of Kleist's *Die Marquise von O.*, *Die Gräfin von Rathenow* (1969), Lange composed two plays on Trotsky, the first *Die Ermordung des Aias oder Ein Diskurs über das Holzhacken* (1971), an elaborate allegory in which the struggle between Stalin and Trotsky for the heritage of Lenin is presented in the form of the rivalry between Ajax and Odysseus for the arms of Achilles before the gates of Troy, the second *Trotzki in Coyoacan* (1972), an account of Trotsky's last days devised to challenge comparison with the work of another partially disillusioned Marxist **Peter Weiss**'s *Trotzki im Exil* (1970).

Lange's next plays are more personal in their focus on characters from different historical periods (in whom, however, their author is recognizable), who are unable to find a role in a society in which a dominant ideology has reached the end of its tether or an ideological vacuum has led to cynicism and apathy (*Staschek oder Das Leben des Ovid* (1973), *Frau von Kauenhofen* (1977), *Pfarrer Koldehoff* (1979)). These plays are accompanied by more convincing works of prose fiction in which further variations on the theme of the artist-intellectual's unease in the recurrent 'deutsche Misere' are elaborated and Nietzsche, instead of Marx, appears as the presiding background presence and in person in the dramatic phantasmagoria *Jenseits von Gut und Böse oder Die letzten Tage der Reichskanzlei* (1975) and in one of the stories collected in *Die Waldsteinsonate* (1984). In some of these recent works (the title-story in *Die Waldsteinsonate*, the *Novelle Das Konzert* (1986) and the play *Der Fall Karlrobert Kreiten* (1987)) familiar figures and motifs from the Third Reich are combined with the theme of the martyr-artist to produce a Grand Guignol effect closer to Thomas **Bernhard**'s dramas than to the more profound and innovative semi-allegorical plays on 'die deutsche Misere' of Heiner **Müller**.

Langgässer, Elisabeth (1899–1950)

Perhaps the most original and durable of the Christian writers of the 'inner emigration' (**Bergengruen**, **Klepper**, von **Le Fort**, **Reinhold Schneider**, **Wiechert**), Langgässer also belonged to the group associated with the magazine *Die Kolonne*, which included Günter **Eich**. As a 'Mischling ersten Grades' she was forbidden to publish by the Nazis. Her Catholicism, in the opinion of some unorthodox, is marked by a strong and vivid sense of sin and demonic natural forces which are seen in relation to figures from classical mythology, as in *Proserpina* (1932). Her work is rooted in her Rhineland home, where she experienced the French occupation after the First World War, reflected in the novel *Der Gang durch das Ried* (1936). Her chief work is *Das unauslöschliche Siegel* (1946) on the grace ensured by baptism to a rationalist Jew through all the vicissitudes of prosperity, homelessness and destitution before, during and after the Third Reich, in which a linear plot and psychological motivation are replaced by a symbolism based on the timeless conflict between God and Satan. In the posthumous *Märkische Argonautenfahrt* (1950) seven very different figures overcome guilt and despair in a pilgrimage from a devastated Berlin to a monastery symbolizing resurrection. Her poems are assembled in the collections *Der Wendekreis des Lammes* (1924), *Die Tierkreisgedichte* (1935) and *Der Laubmann und die Rose* (1947).

Lasker-Schüler, Elsa (1869–1945: the date of birth was not 1874, as she had claimed)

Elsa Schüler was born in Wuppertal, daughter of a Jewish banker; her marriage to J. B. Lasker necessitated a move to Berlin, where she started to write. Her first poems were published in *Die Gesellschaft* in 1899; that year her marriage was dissolved, and she met a Greek, Alcibiades de Rouan, by whom she had a son (born 1900). In 1901 she married George Lewin, a man to whom she gave the name Herwarth **Walden**. In 1902 her poetry was published under the title *Styx*. After the death of Peter **Hille** she published *Das Peter-Hille-Buch* (1906): Peter Hille had said of her: 'Ihr Dichtgeist ist schwarzer Diamant, der in ihre Stirn schneidet und weh tut. Der schwarze Schwan Israels, eine Sappho, der die Welt entzweigegangen ist.' Other collections include *Der siebente Tag* (1905) and *Die Nächte Tino von Bagdads* (1907): the poetry has a highly exotic, intensely imaginative quality which is occasionally irritating in its wilful obscurity and whimsical mythologizing. In 1909 she wrote her play *Die Wupper* (first performed in 1919), which has many expressionist elements; in 1910 she worked with

Walden on *Der Sturm*. She divorced him the following year, and subsequently enjoyed intense relationships with Franz Marc, also Georg **Trakl** and Gottfried **Benn**; the latter, in 1953, called her 'die größte Lyrikerin, die Deutschland je hatte'. In 1911 *Meine Wunder. Gedichte* appeared, to be followed by her novel *Mein Herz. Ein Liebesroman* (1912). Fantastic *personae* are adopted in *Der Prinz von Theben. Ein Geschichtenbuch* (1914); *Die gesammelten Gedichte* appeared in Leipzig in 1917. Karl **Kraus** esteemed her highly, and organized collections of money to relieve her poverty. Her story *Der Malik. Eine Kaisergeschichte* gave the title to the 'Malik-Verlag'. Later collections of poetry (*Hebräische Balladen* (1913, also 1920)) are marked by a diffuse religious yearning, and Jewish themes become prominent. In 1932 she was awarded the Kleist prize; she emigrated to Switzerland in 1933, where her play *Arthur Aronymus und seine Väter* was performed in 1936. In 1941 she settled in Jerusalem; *Mein blaues Klavier. Neue Gedichte* appeared in 1943. Her grave was bulldozed by the Jordanians during the Six-Day War, but the headstone was preserved. The *Gesammelte Werke* (three vols) appeared from 1959 to 1962; *Sämtliche Gedichte* in 1966; *Gedichte und Prosa* in 1967; *Werke* (8 volumes) from 1986.

Lattmann, Dieter (1926–)

Lattmann became a professional writer in 1959 after a period of work in publishing. He was president of the West German Union of Writers (VS) from 1969 to 1974, playing a role in the writers' congress addressed in 1970 by Chancellor Brandt and **Böll**, **Martin Walser** and **Grass** which resolved to join the printing union in an effort to protect the material interests of the profession more effectively. He has edited and contributed to the survey *Die Literatur der Bundesrepublik Deutschland* (1973) and written numerous essays collected in *Die gelenkige Generation* (1957) and *Zwischenrufe* (1967). Two novels in a cinematic style close to traditional realism, in which middle-class men in mid-career cope with typical professional and domestic problems (*Ein Mann mit Familie* (1962), *Schachpartie* (1968)) were followed by a more ambitious work, *Die Brüder* (1985), in which members of a single family settle and develop separate careers in the Federal Republic and the GDR as a result of the political choices made by two generations of brothers; the third brother of the second generation, a teacher of German and school librarian, uses his profession for an understanding between the two German states.

Lautensack, Heinrich (1881–1919)

A student in Munich, Lautensack participated in the *Elf Scharfrichter* cabaret and became a fervent admirer of Frank **Wedekind**. After his move to Berlin he collaborated with Alfred Richard Meyer in the publication of the *Lyrische Flugblätter* and also, with Anselm Ruest, of the *Bücherei Maiandros*. Lautensack excelled at erotica and the scurrilous treatment of religious themes (*Sulamith* (1906); *Medusa–Aus den Papieren eines Mönchs* (1904); *Hahnenkampf* (1908)); the *Documente der Liebesraserei – Die gesammelten Gedichte* (including *Onan* and *Das Lied des Haremwächters*) appeared in 1910. Of his plays *Die Pfarrhauskomödie* (1911) and *Das Gelübde* (1916) should be noted. Lautensack became increasingly interested in the cinema as an art form; his most successful film was an adaptation of Hebbel's *Mutter und Kind*. He was called up in 1914 and fought on the Eastern Front; his knowledge of film technique caused the military authorities to recall him to Berlin in 1917. His mental condition deteriorated, and in 1918, during an attempt to film Frank Wedekind's funeral, he collapsed at the grave. His last months were spent in an asylum near Berlin. The most important of the posthumous publications include *Altbayrische Bilderbogen – Prosadichtungen* (1920) and *Die Samländische Ode* (1926). The *Gesammelte Werke* appeared under the title *Das verstörte Fest* in 1966.

Lebert, Hans (1919–)

A nephew of Alban Berg and an Austrian, Lebert was an opera-singer from 1935 to 1941 and from 1945 to 1950; from 1941 to 1945 he was forced into hiding after arrest for an anti-military offence. His work is limited in scope, but includes, after *Ein Schiff im Gebirge* (1955), two novels which deserve attention for their treatment of the heritage of the Third Reich and for the manner in which they transform the tradition of the *Heimatroman*. In *Die Wolfshaut* (1960) a sailor comes home to a remote Austrian village, brings to light a war crime committed by villagers in the last days of the Second World War, fails to bring the culprits to justice and leaves. In *Der Feuerkreis* (1971) the mythical dimension, present in the first novel in the motif of the werewolf, is more emphatic: Lebert draws on Wagner's *Ring* to add resonance to the story of the confrontation between another home-comer and his half-sister who has been a concentration camp guard; having fallen under her erotic spell he shoots her on hearing her unrepentant revelations of her activities during the Third Reich. Such exposures of psychosocial complexes in rural environments devoid of idyllic features look forward to similar works by Thomas **Bernhard** and **Gerhard Roth**.

Le Fort, Gertrud Freiin von (1876–1971)

Held generally to be a Catholic historical novelist, Gertrud von Le Fort, before her conversion to Catholicism in 1926, had been attracted to Protestantism and was a pupil of the philosopher Ernst Troeltsch, whose work she edited in 1923. She also studied under Jaspers and Bultmann. Her

Hymnen an die Kirche (1924) marked her literary début, although it would be as a prose writer that she achieved success. Her experiences in Rome found expression in *Das Schweißtuch der Veronika* (1928), a psychological study of great sensitivity (a sequel, *Der Kranz der Engel*, was added thirty years later, both parts now being called *Der römische Brunnen*). *Der Papst aus dem Ghetto* (1930) is an admirable picture of twelfth-century Rome, with the Christianized Jew Pierleone as anti-Pope. Gertrud von Le Fort published rhapsodic, patriotic poetry (*Hymnen an Deutschland*) in 1932; her most famous work, however, is the masterly short story *Die Letzte am Schafott* of 1931, a story based on the execution of Carmelite nuns during the French Revolution (it was made into a film scenario by Bernanos and used as a libretto by Poulenc for his *Les Carmélites*). *Die magdeburgische Hochzeit* (1938) is an account of Tilly's attack on the city in the Thirty Years War. Her love for Germany remained deep and sincere, letters to Swiss friends expressed the conviction that National Socialism was a temporary aberration. Her writing continued unabated throughout the 1950s, and her outstanding *Novelle, Am Tor des Himmels* (dealing with Galileo), dates from 1954. Her late essays deal with the special vocation of woman in the age of materialism and technology. *Hälfte des Lebens*, published in 1965, is an autobiography which goes as far as the collapse of Wilhelmine Germany. *Erzählende Schriften* (three vols) appeared in 1956.

Lehmann, Wilhelm (1882–1968)

Lehmann was born in Venezuela; he served in the 1914–18 war and published his first work *Der bedrängte Seraph* in serialized form in 1915 (as a book in 1924). Other novels include *Der Bilderstürmer* (1917), *Die Schmetterlingspuppe* (1918) and *Weingoß* (1921). Lehmann earned his living as a teacher and wrote sporadically: the stories *Der Sturz auf die Erde* and *Die Hochzeit der Aufrührer* appeared in 1923 and 1934 respectively. His prose has met with little interest, but it is as a mystical nature poet, combining detailed description and mythical dimensions, that he made his reputation, particularly after the Second World War. *Antwort des Schweigens* appeared in 1935; the collection *Der grüne Gott* (1942) reveres the 'Green God' of which all things are a cipher. The collections *Entzückter Staub* (1946), *Noch nicht genug* (1950), *Abschiedslust* (1962) and *Sichtbare Zeit* (1967) contain poetry which, although not modernist in any obvious sense, has influenced writers such as **Langgässer**, **Krolow** and **Eich**. Lehmann was a friend of Oskar **Loerke** and initiated with him a school of mythical nature poetry. The confrontation with nature was indispensable and vital to Lehmann, whose poetry compounds 'Erlebnislyrik' and 'Naturlyrik'. Later works include the essays *Dichtung als Dasein* (1956) and *Kunst des Gedichts* (1961) as well as the novels *Ruhm des Daseins* (1953) and *Der Überläufer* (1962). The collection of stories *Verführerin, Trösterin und andere Erzählungen* appeared in 1947. The *Sämtliche Werke* appeared in 1962; *Gesammelte Werke* (eight vols) from 1982 onwards.

Lenz, Hermann (1913–)

Lenz was born in Stuttgart, studied in Heidelberg and Munich, served on the Eastern Front in the Second World War and became an American POW. His career has been uneventful and without involvement in political and literary debate, but the steady appearance of novels and stories has led recently to belated recognition of a talent which in a Proustian manner explores the relation between present and past and in a detached and ruminative style contrasts passive protagonists with artistic sensibility with men of action devoted to efficiency.

Lenz's numerous works may be divided into three groups: a small number of fantastic stories collected in *Das doppelte Gesicht* (1949) and *Spiegelhütte* (1962); historical novels set mainly in Vienna and Swabia, beginning with *Das stille Hause* (1947, first version 1938) and continuing with *Die Augen eines Dieners* (1964), *Der Kutscher und der Wappenmaler* (1972), *Dame und Scharfrichter* (1975), *Die Begegnung* (1979), set in 1848, and *Erinnerung an Eduard* (1981) on the poet Eduard Mörike (cf. **Härtling**, *Die dreifache Maria*). The trilogy *Der innere Bezirk* (1980), which brings together *Nachmittage einer Dame* (1961), *Im inneren Bezirk* (1970) and *Constantins-allee* (1980) and covers the years 1935–48, also belongs to this group. However, Lenz's most substantial achievement is likely to remain the autobiographical cycle *Verlassene Zimmer* (1966), *Andere Tage* (1968), *Neue Zeit* (1975), *Tagebuch vom Überleben und Leben* (1978), *Ein Fremdling* (1983) and *Der Wanderer* (1986). Lenz's poems have appeared in two collections, *Gedichte* (1936) and *Zeitlebens* (1981).

Lenz, Siegfried (1926–)

Born and brought up in the area of the Masurian Lakes in East Prussia, Lenz joined the navy and took part in the mass evacuation at the end of the Second World War. He studied English literature and philosophy until 1948, then worked for the newspaper *Die Welt*. He has been a professional writer since 1951. He belongs with **Böll** and **Grass** to a trend of social realism in the literature of the Federal Republic which combines commitment to democracy and humanitarian causes, strong regional attachment and a debt to the great realists of the nineteenth and twentieth centuries in Britain, France and Russia, as well as, initially, the American short story as represented especially by Hemingway. His work centres on the moral and existential choices made by men (rarely by women) isolated and exposed to the threat of natural forces or political persecution. In his recent works he concentrates on the portrayal of ageing, stubborn and taciturn men unable to adjust to change, whose unattractive features are balanced by a certain monumentality.

His first novel *Es waren Habichte in der Luft* (1951), set in Russian Karelia after the communist take-over at the end of the First World War, is a story of mistrust which almost leads to betrayal; *Duell mit dem Schatten*

(1953) is a confused account of failed 'Vergangenheitsbewältigung' involving the return of a German colonel with his daughter to the Libyan desert in 1952; *Der Mann im Strom* (1957), comparable to Böll's novels of the same time, concerns the professional and domestic problems of an ageing diver, while *Brot und Spiele* (1959) places a journalist's flashbacks from the life of an athlete within the framework of his last race (cf. **Johnson**, *Das dritte Buch über Achim*); in *Stadtgespräch* (1963), related to the play *Zeit der Schuldlosen* (1961, recast as a radio play with the title *Zeit der Schuldlosen/ Zeit der Schuldigen* (1961)), the leader of a resistance group willing to give himself up in order to save the lives of hostages is prevented from doing so and becomes the object of rumours alleging cowardice and irresponsibility. The next novel *Deutschstunde* (1968), which became a bestseller, focuses on the essay assignment undertaken by an inmate of an approved school which expands to an autobiographical account of his relationship to his father, a policeman devoted to duty, and on an artist modelled on Emil Nolde during the Third Reich. In order to ensure compliance with an order forbidding the artist to paint, the policeman destroys some of his works; others are saved by the boy, whose continued 'thefts' after the war lead to his imprisonment. In *Das Vorbild* (1973) three teachers of different ages and backgrounds, having gathered to compile a new teaching anthology, ultimately fail to find satisfactory models for the young. In *Heimatmuseum* (1978) a museum of East Prussian folk-culture transferred to Schleswig-Holstein after the German expulsion is burnt down by its curator when he doubts the possibility of passing on to the future the true spirit that inspired the creation of the objects on display without concessions to racist and nationalist pressures. *Der Verlust* (1981) traces the strains in the relationship between a man and a woman when the former suffers a stroke which robs him of speech. In *Ein Kriegsende* (1984) a mutiny which takes place on a mine-sweeper in the Baltic after the German surrender in 1945 leads to the execution of its leaders. *Exerzierplatz* (1985) is a prolix account of relationships within a family of East Prussian refugees and between its patriarch and Bruno, orphan and simple soul, employed in the family's market-gardening business, from whose point of view the story is told.

Lenz's stories can be divided into two groups: three volumes in lighter vain set in Masuria, Hamburg or at sea (*So zärtlich war Suleyken* (1955), *Lehmanns Erzählungen* (1964), the confessions of a black-marketeer, and *Der Geist der Mirabelle* (1975)); and five collections sharing the themes of the novels (*Jäger des Spotts* (1958), *Das Feuerschiff* (1960), *Der Spielverderber* (1965), *Einstein überquert die Elbe bei Hamburg* (1975) and *Das serbische Mädchen* (1987)).

Leonhard, Rudolf (1889–1953)

Leonhard began his literary career as a poet (*Der Weg durch den Wald* (1913)); during the First World War he became a convinced pacifist, later joined the communist *Spartakusbund* and wrote in the style of the expressionist

J. R. Becher; in *Alles und Nichts. Aphorismen* (1920) he explains: 'Wir schreien mit dem ganzen Blut, in die Ewigkeit, unser ganzes Blut schreit . . .'. The collections *Über den Schlachten* (1914), *Katilinarische Pilgerschaft* (1919), *Spartakussonette* (1922) and *Das Chaos* (1922) chart his growing political commitment. In the 1920s he wrote the plays *Segel am Horizont* (1925), *Tragödie von heute* (1927) and *Traum* (1933). He worked with Erwin Piscator at the *Volksbühne*, was invited by **Hasenclever** to live in Paris and continued to write plays, the best being the comedy *Hitler und Co.* (published 1936). Ill health prevented direct involvement in the Spanish Civil War, although a brief visit to Spain resulted in *Der Tod des Don Quijote. Geschichten aus dem spanischen Bürgerkrieg* (first published in Germany in 1951). Leonhard worked in Paris to ameliorate the lot of German exiles; a selection of his poetry was smuggled into Germany clandestinely. In 1944 a poetry collection (*Deutschland muß leben*) was illegally published in Marseilles. After the war Leonhard lived in East Berlin, where he wrote copiously in defence of the East German government: *Unsere Republik. Bekenntnisbuch zur neuen Ordnung der DDR* appeared in 1951. The *Ausgewählte Werke* (4 vols) appeared 1961–70.

Lernet-Holenia, Alexander (1897–1976)

As a young dragoon officer Lernet-Holenia had joined in the offensive against Russia in the First World War; his work deals predominantly with the imperial Austro-Hungarian army. His early lyrics *Pastorale* (1921) and *Kanzonnair* (1923) betray the influence of Rainer Maria **Rilke**, particularly his *Cornet*. Later volumes of poetry (*Die goldene Horde* (1933); *Die Trophäe* (1946), and *Das Feuer* (1949)) are more classically conventional and reminiscent of Hölderlin: the odes of the latter collection are deliberately reminiscent of Goethe. The plays range from the violence of *Demetrius* (1926) and the dramatic scenes *Saul* and *Alkestis* (also 1926) to the comedies *Olla potrida* (1927) and *Österreichische Komödie* (also 1927); the latter particularly contains a critique of Austrian manners combined with quiet humour. The novels are generally facile: *Die Standarte* (1934) demonstrates the love of a young officer for his standard, the flag which he loves more than his beloved. *Beide Sizilien* (1942) explains: 'Die vollkommensten Erzählungen sind jene, welche bei größter Wahrscheinlichkeit, die sie für sich beanspruchen können, den höchsten Grad von Unwirklichkeit erreichen'. *Graf Luna* (1955) contains realistic and fantastic elements, also an apocalyptic tone which is otherwise lacking in Lernet-Holenia's work. Probably his most successful works are his *Novellen*: *Mayerling* (1960) contains the best of these (including 'Der Baron Bagge', 'Mona Lisa' and 'Maresi'). Lernet-Holenia also served in the Second World War with an army film unit; *Mars im Widder* (1941) describes the campaign in the Balkans. The essay *Adel und Gesellschaft in Österreich* (1957) shows Lernet-Holenia as an acute observer of Austrian *mœurs*.

Lersch, Heinrich (1889–1936)

Lersch, a boiler-maker by trade, joined the group 'Werkleute auf Haus Nyland' (Nyland being the Westphalian farm belonging to Joseph Winckler) in 1905; his poetry praised the new technological age. He portrayed the life of the working man in a rhapsodic, anti-Marxist fashion; the early poetry was collected as *Abglanz des Lebens* in 1914. Lersch became famous with his 'Soldatenlied' of 1914 ('Laß mich gehn, Mutter, laß mich gehn!'), a naïvely sentimental response to war. At the end of 1915 he was buried alive during an artillery bombardment, but survived. Lersch favoured the balladesque form in his poetry ('Brüder', 'Im Artilleriefeuer', 'Massengräber', 'Wenn es Abend wird'); he was later hailed (by Julius Bab) as the 'Feldpostsänger des ersten Weltkrieges'. His collections include *Herz! Aufglühe dein Blut. Gedichte im Krieg* (1916); *Deutschland! Lieder und Gesänge von Volk und Vaterland* (1918) and *Deutschland muß leben* (1935), which demonstrated Lersch's approval of certain aspects of National Socialism. This last collection was reprinted many times, a 'Wehrmachtausgabe' appearing in 1944. The *Ausgewählte Werke* (two vols) appeared in 1965 and 1966.

Leutenegger, Gertrud (1948–)

Born and brought up in Schwyz, central Switzerland, Leutenegger has worked as a nursery schoolteacher, in a psychiatric clinic, as custodian of the Nietzsche house in Sils Maria (part of the setting of her second novel) and as an assistant theatre director. Her novels written in an iridescent prose style convey intense experiences and epiphanies at existential turning-points in their narrators' lives. In *Vorabend* (1975) the evening walk taken by the narrator through streets where a demonstration is due to take place prompts memories and reflections. *Ninive* (1977) is the love-story of the narrator and Fabrizio, who travel together to their home village to view the exhibition of a whale which becomes a dominant but enigmatic symbol. *Gouverneur* (1981) is Leutenegger's most clearly feminist work, the title symbolizing the domineering male and the 'progress' which destroys a balanced relation between human beings and nature, a theme pursued in some of the stories of *Das verlorene Monument* (1985) and the novel *Kontinent* (1985), on the damage to the environment by an aluminium factory. *Komm ins Schilf* (1983) and *Meduse* (1988) represent further variations of the love-story adumbrated in *Ninive*.

Lettau, Reinhard (1929–)

Lettau has taught in American universities and became involved in the *außerparlamentarische Opposition* in Berlin in the late 1960s. His *œuvre* is small but highly idiosyncratic, consisting largely of prose miniatures on the borderline of satire and whimsy which recall both **Kafka**'s pieces of similar length and **Brecht**'s *Keuner-Geschichten* and from 1968 are influenced by a radical political commitment and by the debates on documentary literature. *Schwierigkeiten beim Häuserbauen* (1962) was followed by *Auftritt Manigs* (1963), more concentrated texts in which the title-figure, as insubstantial as a matchstick man, devises predicaments which prompt reflection on life's absurdities. *Feinde* (1968), six short stories directed against militarism and bureaucracy, appeared with the two preceding volumes, together with new texts (poems and portraits), in *Immer kürzer werdende Geschichten* (1973). *Täglicher Faschismus. Amerikanische Evidenz aus 6 Monaten* (1971), a montage of press reports conceived as a contribution to documentary literature, led to *Frühstücksgespräche in Miami* (1978), dialogues in which former dictators from Latin America reminisce in a Florida hotel. *Zerstreutes Hinausschauen* (1980) contain two essays on Kafka.

Lichtenstein, Alfred (1889–1914)

A Jew from Berlin, Alfred Lichtenstein published his first memorable poem in *Der Sturm* in 1910, after which he contributed to *Simplicissimus*, *Die Aktion* and *Pan* (*Die Aktion* published a special Lichtenstein number in October 1913). A first collection of some twenty poems was published under the title *Die Dämmerung* in the same year. Lichtenstein's first book publication was *Die Geschichten des Onkel Krause. Ein Kinderbuch* (Berlin 1910). Lichtenstein was known to his colleagues as a clown, a man marked by a droll, often grotesque sense of humour: his literary *personae* included not only 'Onkel Krause' but also 'Aliwi' and 'Kuno Kohn'. His 'Die Dämmerung' is well known as representing the second expressionist collage-poem ('Zeilengedicht') to appear in print; through discovering Jakob van **Hoddis** Lichtenstein found his own voice ('Der Sturm' is a pastiche of 'Weltende'). His war poetry is honest, simple and totally unheroic ('Gebet vor der Schlacht'); nine days after sending home his 'Die Schlacht bei Saarburg' he died near Reims of a stomach wound, in September 1914. *Gedichte und Geschichten* appeared posthumously in Munich in 1919; during the Second World War his *Nachlaß* was destroyed, apart from four handwritten exercise books. *Gesammelte Gedichte* appeared in Zurich in 1962; the *Gesammelte Prosa* four years later. *Ausgewählte Gedichte* appeared in 1977, *Gesammelte Gedichte* in 1988.

Lienhard, Friedrich (1865–1929)

Born in Alsace, Lienhard studied theology and philosophy and, moving to Berlin, lived as a journalist, editing the literary periodical *Der Türmer* (1920–9). His drama *Weltrevolution* (1889) owes much to naturalism, but this mode he did not find conducive, and he turned to neo-romantic, also regional, literature. In the drama he used historical or legendary German figures (*Till Eulenspiegel* (1896); *Gottfried von Straßburg* (1897); *Wieland der Schmied* (1905); *Münchhausen* (1900)); his best-known work in this field is the *Wartburg* trilogy (1903–6), the Wartburg representing the German Christian tradition. His novels include *Oberlin* (1910) and *Der Spielmann* (1913), which deal with Alsatian, rather than with purely German, themes. He is best known for his essay *Die Vorherrschaft Berlins* (1900) which condemns the unnatural life of that city and calls for a return to rural, unsophisticated values. This was followed by *Neue Ideale* (1901), *Oberflächenkultur* (1904) and *Deutschlands europäische Sendung* (1914). The *Gesammelte Werke* (fifteen vols) appeared from 1924 to 1926.

Lind, Jakov (1927–)

Lind's Ahasverus-like wanderings from Vienna to Holland, Germany (where he survived the Second World War under a false identity), Israel and London, where he has lived since 1954, are traced in his autobiographies (which appeared first in English, then in his own translation) *Counting My Steps* (1969) (*Selbstporträt* (1974)) and *Numbers* (1972) (*Nahaufnahme* (1973)). For him writing is a form of therapy, and the grotesque effects produced by the deformation of reality in his work reflect the traumas of his early life; but they also emerge from the adoption of the point of view of insane and crippled characters such as the lame, one-legged and epileptic figures pursued by a Nazi thug in the title-story of the collection *Eine Seele aus Holz* (1962). However, not only the victims are deformed; so too are the Nazi thug and the corresponding figures in the novels *Landschaft in Beton* (1963) and *Eine bessere Welt* (1966, dramatized in English as *Ergo* (1967)), the latter a satire on post-war conditions in Austria. After *Der Ofen. Eine Erzählung und sieben Legenden* (1973) Lind offered in *Travels to the Emu* (1982) (*Reise zu den Emu* (1983)) in the form of a Pacific island a dystopia loosely modelled on *Gulliver's Travels*, to whose author the book is dedicated.

Linde, Otto zur (1873–1938)

Born in Essen, Otto zur Linde moved to Berlin where, with Rudolf **Pannwitz** he edited the journal *Charon* from 1904 to its demise during the First World War (Charon, who ferried the dead souls across the river Styx without questioning their origins or their destination, became the mythological symbol for the poetic act itself, an act of pure devotion). The 'Charontiker' insisted: 'Wir wollen nichts. . . . Wir sind keine Mystiker sondern wir geben einfache Wirklichkeit'. *Gedichte, Märchen und Skizzen* appeared in 1901, to be followed by *Die Kugel, eine Philosophie in Versen*

(1909) in which a Nietzschean, rhapsodic tone became apparent. The *Charontiker-Mythos* (1913) is a collection of gnomic visions ('Urvater', 'Ballade vom Tod und der nackten Seele', 'An den Wurzeln des Raums', etc.). Of interest is also *Arno Holz und der Charon: eine Streitschrift* (1911). Otto zur Linde emphasized the need for idealism, and saw his task as being 'den deutschen, freiheitsstolzen und weltfrommen Idealismus wieder zu erwecken'. The *Gesammelte Werke* (eight vols) appeared between 1910 and 1924; *Charon. Auswahl der Gedichte* in 1952. *Prosa. Gedichte. Briefe* was published in 1974.

Lissauer, Ernst (1852–1937)

Lissauer is now remembered for his notorious *Haßgesang gegen England*, a venomous patriotic poem composed during the First World War. A Prussian Jew, Lissauer wrote works which could, had he been Aryan, have been accepted as 'Blut und Boden' literature (*Der Acker* (1910), *Der Strom* (1912)); *1813. Ein Zyklus* (1913) and *Bach* (1916) extol great German figures, as do the dramas *Die letzten Stunden Yorcks, Die Anfechtung, Der Royalist* and *Eckermann* (1919). *Der inwendige Weg* and *Pfingsten* (1919) are rhapsodic outpourings. Lissauer published in the Eugen Diederichs Verlag, a right-wing publisher; he bitterly regretted having written the *Haßgesang* and left Germany after the Nazi seizure of power.

Loerke, Oskar (1884–1941)

Son of a West Prussian farmer, Oskar Loerke studied philosophy, history and German in Berlin; in 1907 he terminated his studies and devoted himself to writing. His first publications were in prose, but collections of poems, *Wanderschaft* and *Gedichte*, appeared in 1911 and 1916 respectively. In 1913 he received the Kleist prize and travelled through Algeria and Southern Italy. In 1917 he became a reader for the S. Fischer Verlag. *Das Goldbergwerk*, his most successful *Novelle*, appeared in 1919; the novel *Der Oger* in 1921. Loerke's poetry is sometimes described as expressionist; landscape descriptions verge upon the visionary and the sombre, although the tone is rarely strident. *Pansmusik* (1929) is a reworking of the 1916 collection; *Atem der Erde* (1930) and *Der Silberdistelwald* (1934) contain much remarkable writing. Loerke also wrote on music (Bach und Bruckner). The *Tagebücher 1903–1939* (ed. **Kasack**) give a moving account of Loerke's growing isolation after 1933, the reaction of a sincere and dedicated poet to the new regime; unable to remain as secretary to the Prussian Academy of Arts he notes with bitterness the servility and readiness to conform of Wilhelm **Schäfer** and **Kolbenheyer**, the latter being referred to as 'Das tückische aufgeblasene breiige Nichts . . .'. *Gedichte* (ed. Kasack) appeared in 1954, *Gedichte und Prosa* in 1958; *Reisetagebücher* in

1960. Günther **Eich** made a selection of *Gedichte* in 1963. *Literarische Aufsätze aus der Neuen Rundschau* appeared in 1967.

Loest, Erich (1926–)

Loest served as a soldier in the closing months of the Second World War, worked as a journalist in Leipzig, then became a professional writer in 1950. From 1957 until 1964 he was imprisoned in the GDR for alleged counter-revolutionary activities. Since 1981 he has lived in the Federal Republic, where works which could not be published in the GDR have meanwhile appeared. Loest has throughout his career remained on the margin of the trends and guidelines of GDR literature, adhering consistently to a realism based on his own experiences and observations in an identifiable milieu, usually Leipzig, as in *Es geht seinen Gang oder Mühen in unserer Ebene* (1978), on the differing aspirations of an engineer and his wife and the other factors which lead to their divorce, *Völkerschlachtdenkmal* (1984), a century and a half of Saxon history as reflected in the fortunes of a single family, and *Zwiebelmuster* (1985), on the efforts of a historian and his wife to find a professional excuse to visit the West. Loest has also written novels fairly typical of the 'Ankunftsliteratur' of the early years of the GDR (*Jungen, die übrig blieben* (1950), on the transition from war to peace in the lives of several youths, *Der Westmark fällt weiter* (1952), a black-and-white portrayal of an already divided Berlin, and *Das Jahr der Prüfung* (1955), on a Faculty for Workers and Peasants), novels and stories set in the Third Reich (*Der Abhang* (1968), on the corruption of youth in the SS, the autobiographical 'Pistole mit sechzehn' (1979), the picaresque *Ich war Robert Ley* (1966)), works on the theme of imprisonment (*Schattenboxen* (1973, 1984), the stories 'Etappe Rom' (1975) and 'Zwei Briefe von Rohdewald' (1979), the novel based on the life of the popular nineteenth-century writer Karl May *Swallow, mein wackerer Mustang* (1980) and parts of the autobiography *Durch die Erde ein Riß. Ein Lebenslauf* (1981)). Also worth mention are detective stories written under the pseudonym H. Walldorf, and *Ins offene Messer* (1975), set in Greece under the colonels' regime, and *Froschkonzert* (1987), in which a GDR construction gang permitted to work in the West reduce local wage levels.

Löns, Hermann (1866–1914)

Born in West Prussia, Löns is associated above all with nature descriptions, particularly of the Lüneburger Heide; his portrayal of wildlife is perhaps unequalled in German literature. *Mein grünes Buch* (1901) and *Aus Wald und Heide* (1909) contain sketches and impressions of heathland and forest; Löns also wrote lyric poetry: *Mein goldenes Buch* (1901) and *Der kleine Rosengarten* (1911). He received enormous popularity with *Der Wehrwolf*

(1910), a book which sold well over half a million copies by 1939. The book is set in the Thirty Years War and contains many of the elements associated with 'Blut und Boden' literature: a stubborn peasantry, extirpation of alien peoples, the extolling of the *Volk*. (Löns had also been responsible for the anti-British song: 'Denn wir fahren gegen Engelland'.) Other novels include *Der letzte Hansbur* (1909), *Dahinten in der Heide* (1910) and *Das zweite Gesicht* (1911); *Die Häuser von Olenhof* was published posthumously in 1917. Löns, aged 48, enlisted in 1914 and was killed near Reims in September. *Sämtliche Werke* (eight vols) appeared in 1924 and *Nachgelassene Schriften* in 1928. A five volume *Ausgewählte Werke* appeared in 1986.

Lotz, Ernst Wilhelm (1890–1914)

Lotz became an officer cadet at the age of 17, after which he became a lieutenant in an infantry regiment. His poetry is akin to that of Ernst **Stadler** and undeniably expressionistic in its fervour and intensity. The collection *Und schöne Raubtierflecken* was published in Berlin in 1913; his most famous poems, however, are found in *Wolkenüberflaggt*, published posthumously in Leipzig in 1917 (Lotz was killed on the Western Front in September 1914). 'Hart stoßen sich die Wände in den Straßen' and 'Aufbruch der Jugend' are good examples of his poetry. *Prosaversuche* were published in 1955. His literary remains consist of approximately sixty poems, plus translations from Verlaine and Rimbaud. He was a close friend of the Berlin artist Ludwig Meidner.

Lücken, Iwar von (1874–1939)

Born in Wiesbaden of Baltic nobility, Iwar von Lücken studied briefly in Leipzig (1897) and spent years in Russia before returning to Dresden. An unenthusiastic soldier, he was able to leave military service (thanks to the sympathetic intervention of a Dr. Fritz Neuberger) and lived from 1916 to 1917 in the hostel Felsenburg in Dresden, where he became an associate of **Kokoschka**, **Hasenclever** and Albert **Ehrenstein**. After the war he led an irregular life, often in extreme poverty: a painting by the expressionist Otto Dix in 1926 portrays the sparseness of his surroundings. He met Edwin Muir in 1922 in Hellerau where he taught foreign languages; he was also admired as an expert on Hölderlin. In 1924 he published poems and short pieces of prose in *Querschnitt*, also in the *Zeitschrift für Bücherfreunde*; the Dresden journal *Menschen* (1919–21) also accepted some. A slim volume of his poetry, *Gedichte*, appeared in Berlin in 1928: poems such as 'Trauerfeier', 'Herbst', 'Auftakt' and 'Clematis' show an affinity with Hermann **Hesse** and avoid the hectic features associated with expressionism; the poem 'In Ewigkeit' expresses von Lücken's great love for Hölderlin. He moved from Dresden to Berlin, then emigrated in 1933 to Paris. He lived in such obscurity that his death is normally registered as having taken place in 1935; he briefly visited Berlin after that date, then died in Paris in acute deprivation in the winter of 1939. Descriptions of Iwar von Lücken may be found in the autobiographies of Peter de Mendelssohn and Oskar Kokoschka.

M

Mackay, John Henry (1864–1933)

Born in Greenock, Mackay was brought up in Germany and studied at various universities, settling finally in Berlin. He was one of the so-called 'Moderne', an active member of the club *Durch* and was deeply involved in anarchist circles. He published collections of poetry (*Sturm* (1887) and *Gedichte* (1909), some of which were set to music by Richard Strauss), but was more successful as a prose writer. His *Novellen* include *Schatten* (1887), *Moderne Stoffe* (1888) and *Die letzte Pflicht* (1893); the novel *Die Anarchisten* (1891) is a skilful portrayal of cultural life in Germany at the end of the nineteenth century. Other works include *Albert Schnells Untergang* (1895), *Der Schwimmer* (1901) and *Der Sybarit* (1903); *Der Freiheitssucher* (1920) is a thinly disguised autobiography. Mackay's earlier social concerns gave way to a preoccupation with the individualist philosophy of Max Stirner; in 1898 he published *Max Stirner, sein Leben und sein Werk* and also an edition of *Kleinere Schriften*. As a pederast Mackay sought to achieve tolerance for this proclivity in the *Sagitta Schriften*; *Die Bücher der namenlosen Lieben* appeared in 1977.

Mann, Luiz Heinrich (1871–1950)

Elder brother of **Thomas Mann**, Heinrich Mann was born in Lübeck, son of a wealthy corn merchant; his mother was Brazilian. He was not a successful scholar, and his vocational training (in a bookshop, then with the publisher S. Fischer) was soon broken off in order that he might devote himself to writing. In 1894 he published the novel *In einer Familie*, and three years later *Das Wunderbare und andere Novellen*. He also worked (in Berlin) as a journalist and, in 1895, as editor of the conservative, patriotic journal *Das zwanzigste Jahrhundert*, to which he and his brother contributed. He travelled frequently to Italy, and much of his early writing reflects Italian life and history, particularly the Renaissance: a predilection for violent and often decadent situations prevails. An early influence was also Nietzsche. *Im Schlaraffenland* (1900) is a satire on the literary and fashionable life in the Berlin of the 1890s: especially memorable is an account of the effect of a naturalist play on a blasé audience. The trilogy *Die Göttinnen oder die drei Romane der Herzogin von Assy* (1903) is much indebted to the vogue for d'Annunzio, particularly the depiction of sexuality and power; the element of the grotesque is also in evidence. The novel *Die Jagd nach Liebe* (also 1903), with its sensational portrayal of sexual love and over-reliance on crass effects, brought him his brother's strong disapproval. The year 1905 saw the publication of the *Novellen, Flöten und Dolche*, also the novel *Professor*

Unrat oder das Ende eines Tyrannen (later to achieve world fame as the film *The Blue Angel*), a savage portrayal of petty power-seeking and vindictiveness. An undeniable tendency to caricature characterized Heinrich Mann's work at this time, also a bitterness caused probably through the realization of his younger brother's remarkable literary success (none of Heinrich Mann's books achieved sales of even 5,000 copies in the period up to 1914, whereas over 10,000 copies of *Buddenbrooks* were sold in 1903 alone). The next novel, *Zwischen den Rassen* (1907), described in more sympathetic terms the differences between Northerner and Southerner, a theme very close to Thomas Mann. *Die kleine Stadt* (1909), reminiscent of a five-act drama, is Heinrich Mann's first political novel, depicting the virtue of democracy as opposed to self-interest; a murder towards the end introduces a tragic note. Heinrich Mann attempted (at this time and later) the writing of plays (*Die große Liebe* (1912); *Madame Legros* (1913)); of greater importance, however, are his essays, particularly *Voltaire und Goethe* and *Geist und Tat* (1910) and, above all, *Zola* (1915). It was Heinrich Mann's conviction that the German intellectual, notorious for his arrogant isolation from political matters (his brother included), should look to France as a model, to Zola above all, the embodiment of 'ratio militans'. It was inconceivable to Heinrich Mann (and to many others) that Thomas Mann should not join the ranks of pacifists and denigrators of Imperial Germany, and the rift between the two brothers was never wider than before and during the First World War. Thomas Mann claimed that Heinrich Mann's essay was directed against him rather than against Germany, and would reply with his *Betrachtungen eines Unpolitischen* (1918), an attack above all on the 'Zivilisationsliterat', the political thinker who (in Thomas Mann's eyes) superficially propagated predictable and platitudinous liberalism.

Heinrich Mann's popularity and success as a writer were assured by the publication, in 1918, of *Der Untertan*, part of a so-called *Kaiserreich-Trilogie* (with *Die Armen* (1917) and *Der Kopf* (1925)), a satire on arrogant Kaiser-worship which struck exactly the right note after the ignominious departure of Wilhelm II. Heinrich's fame eclipsed his brother's at this time, albeit temporarily; a severe illness (1922) brought a precarious reconciliation. (His brother's world fame was assured in 1924 by *Der Zauberberg* and in 1929 by the Nobel prize for literature.) In the 1920s Heinrich Mann turned again to *Novellen* (*Kobes* has overtly expressionist elements); further novels include *Mutter Marie* (1927), *Die große Sache* (1930) and *Ein ernstes Leben* (1932), which were, however, not successful. *Eugénie oder die Bürgerzeit* (1928) is a portrayal of Lübeck life after the Franco-Prussian war and contains a disguised portrait of the poet Emanuel Geibel. Frequent speeches and essays date from this time, demanding a moral commitment to Western democracy and expressing a love for French culture above all. In 1931 he became president of the literary section of the Prussian Academy, only to be dismissed immediately in 1933. He took refuge in France, and there wrote his acknowledged masterpiece, the two-part historical novel *Die Jugend des Königs Henri Quatre* (1935) and *Die Vollendung des Königs Henri Quatre* (1938), a depiction of tolerance, good sense and balanced leadership, a deliberate discussion of that which was lacking in Nazi Germany. Polemical writing (*Der Sinn dieser Emigration* (1934) and *Es kommt der Tag* (1936)) showed Heinrich Mann to be a mature political thinker, doyen of the *émigrés* and their natural leader in France.

In 1940 Heinrich Mann escaped to America and settled near his brother in California (he was, to his chagrin, frequently reduced to living off loans from Thomas). He did not find the new environment congenial and later novels, *Lidice* (1943), *Der Atem* (1949) and *Empfang bei der Welt* (1956), although eminently worthy, are second-rate. His memoirs, *Ein Zeitalter wird besichtigt*, give a fascinating account of the literary life in Germany and America with which he was familiar. An unfinished novel *Die traurige Geschichte von Friedrich dem Großen* (published posthumously in 1960) deliberately juxtaposes French political maturity with German hubris. Heinrich Mann accepted the presidency of the newly founded Academy of Arts in the German Democratic Republic, but died before he was able to take up the post.

Heinrich Mann's democratic stance was felt by many to be more convincing than that of his doubtless more famous brother, although the latter's sustained narrative excellence was beyond him. The *Gesammelte Werke in Einzelausgaben* (fifteen vols) appeared from 1958 to 1982, the *Gesammelte Werke* (eighteen vols) from 1965 to 1978, and a *Werkauswahl* (ten vols) in 1976. A collection of *Novellen* appeared in 1970, and *Meistererzählungen* in 1982. Heinrich Mann made a profound impact on the political radicals of the 1960s who preferred his statements to his brother's ironic evasions. The published correspondence between the two gives a clear insight into the relationship between them, never an easy one.

Mann, Klaus (1906–1949)

Eldest son of **Thomas Mann**, Klaus Mann began his literary career as a writer of *Novellen* before becoming theatre critic and *Dramaturg* in Berlin. He collaborated with his sister Erika (1905–1969), Pamela Wedekind and the actor Gustaf Gründgens in the writing of revues, particularly the *Revue zu Vieren* (1926). He was also active as an anthologist of modern prose and poetry (1927–8). He emigrated in March 1933, living in Amsterdam, Paris and Zurich; he edited *Die Sammlung*, the most important journal for German *émigrés*, and also reported on the Spanish Civil War. His novels include *Flucht in den Norden* (1934); *Symphonie Pathétique* (1935, based on the life of Tchaikovsky), *Mephisto. Roman einer Karriere* (1936) and *Der Vulkan. Roman unter Emigranten* (1939). The Mephisto novel is the most notorious, being a thinly veiled account of the career of the actor Gustaf Gründgens during Nazi Germany; the novel appeared in Amsterdam in 1936 and, in 1956, in the German Democratic Republic, Gründgens and his heirs having fought against its publication in the Federal Republic. Pirated editions did, however, appear before the 1981 paperback, and the film (by Iśtvan Szábo) was shown at Cannes that same year. In 1936 Klaus Mann moved to America where he edited (1941–2) *Decision*. He joined the US army in 1942 and became a correspondent for *Stars and Stripes*. His autobiography was published in 1942 as *The turning point. Thirty-five years in this century* (published posthumously in Germany as *Der Wendepunkt* (1952)). He also wrote a substantial study of André Gide. Unable to settle after the war he committed suicide in Cannes. His essays also appeared posthumously (*Prüfungen. Schriften zur Literatur* and *Heute und morgen* (1968 and 1969)). His novels and essays were reprinted from 1976 to 1980; other essays from the *Nachlaß* include *Woher wir kommen und wohin wir müssen*.

Mann, Thomas (1875–1955)

Younger brother of **Heinrich Mann**, Thomas Mann grew up in similar circumstances and sought, at an early age, to emulate his brother and follow a literary career. The imbalance between his parents (the father a Lübeck merchant and prosperous senator, the mother of Brazilian descent) would provide a fruitful motif for much of his writing (see also Heinrich Mann's *Zwischen den Rassen*); the move to Munich (1893) quickened his awareness of the fascinating, as well as the more dubious, aspects of aestheticism. Relinquishing formal study he worked briefly in an insurance office, also on the editorial board of the satirical weekly *Simplicissimus* (1898–9). His first *Novelle, Gefallen*, dates from 1894; after the return from Rome and Palestrina (1896–8) he published his first collection of short stories under the title *Der kleine Herr Friedemann*. In 1901 he published, in two volumes, his first novel, *Buddenbrooks*; the one-volume edition of 1903 brought triumph and fame without precedent (since the appearance of Goethe's *Werther*) in German literature. The book is firmly based on the nineteenth-century realist tradition (Fontane) but is supported by a philosophical substructure; the irony derives from a reluctance to prefer Schopenhauer's views on art and life to Nietzsche's, also from the way in which *Leitmotive* are employed. The decline of the Buddenbrooks family is accompanied by a growth of aesthetic sensibility, and music plays an undeniable part in the process. In 1903 the famous stories *Tristan* and *Tonio Kröger* were published, the former juxtaposing sterile aestheticism (Spinell) against vulgar common attitudes (Klöterjahn), with the music of Wagner occupying a central position, and the latter portraying in a most sympathetic form the 'verirrter Bürger' and the discomfort felt by the protagonist at being neither businessman nor Bohemian (the story has obvious autobiographical elements). In 1905 Thomas Mann married Katja Pringsheim: his new status (established writer, respectable family man) led to much bemused and trenchant speculation on the paradoxical nature of the bourgeois as artist and the relationship between order and disorder, the ethical and the aesthetic. The play *Fiorenza* (1906) was not a success: it dealt with the clash between beauty (the Medicis) and morality (Savonarola), and demonstrated Thomas Mann's tendency, occasionally simplistic, to think in antitheses, antitheses frequently held in an ironic tension. The novel *Königliche Hoheit* (1909) is light-hearted in tone, but also contains a serious theme: the problem of authentic living, of play-acting and the 'Hochstapler'-motif (the novel is also an allegorical portrayal of the 'poet-prince' who only achieves a genuine form of existence after marriage). The novel was coolly received and it was felt by many (including Heinrich Mann) that Thomas Mann had achieved fame too early and was simply writing popular entertainment. The remarkable Novelle Der Tod in Venedig (written in 1911) showed, however, that absolute mastery was still his: the story is a profound statement concerning artistry and order, where concentration on formal perfection is (ironically) shown to be fundamentally amoral. The similarities existing between author and protagonist (Aschenbach) are stressed, certainly as far as their literary output is concerned, but Aschenbach, without the saving gift of irony, is a tragic figure. This story of degeneration is told in a flawlessly classical style which verges at times on the hexameter; Wagner's description (in Mein Leben) of Venice, gondolas and cholera, may well have been known to Thomas Mann at this time; the life of the composer Gustav Mahler, also the fate of Winckelmann and Platen, likewise contributed to the masterpiece. Der Tod in Venedig is the climax of Thomas Mann's concern with aestheticism and decadence; he later referred to himself as 'Chronist und Erläuterer der Dekadenz, Liebhaber des Pathologischen und des Todes, einen Ästheten mit der Tendenz zum Abgrund', a statement relevant to this story, as it was to Wälsungenblut (published in 1906 but withdrawn), an acute depiction of narcissism and perversion.

As early as 1904 Thomas Mann had observed his brother's decision in favour of liberalism and the pursuit of social criticism (see entry under Mann, Heinrich); in 1911 the journal Pan had published Heinrich's essay Geist und Tat, which contained an attack upon those German intellectuals who had no understanding of, or interest in, political freedom. Thomas Mann insisted upon his adherence to an apolitical tradition, a specifically German tradition in his eyes. After the outbreak of war in 1914 Thomas Mann published his essay Friedrich und die große Koalition (December 1914) and attempted to understand, and presumably condone, the violation by Frederick of Saxon neutrality. A letter (April 1915) to the Svenska Dagbladet repeated and stressed the rightness of the German cause: the ideal of 'Das dritte Reich', culled from such thinkers as Bertram, Bondi and Moeller van den Bruck, was adumbrated. Heinrich Mann responded with his essay Zola (November 1915), an attack upon Germany, and also upon his brother. Thomas Mann sought to define his position vis-à-vis Heinrich, and also the democratic, Western tradition; the fruits of his speculation were the Betrachtungen eines Unpolitischen (1918), a reply to his brother's recriminations, and also to the criticisms of such writers as Romain Rolland who were appalled at Thomas Mann's utterances. He, Mann, argued that the German spirit (or Geist) was incommensurate with the shallow ideals of Western democracy and that the German contribution to world culture – music and metaphysics – had nothing in common with the ideals of the French Revolution. The artist must accept the primitive and the vital; he must seek the purifying element of war and not flinch from extolling suffering and hardness. This huge essay (some six hundred pages) is built up of antitheses: it may be called a book full of wrong ideas and splendid insights, often brilliantly expressed. It is an anti-Heinrich work and, remarkably, as a diary entry for 1917 explains, an expression of a 'sexual inversion', an admiration for the blond, blue-eyed German ideal of manhood. It was small wonder that Heinrich Mann, with *Der Untertan* (1918), should have made a much more favourable impression, and the relationship between the two brothers was at its most embittered at this time. The stories *Herr und Hund* and *Gesang vom Kindchen* (in hexameters), both of 1919, show a more relaxed attitude on Thomas Mann's part, although the latter refers, with a hint of reprimand, to the Allied blockade and the shortcomings that it had caused.

'Keine Metamorphose des Geistes ist uns besser vertraut als die, an deren Anfang die Sympathie mit dem Tode, an deren Ende der Entschluß zum Lebensdienste steht.' Thomas Mann's more sympathetic appraisal of his brother's position, and the realization of the dangers inherent in an extremely nationalistic, German, romantic attitude led to a salutary change of direction in his thinking. The murder of Walther Rathenau (1922) shocked him deeply, and his address in memory of the statesman acknowledged the need for vigilance and political awareness; his Berlin oration *Von deutscher Republik* (1922) bestowed his blessing on the new form of government, albeit in a highly personal manner. The *rapprochement* between the two brothers followed, particularly after Heinrich's severe illness. In 1924 there followed the second great novel, *Der Zauberberg*, an intellectual masterpiece of the highest sophistication, a rich fabric of many strands, the most important of which being the education of Hans Castorp, a 'Sorgenkind des Lebens' and symbol for Germany, 'das Land der Mitte'. In 1915 Thomas Mann had stressed the 'Sympathie mit dem Tode' which his novel would express; later he took stock of this 'fascination with death' and ironically reassessed many of his earlier attitudes (the 'aristocracy of sickness' being the most important). The *Berghof* sanatorium becomes a Europe in microcosm, and aestheticism is rejected in favour of life; this profound, complex and highly entertaining novel seeks a balance between facile humanism and the romantic abyss. Thomas Mann's magnanimity of spirit is seen in the fact that his earlier views are here put into the mouth of the sinister Naphta, whereas his brother's are expressed by Settembrini, a man predictable and worthy in his beliefs, yet fundamentally decent. Naphta's suicide demonstrates the self-destructive nature of those doctrines of mysticism and terror which may be fascinating, but also irresponsible. Castorp passes through the carnage of Armageddon; the novel leaves little hope for his survival, but his intellectual and emotional experiences in the sanatorium have taught him to see clearly the dangers of irrationalism and the need for balance. The book is also a highly ironic *Bildungsroman*: Castorp's progress is viewed in a detached manner, as are the antics of the other *habitués* of the *Berghof*. *Der Zauberberg* confirmed Thomas Mann's position as Germany's leading novelist, and the Nobel prize (1929) acknowledged his European stature. The short story *Unordnung und frühes Leid* (1926) portrays a domestic situation with acute psychological penetration; *Mario und der Zauberer* (1930) demonstrates a keen awareness of the roots of fascism and its kinship with perverted aestheticism.

In February 1933 Thomas Mann delivered his lecture on Wagner (*Leiden und Größe Richard Wagners*) in Munich; his description of the more questionable aspects of the composer's work led to an outcry in political circles and he was advised not to return to Germany after his lecture tour. His speeches *Deutsche Ansprache* and *Ein Appell an die Vernunft* (1930) had sought to warn his fellow-countrymen of the dangers of irrationalism, and the triumph of Nazism in 1933 confirmed his worst fears. He moved to Sanary-sur-mer and from there to Küsnacht near Zurich. In that year, 1933, he published the first part of his tetralogy *Joseph und seine Brüder*, entitled *Die Geschichten Jaakobs*; parts two and three, *Der junge Joseph* and *Joseph in Ägypten* were published in 1934 and 1936, and the fourth part, *Joseph der Ernährer*, in 1943. These novels represent the summit of Thomas Mann's achievement, and the creative use of myth found in them is meant as an answer to its wilful distortion by hysterical demagogues in Germany. To find a German writer in the 1930s who treated the origins of the Jewish race with sympathy, humour and enormous erudition was also gratifying. The figure of Joseph embodies the grace, the insouciance and the trusting self-confidence of the later 'rogue' Felix Krull, and benediction and ultimate wisdom prevail: a salutary antidote to the sombre violence of the times. *Lotte in Weimar* (1939), a playful account of the meeting between the elderly Charlotte Buff and the sage of Weimar, drew the world's attention to a different, cultured, Germany (but Goethe's shortcomings are also depicted). In 1939 Thomas Mann moved to a professorship in Princeton, New Jersey; he moved to California in 1942, where he was to remain for ten years. He became a US citizen in 1944 (he had been Czech since 1936); he also made many radio broadcasts to Germany (*Deutsche Hörer! 55 Radiosendungen nach Deutschland*) in 1945. It was entirely appropriate that Thomas Mann's preoccupation with Goethe should give way to an awareness of the possibilities of using the Faust legend to describe the apparently Satanic temptation into which Germany had fallen; the basic themes of Thomas Mann's *œuvre* – the relationship between art and disease, the tension between Germany and Western Europe, the special and ambiguous nature of music within the arts – are taken to extremes in his last great novel *Doktor Faustus. Das Leben des deutschen Tonsetzers Adrian Leverkühn, erzählt von einem Freunde* (1947). The figure of Adrian Leverkühn, so closely modelled on Nietzsche, exemplifies in Thomas Mann's view the modern artist who, threatened by sterility, turns to diabolic influences for the gift of creativity, the *Durchbruch* which Germany also achieved, but at fearful cost. Thomas Mann puts the story into the mouth of Serenus Zeitblom, representative of German bourgeois culture at its finest: the tension between narrator and subject matter (genius, syphilis and madness) is apparent, and Thomas Mann is able to parody his own prolix verbosity and mandarin dignity in Zeitblom's style of discourse. The book is a sombre portrayal of German irrationalism and violence, but lightened also by the belief that the greatest sinner may find absolution. A light-hearted variation on the theme of the great sinner and his forgiveness is *Der Erwählte* (1951), a reworking of Hartmann von Aue's *Gregorius*. Thomas Mann's consummate skill at dealing with potentially offensive material is also seen in the story *Die Betrogene* (1953), where nature is depicted as not being entirely devoid of ambiguity. The last work of fiction, written at the end of his life, is the *Bekenntnisse des Hochstaplers Felix Krull. Der*

Memoiren erster Teil (1954), a highly entertaining novel which charts the fortunes of 'Felix', the happy one who moves through society as a charming trickster, a final and humorous variation on the theme of the amoral artist-figure. The *Versuch über Schiller* (1955), a tribute to the great dramatist, is a collection of speeches, made shortly before Thomas Mann's death.

Thomas Mann's magisterial stance, his immense erudition, psychological finesse and ironic subtlety have little equal in German, in world literature. Heir to the nineteenth-century tradition, he, the apparently conservative writer, remained aloof from the more extreme experiments in the modern novel, yet his use of parody and his awarenes of the dichotomy between author and fictional world make him a highly sophisticated writer. A self-conscious element is undeniable, also occasional mannerisms and a not infrequent pomposity ('Wo ich bin ist Deutschland'). His position as one of Germany's greatest novelists is unassailable. The *Gesammelte Werke* appeared between 1922 and 1925 (ten vols), and were reprinted in 1929. The Stockholm *Gesamtausgabe* (twelve vols) was published from 1938 to 1956, and *Gesammelte Werke* (twelve vols) appeared in 1955, to be followed by a thirteen-volume edition in 1974. *Das erzählerische Werk* (twelve vols) appeared in 1975, the *Ausgewählte Essays* in 1972. The *Gesammelte Werke* (twenty vols) was published from 1980, and the *Tagebücher* (7 vols) from 1980 to 1989.

Martens, Kurt (1870–1945)

Martens, formerly a civil servant, made his reputation in 1898 with his novel *Roman aus der Décadence*, an exemplary *fin de siècle* portrayal of decadent attitudes (Martens had also published, in *Die Jugend*, poems dealing with cruelty and perversion). From 1899 to 1927 he lived in Munich and associated with most of the literary figures in that city: he was a friend of **Thomas Mann**, who had wished to use the title of Martens's book as a subtitle for *Buddenbrooks*. Other novels include *Die Vollendung* (1902), *Kreislauf der Liebe* (1906), *Jan Friedrich* (1916), *Gabriele Bach* (1935), *Die junge Cosima* (1937) and *Verzicht und Vollendung* (1941): these met with little success. A volume of *Novellen, Katastrophen*, appeared in 1904. He also wrote a play on the figure of Kaspar Hauser. The autobiography *Schonungslose Lebenschronik* (1921–4), in two volumes, gives a memorable account of the literary Bohemia of Munich. Martens settled in Dresden after 1927; after the air raid on that city (February 1945) he committed suicide.

Marti, Kurt (1921–)

Marti has since 1961 been a Protestant parish priest in Berne, Switzerland. Since 1959 he has written poetry which in form approaches the concrete style of **Gomringer** but in content reflects an engagement with contemporary issues inspired by the gospels, *republikanische gedichte* (1959), *gedichte am* *rand* (1963), notes in the margin of St Mark's gospel, *leichenreden* (1969), unconventional funeral speeches, and poems in Bernese dialect *rosa loui* (1967) (i.e. pink avalanche) and *undereinisch* (1973). A selection of poems written between 1959 and 1980 (*Schon wieder heute*) appeared in 1982.

Marti's prose includes *Dorfgeschichten 1960* extended as *Wohnen zeitaus. Geschichten zwischen Dorf und Stadt* (1965), character sketches of villagers in various short forms, *Paraburi* (1972) and *Abratzki oder Die kleine Brockhütte. Lexikon in einem Band* (1971), both with a strong element of fantasy, and the political diary *Zum Beispiel Bern 1972* (1973), in which he joins his writing compatriots **Frisch** and **Muschg** as a critic of his homeland.

Maurer, Georg (1907–71)

Born in the German-speaking enclave in Romanian Transylvania, Maurer studied from 1926 to 1934 in Germany, became a journalist, soldier and Soviet POW, returning to Germany in 1945. Maurer's work forms an important link between **J. R. Becher** and the younger generation of GDR poets, several of whom (**Braun**, **Rainer** and **Sarah Kirsch**) he influenced directly as a teacher at the Johannes R. Becher Institute of Literature in Leipzig. However, he is barely known in the West, partly because his work has been inaccessible, partly because poets in the Federal Republic found an alternative strand of GDR poetry with its roots in **Brecht** more appealing and adaptable to their aims. His early work draws on **Rilke** and even after his contact with Marxism, which influenced his choice of subject and attitude – celebration of man's achievements, including occasionally industrial projects on the Soviet model – he remained loyal to traditional hymnic forms which allow the direct expression of emotion, especially in the key transitional work *Gesänge der Zeit* (1948), containing religious poems modelled on Hölderlin and sonnet cycles conveying a belief in man as part of nature and able to master it. Of his numerous other collections *Die Elemente* (1955) evoking the four elements of earth, air, fire and water in conjunction with the human capacities evident in art, love and work, the popular *Drei-Strophen-Kalender* (1961), in the form of an almanach, *Das Unsere* (1962), perhaps his most substantial work, *Erfahrene Welt* (1972), in which Achilles, Frederick the Great and Macbeth represent man's warlike proclivities, and *Variationen* (1965), on poems by Shakespeare, Schiller and Brecht, deserve mention. *Werke* in two volumes appeared in 1987.

Mayröcker, Friederike (1924–)

Born in Vienna, Mayröcker taught English in secondary schools there from 1946 to 1969 and has been associated with the *Wiener Gruppe*, the *Grazer Autorenversammlung* and above all with Ernst **Jandl**, with whom she has collaborated on four radio plays and a television film. Her work is difficult to categorize; based on the Wittgensteinian notion of 'Welt als Sprache' and marked by free association, even 'écriture automatique' in the manner of the surrealists, quotation, montage, dislocation of syntax, it relies heavily on dreams and the shifting mental states induced by introspection and moves steadily away from direct expression of emotion, metamorphosis being a key term for its understanding. *Ausgewählte Gedichte*, containing poems written between 1944 and 1978, appeared in 1979. In her prose works the vicissitudes of personal relations between the sexes are registered; of these *Reise durch die Nacht* (1984) is typical. Her radio plays are collected in *Fünf Mann Menschen* (1971) and *Schwarmgesang. Szenen für die poetische Bühne* (1978).

Meckel, Christoph (1935–)

The son of the writer Eberhard Meckel (1907–69), the discovery of whose diaries led to the composition of *Suchbild. Über meinen Vater* (1980), the character portrait of a cultural fellow-traveller in the Third Reich, Christoph Meckel grew up in Freiburg, the destruction of which by Allied bombs in 1944 is the subject of the story 'Der Brand'. He studied graphic art and travelled extensively, teaching at American universities. His numerous works in verse and prose, several of which are illustrated by his own graphics, are marked by a childlike, whimsical and grotesque imagination, occasionally by a preoccupation with death (*Manifest der Toten* (1960, 1971)) and a predilection for adventurers and vagabonds (*Der wahre Muftoni* (1982)). The state of Germany is the subject of some poems, implicit also in the dialogue of ten sonnets with fellow-poet Volker von **Törne**, *Die Dummheit liefert uns ans Messer* (1967, 1983). Typical of his prose works are *Tullipan* (1965), in which the author is confronted by a creature of his own imagination whose failure to adjust to reality turns him into a social outsider who eventually disappears, except for occasional manifestations in the author's dreams, and *Bockshorn* (1973), about the fantastic journey of two small boys in search of a guardian angel. In *Nachricht für Baratynski* (1981) a nineteenth-century Russian poet is commemorated in an original mixture of genres. Episodes from a failed love-affair related in the prose work *Licht* (1978) appear in the poems of *Säure* (1979) and *Souterrain* (1984). Meckel's stories are collected in *Der glückliche Magier* (1967) and *Ein roter Faden* (1983) and a selection of his poems forms *Ausgewählte Gedichte 1955 bis 1978*, while *Werkauswahl. Lyrik, Prosa, Hörspiel* (1971, 1981) offers a cross-section of work in three genres.

Mehring, Walter (1896–1981)

Mehring's work is typical of the 'neue Sachlichkeit' which was the main cultural trend during the Weimar Republic and received belated recognition on its republication shortly before his death. His roots lie in expressionism –

his first poems and plays appeared in *Der Sturm* before the First World War, in which he served – and in Berlin Dada, which he helped to found. He worked for the cabarets *Schall und Rauch* and *Wilde Bühne*, where his satirical talent found scope in chansons combining attacks on the reactionary ballast of the Weimar system with formal experimentation (collage, jazz rhythms, travesty of traditional forms). His play *Der Kaufmann von Berlin*, subtitled 'Ein historisches Schauspiel aus der deutschen Inflation', caused a scandal when it was produced by Erwin Piscator in 1929, and the play *Die höllische Komödie* (1932) could not be performed in Germany. Mehring's exile took him to Paris, then after internment in France in 1940–1 to the USA, from which he returned to Europe an American citizen in the late 1950s. The poems and chansons written in Berlin, *Ketzerbrevier* (1921), *Die Gedichte, Lieder und Chansons des W. M.* (1929) and *Arche Noah SOS – ein neues trostreiches Liederbuch* (1931), were republished in the two volumes of *Chronik der Lustbarkeiten* (1983), the later poems in *Staatenlos im Nirgendwo* (1981). Mehring's fiction includes the novels *Paris in Brand* (1927), set in seventeenth-century France but aimed at the gutter press, *Müller. Chronik einer deutschen Sippe* (1935), in which the recurrence of the servile spirit in German history is traced through generations of the title-family from Tacitus to Hitler, *Die Nacht des Tyrannen* (1937) and the Novelle, *Algier oder die 13 Oasenwunder* (1927). *Die verlorene Bibliothek* (1952, extended 1964) combines autobiography and literary criticism.

Meister, Ernst (1911–79)

Meister's life apart from war service was uneventful and his work outside the main stream. His poems, published in numerous collections between 1953 and his death (apart from *Ausstellung* of 1932), is laconic, hermetic, meditative, melancholy, close to Hölderlin and **Celan** in form – the collection *Sage vom Ganzen den Satz* (1972) was inspired by the coincidence of Hölderlin's two-hundredth birthday and Celan's death – and especially in the later volumes, close to Pascal, Montaigne, Nietzsche and Kierkegaard in its focus on the themes of transience and death. His plays are also bleak, e.g. in the radio play *Die Botschaft* (1970) poor desert dwellers learn that their home is about to become the site of an atom bomb test. Meister also wrote in French and painted. *Ausgewählte Gedichte*, containing poems written between 1932 and publication date, appeared in 1977 and 1979. A complete edition, *Sämtliche Gedichte*, followed in 1981.

Mell, Max (1882–1971)

Born in Marburg, Southern Styria (now Maribor), Max Mell moved to Vienna; his first volume of prose, *Lateinische Erzählungen*, appeared in 1904. This was followed by the *Novellen, Die Grazien des Traumes* (1906),

Jägerhaussage (1910) and the poems *Das bekränzte Jahr* (1911). Mell served in the army in the First World War; after 1918 his writing became predominantly religious in tone, the expression of a desire to uphold Christian values. *Das Wiener-Kripperl von 1919* (1921) describes the appearance, on Christmas Eve, of angels in a Viennese tram-car. His most successful play was *Apostelspiel* (1922), where innocence and love triumph over criminality. *Schutzengelspiel* (1923) portrays salvation through humility; *Nachfolge-Christi-Spiel* (1927) shows again the redemptive power of love. Mell uses *Knittelvers* in these 'Spiele', which are best seen as modern mystery plays. In *Die Sieben gegen Theben* (1932) he reworks the classical Greek story; *Spiel von den deutschen Ahnen* (1935) stresses the traditional rural values. *Der Nibelunge Not* (1951) stresses the vision of Dietrich von Bern; *Jeanne d'Arc* (1956) is a specifically Christian drama; *Paracelsus und der Lorbeer* (1964) speaks again of the power of vision. In his poetry Max Mell evokes the Styrian landscape ('Die Stadt auf dem Hügel', 'Der milde Herbst von Anno 45', 'Bauernhof in den Alpen', etc.). The prose works include *Barbara Naderers Viehstand* (1914), *Morgenwege* (1924) and *Das Donauweibchen* (1938). *Steierischer Lobgesang* (1939) again portrays the Styrian countryside; the collection *Verheißungen* attempts a Stifter-like simplicity. Mell was also an active editor and anthologist. His *Gesammelte Werke* (four vols) appeared in 1962; *Herz werde groß. Gedichte und Dramen* in 1982.

Meyrink, Gustav (pseudonym of Gustav Meyer, 1868–1932)

Illegitimate son of a Swabian aristocrat and a Bavarian actress (he took his mother's name before using the pseudonym), Meyrink is famous above all for *Der Golem*, a fantastic novel set in the Jewish ghetto in Prague. He had also published a collection of mainly satirical stories (see 'Das Wildschwein Veronika') under the title *Des deutschen Spießers Wunderhorn* (three vols) in 1913 (reprinted in 1981). A devotee of the occult, Meyrink was well known in Prague in the years before the First World War for his eccentric behaviour and necromantic practices. He was closely associated with **Kubin**, whose *Die andere Seite* was inspired by the opening sketches for *Der Golem*. After 1911 Meyrink, whose banking ventures met with no success, lived in isolation near Munich. His later novels include *Das grüne Gesicht* (1916), *Walpurgisnacht* (1917), *Der weiße Dominikaner* (1921) and *Der Engel vom westlichen Fenster* (1927). Meyrink was also an accomplished translator (of Charles Dickens above all). Theoretical writings include *An der Grenze des Jenseits* (1923). His plays met with no success. The *Gesammelte Werke* (six vols) appeared in 1917; the *Werke* were published in 1983.

Miegel, Agnes (1879–1964)

Known as the 'Patrona Borussiae', Agnes Miegel was born and lived most of her life in Königsberg. Encouraged by Börries von **Münchhausen**, who would later call her 'zweifellos der größte lebende Balladendichter', she published poetry in his *Göttinger Musenalmanach* (1901); in 1902 she went to Clifton College for Girls as a teacher of German and wrote 'Die Nibelungen', one of her most successful ballads. On her return to Königsberg she worked as a journalist for the *Ostpreußische Zeitung*; *Balladen und Lieder* were published in 1907. In 1913 she received the Kleist prize. She also studied and emulated the *Volkslied*, turning her attention particularly to East Prussian themes. She received an honorary doctorate of the University of Königsberg in 1924; in 1926 she published a prose work, *Geschichten aus Altpreußen*. In the following year her *Gesammelte Gedichte* appeared; in the 1930s she published many stories, frequently in groups. Becoming more and more associated with her East Prussian background she was greeted by the Nazis as an exemplary regional writer; in the journal *Ostland* she published a poem 'An den Führer' (1940) with obligatory praises. In February 1945 she was forced to flee Königsberg (in *Gespräch mit den Ahnen* (1936), she had prophesied its destruction) and was interned in Denmark; the story *Fischtag im Lager* and the poems of *Du aber bleibst in mir* (1953) describe her experiences. Religious themes predominate in her late work. East Prussian nationalistic *Landsmannschaften* claimed her support in the 1950s, but she remained free of chauvinistic excesses and anti-Soviet feeling. She died in Bad Salzuflen in 1964. *Gesammelte Werke* appeared between 1952 and 1955; *Gedichte. Erzählungen. Erinnerungen* in 1965.

Mombert, Alfred (1874–1942)

A lawyer who turned to writing, Mombert lived most of his life in Heidelberg. He is above all a lyric poet, fervent and dedicated to spiritual realities. The early collection *Tag und Nacht* (1894) contains impressionist-naturalistic elements, plus a *Jugendstil* tendency; *Der Glühende* (1896) is dedicated to Richard **Dehmel** and also met with the enthusiastic praise of **Przybyszewski** and Martin Buber. Nietzschean imagery predominates, also an ecstatic, cosmic atmosphere. The collection *Die Schöpfung* (1897) contains the famous 'Stürz' ein, o Seele, und erwache im Chaos'; the rhapsodic sweep of many of the poems is akin to certain aspects of expressionism (Herwarth **Walden** organized a reading of Mombert's poetry in 1906 in Berlin). An oriental element becomes apparent in Mombert's work, Persian mysticism above all. The cycle *Der Denker* (1901) is dedicated to the constellation of Orion. *Der Sonne Geist* (1905), entitled 'Mythos', is similar to the work of **Däubler**. Mombert also turned to lyrical drama; after *Die Blüte des Chaos* (1905) he worked at *Aeon. Dramatische Trilogie* (1907–11), a *Stationendrama* with mystical dimensions. The concept of 'Sfaira', emerging in this trilogy, is best understood as a creative, spiritual act. Mombert's need to view all human experience *sub specie aeternitatis* is seen above all in *Der Held der Erde* (1914–19) and *Atair* (1925).

Mombert lived in increasing isolation; as a Jew he was expelled from the Prussian Academy in 1933. In 1936 the publication of his *Sfaira der Alte* was greeted with derision, although Hans **Carossa** had the courage to honour his work. In 1940 he was seized by the Gestapo and taken to the French detention camp at Gurs. He was allowed entry into Switzerland in 1941 but died shortly afterwards. The second part of *Sfaira der Alte* describes in mythological terms the horrors of imprisonment and torture, but the collection ends on a note of mystic rapture. *Ausgewählte Werke* appeared in 1952; *Der himmlische Zecher* (published originally in 1909, and enlarged in 1922) was reprinted in 1951. *Dichtungen* (three vols) were published in 1963.

Morgenstern, Christian (1871–1914)

Son of an artist, Morgenstern studied at Breslau University and later turned to translation (of Ibsen predominantly), journalism (in Berlin) and writing. He was greatly influenced by Nietzsche in his early poetry (*In Phanta's Schloß* (1895) is dedicated to him), although a humorous quality is also frequently at play. The Norwegian experiences (he had travelled to Norway to meet Ibsen) are also reflected in the early poems; these, plus Nietzschean images, convey a mythical world of mountain, ice and fire. Morgenstern turned to Buddhism, also to the theosophy of Rudolf Steiner: the last collection of poems, *Wir fanden einen Pfad* (1914), is dedicated to him. In the winter of 1905–6 Morgenstern underwent certain mystical experiences after reading Meister Eckhart, and began his *Tagebuch eines Mystikers*; the anthologies *Melancholie* (1906), *Einkehr* (1910) and *Ich und Du* (1911) chart the poet's spiritual development, a path leading towards a Christian mysticism tinged with anthroposophy. Morgenstern wrestled with tuberculosis for most of his life, but remained basically an optimist: humour and grotesque situations are found in the well-known poems *Galgenlieder* (1905), *Palmström* (1910) and the posthumous *Palma Kunkel* (1916), *Der Gingganz* (1919) and *Die Schallmühle* (1928). *Alle Galgenlieder* were published in 1932 and made the hapless Palmström and Korf known throughout Europe. Morgenstern is, however, basically a serious poet who sought to express spiritual verities. As a member of the Anthroposophical Society he travelled to Oslo and Budapest to hear Steiner lecture; after his death in the spring of 1914 he was cremated, his ashes being later deposited in the Goetheanum at Dornach. In 1965 the *Gesammelte Werke* appeared, to be followed by *Sämtliche Dichtungen* (seventeen vols) between 1971 and 1979. A *Jubiläumsausgabe* (four vols) was also published in 1979. Werke and Briefe (*Stuttgarter Ausgabe*) began to appear in 1987.

Morgner, Irmtraud (1933–90)

After studying at the Leipzig Institute of Literature and helping to edit the magazine *Neue Deutsche Literatur* Morgner published her first story in 1959 a year after becoming free-lance. Her early works conform to the conventions of socialist realism, although the unpublished *Rumba auf einen*

Herbst breaks new ground by treating a then taboo subject, the disillusionment of the younger generation after Khrushchev's denunciation of Stalin in 1956. With *Hochzeit in Konstantinopel* (1968) she turned to what has remained her principal theme, on which she has developed increasingly complex and imaginative variations, the conflict of rationality and fantasy in relation to the male-female polarity in history, legend and the present. In *Gauklerlegende. Eine Spielfrauengeschichte* (1970), *Die wundersamen Reisen Gustav des Weltfahrers. Lügenhafter Roman mit Kommentaren* (1972), drawing on a submerged literary tradition (the picaresque novel and the open-ended fantasy of Jean Paul), she has devised a specifically GDR form of magic realism, which has been further elaborated in the first two parts of a planned trilogy, *Leben und Abenteuer der Trobadora Beatriz nach Zeugnissen ihrer Spielfrau Laura* (1974) and *Amanda. Ein Hexenroman* (1983). In *Trobadora Beatriz* the title-figure, a time traveller from the Middle Ages, accompanies a journalist whom she meets during the Paris *événements* of 1968 to the GDR in order to test his claim that women have attained emancipation there. Disappointed on arrival, she engages as her 'Spielfrau' Laura Salman, mother of two and *S-Bahn* driver, and together they go in search of men who might fulfil their expectations of a balanced partnership. Only Laura finds the object of her desire, while Beatriz accidentally falls to her 'death' after her return to Paris. *Amanda* is more fantastic in its radical renewal and critical reinterpretation of German folk mythology. The witch Amanda, who is Laura's *alter ego*, persuades her to resume her alchemical studies in preparation for a general revolution of witches against the patriarchal domination represented by the chief devil, Kolbuk, whose domain, the Blocksberg, becomes the officially licensed scene of tame revels during *Walpurgisnacht*, while the Hörselberg, once the home of fully emancipated witches, has become a brothel for Kolbuk's underlings. Laura, faced with the prospect of marriage either to Kolbuk or to the equally patriarchal chief angel Zacharias, flees in search of a suitable male identification-figure for her son. She finds him in the person of her former boyfriend, who however is captured by Kolbuk. A postlude presents Amanda triumphant as President of the Blocksberg after a successful revolution by the witches, to be related in the third part of the trilogy. This, judging from its two published parts, should rank with similar works by **Grass**, **Stefan Heym** and **Stefan Schütz** as a contribution to the revival of fiction in the German Romantic tradition by recourse to myth, legend and folklore which is such a marked feature of recent German literature.

Mühsam, Erich (1878–1934)

Son of middle-class Jewish parents, Mühsam became an anarchist and took part in the Bavarian soviet revolution of 1918–9. He had published poetry and narrative prose before 1914 (*Die Wüste. Gedichte* (1904) and *Der Krater* (1909)) but turned his attention increasingly to political agitation. He edited *Kain. Zeitschrift für Menschlichkeit* from 1911–25, was imprisoned for his anarchist activities and, on his release, sought to organize a united front against the threat of fascism. The story *Die Affenschande* (1923) mocked the Nazi racial doctrines, as did his last play *Alle Wetter* (1930), which also satirized the so-called 'Workers' Racial Party'. A chanson, *Republikanische National-hymne* (1924) is a scurrilous attack on the legal system. In 1925 he published *Revolution. Kampf-, Marsch- und Spottlieder*; he edited *Fanal. Anarchistische Monatsschrift* from 1926 to 1933 and in 1928 published *Staatsräson. Ein Denkmal für Sacco und Vanzetti. Sammlung 1898–1928* (1928) is a collection of poetry and prose, plus a 'Selbstbiographie'. Mühsam, being Jewish, anarchist and a virulent opponent of fascism, was an obvious target for the Nazis; he was arrested a few hours after the burning of the Reichstag (1933). For over a year he was tortured and humiliated: pieces of his beard were torn out to make him appear the 'typical Jew' of *Der Stürmer* and other anti-Semitic tracts. His mutilated corpse was found hanging in a latrine at Oranienburg concentration camp (10 July 1934). The *Ausgewählte Werke* (two vols) appeared in 1958; a *Gesamtausgabe* (five vols) in 1977; a further *Ausgewählte Werke* (again two vols) in 1978. *Ich möchte Gott sein und Gebete hören. Prosa, Gedichte, Stücke* (two vols) appeared in 1981, the *Gesammelte Aufsätze* in 1989.

Müller, Heiner (1929–)

After work as a journalist and editor, Müller became a professional writer in 1959 and has since been employed at different times as literary adviser at all the major theatres in East Berlin. In recent years he has been able to move freely between East and West, where he has exerted considerable influence as director of his own and others' plays (e.g. **Brecht**'s *Fatzer* fragment). Two traumatic experiences, the arrest and imprisonment of his father by the Nazis in 1933 and later, and the suicide of his wife Inge in 1966 have left their mark directly, in certain poems, and indirectly on his work. An account of his *œuvre* presents special difficulties, as some of his plays were conceived long before their first performances and written and occasionally revised over a long period. In most instances publication and première in East and West do not coincide. For long Müller shared with **Lange**, **Hacks** and **Volker Braun** the label of successor to Brecht, and he has been engaged through much of his career in a creative debate with him, adapting and developing his themes and forms, especially those of the *Lehrstücke*, so that *Mauser* can be related to *Die Maßnahme*, *Der Horatier* to *Die Horatier und die Kuriatier*, *Die Schlacht* to *Furcht und Elend des Dritten Reiches*, while in *Der Lohndrücker* (written in collaboration with his wife) he offers his own perspective on a real event treated by Brecht in his *Büsching* fragment, as well as by the GDR writers Eduard Claudius and Karl Grünberg. Although, in view of the experimental nature of Müller's work, his view of performance as a process generating an on-going open-ended interaction with the spectator any construction of creative phases and chronological divisions is artificial, it is possible to distinguish four groups of plays: first, those collected in the two volumes *Geschichten aus der Produktion*, including *Die Korrektur* (also written with Inge Müller, in two versions, 1957 and 1958), in which during the construction of a *Kombinat* in 1956 a Nazi foreman guilty of falsifying production figures is forced to leave the brigade, but the brigade leader is warned by the party secretary against outright rejection of those who appear compromised by their role in the Third Reich. *Der Bau* (two versions, 1963, 1964), based on *Spur der Steine* by Erik **Neutsch**, concerns the difficulties encountered during the transition to socialism on a major building site; *Traktor* (1974, written between 1955 and 1961) and *Die Umsiedlerin* (written between 1956 and 1961, published in 1975 in a new version as *Die Bauern*) deal with the same process in agriculture. The problems of critical decision-making in extreme situations of war and revolution are the subject of a 'Versuchsreihe' or series of experiments consisting of *Mauser* (1970), *Philoktet* (1966), *Der Horatier* (1973), *Zement* (1974), *Wolokolamsker Chaussee I–V* (1988). *Philoktet* and other adaptations of the classics (*Prometheus* (Aeschylus) (1968), *Ödipus Tyrann* (Sophocles) (1969), *Herakles 5* (1966)), unlike those of Hacks, focus on the brutal struggles of history rather than on the prospect of harmony in a future Utopia. Müller turned to German history in *Die Schlacht* (1975), five scenes showing the dehumanization suffered during the Third Reich, *Germania Tod in Berlin* (written between 1956 and 1971, published in 1977), a collage of scenes set in the Berlin of 1918, the day of the GDR's foundation in 1949 and 17 June 1953, a juxtaposition of turning-points in German history which aims to convey its special tensions with the aid of surrealistic and burlesque interludes, culminating in a fragile but positive vision of the future. The critique of the Prussian ethos present in this play is expanded in more grotesque form in the 'Greuelmärchen' *Leben Gundlings Friedrich von Preußen Lessings Schlaf Traum Schrei* (1977), which offers variations on the theme of the intellectual's enforced subordination to the power of the state. With the Shakespeare adaptations *Macbeth* (1972), *Hamletmaschine* (1978) and *Anatomie Titus Fall of Rome* (1985), the last a version of *Titus Andronicus* Müller undertakes an ever more radical dissolution of traditional dramatic form continued in *Bildbeschreibung* (1985) and *Verkommenes Ufer Medeamaterial Landschaft mit Argonauten* (1983), which like the five parts of *Wolokolamsker Chaussee* (1988) read more like scenarios or extended stage directions than conventional plays. With these and with *Der Auftrag* (1979), based on one of Anna **Seghers**'s Caribbean stories, in which three men, two white and one black, deputed by the new French Republic to foment a slave uprising in the British colony of Jamaica, face the choice between commitment and betrayal when their commission is revoked, and *Quartett* (1981), an adaptation of Laclos's *Les liaisons dangereuses*, Müller may be said to have joined the main stream of international post-modernism. Yet interest in revolution and awareness of its potential have not diminished, finding expression now in treatment of Third World themes in *Der Auftrag* and the 'Nord-Süd-Stück' *Anatomie Titus Fall of Rome*. The thematic range and formal originality of his work, together with his influence on other past and present GDR dramatists (**Brasch**, **Stefan Schütz** and Volker **Braun**), make Müller one of the most important authors of the GDR and perhaps the most significant German-speaking dramatist of the present.

Münchhausen, Börries Freiherr von (1874–1945)

A descendant of the famous 'Lügenbaron', Börries von Münchhausen studied at different universities, served in the Horse Guards in the First World War and then settled down as a landed gentleman to cultivate the writing above all of ballads. From 1898 to 1923 he edited the *Göttinger Musenalmanach*; he encouraged the writer Agnes **Miegel** and was a friend of Lulu von **Strauss und Torney** and her husband, the right-wing publisher Eugen Diederichs, founding the so-called 'Göttinger-Kreis'. In 1900 he published *Balladen* and *Juda*, a collection of Old Testament ballads; *Ritterliches Liederbuch* followed in 1904. Other collections include *Das Herz im Harnisch* (1911), *Die Standarte* (1916) and *Schloß in Wiesen* (1921). A theory of the ballad form is set out in *Meisterballaden* (1923). *Fröhliche Wochen mit Freunden* (1922) is a light-hearted autobiography. Börries von Münchhausen cultivated successfully the pose of English country gentleman; his conservative stance was fundamentally apolitical and his welcome of the new regime in 1933 was tepid. Fearing the advance of the Russians in 1945 he committed suicide. *Das dichterische Werk* (two vols) appeared between 1950 and 1953; the *Ausgabe letzter Hand* from 1959.

Muschg, Adolf (1934–)

Muschg has combined a writing career with a number of academic posts in Tokyo, Göttingen, Ithaca (New York), Geneva and Zurich. A cosmopolitan Swiss, Muschg concentrates in his fiction on the personal and professional predicaments of intellectuals which he views with detachment, psychological acuteness and remarkable linguistic virtuosity. Art as illusion and necessary compensation for maladjustment to reality is the theme of the Frankfurt literature lectures *Literatur als Therapie?* (1981), as of several works. These features bring Muschg closer to the Anglo-American mainstream of fiction than any other German-speaking writer except **Martin Walser**.

In *Im Sommer des Hasen* (1965) six journalists visit Japan, each with the commission to write a personal account of the country for the Swiss firm which is financing them. In *Gegenzauber* (1967) a group of Bohemians save the inn which had become their meeting-place from demolition, but only by declaring it a museum. *Mitgespielt* (1969) concerns a homosexual teacher and the mysterious disappearance of his favourite pupil. In *Albissers Grund* (1974) a school-teacher shoots at his psychiatrist, whom the authorities expel because his radical ideas are seen as socially disruptive. In *Noch ein Wunsch* (1979) a middle-aged lawyer fails to renew a relationship with a much younger women to his own satisfaction. *Baiyun oder die Freundschaftsgesellschaft* (1980) varies the theme of Muschg's first novel by presenting the reactions of members of an eight-strong delegation to China when one of them is poisoned. In *Das Licht und der Schlüssel* (1984) the narrator portrays himself as a vampire practising nature therapy.

Two plays deserve mention: *Rumpelstilz* (1968), in which a hypochondriac

German teacher exploits his wife and daughter, and *Kellers Abend* (1975), in which Gottfried Keller, Ferdinand Lassalle and Georg Herwegh are shown in their response to the failure of the 1848 revolution. Keller is also the subject of a 1977 biography. Muschg's stories are collected in the volumes *Fremdkörper* (1968), *Liebesgeschichten* (1972), *Entfernte Bekannte* (1976), *Besuch in der Schweiz* (1978), *Leib und Leben* (1982) and *Der Turmhahn und andere Liebesgeschichten* (1987).

Musil, Robert (1880–1942)

Son of an engineer, Musil was born in Klagenfurt; he was a pupil at the military boarding-school at Mährisch-Weißkirchen and later (1897) studied at the Military Academy of Technology in Vienna. He studied machine construction at the Technological University in Brünn (Brno) where his father was professor, moved from there to Stuttgart (1902–3) and thence to Berlin, where he followed lectures on philosophy, mathematics, physics and experimental psychology at the university. In 1906 he published his first novel, *Die Verwirrungen des Zöglings Törleß*, a penetrating study of the problems of puberty and a sophisticated portrayal of the dual nature of things, where language is seen as inadequate in its attempt to define and delineate (a film version was made in 1966). In the same year Musil constructed a chromatometer for use in testing colour perception. He obtained his doctorate in 1908 with a thesis on Ernst Mach, but declined an academic post offered by the University of Graz. Between 1908 and 1910 he was involved in the literary activities in Berlin, but moved to Vienna in 1910 and worked as librarian at the Technological University. In 1911 he published *Vereinigungen*, two stories which, he claimed, 'leiteten, vielleicht durch Irrtum, den literarischen Expressionismus in Deutschland ein'. He contributed to the leading periodicals (including *Die neue Rundschau*) and published his first essay, 'Das Unanständige und Kranke in der Kunst'. Musil served as an officer in the army during the 1914–18 war, experiencing the fighting on the Italian front. He worked at a clerical post in the Foreign Office from 1919–20; in 1921 he met Ernst Rowohlt, who would become his publisher. During the 1920s he worked as a theatre critic in Vienna: in 1921 he published his first play *Die Schwärmer* and two years later his farce *Vinzenz oder die Freundin bedeutender Männer*. The three stories *Drei Frauen* (*Grigia, Die Portugiesin* and *Tonka*) were published in 1924; the precision and elegance of Musil's style were praised by **Döblin** who had recommended Musil for the Kleist prize in the previous year. In 1927 he read the memorial address for **Rilke** in Berlin. 1930 saw the publication of Book One of his vast novel *Der Mann ohne Eigenschaften* (a second volume, Book Two, would be published in 1933, and a third, unfinished, appeared in 1943 after Musil's death). This is a mercilessly precise, witty and sophisticated analysis of Austria-Hungary ('Kakanien') during its last months, observed by a 'man without qualities' who moves as a detached observer through the Viennese salons and registers the attitudes struck, the posturing and the rodomontade. The book is an acute study of a bankrupt society, yet also posits a mystical dimension, a journey 'ins tausendjährige Reich', where the protagonist experiences with his sister an ever-increasing intimacy. Musil believed that life was not to be grasped by ideologies and structured beliefs; an 'essayistic' life-style with its perspectivism and open-mindedness is infinitely preferable to the dogmatic and the categoried. The work is also an enormous *roman-à-clef* (there are portraits of Walther Rathenau, Ludwig Klages, Frank **Werfel** and others); Nietzschean histrionics and Wagnerian excess are also castigated. The fluid is extolled at the expense of the schematic; the gigantic work was, as Musil well knew, unfinishable. In 1934 the Musil Society in Berlin was dissolved and a similar society was founded in Vienna; between 1935 and 1936 Musil spoke at the International Conference of Writers for the Defence of Culture in Paris, and also went on a lecture tour of Switzerland, where he met **Thomas Mann**. *Nachlaß zu Lebzeiten* appeared in 1936. After the *Anschluß* (1938) Musil emigrated to Italy, then Switzerland; in 1939 he moved to Geneva, where he died of a stroke in 1942. In 1952 an extended version of *Der Mann ohne Eigenschaften* was edited by Adolf Frisé; this met with much controversy. *Tagebücher, Aphorismen, Essays und Reden* appeared in 1955, as did *Prosa, Dramen und späte Briefe*. The *Tagebücher* (two vols) of 1976 provided a fascinating quarry of intellectual insights, with 'M. le vivisecteur' as a dispassionate, analytic observer of phenomena. In 1978 a nine-volume pocket-book edition of the *Gesammelte Werke* appeared, containing a number of texts previously missed; a radically new presentation of the posthumous portions of *Der Mann ohne Eigenschaften* was also included. *Briefe* (two vols) appeared in 1980; *Gesammelte Werke* (two vols) in 1983; *Tagebücher* (two vols) also in 1983.

Mynona (pseudonym of Salomo Friedländer, 1871–1946)

A Jew from West Prussia, Salomo Friedländer studied medicine in Munich and philosophy in Berlin and Jena; he gained his doctorate in 1902 with a thesis on Schopenhauer's interpretation of Kant's *Kritik der reinen Vernunft*. In Berlin he published, under the pseudonym Mynona, in several of the expressionist journals; Franz Pfemfert dedicated to him the first issue of *Die Aktion* in 1913 and Herwarth **Walden** published many of his so-called 'Grotesken' in *Der Sturm*. Mynona also produced, with his cousin Anselm Ruest, his own periodical *Der Einzige* (1919–25). His most important philosophical tracts were *Friedrich Nietzsche. Eine intellektuelle Biographie* (1911), *Schöpferische Indifferenz* (1918) and *Der Philosoph Ernst Marcus als Nachfolger Kants* (1913): these works stress the importance of individual insight and insist upon a principle of polarity ('Indifferenz'). Apart from the 'Grotesken' in *Der Sturm* and elsewhere (*Gute Nacht, Aerosophie, Für Hunde und andere Menschen, Willi Willi, Beschreibung meiner Braut*, etc.) the following should be mentioned: *Durch blaue Schleier* (poems, 1908); *Rosa, die schöne Schutzmannsfrau* (1913); *Hundert Bonbons* (grotesque sonnets, 1918); the novel *Die Bank der Spötter. Ein Unroman* (1919); *Mein Papa und die Jungfrau von Orleans* (1921); the parody *Tarzaniade* (1924); *Hat Erich Maria Remarque wirklich gelebt?* (1929); *Der Holzweg zurück oder Knackes Umgang mit Flöhen* (1931). In September 1933 Mynona moved to Paris where he died in great poverty in 1946. *Rosa die schöne Schutzmannsfrau und andere Grotesken* was published in Zurich in 1965 in the series 'Frühe Texte der Moderne'. *Prosa* (two vols) was published in 1980 (vol. I: *Ich verlange ein Reiterstandbild*; vol. II: *Der Schöpfer*). *Das Eisenbahnunglück oder Der Anti-Freud* appeared in 1988, and *Graue Magie* in 1989.

N

Nebel, Otto (1892–1973)

Born in Berlin, Otto Nebel studied structural engineering before turning to acting, at the *Lessing-Theater*. His teacher, Rudolf Blümner, brought him into contact with the *Sturm* circle, and Nebel published his first work in *Der Sturm*, after spending four years in active service, in 1919. *Zuginsfeld* is acknowledged to be the most substantial attack on war in that journal, a satirical denunciation of the corruption of language encountered above all in military circles. In 1925 Nebel's second major contribution was *Runenfuge Unfeig*, later to be reworked and extended as *Das Rad der Titanen* (1957) and further as the unfinished *Sternendonner*. The 'Runen' system is a grotesque play with language which has certain similarities to the preoccupations of the Dadaists. Nebel constantly revised his work, particularly *Zuginsfeld*, which appeared in an extended version in 1974. *Das dichterische Werk* (three vols) was published in 1979.

Neumann, Alfred (1895–1952)

After Lion **Feuchtwanger**, with whom he shared in California part of his exile, Alfred Neumann was the most successful historical novelist of his generation. He supplied numerous variations of Feuchtwanger's early theme of the temptations of power as represented by the rise and fall of determined, dubious and ultimately vulnerable men, such as the 'Jud Süß' figure who becomes the power behind the throne in a German grand duchy around 1830 in *König Haber* (1926, dramatized as *Haus Danieli*, 1930). A similar character becomes the creature of Ludwig XI of France in *Der Teufel* (1926). *Rebellen* (1927) and *Guerra* (1928) concern the activities of the Carbonari in pre-Risorgimento Italy, while *Der Held* (1930) examines the psychology of an ex-officer who murders a minister modelled on Walther Rathenau. After *Narrenspiegel* (1932), on a dissipated petty princeling of the sixteenth century, Neumann produced his chief work, a trilogy on the life of Napoleon III, culminating in the events of 1870–1, in which a sixteen-year-old revolutionary apprentice involved in the Commune is made to epitomize the theme of the sudden change of fortune (*Neuer Cäsar* (1934), *Kaiserreich* (1936), *Die Volksfreunde* (1941) which was later entitled *Das Kind von Paris* (1952)). *Die Goldquelle* (1938), on a minister who falls victim to a financial scandal, and *Der Pakt* (1950), on the political confidence trickster Colonel Walker whose violent establishment of an independent republic in California is followed by a reign of terror as dictator of Nicaragua, mark a return to Neumann's first theme. *Es waren ihrer sechs* (1944), on the resistance group led by Hans and Sophie Scholl, became a bestseller in the USA, but was written too close in time and too far in space from the events on which it is based.

Neumann, Robert (1897–1975)

Born in Vienna, Neumann became suddenly famous on the publication of his parodies after years of struggle as a writer and work in business. Having ridiculed the Nazis, who publicly burned his books, he emigrated to Britain in 1932, settling at Cranbrook, Kent, moving later to Locarno, Switzerland. Like his namesake, **Alfred Neumann**, Robert Neumann was fascinated by the rootless confidence trickster, but he portrayed him (or her) in a less sinister light and in a twentieth-century setting. His mastery of the art of parody, for which he is now remembered (*Mit fremden Federn* (1927), *Unter falscher Flagge* (1932), both volumes combined with seventy new parodies in *Die Parodien* (1962)) is also evident in his fiction, especially works in which a fictional narrator tells his/her own life story in a distinctive style (*Hochstapler-Novelle* (1930), as *Die Insel der Circe* (1952), *Karriere* (1931), confessions of a Hungarian courtesan who is adopted by an English lord, *Olympia* (1961), the autobiography of the sister of **Thomas Mann**'s Felix Krull), and in which the style of famous authors is adopted (Boccaccio in the collections of 'Novellen' *Die Pest von Lionara* (1927), Joyce in the novel *Bibiana Santis. Der Weg einer Frau* (1950; published in English as *The Inquest*, 1945)). His other novels, mainly based on contemporary events, include *Sintflut* (1929) on inflation in Austria, *Die Macht* (1932) on the activities of forgers and the ambitions of Nazis, *Children of Vienna* (1946; *Kinder von Wien*, 1948) on the deprivation suffered by children at the end of the Second World War, *Bibiana Santis* on the exile odyssey of a woman, *Die Puppen von Poshansk* (1952) set in the Soviet Gulag, and *Der Tatbestand oder Der gute Glaube der Deutschen* (1965) on the failure of the Federal Republic's judicial system to deal adequately with Nazi crimes. Other works are the historical novel *Struensee* (1935; as *Der Favorit der Königin*, 1953), on the Danish minister ousted from power in 1772, and *By the Waters of Babylon* (1939; *An den Wassern von Babylon*, 1945), ten stories about Jews down the ages.

Neutsch, Erik (1931–)

Neutsch, who has been a member of the SED since 1949 and, after a period as a journalist and party activist, a writer since 1960, can be considered, along with **Strittmatter**, the most successful and prolific of the officially approved socialist realists, who combines a detailed portrayal of the working environment with unstereotyped characterization. The twelve *Bitterfelder*

Geschichten (1961) present the work of socialist brigades according to the formula put forward at the Bitterfeld Conference of 1959 that writers should gain first-hand experience of working practices and reflect them in their fiction. The monumental *Spur der Steine* (1964), set on a huge construction site, reflects changes in the organization of work introduced by the new economic system and the consequent switch of focus from the labourer to the technical expert. A team leader is forced to abandon Stakhanovite working practices when shift-work is introduced by the party secretary, who is succeeded in his post by a zealous dogmatist when he fails to stand by the woman he has made pregnant. Neither of these men, nor the title-figure of *Auf der Suche nach Gatt* (1973) can be described as a positive hero; Gatt's progress from miner to hardline journalist who becomes alienated from his wife and drives her employer to flee the country culminates in divorce, breakdown, three years in a sanatorium and a return to the mine, when his career takes another upturn. Neutsch has since been occupied with the *roman-fleuve Der Friede im Osten*, planned to consist of six volumes, three of which have appeared (1974, 1978, 1986).

Nossack, Hans Erich (1901–77)

Born in Hamburg, Nossack studied law and literature in Jena, worked in various jobs, including journalism, then, having been forbidden to publish by the Nazis, entered his father's import firm, where he remained until 1956. He then moved to South Germany, eventually settling in Darmstadt in 1962. In 1943 his early manuscripts and diaries fell victim to the flames during the bombing of Hamburg, a traumatic experience which left a permanent mark on his work. His type of magic realism, which is similar to that of **Kasack** and the early **Jens** and is as symptomatic of its time as 'Kahlschlagliteratur' and **Borchert**'s expressionism, has not worn as well as these, partly because Nossack chose to remain detached from the literary debates and groupings of his time and out of step with the general development towards social realism, preferring to the end of his career a bleak existentialism, which led to his promotion in France by Sartre, and the exploration of a metaphysical dimension by means of myth, allegory and futuristic fantasy. *Nekyia* (1947), based on the episode in the *Odyssey* in which Ulysses descends to Hades and makes a sacrifice to the dead, was inspired, like 'Der Untergang', by the destruction of Hamburg, the latter a realistic account and one of ten pieces, some based on myth, *Märchen* and science fiction motifs, assembled in *Interview mit dem Tode* (1948), which later appeared under the title *Dorothea* (1950, extended 1963). Nossack linked five more stories as the waking dreams of the central figure in *Spirale. Roman einer schlaflosen Nacht* (1956). With one exception these were republished with ten more stories in the collection *Begegnung im Vorraum* (1958, 1963). His first novel *Spätestens im November* (1955) on a love-affair between a businessman's wife and a poet narrated by her after her death can be related to the story *Das kennt man* (1964) on the fantasies of a dying prostitute as she becomes aware of a post-mortem existence. *Der jüngere Bruder* (1958) describes a man's search after his wife's death for the title-figure, who emerges as an *alter ego*. The mysterious dystopia *Nach dem letzten Aufstand* (1961) invites comparison with **Kafka**'s 'In der Strafkolonie' in its portrayal of attitudes before and after the uprising of the title. In *Der Fall d'Arthez* (1968) two friends, artist-intellectuals, succeed in defeating the machinations of a secret service. In *Dem unbekannten Sieger* (1969) a historian discovers by accident his father's identity with the leader of a revolution in Hamburg after the First World War, while in *Die gestohlene Melodie* (1972) the melody of the title is traced to its source in a dimension beyond death. *Bereitschaftsdienst. Bericht über eine Epidemie* (1973) concerns the reaction of officialdom to a suicide epidemic, and *Ein glücklicher Mensch. Erinnerungen an Aporée* (1979) is a post-nuclear dystopia. In *Das Testament des Lucius Eurinus* (1964), a story in which Nossack's aristocratic nihilism is succinctly conveyed, the title-figure commits suicide in the name of a stoic individualism when he recognizes his wife's conversion to Christianity as a sign of the times.

Otten, Karl (1889–1963)

Novelist, poet and editor of expressionist poetry, Karl Otten studied sociology and art history between 1910 and 1914; the meeting with Erich **Mühsam**, **Heinrich Mann**, Carl **Sternheim** and Franz **Blei** was, he explained, 'politisch und künstlerisch richtunggebend'. A fervent pacifist and advocate of a messianic communism, Otten spent much of the First World War in prison; in 1918 he edited the Viennese journal *Der Friede* before moving to Berlin and contributing to *Die Aktion*. The most successful early anthology was *Thronerhebung des Herzens* (1917); the psychological study *Der Fall Strauß* (1925) and the biography of Toussaint Louverture *Der schwarze Napoleon* (1931) deserve mention. In 1933 Otten fled to Majorca, where he lived till 1936; the novel *Torquemadas Schatten* (1938) describes the fascist reign of terror on that island and the reluctant decision to use force to combat evil (the spirit of Torquemada haunts the novel in the shape of the leader of the Blueshirts). In 1936 Otten moved to London, where he fought ceaselessly to denounce National Socialism and to promote world peace. He became blind in 1944. He moved to Switzerland after the war, and became famous as the editor of such anthologies as *Ahnung und Aufbruch. Expressionistische Prosa* (1957); *Schrei und Bekenntnis. Expressionistisches Theater* (1959) and *Ego und Eros. Meistererzählungen des Expressionismus* (1963). He also edited *Albert Ehrenstein. Gedichte und Prosa* (1961). *Herbstgesang. Gesammelte Gedichte* appeared in 1961.

P

Panizza, Oskar (1853–1921)

Panizza was born in Bad Kissingen of a partly Italian, Catholic father and a devoutly pietist mother of Huguenot extraction who had published novels under the pseudonym 'Siona'. Panizza studied medicine in Munich and Paris: he worked in the *Oberbayrische-Kreis-Irrenanstalt* between 1882 and 1884. In 1886 he published *Düstre Lieder*; *Londoner Lieder* followed in 1887 after a sojourn in England. Panizza's predilection for the macabre is seen in the collection of stories *Dämmerungsstücke* (1890) which are reminiscent of Edgar Allen Poe. He contributed to Michael Georg Conrad's *Gesellschaft* and achieved notoriety with his satirical attack *Die unbefleckte Empfängnis der Päpste* (1893). His greatest scandal was the farcical *Das Liebeskonzil. Eine Himmels-Tragödie in fünf Aufzügen* (1894), which portrayed God as an imbecile, Mary as a whore and Christ as a consumptive half-wit; the introduction of syphilis into the court of Pope Alexander VI is depicted in scurrilous detail. Panizza was arrested and served one year's imprisonment for blasphemy and obscenity. He settled in Switzerland, founded his own publishing house ('Zürcher Diskussionen') and attacked the Catholic Church with an almost demented intensity, particularly in the *Dialoge im Geiste Huttens* (1897). He also published in Zurich his *Psichopatia criminalis* (1898) and the tragedy *Nero* (1898). He moved to Paris, where he wrote his *Parisjana* (1899), the last book that he was to publish, an uneven collection of political-satirical poetry, reminiscent of Heine. Signs of mental instability became increasingly apparent; he suffered persecution mania in Paris, returned to Munich and, in 1905, was admitted to the mental home in Bayreuth, where he was incarcerated until his death. A private edition of *Das Liebeskonzil*, with illustrations by **Kubin**, appeared in 1913; a collection of stories, *Visionen der Dämmerung*, with an introduction by Hanns Heinz **Ewers** was published in 1914. *Der Korsettenfritz. Gesammelte Geschichten* appeared in 1981; in 1982 Luchterhand published *Das Liebeskonzil: Materialien zum Film von Werner Schroeter*.

Pannwitz, Rudolf (1881–1969)

Co-founder, with Otto zur **Linde**, of the journal *Charon* and editor from 1904 until its demise during the First World War, Rudolf Pannwitz worked as a private tutor before devoting his life to study and scholarship. His writings on European civilization (*Die Krisis der europäischen Kultur* (1917); *Der Nihilismus und die werdende Welt* (1951); *Beiträge zu einer europäischen Kultur* (1954)) are much indebted to Nietzsche, whom he revered (Nietzsche being 'mein einziger Freund'). Nietzsche's dithyrambic style is also seen in Pannwitz's *Prometheus* (1902) and the *Dionysische Tragödien* (1913) and *Die Erlöserinnen* (1922). The verse *Mythen* (1919–21) are characterized by a diffuse and high-flown rhetoric. The second mentor was Stefan **George**; Pannwitz had been a close associate of Karl **Wolfskehl** before joining Otto zur Linde and tirelessly extolled George's discipline and order ('George bändigte das chaos und schuf normen') and kept his orthography and punctuation. Similarly to **Mombert** and **Däubler**, Pannwitz experienced Venice as a myth rather than reality; he lived on the Dalmatian island of Koločep before moving to Switzerland. An autobiography, *Nach siebzig Jahren* (1951), is included in *Über den Denker Rudolf Pannwitz* (U. Rukser, 1970).

Paquet, Alfons (1881–1944)

Son of a cloth merchant, Paquet was sent as a young man to London to learn the business; the sight of poverty and deprivation moved him deeply, and he turned his attention increasingly to writing (a phrenologist in Ludgate Circus prophesied a life devoted to literature rather than commerce). His first publications were collections of poetry (*Schutzmann Mentrup und Anderes* (1902); *Lieder und Gesänge* (1902); *Held Namenlos* (1912)), much of it written in free rhythm similar to Whitman and **Werfel**. Paquet travelled widely and later described his journeys to Mongolia, Siberia and the Far East. A convinced pacifist (later a Quaker), Paquet greeted the Russian Revolution in 1917 and was a keen observer of the Soviet scene (*Im kommunistischen Rußland*; *Aus dem bolschivistischen Rußland*; *Der Geist der russischen Revolution* (all 1919)). His utopian visions were later tempered by an awareness of violence and excess, but his more successful works are overtly left-wing in their political stance. His best-known play is *Fahnen* (1923), a portrayal of the infamous Chicago Haymarket trial (the arrest and execution of certain anarchists); Paquet deliberately stressed the travesty of justice in Chicago and drew parallels with the contemporary problem of social injustice in the Weimar Republic. The play achieved notoriety in 1924 when Paquet collaborated with Erwin Piscator in its production. Other plays which were associated with expressionism are *Markolph* (1924) and *Sturmflut* (1926); the cycle of poems *Amerika. Hymnen. Gedichte* (1925) again shows the influence of Werfel. Paquet was not so successful in narrative prose: the two-volume novel *Kamerad Flemming* appeared in 1911 (reprinted in 1921); *Von November bis November* (1931–5) remained unpublished. Paquet also wrote on William Penn and, in later life, undistinguished verse on the Rhine and the cities associated with it (for example *Ode vom Rhein. Dank des nun Sechzigjährigen* (1941)). *Gesammelte Werke* (three vols) appeared in 1970.

Penzoldt, Ernst (1892–1955)

Penzoldt originally made his reputation as a Munich sculptor and artist; he turned to literature and wrote with elegance and assurance. His poetry is largely unmemorable (*Der Gefährte* (1922); *Zwölf Gedichte* (1937)) and his plays undistinguished (*Karl Ludwig Sand* (1931), a tragedy, also two comedies, *So war der Herr Brummell* (1933) and *Die verlorenen Schuhe* (1946)), but his narrative prose is eminently readable. His most successful novels are *Der arme Chatterton* (1928), an imaginative account of the life and death of the English poet, and *Die Powenzbande* (1930), a 'Zoologie einer Familie, gemeinverständlich dargestellt', which portrays, in pseudo-sociological manner, the scurrilous rise and fall of Baltus Powenz. Other novels include *Der Zwerg* (1927), *Kleiner Erdenwurm* (1934) and *Der Kartoffelroman* (1948). Penzoldt was one of those writers who were able to write with equal ease before and after 1945, being prolific in the 1930s and 1940s. Shorter prose works include *Die Portugalesische Schlacht* (a collection of stories, 1930), *Idolino* (1935), *Zugänge* (1947), *Bitternis* (1951) and *Squirrel* (1954). He was also an essayist who wrote urbane and witty sketches. *Das Nadelöhr* (1948) is a series of reminiscences. *Gesammelte Schriften* (four vols) appeared between 1949 and 1962; *Die schönsten Erzählungen* (five vols) in 1981.

Piontek, Heinz (1925–)

Born in Silesia, Piontek settled in Munich after the war. He is known primarily as a lyric poet in a traditional mould, continuing the line of nature poetry represented by **Lehmann** and **Britting**, although his laconic free verse occasionally suggests more modern affinities. In programmatic statements he has adopted a conservative position *vis-à-vis* experimentalists (e.g. **Heißenbüttel**) and politically engaged poets. Although his work is marked by a non-rational approach to imagery and by an existentialism with Christian overtones, he has written narrative poems, including 'Die Verstreuten' on the flight of refugees from the East at the end of the Second World War, and has edited the anthology *Neue deutsche Erzählgedichte* (1964). Since *Gesammelte Gedichte* (1975), which assembles poems from six volumes published between 1952 and 1971, four further volumes have appeared. Piontek has also written four novels, *Die mittleren Jahre* (1967), on the mid-life crisis of the narrator, a prematurely retired teacher, who looks back on episodes from his life, especially relationships to wife, daughter and lover, *Dichterleben* (1976), in which the decision made by a fifty-year-old writer to abandon his profession is reversed after encouragement by a younger man on the threshold of a similar career, *Juttas Neffe* (1979) and *Zeit meines Lebens* (1984), the latter an autobiographical novel. These, together with numerous essays (e.g. *Buchstab Zauberstab* (1959), *Männer die Gedichte machen* (1970) and *Das Handwerk des Lesens* (1972)), short stories, plays, mainly for radio, and the poems, have been collected in *Werke in 6 Bänden* (1985).

Plenzdorf, Ulrich (1934–)

Born in Berlin, Plenzdorf has studied in Leipzig and worked in the theatre, but since 1959 he has been employed mainly in the GDR film industry as a writer of scenarios. His name and reputation remain associated with the sensationally successful *Die neuen Leiden des jungen W.* which having originated as a film scenario appeared in the periodical *Sinn und Form* in 1972 and was published in a modified version in book form the following year. A dramatization was premièred in Halle in 1972 and was filmed in the Federal Republic in 1976. The ingredients of this success include an anti-hero with whom many, especially the young, can identify, the skilful use of quotations from Goethe's *Die Leiden des jungen Werthers* which both confirm the parallel and produce an ironic effect, mild concessions to literary modernism in the form of flashbacks – the story is told by the central character after his death (cf. **Nossack**, *Spätestens im November*) – and adaptability to different genres and media. Its appearance and acceptance signalled a temporary relaxation of official cultural policy at the beginning of the Honecker era. Since then some of Plenzdorf's scenarios, *Die Legende von Paul und Paula* (1974) and the two stories *Karla. Der alte Mann, das Pferd, die Straße* (1978), have appeared in book form, and the *Legende*, a romantic love-story set in proletarian Berlin, has been extended to novel length in *Legende vom Glück ohne Ende* (1979). The formally advanced story *kein runter kein fern* was awarded the Ingeborg Bachmann prize in 1978, receiving independent publication in 1984. Plenzdorf has also written plays based on works by Günter de **Bruyn**, *Buridans Esel* (1976) and *Freiheitsberaubung* (1988).

Plessen, Elisabeth (1944–)

Born and brought up in Schleswig-Holstein on the estate of her ancient aristocratic family, Plessen studied in Berlin and edited with Michael Mann the memoirs of **Thomas Mann**'s wife Katja in 1974. In her first novel, the autobiographical *Mitteilung an den Adel* (1976), the death of the narrator's father prompts an evocation of the factors in her upbringing which had led to a growing estrangement and a painful struggle for independence and distinct identity during the years of the *Studentenbewegung*. *Kohlhaas* (1979) offers an alternative account of the historical figure on whom Heinrich von Kleist based his most substantial story *Michael Kohlhaas* and remains closer to documentary evidence unavailable to him. *Stella Polare* (1984) deals with the problems of a female writer unable to reconcile her wish to pursue her art with the demands of her relationship with another writer.

Plievier (sometimes Plivier), Theodor (1892–1955)

Son of a worker of Dutch origin, Theodor Plievier was born in Berlin-Wedding and grew up under harsh conditions. In 1909 he published a short story *Proletariers Ende* in the anarchist journal *Der freie Arbeiter*; after a vagrant existence he joined the German navy and, in 1918, was active in the uprising in Wilhelmshaven. After the war he associated with various left-wing literary circles (with **Mühsam** and **Toller**), editing *Die Republik* and studying Stirner, Kropotkin and Gustav Landauer. His first novel, inspired by Remarque's *Im Westen nichts Neues*, was *Des Kaisers Kulis* (1930), which was translated into eighteen languages (the collection of short stories, *Zwölf Mann und ein Kapitän*, had appeared the previous year). With the motto 'Der Getretne schreit!' Plievier threw himself into literary activity: subsequent novels include *Der Kaiser ging, die Generäle blieben* (1932), *Das große Abenteuer* (Amsterdam, 1936), *Im letzten Winkel der Erde* (Moscow, 1941) and *Haifische* (Moscow, 1941). Plievier lived in Russia during the Second World War; he achieved his greatest success with the novel *Stalingrad* (1945), to which he added, as a trilogy, *Moskau* (Munich, 1952) and *Berlin* (Munich, 1954). In 1947 Plievier fled the Russian zone of occupation and moved to the American zone. The last three novels particularly reached enormous sales, the realistic and gripping descriptions of warfare being written in an easily accessible style. Rudolf **Hagelstange** said of him: 'Für die Politiker war er ein Literat. Für die Literaten ein politischer Schriftsteller. Dem Bürger war er immer etwas verdächtig'. *Werke in Einzelausgaben* appeared from 1981.

Polgar, Alfred (1873–1955)

Son of a Jewish piano teacher (the family name, Polak, was changed in 1914), Alfred Polgar worked as a reporter in Vienna, but soon frequented literary cafés and contributed to anarchist journals, particularly *Die Zukunft*. He also became theatre critic for the *Wiener Allgemeine Zeitung* and wrote satirical sketches for *Simplicissimus*; in 1905 he collaborated with Egon Friedell in the two satires *Goethe im Examen* and *Das Soldatenleben im Frieden*. Collections of *Novellen* include *Der Quell des Übels* (1908), *Bewegung ist alles* (1909), *Hiob* (1912) and *Gestern und heute* (1922). During the First World War Polgar worked sporadically in the War Archives; a series of essays under the title *Kleine Zeit* appeared in 1919. As theatre critic and satirist Polgar was avidly read, and particularly successful were *An den Rand geschrieben* (1926) and *Ja und Nein* (1926–7). His play *Die Defraudanten*, an adaptation of Katajev's novel, was staged in Hamburg in 1931 and filmed in the following year under the title *Der brave Sünder*. Polgar fled to Prague in 1933 and later to Switzerland and France; he published further collections of essays and sketches, *In der Zwischenzeit* (1935), *Sekundenzeiger* (1937) and *Handbuch des Kritikers* (1938). At the invasion of France he moved with **Heinrich Mann**, Franz **Werfel** and

Leonhard **Frank** across the Spanish frontier and finally reached New York in October 1940. He worked briefly in Hollywood for Metro Goldwyn Mayer, becoming a US citizen in 1945. After the war he returned to Europe and translated English and American plays for the German stage. Later collections include *Im Vorübergehen* (1947), *Standpunkte* (1953) and *Fensterplatz* (1959), the latter appearing posthumously, Polgar having died in a Zurich hotel room in 1955. *Prosa aus vier Jahrzehnten* appeared in 1968, and *Bei Lichte betrachtet* in 1970. *Die Mission des Luftballons* was published in 1975, *Kleine Schriften* (four vols) from 1982.

Ponten, Josef (1883–1940)

Descended from an artisan family living near the Belgian border, Josef Ponten studied at several universities, but also strove to identify himself with his family and his birthplace (Raeren, near Eupen): 'Herkunft aus dem niederen arbeitenden Volke schuf das tiefe Behagen an völkischem Denken, Sprechen und Schaffen'. He excelled at historical and regional novels (*Jungfräulichkeit* (1906); *Siebenquellen* (1909)); he is best known for *Der babylonische Turm* (1918), a successful portrayal of the Großjohann family and the tensions within it. The *Novellen Die Bockreiter* (1919) and *Der Gletscher* (1923) should be noted, the former dealing with the legends of the Lower Rhine, the latter being 'Eine Geschichte aus Obermenschland'. The novels *Salz* (1921–2) and *Die Studenten von Lyon* (1927) are less successful. Ponten travelled widely and was skilful in his descriptions of landscape (*Griechische Landschaften* (1915) and *Europäisches Reisebuch* (1928)). His most ambitious project was the account, entitled *Volk auf dem Wege*, of German settlement in foreign countries. Six novels were published from 1934 to 1942, the most readable of which is *Im Wolgaland*, dealing with the life of the Volga Germans. Ponten settled in Munich and became a friend of **Thomas Mann**, who admired his conservative stance. Alfons **Paquet** wrote a tribute to Ponten on his death.

Preradović, Paula von (1887–1951)

Granddaughter of Petar Preradović, general in the Austro-Hungarian army and leading poet of the Croatian national revival, Paula von Preradović was born in Vienna, lived in Pola and was educated in St Pölten. She began writing about 1910 and was soon praised by **Hofmannsthal**. In 1916 she married Ernst Molden, later editor of the *Wiener Freie Presse*, and lived for the rest of her life in Vienna. Her first successful collection of poetry, *Südlicher Sommer*, appeared in 1929; the next, *Dalmatinische Sonette* (1933), contains the sonnet-cycle 'Die Engel der Toten', inspired by the work of the Croatian sculptor Ivan Meštrović. Neo-romantic nostalgia for Dalmatia, plus a devout catholicism characterize her writing; the influence of **Rilke** is also discernible in her third collection *Lob Gottes im Gebirge* (1936). Her prose works include the novel *Pave und Pero* (1940) and the *Novellen Königslegende* (1950) and *Die Versuchung des Columba* (1951), the former being a classical *Novelle* set in eleventh-century Dalmatia, the latter telling of the purification of St Columba. During the Second World War Paula von Preradović was an active member of the anti-Nazi resistance; in February 1945 she and her husband were arrested, but released as the Russians entered Vienna. After the war she took a keen interest in the *Europäisches Forum Alpbach*, of which her eldest son was the co-founder. Her poem 'Land der Berge, Land am Strome' has been adopted as the Austrian national anthem. The *Gesammelte Werke* appeared in 1967.

Przybyszewski, Stanisław (1868–1927)

Born in a small village in Prussian Poland, Przybyszewski studied medicine and architecture in Berlin. In 1892 he published *Zur Psychologie des Individuums*, a highly subjective appraisal of Nietzsche, Chopin and Ola Hansson. He became the centre of the Berlin Bohemia, an *habitué* of the wine-cellar *Zum schwarzen Ferkel*, where he consorted with August Strindberg, Edvard Munch and Richard **Dehmel**. His 'poems in prose' include such sensational works as *Totenmesse* (1893), *Vigilien* (1894), *De profundis* (1895), *Epipsychidion* (1900) and *Androgyne* (1906). He was active in founding the journal *Pan*, and contributed to *Die Fackel* ('Das Geschlecht' (1907)); he became increasingly involved in Satanism and anarchism. His novel trilogy *Homo Sapiens* includes *Unterwegs* (1895), *Über Bord* (1896) and *Im Malstrom* (1896); *Erdensöhne* appeared in 1905, *Der Schrei* in 1918 and *Satanskinder* in 1919. His plays, less successful, include *Totentanz der Liebe* (1902) and *Schnee* (1903). Przybyszewski edited the Polish literary periodical *Życie* between 1898 and 1900 and became a leading member of the Young Poland movement; he lived in Munich from 1906 to 1919 before returning to independent Poland. Przybyszewski made an indelible impression on his German contemporaries, and is frequently portrayed in the literary works of the time. His writings in Polish are of less significance; informative, however, are his memoirs *Moi współcześni* (two vols, 1926–30: volume one appearing later in German as *Erinnerungen an das literarische Berlin*). The collected works appeared in Moscow (four vols, 1904–6, then ten vols, 1905–11); later in Warsaw (twelve vols, 1923–9). Of the works in German *Der Schrei* (1986) and *De Profundis* (1989) have been reprinted. Przybyszewski was married to Dagne Jule, whom Edvard Munch frequently painted; she was later murdered in Tiflis.

Qualtinger, Helmut (1928–86)

Although better known as a performing artist, especially in Viennese *Kabarett*, than as a writer, Qualtinger deserves to be remembered as the creator, with Carl Merz, of Herr Karl, a cynical opportunist, a Vicar of Bray figure, who survives the political upheavals in Austria between 1927 and 1955 and tells his story in the form of a long monologue, first performed by Qualtinger himself (*Der Herr Karl* (1962)). Other works for stage and television include *Die Hinrichtung* (1964, also with Merz), in which the attempt by an unhappily married father of three to escape poverty and his humdrum existence by arranging his own execution misfires when public interest wanes and the guillotine develops a technical failure, and *Alles gerettet* (1963), on a fire disaster at a Viennese theatre in 1881 in which the incompetence of the fire service resulted in several hundred deaths. Qualtinger can be placed firmly in the tradition of Austrian satire represented by the nineteenth-century *Volksstück*, Karl **Kraus** and Jura Soyfer.

R

Reger, Erik (pseudonym of Hermann Dannenberger, 1893–1954)

Reger was during most of his later career a newspaper editor, but spent the years 1919 to 1927 as a public relations employee with the Krupp steel firm in Essen, where he gained the inside knowledge on which is based his best-known work *Union der festen Hand* (1931), a documentary novel typical of 'Neue Sachlichkeit' in which the ramifications of industry, big business and politics are traced through the First World War, the 1918 revolution, the Kapp *putsch*, the French occupation of the Ruhr, inflation and mass unemployment. The concentration of economic power in a few hands at the expense of the Social Democrats and the Communists and the failure to recognize the danger represented by the early progress of Nazism are the main themes of the work, which also aims to provide a cross-section of an industrial community through typical figures from all its social strata. Reger produced several other novels set in the Rhineland, of which only *Das wachsame Hähnchen* (1932), a satirical portrait of an opportunist against the background of the 1923 inflation, remains of interest.

Rehn, Jens (pseudonym of Otto Jens Luther, 1918–83)

A Berliner, Rehn studied music, became a submarine officer, began writing in 1947 and worked for radio in Berlin from 1950. He is remembered for three novels which present human beings in extreme situations, exposed to the elements in a condition of existential solitude. *Nichts in Sicht* (1954), set in 1943, brings together a German U-boat commander and an American airman, who, both wounded, drift in a dinghy in the Atlantic and slowly die of thirst. In *Feuer im Schnee* (1956) an old schoolteacher who has joined a refugee trek at the end of the Second World War turns back east, only to lose his way when his compass fails, while *Die Kinder des Saturn* (1959) concerns three survivors of an atomic explosion who having emerged from their bunker experience a steady decline to madness and death on the desolate surface of the earth.

Reimann, Brigitte (1933–73)

Reimann's career, tragically curtailed by cancer, is symptomatic of a general development in GDR fiction in the 1960s and early 1970s from a positive celebration of socialist achievements in 'Ankunftsliteratur' (a term derived from her first major novel *Ankunft im Alltag* (1961), in which a group of young intellectuals come to terms with life on the shop-floor during the period of socialist reconstruction) to the concentration on the fate and inner development of a single character in a form of fiction which traces in a more complex manner the interaction of individual and society and contains some features of the German *Bildungsroman* (e.g. Hermann **Kant**, *Die Aula*, **Christa Wolf**, *Nachdenken über Christa T.*). Her second, incomplete, novel *Franziska Linkerhand* (1974), in which an enthusiastic girl of middle-class background joins a team of architects constructing a new town and gradually progresses towards sexual and professional independence via an uneasy marriage to a worker and relationships to colleagues with differing attitudes to their job and to society in general, exemplifies the latter type.

Reinig, Christa (1926–)

From a Berlin working-class background, Reinig studied from 1953 to 1957 at the Humboldt University in East Berlin, then worked at the *Märkisches Museum* there, moving to the Federal Republic in 1964 when she was awarded the Bremen literary prize for her *Gedichte* (1963). Other volumes of poetry are *Die Steine von Finisterre* (1960), containing poems written between 1947 and 1959, and *Die Schwalbe von Olivano* (1969), inspired by the experience of Italy. Her poems are marked by the influence of **Rilke** and **Brecht** and a predilection for outcast figures, as in the well-known 'Ballade vom blutigen Bomme'. After the experimental autobiographical novel *Die himmlische und die irdische Geometrie* (1975), in which anecdotal reminiscences of family life in the GDR alternate with imaginary dialogues between great cultural figures of the past, Reinig began a feminist phase with *Entmannung* (1977), a novel which reverses active-passive stereotypes in relations between the sexes in a series of revenge fantasies. The story collections *Der Wolf und die Witwen* (1980) and *Die ewige Schule* (1982) were followed in 1984 by *Die Frau im Brunnen*, concerning the relationship between two women of different personalities and interests. Reinig adopts satire and black humour to convey the notion that women have been the victims of physical and psychological violence at the hands of men and that they are ill-equipped to reverse this situation.

Reinshagen, Gerlind (1926–)

After studying pharmacy and art, Reinshagen wrote children's books and radio plays on everyday themes, before her first play for the theatre, *Doppelkopf*, was premièred in 1968. Her politically untendentious social realism focuses on the intrigues, gossip and petty rivalries of the business world at various levels, as in the above play, in which during the period of the economic miracle during an office party a careerist is exposed by means of a 'play within a play' device, or in *Das Frühlingsfest* (1980), a social panorama of the 1950s, *Eisenherz* (1982) and the novel *Rovinato* (1981), in both of which a naïve apprentice confronts an office hierarchy. Reinshagen's other plays are centred on female characters: whether a teenage girl observing how family and friends come to terms with the Third Reich in *Sonntagskinder* (1976); the film star in *Leben und Tod der Marilyn Monroe* (1971) – here the mechanism by which the public's desires are projected on to an image and the tragic consequences for the victim of the star cult are revealed by assigning the role of Monroe to three actresses; the tough independent woman forced to take stock of her life while suffering from a terminal illness in hospital in *Himmel und Erde* (1974); or the ageing actress in *Die Clownin* (1985), who after reviewing her past and encountering in her imagination Emily Brontë and Charlie Chaplin becomes a circus clown and falls from a tight-rope. The novel *Die flüchtige Braut* (1984) presents the disintegration of a company of artists and drop-outs in Berlin at the end of the 1970s.

Remarque, Erich Maria (pseudonym of Paul Remark, 1898–1970)

The son of a bookbinder in Osnabrück, Remarque was called up in 1916; after the war he worked as a teacher and journalist. He published his first novel, *Die Traumbude*, in 1920, but it was with *Im Westen nichts Neues* (1929) that he achieved instant, international success (some three and a half million copies were sold within eighteen months). The book was greeted by many as a salutary indictment of the folly of war; nationalist circles were incensed. Further novels include *Der Weg zurück* (1931), *Drei Kameraden* (1938), *Liebe deinen Nächsten* (1941) which were far less effective. Remarque left Germany in 1929, lived in Ascona and settled in New York in 1939; his books were publicly burned by the Nazis in 1933. Remarque acquired US citizenship and achieved a second great success with the American bestseller *Arc de Triomphe* (1946), a sensational account of the murder by a refugee German doctor of a concentration camp sadist. Other novels followed, some dealing with the Second World War (*Der Funke Leben* (1952); *Zeit zu leben und Zeit zu sterben* (1954); *Der schwarze Obelisk* (1956); *Der Himmel kennt keine Günstlinge* (1961); *Die Nacht von Lissabon* (1961); *Schatten im Paradies* (1971)), but none has the vitality and conviction of *Im Westen nichts Neues*. Remarque also attempted drama (*Die letzte Stadt* (1956) and *Drei Kameraden* (1960)).

Renn, Ludwig (pseudonym of Arnold Vieth von Golßenau, 1898–1979)

Renn came from a Saxon aristocratic background and joined the army in 1910; during the First World War he served as a company and battalion commander. After a period in the *Freikorps* he left the army in 1920 to study Russian, law, economics and art history. He became a free-lance writer and joined the Communist Party after publishing his first book, *Krieg*, in 1928. The novel is a sober, factual account of an infantryman's experiences at the front; the tone is deliberately unsensational. In the same year Renn became secretary of the Alliance of Proletarian Revolutionary Writers, a post which he held until 1932; he also edited the communist journal *Linkskurve*. The novel *Nachkrieg* (1930) dealt with the security forces of the Weimar Republic; *Rußlandfahrten* (1932) described a visit to the Soviet Union made in 1929. Renn was arrested on 27 February 1933 and spent two-and-a-half years in prison. In 1936 he succeeded in fleeing to Switzerland and later joined the Eleventh International Brigade in the Spanish Civil War. (The novels *Die Schlacht bei Guadalajara* and *Der spanische Krieg*, both of 1955, describe these experiences.) Renn was interned in France in 1939, released in 1940, and then moved to Mexico, becoming professor of European history and languages at the University of Morelia. He was a leading figure in the periodical *Freies Deutschland* and, after the war, moved to East Germany in 1947, where he became professor of anthropology at the Technical High school, Dresden. He was appointed honorary president of the East German Academy of Arts in 1969. His later novels are unashamedly partisan; the theoretical writings plead for pacifism. The *Gesammelte Werke* (ten vols) appeared between 1964 and 1969, a twelve volume edition from 1989.

Reuter, Gabriele (1859–1941)

Born in Egypt, Gabriele Reuter's first attempts at writing were based on her experiences in Alexandria. In 1889 she met Ibsen in Munich; in Berlin she became a close friend of John Henry **Mackay** and was associated with many of the naturalists. Her first literary success was the novel *Aus guter Familie* (1895), which criticized the subservient role of women in the middle-class family of the times. Other novels (*Ellen von der Weiden* (1900) and *Das Tränenhaus* (1909)) attack the traditional concepts of marriage and motherhood. *Gunhild Kersten* (1904) and *Frühlingstaumel* (1911) deal with the conflicting claims of home and profession. Her plays were not successful; eminently readable, however, are her essays on Marie von Ebner-Eschenbach and Annette von Droste-Hülshoff (both 1905). *Das Problem der Ehe* (1907) and *Liebe und Stimmrecht* (1914) show her to be a vigorous campaigner for women's rights. *Vom Kinde zum Menschen* (1922) and *Grüne Ranken um alte Bilder* (1937) are autobiographical.

Richter, Hans Werner (1908–)

Richter began writing late, after a period as a bookseller, a brief emigration, war service from 1940 to 1943, capture in Italy and internment in a POW camp in the USA. With Alfred **Andersch** he edited *Der Ruf* (originally the name of a camp newspaper) from 1946 to the following year, when it was effectively banned by the American occupation authorities. Having received no licence for the literary periodical *Der Skorpion* which was to succeed it, Richter founded *Gruppe 47*, which consisted originally of former contributors to *Der Ruf*, but proceeded to expand to include almost the entire West German literary élite. Richter remained the *spiritus rector* of the group until its dissolution in 1966. He edited an anthology of verse by prisoners of war, *Deine Söhne, Europa*, in 1947. Richter's early novels can be associated with 'Kahlschlagliteratur', as they portray the reality of war without ideological commitment and from the standpoint of the common soldier or the average citizen; however, they lack the laconic understatement and formal sophistication of some 'Kahlschlag' authors, although *Sie fielen aus Gottes Hand* (1951), in presenting in turn the experiences of twelve persons of different national, social and political origin, approaches in technique the multiple perspectives of, e.g. Andersch's *Sansibar*. Richter's first novel *Die Geschlagenen* (1949) resembles in subject another novel by Andersch, *Die Kirschen der Freiheit*, in tracing the odyssey of a German corporal from capture at Monte Cassino to POW camp in the USA. *Du sollst nicht töten* (1955) follows the course of the Second World War in its effect on the Lorenz family. *Spuren im Sand* (1953) is an account of Richter's childhood and youth in a Baltic seaside resort in novel form, while *Linus Fleck* (1959) represents a new departure, a satirical picaresque novel in which an opportunist climbs up the ladder of West German society during the years of the economic miracle. *Rose weiß Rose rot* (1971) portrays Berlin in the closing years of the Weimar Republic, and *Die Stunde der falschen Triumphe* (1981) offers within a wider temporal framework spanning the period between the Second Reich and the years after the Second World War two stories linked by the figures of a teacher and a barber related by marriage. In *Ein Julitag* (1981) the central character looks back to experiences shared with the widow of his younger brother during the Third Reich after renewing their relationship at the latter's funeral, and *Die Flucht nach Abanon* (1980) describes the meetings between the narrator, an ageing writer and an actress who withdraws into a private world and eventually commits suicide.

Rilke, Rainer Maria (1875–1926)

Born in Prague as the son of an Austrian official, Rilke reluctantly served in the military academy at Sankt Pölten from 1886 to 1891 before studying sporadically in Linz, Prague and Munich (where he met Lou **Andreas-Salomé**), and Berlin. His early work is frequently derivative and is characterized by neo-romantic effusion and mawkishness: the stories and lyrical prose include *Am Leben hin* (1898); *Zwei Prager Geschichten* (1898); *Vom lieben Gott und anderes* (1900); *Die Letzten* (1902). The poetry is represented by *Leben und Lieder* (1894), *Wegwarten* (1896), *Larenopfer*

(1896), *Traumgekrönt* (1897), *Advent* (1898) and *Mir zu Feier* (1899). Rilke
also attempted plays: *Jetzt und in der Stunde unseres Absterbens* (1896), *Im
Frühfrost* (1897) and *Die weiße Fürstin* (1902). The verse consists of little
more than sentient waves of feeling, whilst the plays attempt a fusion of
Ibsen and Maeterlinck. *Das Buch der Bilder* (1902) is an anthology of early
poetry which contains many of Rilke's most popular poems. In 1899 and
1900 Rilke journeyed to Russia with Lou Andreas-Salomé: *Das Stundenbuch* (1905) describes the impact of this country, where the poet, speaking
through the mouth of an imaginary Russian monk, blesses and affirms
existence (a typically neo-romantic confusion between aesthetic and
religious concepts is clearly noticeable); a vapid spirituality predominates. In
1900 Rilke made contact with the artist colony in Worpswede and, in 1901,
married the sculptress Clara Westhoff. He settled in Paris in the following
year; further travels included visits to Italy, Denmark and Sweden. Between
1905 and 1906 he worked as a secretary for Rodin, whose method of work
and emphasis on form helped Rilke to overcome much of his earlier artistic
self-indulgence: a clearer, harder line in his writing would become apparent,
and the misty effulgence of the juvenilia recedes. The *Weise von Liebe und
Tod des Cornets Christoph Rilke* (1906), enormously popular through its
musicality and its sentimental portrayal of the love and death in battle of a
young aristocratic cadet, marked the culmination of what may be called
Rilke's pre-Rodin poetry. It was with the publication of the *Neue Gedichte*
(1907/1908) that Rilke emerged as a major European poet; precision is
combined with an elusive symbolic extension, and the stale, neo-romantic
clichés are expunged. The famous 'Dinggedichte' ('Der Panther', 'Die
Flamingos') show the influence of Rodin in their objectivity and plasticity.
The *Requiem* of 1909 contains Rilke's newly-won belief in objectivity and
the need to transcend emotional surrender. The concept of 'Sagen' emerges,
precise statement which is extolled at the expense of 'Sich beklagen'
(complaint).

   The novel *Die Aufzeichnungen des Malte Laurids Brigge* (1910), dealing
with the experiences of a twenty-eight-year-old Dane in Paris, is a
remarkable conglomerate of childhood memories, reminiscences culled from
journeys to Scandinavia and Russia, literary associations and above all the
portrayal of existentialist dread and the overwhelming impact made by the
modern city and its ugliness. Precision (the description of the wall of a house
in the slums) is conveyed with an almost morbid sensitivity. The disjointed,
associative narration, the introspection and apparently arbitrary concatenation of disparate reflections and memories put the novel in the vanguard of
modern, experimental prose fiction: a fragmentary, more tenuous and
tentative form of writing is preferred. The true artist, it appears, is not the
one who escapes into rarefied worlds but who observes the sick and the
dying, the deformed and the rejected, and yet who transforms all this
through the manipulation of appropriate images into an objectified,
recreated reality. The sensibilities of aestheticism and the precision of
naturalism fuse at this stage of Rilke's art into a unique synthesis: nuance
and exactness, imagination and precision coexist.

   The creation of perfect art forms (the sonnets of the *Neue Gedichte*),
although demonstrating mastery, begins to give way in the years preceding

the outbreak of the First World War to a realization that 'seeing' must give way to 'heart-work', by no means a return to earlier self-indulgence, but a realization that a radical reinterpretation of existence, a new 'poetic' reappraisal of traditional concepts and ways of feeling, were required. The poetry becomes 'modern' in that it can no longer rely on a traditional, universally held picture of reality. Rilke's *Duineser Elegien*, published in 1923, were begun in 1912: they represent the summit of his poetic achievement. Tentative and hesitant (there are ten of them) they pose an 'angelic' order, the Angel being the yardstick against which man measures his achievements and insufficiencies. Trapped within the flux and turmoil of transient phenomena it seems that man cannot embrace and accept as the Angel does. Yet Rilke knows that there are certain moments of human existence which do possess an authenticity and an integrity such that the Angel must needs be aware of them. Mystical concepts (the realm of death, the young dead) alternate with an awareness of the wretchedness of modern life (technology and vulgarization) and the creation of new myths (the unrequited lovers, the *Umschlag* or turning-point). The tone of the ten elegies alternates between resignation, depression, longing and even defiance: written over a period of ten years, a period that straddled the war years (1914–18), the *Elegien* represent one of the greatest poetic statements of this century. The hymn-like rapture looks back to Klopstock and to Hölderlin, whereas the content (man's ontological inauthenticity, plus the need for an almost Nietzschean transvaluation) belongs very much in the modern canon.

Apart from a brief period spent in the military archives in Vienna, Rilke spent the war years in Munich; the elegies were completed at Muzot in Switzerland. At this same time he composed his *Sonette an Orpheus* (1923), a luminous cycle of poems which extol the Orphic principle, the identification of artistic subjectivity and objective reality. The turmoil of the elegies is not found here, and a serenity prevails, one which, however, is not unruffled by fundamental questions concerning human life. Existential difficulties and strained injunctions are, however, rare, and a pellucid, Mediterranean atmosphere prevails. Late poems continue to praise in an almost mystical remoteness, yet the problems of pain, parting and death are not absent. Rilke also wrote, in his last years, poems in French; comparisons with the work of Valéry are frequently made. He died of leukaemia near Montreux at the end of 1926.

In Rilke's hands the German language achieved a suppleness and refinement hitherto unknown. The occasional mannerisms which mar such collections as *Das Marien-Leben* (1913), and the pretentious attitudinizing and sycophancy in letters to wealthy aristocratic ladies cannot detract from his poetic stature. The final line from his *Requiem* ('Wer spricht von Siegen? Überstehn ist alles') was praised by Gottfried **Benn** in 1949 as the one line that his own generation could never forget. The early poetry is known, loved and anthologized; the later work is central in any discussion of modern European poetry. The *Gesammelte Werke* (six vols) appeared in 1927, *Verse und Prosa aus dem Nachlaß* in 1929, *Ausgewählte Werke* (two vols) in 1938. Four volumes *Aus R. M. Rilkes Nachlaß* were published in 1950, and *Sämtliche Werke* (six vols) appeared between 1955 and 1966. *Der andere*

Rilke. Gesammelte Schriften aus dem Nachlaß appeared in 1961, and a three-volume *Werke* in 1966. A selection, *Ausgewählte Gedichte 1902–1917*, was published in 1975 and the centenary *Sämtliche Werke* (twelve vols) also in 1975. A six volume *Sämtliche Werke* appeared in 1987. Rilke was also an accomplished translator (mainly from the French); his correspondence was considerable (and carefully cultivated), and much has been published.

Ringelnatz, Joachim (pseudonym of Hans Bötticher, 1883–1934)

Son of a writer and illustrator of children's books, Ringelnatz went to sea after having left school, became (briefly) a businessman and, in 1909, joined the satirical Munich cabaret *Simplicissimus*. *Was ein Schiffsjungentagebuch erzählt* (1911) and *Ein jeder erlebt's* (1913) describe these experiences. He served in the navy during the First World War, after which he appeared again in cabaret. His poetry (*Stumpfsinn in Versen* (1912) and *Kuttel-Daddeldu* (1920)) contains scurrilous, amusing and grotesque elements; *Turngedichte* (1920) have a lightness of touch which dispels the charge of obscenity. Witty autobiographical works (*Als Mariner im Krieg* (1928), and *Mein Leben bis zum Kriege* (1931)) show much irony and a delight in caricature and self-deprecation. Ringelnatz (the name means grass-snake) excelled as clown and raconteur, although later poetry (*Gedichte dreier Jahre* (1932)) contains a more genuine lyrical tone. In 1933 he was forbidden to appear on the stage, and his flippancy and iconoclasm were deplored. *Gedichte Gedichte Gedichte* appeared in 1934, and *Der Nachlaß von Joachim Ringelnatz* in the following year. The *Gesammelte Gedichte* were published in 1950, and the *Kunterbunte Nachrichten. Dreiundzwanzig Briefe aus Berlin* in 1963. *Das Gesamtwerk* (seven vols) appeared from 1982.

Rinser, Luise (1911–)

Having studied in Munich and worked as a schoolteacher from 1935 to 1939 Rinser was forbidden to write by the Nazis in 1941 and was imprisoned in 1944 for treason and undermining military morale, an experience documented in her *Gefängnis-Tagebuch* (1946). Imprisonment remains an important theme in her later work, e.g. in the story *Daniela* (1946) and the novels *Die Stärkeren* (1948), *Mitte des Lebens* (1950), *Der Sündenbock* (1955) and *Die vollkommene Freude* (1962). Many of her novels and stories, e.g. *Die gläsernen Ringe* (1941), *Erste Liebe* (1946), *Ich bin Tobias* (1966), *Mirjam* (1983), concern the passage of women from childhood to adulthood with its attendant social and psychological adjustments and the search for a satisfying religious faith which takes the form of a left-wing Catholicism. The semi-autobiographical *Mitte des Lebens* (1950) and the epistolary novel *Abenteuer der Tugend* (1957) were combined in 1967 to form *Nina*, whose life from 1929 to 1948 and marriage to an alcoholic drug-addicted artist form the subjects of the two parts. *Jan Lobel aus Warschau* (1948) and sections of *Die Stärkeren* (1948) and *Der schwarze Esel* (1974) are set in the Third Reich. *Die vollkommene Freude* (1962) offers a further variation on the theme of conjugal devotion to a difficult partner. Rinser is also known for her diaries, *Baustelle* (1970), *Grenzübergänge* (1972) on the USSR and Poland, *Kriegsspielzeug. Tagebuch 1972–78* (1978), *Wenn die Wale kämpfen* (1976), both on South Korea, *Nordkoreanisches Tagebuch* (1981) on North Korea, and *Aufzeichnungen 1979–82. Winterfrühling* (1982).

Roda Roda (pseudonym of Sandór Friedrich Rosenfeld, 1872–1945)

Son of an estate manager in Slavonia (now Yugoslavia), Roda Roda served (between 1892 and 1902) as an officer in the Austrian army; he later worked as a journalist before devoting himself to writing. In 1905 he moved to Berlin, later to Munich; he also travelled widely in the Balkans. In the First World War he was a war reporter; he settled in Munich again in the 1920s, contributing to satirical periodicals (*Simplicissimus* and *Die Ente*) and reaching a wide readership with his light and humorous account of life in Old Austria, particularly amongst the officer corps. His novels were unsuccessful, but his collections of anecdotes were very popular (*Der gemütskranke Husar* (1903); *Soldatengeschichten* (1904); *Adlige Geschichten* (1906); *Der Schnaps, der Rauchtabak und die verfluchte Liebe* (1908); *Milan reitet durch die Nacht* (1910); *Kaiserliche Kämmerer* (1912) and others). The most famous of his comedies was *Der Feldherrnhügel* (written in collaboration with Carl Rößler in 1910). He also collaborated with Gustav **Meyrink**. Autobiographical works include *Irrfahrten eines Humoristen* (1920) and *Roda Roda erzählt* (1925). Karl **Kraus** attacked him remorselessly as a glib and meretricious writer. In 1933 he emigrated to Austria, later to Switzerland and, in 1940, to the USA, where he lived until his death. *Ausgewählte Werke* (three vols) appeared between 1932 and 1934, to be followed by *Das große Roda Roda Buch* in 1949; *Großmutter reitet*, a selection, appeared in 1981.

Rosei, Peter (1946–)

Born in Vienna, Rosei has been a professional writer since 1972. In his early works *Landstriche* (1972), *Alben* (1973), *Wege* (1974) and *Entwurf für eine Welt ohne Menschen. Entwurf zu einer Reise ohne Ziel* (1975) men appear as tormented victims of themselves and one another and bleak landscapes are metaphors for a pessimistic view of the world, while *Bei schwebendem Verfahren* (1973) is a Kafkaesque dystopia. In *Wer war Edgar Allan?* (1977), *Von hier nach dort* (1978) and *Das schnelle Glück* (1980) narrators cut themselves off from a familiar reality, whether under the influence of drugs, or as motor-bike drop-outs or in the passage from unemployment to prostitution. *Die Milchstraße* (1981) consists of seven independent books held together by the figure of Ellis who observes the disturbed relationships of casual acquaintances. Relationships are also the subject of four of the five following novels, part of a cycle (*Komödie* (1984) the narrator's relation to a girl waif, *Mann & Frau* (1984) their lives after separation, *Die Wolken* (1986) the eternal triangle in a remote village and *Der Aufstand* (1987) about a disillusioned professor and a student activist), but at its centre stands *15 000 Seelen* (1985), a dystopia in which the human passion for records leads to ecological catastrophe.

Roth, Gerhard (1942–)

Roth studied medicine, then worked in a computer centre in Graz from 1966 to 1977, since when he has been a professional writer living in Graz and south-west Styria. He is a member of the *Grazer Autorenversammlung*, a group associated with Alfred Kolleritsch and the magazine *manuskripte*. He visited the USA several times between 1972 and 1981. After early experiments (*Der Ausbruch der ersten Weltkriegs und andere Romane* (1972)) which followed the example set by the *Wiener Gruppe*, Roth wrote *die autobiographie des albert einstein* (1972) and *Der Wille zur Krankheit* (1973), which explore mental illness from the point of view of the sufferer. These were followed by two novels set in the USA, *Der große Horizont* (1974) in which the hero identifies with Philip Marlowe, and *Ein neuer Morgen* (1976) in which the paranoid fantasies of flight and pursuit in the previous novel are translated into reality. Flight is also the subject of *Winterreise* (1978), set in Italy, and of *Der stille Ozean* (1980) which along with *Landläufiger Tod* (1984) and *Am Abgrund* (1986) presents life in the countryside of south Styria. Roth has also written plays *Lichtenberg* (1973), *Sehnsucht* (1976) and *Dämmerung* (1977). Although Roth's themes and settings can be related to those of **Handke** in his middle period (cf. the USA in *Der kurze Brief zum langen Abschied* and the flight from routine of a character who develops a disturbed relation to reality in *Die Angst des Tormanns beim Elfmeter*) Roth has built up a substantial *œuvre* which shows that he does more than merely follow in his compatriot's footsteps.

Roth, Joseph (1894–1939)

Born in Galicia, Roth studied in Lemberg and Vienna; he served in the Austrian army from 1916 to 1918 and became a journalist after the war. His articles showed a committed, left-wing stance which became modified after a visit to the Soviet Union in 1926. The novels *Das Spinnennetz* (1923), *Hotel Savoy* (1924) and *Die Rebellion* (1924) demonstrate an acute political awareness of resurgent militarism and arrogant authoritarianism. *Die Flucht ohn Ende* (called 'Ein Bericht', 1927) is a sharp analysis of the political and cultural situation of his day; it is also characterized by a growing scepticism. *Der stumme Prophet* (1929) casts a disenchanted eye on the Russian Revolution. Roth's success as a novelist began with *Zipper und sein Vater* (1928) and *Hiob* (1930), where the political element recedes and personal, particularly Jewish, themes are dealt with. His greatest achievement was *Radetzkymarsch* (1932), which describes four generations in the life of the Trotta family, from the battle of Solferino (1859) to the death of Franz Joseph in 1916. Particularly memorable are the descriptions of those eastern parts of the Austro-Hungarian Empire which Roth knew well. In 1933 Roth moved to Nice, Marseilles and finally Paris. *Die Büste des Kaisers* (1934, originally written in French) attacks the nationalistic fanaticism of the day and extols, in a somewhat utopian manner, the old empire with its multiplicity of races. *Die Kapuzinergruft* (1938) attempts, unsuccessfully, to be a sequel to *Radetzkymarsch* (it continues the portrayal of the Trotta family up to the *Anschluß*). Roth became increasingly sceptical about the age and the prospects for the future, and died an alcoholic. *Werke* (three vols) appeared in 1956; *Ausgewählte Werke* (four vols) in 1975 and *Romane und Erzählungen* (four vols) in 1982. A six volume *Werke* is in preparation.

Rubiner, Ludwig (1881–1920)

Rubiner made his literary début with the novel *Die indischen Opale* (1911), published under the pseudonym Ernst Ludwig Gombert. He turned his attention to poetry, and wrote the *Kriminalsonette* (1912), a collection greatly influenced by van **Hoddis**; during the war he fled to Switzerland and contributed to *Die Aktion* and *Die weißen Blätter*. The poems *Das himmlische Licht* (1916) document his turning towards left-wing, politically committed expressionism. His utopianism is also seen in the essay *Der Mensch in der Mitte* (1916) and his play *Die Gewaltlosen* (1919). Rubiner joined the Communist Party in 1919 and was active above all as editor and translator of Tolstoy and Voltaire. An anthology of his writing, *Der Dichter greift in die Politik. Ausgewählte Werke 1908–1919*, appeared in 1976.

Rühm, Gerhard (1930–)

Having studied music, Rühm formed, along with **Achleitner**, **Artmann**, **Bayer** and **Wiener**, the *Wiener Gruppe* and proved to be with Artmann its most productive, versatile and accessible member, besides providing the theoretical underpinning of the group's work in his introduction to the representative collection of texts he edited, *Die Wiener Gruppe* (1967). On the dissolution of the group in 1964 he moved to Berlin, in 1975 to Cologne, having become in 1972 professor of design at the Hamburg *Hochschule für bildende Kunst*. Rühm's work consists of sound poetry, pieces in Viennese dialect (*hosn rosn baa* with Achleitner and Artmann (1959)), montages (*montagen* with Artmann and Bayer (1956), *daheim* (1967)). At the same time as **Gomringer** he developed in *konstellationen* (1961) the type of asyntactic word composition which has become the most familiar form of concrete poetry. The 'Lesetexte' *fenster* (1968), *rhythmus r* (1968) and above all *die frösche* (1958) in which frog noises induce a revulsion which overwhelms the narrator, and the 'Hörtexte' *abhandlung über das weltall* (1966) in which words suffer entropy like the universe they describe, and *zensurierte rede* (1969), an exposure of censorship, show Rühm's mastery of a new form of performance art, evident also in the radio plays *ophelia und die wörter* (1969, published 1972, television version 1972) in which the speeches of Shakespeare's heroine dissolve into words which take on a dramatic life of their own, *wintermärchen, ein radiomelodram* (1976, 1984) in which a man abandoned naked in a forest as part of a cruel practical joke freezes to death, and *wald, ein deutsches requiem* (1983) on the death of the forest through acid rain. Here and in other works Rühm has demonstrated that experimental word play can be harnessed to the presentation of serious social issues. Collections of his works are contained in *Gesammelte Gedichte und visuelle Texte* (1970) and *Ophelia und die Wörter. Gesammelte Theaterstücke 1954–1971* (1972).

Rühmkorf, Peter (1929–)

Rühmkorf studied in Hamburg, where he has continued to live. From 1958 to 1964 he was a reader for the Rowohlt publishing firm. He has combined his work as a poet throughout with polemical literary journalism since contributing in the 1950s to *Studentenkurier* and *konkret*. With Werner Riegel (1925–56) he proclaimed 'Finismus' as the last of the -isms in *Zwischen den Kriegen. Blätter gegen die Zeit* (1952–6), which were followed by *Heiße Lyrik* (1956) and the anthology *Irdisches Vergnügen in g* (1959). Later essays include *Über das Volksvermögen* (1967), *Walther von der Vogelweide, Klopstock und ich* (1975), *Strömungslehre I* (1978), the Frankfurt poetry lectures *agar-agar-zaurzaurim. Zur Naturgeschichte des Reims* (1981) and *Bleib erschütterbar und widersteh* (1984).

Rühmkorf's poetry, which has appeared in the collections *Kunststücke* (1962), *Gesammelte Gedichte* (1976), *Phönix – voran!* (1978), *Haltbar bis Ende 1999* (1979) and *Einmalig wie wir alle* (1989), was initially marked by a love-hate relationship to a dominant influence in the early post-war years – Gottfried **Benn**, but throughout there is a characteristic fusion of the traditional and the modern: on the one hand poems on love, nature, evening, lullabies in regular rhyming stanzas or in a form of free verse which recalls the hymns and odes of eighteenth- and nineteenth-century poets, on the other hand poems in racy rhythms and multiple registers, full of slang and abstruse recondite diction, including an element of parody in modern variations on certain poems of the past of classic status.

Rühmkorf made a brief excursion into drama in the 1970s in three plays which owe much to **Brecht**: in *Lombard gibt den Letzten* (1972) business competition leads to the ruin of two publicans and a takeover by a restaurant chain, in *Was heißt hier Volsinii?* (1973) the conflict between rich and poor in an ancient Etruscan city results in Roman intervention (cf. Brecht's *Coriolan*), and in *Die Handwerker kommen* (1974) a family of six disintegrates as their living-room is converted – an allegory of the chaos produced by rampant individualism.

More recently Rühmkorf has turned his attention to the fairy-story in the tradition of E. T. A. Hoffmann in *Auf Wiedersehen in Kenilworth* (1980), in which the castle custodian and his cat undergo a metamorphosis by a ghost, and in the thirteen *Märchen* of *Der Hüter des Misthaufens* (1983). The autobiography *Die Jahre die Ihr kennt* (1972) offers a portrait of the radical chic scene in Hamburg during the 1960s.

S

Sachs, Nelly (1891–1970)

Sachs grew up in a liberal Jewish household in Berlin, where she was privately educated. She and her mother were able through the mediation of Selma Lagerlöf to take refuge in Sweden in 1940. After conventional beginnings (*Legenden und Erzählungen* (1921)) her work was transformed by seven years under Nazism and the period of emigration. She was awarded the Nobel prize for literature in 1966. The volumes *In den Wohnungen des Todes* (1947) on the Holocaust and the experience of exile and *Sternverdunklung* (1949) containing poems dedicated to Abraham, Jacob, Job, David and Saul, were followed by three further collections between 1957 and 1961; all her poems were eventually assembled in *Fahrt ins Staublose* (1961) and *Suche nach Lebenden* (1979). Sachs draws on the Old Testament, especially the prophets and the psalms, the Kabbala, Hasidic writings and Jakob Böhme to convey in free verse the themes of flight, persecution and death. She aims to commemorate and conciliate, to sound the mysteries of suffering and death and develop a strategy for personal survival. Of her seven plays collected in *Zeichen im Sand. Die szenischen Dichtungen* (1962) the most important is *Eli. Ein Mysterienspiel vom Leiden Israels* (1951, but written in 1943); in it survivors of the Holocaust rebuild a destroyed town in Poland and the murderer of the shepherd boy Eli dissolves into dust when discovered.

Sack, Gustav (1885–1916)

Sack studied German language and literature from 1906 to 1910, then science; his early writing (*Olof* (1904) and *Die drei Reiter*, not published until 1958) contains mostly neo-romantic topoi. Sack was in Switzerland at the outbreak of war, but joined the army after initial hesitation. He was killed in Romania in 1916. The novel *Ein verbummelter Student* appeared posthumously in 1917; expressionistic elements may be seen in its cult of violence and its vitalism ('brausendes, riesenfäustiges Leben'). The phrase 'Lieber verroht als vergeistigt' is seen with hindsight to have a sinister ring: **Goebbels**'s novel *Michael* copies Sack almost to the point of plagiarism. *Ein Namenloser* (1919) portrays insoluble conflict, the hero's inability to find solace in nature or science. The fragmentary novel *Paralyse* (published 1978) is greatly indebted to Nietzsche ('dementia paralytica', 'Wahnideen', etc.), as is the drama *Der Refraktär*. The war experiences are portrayed in *In Ketten durch Rumänien*. The *Gesammelte Schriften* (two vols) appeared in

1920; *Gustav Sack. Einführung in sein Werk und eine Auswahl* in 1958. *Prosa. Briefe. Verse* was published in 1962 and *Paralyse. Der Refraktär* in 1978.

Salomon, Erich von (1902–72)

After leaving the élite army cadet school at Berlin-Lichterfelde von Salomon took part immediately after the First World War in fighting in the eastern border areas as a member of a *Freikorps* or paramilitary group dissatisfied with the Versailles settlement. Having been involved in the murder of the Foreign Minister Walther Rathenau, who in the early years of the Weimar Republic became a right-wing scapegoat, he was sentenced to five years imprisonment. He gave a fictional account of his experiences at this time in *Die Geächteten* (1930), following it with the more directly autobiographical *Die Kadetten* (1933). *Die Stadt* (1932) observes Berlin of the late Weimar Republic through the eyes of a provincial newspaper editor. Von Salomon's most important work is undoubtedly *Der Fragebogen* (1951); in it the demand by the Allied occupation authorities after 1945 that those suspected of complicity with Nazism should answer the 131 questions in a standard form is taken as the point of departure for a candid account of his life from 1919 onwards. His later works include *Die schöne Wilhelmine* (1965), a Prussian rococo novel, and *Der tote Preuße* (1973), a lengthy fictional attempt to come to terms with the decline and fall of the Prussian ethos. Together with Ernst **Jünger** von Salomon is perhaps the most significant literary representative of the non-Nazi right in the first half of this century.

Salten, Felix (pseudonym of Siegmund Salzmann, 1869–1947)

Born in Budapest, Salten became a journalist, contributed to the *Allgemeine Kunst-Chronik* and became theatre critic for the *Wiener Allegemeine Zeitung* and the *Neue Freie Presse*. He became closely associated with **Beer-Hofmann**, **Hofmannsthal** and **Schnitzler**; his writing has a facility and ease of expression which led to great popularity. He was frequently (and savagely) attacked by Karl **Kraus** for the apparent triviality of his work (some fifty novels and short stories, six plays); he has, however, also been credited with the writing of the hilariously pornographic *Lebensgeschichte einer wienerischen Dirne, genannt Josefine Mutzenbacher, von ihr selbst erzählt* (1906). His most successful story was *Bambi. Eine Lebensgeschichte aus dem Walde* (1923), which achieved world fame when made into a cartoon by Walt Disney (1941–2). Salten emigrated to Hollywood in 1938 and attempted to cash in on the Bambi vogue with the sequel *Bambis Kinder* (1941) and *Djibi das Kätzchen* (1946). Salten should also be remembered as a vigorous champion of Gustav Klimt; the *Schauen und Spielen. Studien zur Kritik des* *modernen Theaters* are informative and readable. The *Gesammelte Werke* (six vols) appeared from 1928 to 1932. Salten returned to Europe at the end of the Second World War and died in Zurich.

Schaeffer, Albrecht (1885–1950)

Schaeffer studied classical philology in Munich and Berlin, also German literature; he settled in Hanover in 1913 to devote himself to writing. His early poetry, *Die Meerfahrt* (1912), *Attische Dämmerung, Heroische Fahrt* (both 1914) is reminiscent of Hölderlin; the epic writing (*Parzival* (1922)) shows an interest in the German medieval past. His most well-known novel is *Helianth* (1920), a *Bildungsroman*. After the First World War Schaeffer moved to Bavaria; in 1939 he emigrated to the USA. He gained considerable popularity through his prolific and accessible writing, but is best regarded as an epigone. His essays *Dichter und Dichtung* appeared in 1923, a second collection, *Mythos* in 1958. Collected editions include *Das Prisma* (1925) and *Gedichte aus den Jahren 1915–1930* (1931).

Schäfer, Wilhelm (1868–1952)

Son of a farmer, Schäfer worked as a teacher for seven years near Düsseldorf, where he edited the conservative journal *Die Rheinlande*. He moved to Berlin where he was befriended by Richard **Dehmel**. His first attempts at writing were plays greatly influenced by naturalism (*Ein Totschläger* (1894)), but he was more successful in the writing of anecdotes dealing with peasant life (his model was Johann Peter Hebel). These include *Mannsleut. Westerwälder Bauerngeschichten* (1895), *Anekdoten* (1907) and *Rheinsagen* (1908). His writing became increasingly patriotic (*Die dreizehn Bücher der deutschen Seele* (1922); *Deutsche Reden* (1933); *Auf den Spuren der alten Reichsherrlichkeit* (1933)) and his concept of the 'deutsche Sendung' was greeted by the Nazis. His autobiography *Mein Leben* was published in 1934; a *Rechenschaft* followed in 1948. Four volumes of *Erzählende Schriften* appeared in 1919; the *Gesamtausgabe der Anekdoten* in 1943.

Schaffner, Jakob (1875–1944)

Born in Basel as the son of a gardener, Schaffner was largely self-taught, working as a labourer in several countries. His prose is influenced by Gottfried Keller (*Die Irrfahrten des Jonathan Bregger* (1905); *Die Laterne*

(1907); *Hans Himmelhoch* (1909)); later novels may be seen as exemplifying a religious *Heimatdichtung*. The autobiographical trilogy *Johannes – Die Jünglingszeit des Johannes Schattenhold – Eine deutsche Wanderschaft* was published between 1920 and 1933. A collection of *Meisternovellen* was produced in 1936; *Kampf und Reife: eine Roman-Tetralogie* followed in 1939. Schaffner felt drawn to certain aspects of National Socialism: he was present at the first performance of *Schlageter* by Hanns **Johst**. He was killed in an air-raid on Strasburg in September 1944.

Schaper, Edzard (1908–84)

Born in Prussian Poland, Schaper led a restless life (actor, musician, gardener, sailor); he lived in Estonia, fled to Finland in 1940 and thence to Sweden. His novels and stories deal almost exclusively with the Baltic, and with religious problems, faith and martyrdom. *Die sterbende Kirche* (1935) describes the assault upon a Christian community in Estonia after the Russian Revolution (the need for stoicism and religious commitment in the face of oppression would also be relevant to the situation of the church in Hitler's Germany); *Der letzte Advent* (1949) would be a sequel. *Der Henker* (1940, published also as *Sie mähten gewappnet die Saaten* (1953)) deals with the crisis of conscience of a German-Baltic officer after the uprising of 1905. *Die Freiheit des Gefangenen* (1950) and *Die Macht der Ohnmächtigen* (1951) are set in Napoleonic times. Other novels and stories (*Am Abend der Zeit* (1970)) focus on the struggle in the Baltic during the First World War. Later novels touch on Swiss themes (Schaper moved to Switzerland in 1947). The style of his writing is deliberately archaic and eschews experimentation. His essays include *Der Mensch in der Zelle* (1951), *Untergang und Verwandlung* (1952) and *Wagnis der Gegenwart* (1965). The *Gesammelte Erzählungen 1938–1962* appeared in 1965; the *Geschichten aus vielen Leben* in 1977.

Scharang, Michael (1941–)

Scharang studied in Vienna, gained a doctorate with a dissertation on Robert **Musil** and became a member of the *Grazer Autorenversammlung*. Although he is less self-consciously experimental than its other members, the relation of the author/narrator to reality is problematized in his work. After the experimentalism of *Verfahren eines Verfahrens* (1969) he developed a form of politically engaged social realism in accordance with the ideas of Walter Benjamin, whose influence is also evident in the essays collected in *Die Emanzipation der Kunst* (1971). In *Charly Traktor* (1973) the individualistic rebellion of a piece-worker, told from his point of view and in his language, leads to dismissal, but with the help of a communist fellow-worker Charly comes to see the need for solidarity. In *Der Sohn eines Landarbeiters* (1976), on the other hand, a similar proletarian protagonist proves unable to attain the same awareness and commits suicide. In *Harry. Eine Abrechnung* (1984) the central figure, Charly's 25-year-old illegitimate son, tells in a monologue the story of a life in which circumstances which deprive him of family and friends and loyalty to his own notion of personal independence lead to growing isolation. Scharang has also written radio and television plays and a novel on a bank robbery *Der Lebemann* (1979), which departs from the critical realism of his other fiction.

Schaukal, Richard von (1874–1942)

Schaukal studied law in Vienna and became a civil servant, achieving the patent of nobility in 1918. He is best known as the author of *symboliste* poetry, frequently of elegiac mood; he translated skilfully from the French (Verlaine, Baudelaire and Mallarmé). His poetry is sensitive, musical and delicate. The *Gedichte* of 1893 set the tone, and the later work remained basically backward-looking. The collection *Tristia* (1898) is probably his best known. The stories *Von Tod zu Tod* (1902) and *Eros Thanatos* (1906) are good examples of Viennese *fin de siècle* writing. His plays include *Rückkehr* (1894) and *Vorabend* (1902). Schaukal also wrote essays on literary figures (E. T. A. Hoffmann, Wilhelm Busch, Adalbert Stifter and Richard **Dehmel**). His memoirs concern the Austro-Hungarian Empire, which he loved and whose loss was a trauma for him. The *Werke in Einzelausgaben* appeared from 1965.

Scheerbart, Paul (1863–1915)

Scheerbart was born in Danzig; he studied philosophy and art history in Leipzig, Halle, Munich and Vienna. He moved to Berlin in 1887 where he founded the 'Verlag deutscher Phantasten'. He is regarded as one of the most eccentric precursors of expressionism and Dadaism, concentrating above all on the grotesque and the bizarre. Social criticism is also to be found: *Rakkóx, der Billionär. Ein Protzenroman* (1900) is a thinly veiled attack on Wilhelm II. Ernst Rowohlt and Herwarth **Walden** greatly admired his work; Walden published Scheerbart's ideas on 'Glasarchitektur' in the 'Verlag der Sturm' in 1914. A 'Monument des neuen Gesetzes' is posited, a shrine of glass to be inscribed with the laws of a utopian future. 'Glasarchitektur' also forms the central motif in the two stories *Kapitän Junker auf der Insel Temuso* and *Das Ozeansanatorium für Heukranke*. Scheerbart also attempted poetry (*Katerpoesie* (1909)) and plays (*Kometentanz* (1902)). **Kokoschka** twice sketched him for *Der Sturm* (in

'Menschenköpfe'). He died an alcoholic. *Eine Einführung in sein Werk und eine Auswahl* appeared in 1955; *Dichterische Hauptwerke* in 1962. A ten volume *Gesammelte Werke* appeared in 1986.

Schickele, René (1883–1940)

Born of an Alsatian father and French mother, Schickele was born in Oberehnheim, Alsace, studied philosophy in Strasburg, Munich, Paris and Berlin. With Otto **Flake** and Ernst **Stadler** he edited the Alsatian journal *Der Stürmer* (1902); his main preoccupation was with the removal of national prejudices, particularly the animosity between France and Germany. The early poetry (*Pan. Sonnenopfer der Jugend* (1902)) is undistinguished; it was as the publisher in Zurich during the First World War of the expressionist journal *Die weißen Blätter* that Schickele's reputation was assured. His drama *Hans im Schnakenloch* (1916) deals again with the Alsatian 'Grenzland': Schickele was acquainted with James Joyce in Zurich and suggested to him that he might translate this play into English. The essays *Schreie auf dem Boulevard* (1913) show Schickele to be an accomplished journalist. After the war Schickele moved away from the somewhat expressionistic style of writing to more sober descriptions and documentation, akin to 'Neue Sachlichkeit' (*Das Erbe am Rhein* (1925); *Symphonie für Jazz* (1929); *Der Wolf in der Hürde* (1931)). The Provence novel *Die Witwe Bosca* (1933) should also be noted. Schickele was also an energetic anthologist. His *Werke* (three vols) appeared in 1959, and (four vols) in 1975; *Romane und Erzählungen* appeared in 1983.

Schlaf, Johannes (1862–1941)

Schlaf made his reputation with Arno **Holz** as one of the exponents of 'konsequenter Naturalismus'; the two collaborated on *Papa Hamlet* (1889), *Die Familie Selicke* (1890) and *Neue Gleise* (1892). Schlaf's drama *Meister Oelze* (1892) is regarded as one of the triumphs of German naturalism. Schlaf turned away from this form of writing, and engaged in a bitter polemic with Holz which lasted many years. He advocated an 'intimes Theater' (here Strindberg's influence is noticeable), and turned more and more to mysticism and *Naturphilosophie*. His contributions to the journals *Pan*, *Jugend* and *Simplicissimus* show a *Jugendstil* tendency in his prose (viz. the sketch *Sommertod* (1897)). The novel *Das dritte Reich* (1900) expresses a monistic viewpoint. Schlaf suffered increasingly from nervous disorders: his speculative thinking took an increasingly eccentric direction, particularly the attempt to discredit a heliocentric cosmogony (*Die Erde – nicht die Sonne* (1919), and *Die geozentrische Tatsache als unmittelbare Folgerung aus dem Sonnenfleckenphänomen* (1925)). Schlaf spent much time in sanatoria before settling in Weimar, befriended by Paul **Ernst**. He died in his home-town Querfurt. His translations of Whitman, Balzac and Zola were widely acclaimed. The *Ausgewählte Werke* (two vols) appeared from 1934 to 1940.

Schlesinger, Klaus (1937–)

Born in Berlin, Schlesinger has spent most of his life in the GDR, where he began writing in the late 1950s, but has lived since 1980 in West Berlin. In his first novel *Michael* (1971 in GDR, 1972 under the title *Capellos Trommel* in Switzerland, then in the Federal Republic) he succeeded in treating with remarkable narrative verve a theme which in one form or another has received attention from other German writers of his generation, e.g. Günter **Herburger** in *Die Messe*: the complications arising in a father-son relationship from the suspicion that the father had committed officially approved crimes during the Third Reich. In *Alte Filme* (1975) a film enthusiast discovers that his aged neighbour is a former star; suddenly made aware of the effects of time he plunges into a hectic round of new pleasures. The stories collected in *Berliner Traum* (1977) include 'Die Spaltung des Erwin Racholl', a Kafkaesque fantasy in which a man due for promotion finds himself conveyed by *S-Bahn* to West Berlin, then forced to justify this enforced departure from the norm before an anonymous court. In *Leben im Winter* (1980) a grandmother's seventieth birthday party brings together friends and relations from East and West Berlin, while in *Matulla und Busch* (1984) an old man unexpectedly inherits a house in Berlin and discovers on arrival that it is occupied by squatters.

Schmidt, Arno (1914–79)

Having briefly studied mathematics, Schmidt worked from 1934 to 1939 in the textile industry, served in the army between 1940 and 1945, for a time as a cartographer in Norway, became a POW, then an interpreter. He eventually settled as a professional writer in the village of Bargfeld in the Lüneburg heath, where he remained totally dedicated to his work until his death. In theme and content his early works are similar to those of his contemporaries inspired by the post-war situation of ideological vacuum, material shortage and existential insecurity. In style, however, he went from the beginning his own way, preferring the microscopic examination of particulars to the broad flow of conventional narrative, at the same time allowing several narrative strands to proceed simultaneously. With the exception of *Das steinerne Herz* (1956), the story of an unscrupulous book-collector set in 1954, and part of *KAFF* all Schmidt's works to the end of the 1960s present characters from the ancient world (Gadir and Enthymesis in *Leviathan* (1949), Alexander in *die umsiedler* (1953), *Kosmas* (1955)), the Third Reich and its aftermath (the title-stories of *Leviathan* and *die umsiedler*, *Aus dem Leben eines Fauns* (1953) and the first story in *Brand's Haide* (1951)) and after a nuclear war (the second story in *Brand's Haide*, *Schwarze Spiegel* (1963), *Die Gelehrtenrepublik* (1957) and the second narrative strand of *KAFF auch Mare Crisium* (1960)). Although these themes prompt comparison with **Kasack** and **Nossack** Schmidt lacks their concern with a metaphysical dimension beyond the phenomenal world; he aims instead at a total and precise reproduction of mental processes in all their variety, including the interaction of the conscious with the unconscious mind as it finds expression in the multiple and subliminal meanings of words and word combinations. Basing himself on the theories of Freud and the practice of a host of writers, especially Laurence Sterne, Lewis Carroll and James Joyce, Schmidt has developed the notion of the 'etym', according to which man uses language on two levels, as a means of correct communication between conscious minds and as a reservoir of fragments which emerge from the unconscious to form unexpected neologisms for the normally censored expression of sexual intentions. Having in *KAFF* separated the two strands into distinct columns, he increases their number to three in *Zettel's Traum* (1970), so that the core story of a visit on a single day in summer 1968 by Wilma and Paul Jacobi with their daughter Franziska to the hermit scholar Daniel Pagenstecher to gain advice on their planned translation of the works of Edgar Allan Poe is flanked by quotations and digressions. In this *magnum opus* consisting of 1,334 A3 typescript pages weighing eight kilos in its first edition and based on 130,000 filing cards the 'etym' theory is demonstrated in analyses of the life and works of Poe, whose *Das Gesamte Werk in 10 Bänden* (1966–72) was translated by Schmidt with Hans **Wollschläger**. The late works *Die Schule der Atheisten* (1972) set in the year 2014 after yet another nuclear catastrophe and *Abend mit Goldrand* (1975) which, laid out in the typescript format of his chief work, offers a review of his past life in the form of a mythical phantasmagoria, can be described as comic Utopias, to which the posthumous fragment *Julia, oder die Gemälde* (1983) represents a subdued coda. Schmidt's works may be compared to tower blocks, their multilevel structures rising from the narrow foundations of an exiguous plot involving a small number of characters. Yet few would deny that he is a worthy successor to the long line of obsessive wordsmiths who both provide impulses for his fiction and form the subjects of the essay collections *Dya Na Sore* (1958), *Belphegor* (1961), *Die Ritter vom Geist* (1965), *Der Triton mit dem Sonnenschirm* (1969) (the last on British writers) and of the biographies *Fouqué und einige seiner Zeitgenossen* (1958, extended 1959) and *Sitara und der Weg dorthin* (1963) on Karl May.

Schnabel, Ernst (1913–86)

Schnabel went to sea at the age of 17, sailed the world for twelve years and served in the navy throughout the Second World War. He then worked for radio from 1946 onwards. His maritime experiences are reflected in the novels *Die Reise nach Savannah* (1939) and *Nachtwind* (1941), the stories *Sie sehen den Marmor nicht* (1949) and the travel book *Die Erde hat viele Namen* (1955), as well as in his best-known work *Der sechste Gesang* (1956) in which the contemporary theme of the return home from war is presented through the person of Odysseus. This was followed by a similar modern recreation of Greek myth *Ich und die Könige* (1958) on Daedalus, the 'first engineer'. Schnabel is also remembered for his development of the radio feature, a combination of document, reportage, dialogue, dramatic scenes and realistic sound effects, exemplified at its most original by *Der 29. Januar 1947* (1947), based on thousands of letters describing listeners' experiences on that day – an experiment repeated thirty years later in *Der 29. Januar 1977* (1977).

Schnack, Anton (1892–1973)

Born in Rieneck, Mainfranken, Schnack is regarded as one of the most outstanding poets of the First World War. He began publishing in *Die Aktion* in 1915: his first war poem is 'Schwester Maria' (*Die Aktion*, 1917). Three collections of war poems appeared in 1919 (*Strophen der Gier, Die tausend Gelächter* and *Der Abenteurer*); in 1920 his most important collection *Tier rang gewaltig mit Tier* was published in a limited edition. Schnack wrote predominantly in long rhymed lines in free rhythm which approximate to the sonnet form. Most successful are 'Schwester Maria' and 'Nächtliche Landschaft'. Of this collection Schnack wrote: 'Das Buch enthält keine hurrapatriotischen Gedichte, sondern es ist vielmehr ein Buch des Weinens und der Trauer'. Schnack later turned to popular, light-hearted fiction (*Kleines Lesebuch* and *Die fünfzehn Abenteuer* (1935)). His writing during the Second World War was largely trivial; the two novels *Zugvögel der Liebe* (1936) and *Der finstere Franz* (1937) should also be noted. In the 1950s he published *Die Reise aus Sehnsucht* (1954) and *Flirt mit dem Alltag* (1956).

His brother, Friedrich Schnack (1888–1977) was famous for popular books on natural history, travel accounts (to Madagascar) and children's literature. His *Gesamtausgabe des poetischen Werkes* appeared from 1950 to 1954, and the *Gesammelte Werke* (two vols) in 1961.

Schneider, Michael (1943–)

Having studied in Freiburg, Berlin and Paris, Michael Schneider wrote a doctoral dissertation on Marx and Freud and contributed to various periodicals (*konkret, Kursbuch, Literaturmagazin*) essays (e.g. 'Gegen des linken Dogmatismus') based on a retrospective awareness of the weaknesses and failures of the student movement and on insights derived from ideas the movement had itself advocated, later collected in *Die lange Wut zum langen Marsch* (1975). He takes issue with further intellectual and cultural trends in the later volumes of essays *Den Kopf verkehrt aufgesetzt oder Die melancholische Linke. Aspekte des Kulturzerfalls in den siebziger Jahren* (1981) and *Nur tote Fische schwimmen mit dem Strom* (1984). The play *Die Wiedergutmachung* (première 1977, published 1985) concerns the activities during the Third Reich of Friedrich Flick, who became the richest manufacturer in the Federal Republic. It was followed in 1982 by *Luftschloß unter Tage* on the disintegration of a residential commune and of the utopian dreams which had led to its foundation. Schneider's fiction begins with *Das Spiegelkabinett* (1980), which can be interpreted as an answer to 'Der große und der kleine Bruder' by his brother **Peter Schneider**. In it the feat which brings the magician Alfredo cult status turns out to be a fraud in which his brother acts as double, whereupon the latter begins his own career as an 'anti-magician' who explains his tricks to his audience. *Die Traumfalle* (1987) consists of three stories ('Balzacs Totenklage', 'Suchbild Woyzeck. Eine Theaternovelle' and 'Die Unbeschreibliche. Bekenntnisse eines Literaten') in which the mask of genius is stripped from the tormented artist in a manner which recalls the psychological subtlety of **Thomas Mann**'s treatment of the same theme.

Schneider, Peter (1940–)

Peter Schneider studied at several German universities before becoming a professional writer in 1967. He has lived in Berlin since 1961, apart from interruptions in England and Italy. His involvement in the student movement of the late 1960s and in the controversies on the role of literature which arose in its context can be traced in the essays collected in *Ansprachen, Reden, Notizen, Gedichte* (1970) and in contributions to *Kursbuch*, the periodical edited by Hans Magnus **Enzensberger** from 1965 to 1975 which played a key role in West German intellectual life in this period of political transition. Schneider's first work of fiction *Lenz* (1973), which sold 123,000 copies in seven years and is perhaps the most important work to emerge from the aftermath of the student movement, concerns the personal and political failures of a radical student before he finds temporary refuge from the stridencies of the German political scene in the close community life of Italian workers. Although the central figure differs from his model, the *Sturm und Drang* writer J. M. R. Lenz in Georg Büchner's account of his descent into madness, the story stands in a long German tradition in which the maladjustments of a sensitive youth to social and political reality are the subject of fiction. . . . *schon bist du ein Verfassungsfeind* (1975) aims to show the effects of government measures (the so-called 'Radikalenerlaß') intended to counter what it saw as subversion of schools and other public institutions by persons committed to the revolutionary overthrow of parliamentary democracy by tracing the efforts of the teacher Kleff to gain employment. *Die Wette* (1978) contains the story 'Der große und der kleine Bruder' on the conflict between two brothers, both magicians (cf. **Michael Schneider**, *Das Spiegelkabinett*). *Der Mauerspringer* (1982) is a collection of stories and reports about people who contrive for various reasons to cross the Berlin Wall from east to west and vice versa and often back, presented without commitment to either side. *Vati* (1987), about the son of a Nazi mass murderer, draws on the case of the notorious concentration camp doctor Mengele. The play *Totoloque* (1985) concerns the conflict between Aztecs and Spaniards in Mexico, culminating in the bloodbath of Tenochtitlan in 1520. Schneider's later essays are collected in *Atempause* (1977) and *Die Botschaft des Pferdekopfs* (1981).

Schneider, Reinhold (1903–58)

Reinhold Schneider travelled extensively in Europe between 1928 and 1939, then lived in Potsdam from 1932 to 1937 and in Freiburg from 1938 to his death. The son of a Protestant father and a Catholic mother he came to an undenominational Christianity after a reading of Unamuno's *The Tragic Sense of Life* enabled him to place an already strong tragic awareness – early melancholy had led to a suicide attempt – in the context of history, and contact with the works of Kierkegaard supplied an existential interpretation of the same feeling. His early historical works show the conflict or interaction between political power and the religious spirit in the lives of prominent rulers (*Philipp II oder Religion und Macht* (1931), *Innozenz der Dritte* (written 1930–1, published 1960), *Die Hohenzollern* (1933)). Questions of guilt, atonement and grace begin to emerge in the survey of English history *Das Inselreich* (1936) and continue to preoccupy Schneider in *Kaiser Lothars Krone* (1937) on a twelfth-century German emperor, and above all in one of the most important works of the Christian inner emigration *Las Casas vor Karl V* (1938), in which the Dominican monk defends the interests of the South American Indians before the king. In thus giving natural law priority over the law of the state Schneider offered a disguised protest against Nazi anti-Semitism. Despite a ban on publication from 1942 a flood of religious essays, stories, poems and historical reflections reached the public and the army in the closing years of the Third Reich, while the story 'Der Tröster' in the collection *Die dunkle Nacht* (1943) was inspired by the first reports of Dachau. After the end of the war Schneider turned to drama in further variations on the theme of conflict between secular power and religious calling: *Der große Verzicht* (1950, dramatized for radio 1954, for the theatre 1958) on the hermit Petrus of Murrhone who having been raised to the papacy prefers abdication to becoming an instrument of secular power, *Innozenz und Franziskus* (1953) on the most powerful medieval pope and the most influential medieval saint, *Der Traum des Eroberers* (1951) on William the Conqueror, *Zar Alexander* (1951, performed under the title *Die Abrechnug* 1954) and *Die Tarnkappe* (1951), a Nibelungen play in which Siegfried appears as the first Christian.

Schneider, Rolf (1932–)

Rolf Schneider studied in Halle and edited the periodical *Aufbau* in Berlin from 1955 to 1958, since when he has been a professional writer. Although he was excluded from the GDR Writers Union after signing the protest against the expatriation of Wolf **Biermann** he was able to leave and return to the GDR at will and has worked as a literary adviser to the theatre in Mainz. He began with parodies, *Aus zweiter Hand* (1958), and a talent for pastiche is evident in his fiction, whether in the story collections *Brücken und Gitter* (1965) and *Nekrolog* (1974, West German title *Pilzomelett*) or the novel *Der Tod des Nibelungen* (1970), which adopts the model of *Der Fragebogen* by Ernst von **Salomon** in order to document the progress of a fictional sculptor to prominence during the Third Reich. In *Die Tage in W.* (1965) a detective story is made the vehicle for the exposure of conditions in a provincial town during the closing years of the Weimar Republic, while *Das Glück* (1976) traces the life of a woman from the humblest origins to a position as schoolteacher in the GDR; the private cost of her emancipation is the happiness which eludes her. In *Die Reise nach Jaroslaw* (1974) the failure of a teenage girl to make headway in the GDR education system prompts her to escape the pressures of home by hitch-hiking through Poland; by allowing his central character to act as narrator Schneider is able to reproduce the slang of a distinct generation in the manner of **Plenzdorf**'s *Die neuen Leiden des jungen W.* In *November* (1979) a woman writer after protesting against the expatriation of a colleague retains the accustomed privileges of her life in the GDR, but her ambivalent and resigned attitude alienates her son. Although manifestly inspired by the **Biermann** affair the novel is according to Schneider not a *Schlüsselroman* or work of disguised identities. Schneider's numerous plays, mainly for radio and television, cover a wide range of historical periods and geographical settings, but the best concern the confrontation of intellectuals with questions of conscience in the context of the struggle against Nazism or the cold war, as in *Prozeß Richard Waverly* (1961) on the commitment to a mental institution of the commander of the atom bomb sortie to Hiroshima, *Die Rebellion des Patrick Wright* (1966) in which the protagonist refuses command of the bombardment of Dresden, and *Der Mann aus England* (1963) in which a British teacher becomes the victim of West German attempts to cover up the Nazi past. *Prozeß in Nürnberg* (1967) is a documentary play in the manner of **Peter Weiss**, **Hochhuth** and **Kipphardt**.

Schnitzler, Arthur (1862–1931)

Son of an eminent Jewish Viennese throat specialist, Schnitzler qualified as a doctor at the medical school of Vienna University; his father's contact with many leading actors gained him access to the *Burgtheater* and many fashionable salons. The short play *Liebelei*, a tragicomedy of erotic entanglements (written in 1894) was performed there in 1895; *Anatol*, a cycle of seven one-act plays was performed as a cycle first in Prague in 1893 and Vienna in 1910. The latter work is a series of episodes from the life of a man about town: Schnitzler's wit, irony and scepticism are well to the fore. *Reigen*, a cycle of ten dialogues (1900) was banned because of the remarkable frankness with which sexuality is treated; it became widely known as the French film *La ronde*. Sex is seen as the great leveller: the work may be interpreted as a satire, although its detractors may deplore its supposedly cynical immorality. Schnitzler also gained a reputation as a prose-writer: *Leutnant Gustl*, a short *Novelle* written in 1900, is experimental in its use of interior monologue: it was seen as a satirical attack on the military code of honour, and the scandal it caused forced Schnitzler to resign his commission in the medical corps (he would later use the same technique in the story *Fräulein Else* (1924)). He rapidly became known in the avant-garde circles in Vienna: the sophistication of his irony, however, precluded an unequivocal commitment to modernism. A salutary scepticism, also a tolerance born of deep understanding of human behaviour, characterized much of his writing. He published many of his stories in the *Neue Freie Presse*, and was on friendly terms with **Hofmannsthal**, **Beer-Hofmann** and Hermann **Bahr**; Freud greatly admired him, going as far as to claim that Schnitzler was his 'Doppelgänger'. In the plays *Das Märchen* (1894) and *Freiwild* (1898) Schnitzler criticized hypocrisy and an ossified code of values; *Der einsame Weg* (1904) is a conversation piece in which death (the suicide of the daughter – a premonition of the death of Schnitzler's own) seems omnipresent. Schnitzler excelled at dialogue, the subtle uncovering of hitherto unknown tendencies; his verse-dramas were not successful. The problem of anti-Semitism is faced in *Professor Bernhardi* (1912), a play banned in Austria-Hungary because of its supposed anticlericalism.

Schnitzler's position as a writer is paradoxical: attached so closely to his Viennese environment, he could also criticize it; an established figure, he could also appear subversive. Hofmannsthal described him as 'Arzt und Sohn eines Arztes, also Beobachter und Skeptiker von Beruf': his gaze, although disenchanted, was never censorious. The stories of *Doktor Graesler, Badearzt* (1917) best exemplify his stance, part *fin de siècle* hedonist, part moralist, a man whose judgement is always tempered by sympathy. An autobiography was planned, but remained a fragment (*Leben und Nachklang: Werk und Widerhall*): Schnitzler's son edited the work which was published as *Jugend in Wien* in 1968.

Seven volumes of *Gesammelte Werke* appeared in 1912 (nine vols from 1922 to 1926); *Gesammelte Werke in Einzelbänden: Die erzählenden Schriften* (two vols) appeared in 1961; *Die dramatischen Werke* (two vols) in 1962; *Aphorismen und Betrachtungen* in 1967; *Entworfenes und Verworfenes* in 1977. *Werke* (6 vols) appeared in 1981. The diaries *Tagebücher 1879–1931* began publication in 1981.

Schnurre, Wolfdietrich (1920–89)

Born in Berlin, Schnurre served throughout the war in the army, and passed the rest of his life in his home city as a professional writer. His reading of the short story 'Das Begräbnis' initiated the activities of *Gruppe 47* and concluded the group's thirtieth anniversary celebration. He began as a writer of 'Kahlschlagliteratur' (cf. **Böll**, **Bender**, **Weyrauch**) whose preferred and most successfully cultivated form was the short story in the dead-pan style of Hemingway. His themes were war and its aftermath viewed from the point of view of its victims whose spontaneous acts of mercy lead to death, the difficulties of demobilized soldiers adjusting to civilian life, guilt and responsibility in everyday post-war situations and in the Third Reich. Pieces from the collections *Man sollte dagegen sein* (1960), *Die Rohrdommel ruft jeden Tag* (1950), *Eine Rechnung, die nicht aufgeht* (1958), *Funke im Reisig* (1963), *Ohne Einsatz kein Spiel* (1964) were assembled in *Die Erzählungen* (1966) and *Erzählungen 1945–1965* (1977). In *Das Los unserer Stadt* (1959) and its sequel *Richard kehrt zurück* (1970) he developed a form of magic realism comparable to that of **Nossack** and **Kasack** in order to present an allegory of the post-war situation in Berlin. His one major novel is *Ein Unglücksfall* (1981), a deeply felt investigation of the German-Jewish relationship during the Third Reich. In it a Berlin rabbi reconstructs events leading to the death of a glazier engaged in the installation of a Misrach window in a synagogue destroyed during the 'Kristallnacht'; the lengthy flashbacks to the years of the Third Reich reveal the glazier, who had given shelter to a Jewish couple but had been unable to prevent their suicide, as a man who did the right thing for the wrong reason. The other most significant work of Schnurre's later years is *Der Schattenfotograf* (1978), autobiographical notes which include illuminating accounts of works by admired authors, e.g. Montaigne, **Kafka**, Ernst Bloch. He also produced numerous lighter works, some with his own illustrations, such as *Als Vaters Bart noch rot war* (1958) in which a proletarian milieu in the north of Berlin during the 1920s and 1930s is viewed from the perspective of a growing child and his father, *Aufzeichnungen des Pudels Ali* (1962, originally published as *Sternstaub und Sänfte* in 1951), an ambivalent satire of the ivory-tower artist, to which can be compared the animal fables in *Protest im Parterre* (1957). His poems are collected in *Kassiber* (1956, 1964, 1979).

Scholz, Wilhelm von (1874–1969)

Son of Bismarck's last Minister of Finance, Scholz studied literature and philosophy, served briefly in the army (1894), then devoted himself to writing. His early poetry (*Frühlingsfahrt* (1896)) is influenced by Liliencron, whom Scholz admired; he felt a great affinity with the theatre, however, and was *Dramaturg* in Stuttgart from 1914 to 1922. He became associated with Paul **Ernst** and put forward his views on neo-classicism in 1915 (*Gedanken zum Drama*). His most famous play was *Der Wettlauf mit dem Schatten* of 1921, a work in which Scholz's interest in the occult is plainly seen. Of the novels, *Perpetua* (1926) was the most successful, an account of two sisters in Augsburg in 1500, the one an abbess, the other (ostensibly) a witch. Scholz retired to his estate near Konstanz and devoted himself to a study of mysticism (*Deutsche Mystiker* (1908)); essays on literary figures (Annette von Droste-Hülshoff and Friedrich Hebbel) are also memorable. Scholz also edited the *Deutsches Balladenbuch* (1905) and three volumes of *Deutsche Dramaturgie* (1907–12). Five volumes of *Gesammelte Werke* appeared in 1924; *Ausgewählte Schauspiele* in 1964.

Schönherr, Karl (1867–1943)

Son of a teacher in the Tyrol, Schönherr studied medicine in Vienna, but gave up practising in 1905 to concentrate on writing. His plays may be seen as exemplifying Austrian naturalist *Heimatdichtung*, dealing principally with the peasant and his fight to save his land. Typical here is *Erde* (1908), produced successfully in the *Burgtheater* with Josef Kainz in the lead; *Glaube und Hoffnung* (1910) has a religious theme. *Volk in Not* (1915), *Passionsspiel* (1933) and *Die Fahne weht* (1937) are overtly nationalist in tone; Schönherr drew on his medical knowledge for certain late plays: *Es* (1923), with only two actors, concerns the sanctity of the unborn child. He also wrote poems in dialect (*Innthaler Schnalzer*, and *Tiroler Marterln* (both 1895)). His prose is best represented by the *Tiroler Bauernschwänke* (1913). He was awarded several prizes for his writing (the Bauernfeld, Schiller and Grillparzer prizes). The *Gesamtausgabe Bühnenwerke* appeared in 1967 and the *Lyrik and Prasa* in 1969.

Schröder, Rudolf Alexander (1878–1962)

Born into a wealthy Bremen patrician family, Schröder studied architecture in Munich and worked in Berlin, where he was associated with the art historian Julius Meier-Graefe. His lyrical work first exemplified neo-romantic attitudes (*Lieder an eine Geliebte* (1900); *Sonette zum Andenken an eine Verstorbene* (1904)), but soon became deliberately traditional in form, eschewing modernist techniques. During the First World War Schröder worked for the censor in Brussels; his conservative, patriotic stance is seen in the *Deutsche Oden* (1913) and *Heilig Vaterland* (1914). Schröder came to see his task as the preservation of traditional values in the face of a threatening future; a fervent Protestant, he wrote and lectured frequently on Lutheran theology. He settled in Bavaria (Chiemsee) and took up landscape-painting; *Die weltlichen Gedichte* (1940) are remarkable for their mastery of several traditional lyric styles. During the Second World War he was in contact with Pastor Niemöller and the Confessing Church: *Die geistlichen Lieder* (1949) express his religious convictions. Schröder was also a prolific essay-writer and editor; his translations, especially of the classics, should also be noted. He became the acknowledged guardian of the values of the 'other Germany' after 1945, and received innumerable honours. Eight volumes of *Gesammelte Werke* appeared from 1958 to 1965; *Ausgewählte Werke* (three vols) from 1965 to 1966.

Schütz. Helga (1937–)

Born in Silesia, Helga Schütz attended the film school in Potsdam from 1958 to 1962 and has since combined the writing of fiction with work, usually with the director Egon Günther, on scenarios for the GDR film company DEFA. Three collections of stories, *Vorgeschichten oder Schöne Gegend Probstein* (1970), *Das Erdbeben bei Sangershausen und andere Geschichten* (1972), *Festbeleuchtung* (1974) and the novel *Jette in Dresden* (1977, published 1978 in the Federal Republic as *Mädchenrätsel*) follow the lives of a few members of a small rural community uprooted from Silesia at the end of the Second World War and scattered to different parts of the two Germanies. They focus on Jette who, coming from Dresden and returning there after the war, observes events without village preconceptions and can be identified with the author's former self at different ages. In the novel *Julia oder Erziehung zum Chorgesang* (1983) the years of reconstruction in the GDR are viewed retrospectively in 1979 when the title-figure makes a journey to her roots in connection with a film project. The most recent novel *In Annas Namen* (1987) shows the effects on a triangular relationship of divisions between the two German states. Helga Schütz's strength lies in her ability to show the impact of large events on characters whose range of experience is limited by their confinement to rural backwaters.

Schütz, Stefan (1944–)

Schütz trained and worked as an actor in various GDR theatres, then as a production assistant and adviser with the *Berliner Ensemble* and the *Deutsches Theater* in Berlin. Having begun to write plays in 1970 he moved to the Federal Republic in 1980. Two themes are present throughout his work: the conflict between the individual and authority and the socio-political dimension of relations between the sexes. In dealing with the former Schütz is inspired by the problem of the writer in the GDR and other regimes he sees as born of a failed revolution, leading to a split personality in *Majakowski* (1971), *Stasch* (1978) and *Die Seidels* (1983). In *Kohlhaas* (1975–6) the figure known to German readers from Heinrich von Kleist's story appears at the end as one whose disillusioned view of man's addiction to power prevents him pursuing the revolution further. Similar views inform *Odysseus Heimkehr* (1972) in which the inhabitants of Ithaca are shown afflicted with a skin disease, a symbol of stagnation, and Odysseus's proposed cure is adopted by his rivals in order to secure a monopoly of power. The critique of hidebound communism implied here may also be present in *Laokoon* (1979) in which the Trojans refuse to heed the warnings of the title-figure, preferring illusion to reality, faith to critical doubt. *Sappa* (1980) and *Die Schweine* (1981), in which the mythical mask is abandoned, are more clearly directed against conditions in the GDR. Schütz's critique of the patriarchal system, seen as present under both communism and capitalism, finds radical expression in the plays *Antiope und Theseus* (1974) and *Heliosa und Abaelard* (1975), in which the female figures are more firmly committed to the absolute claims of love than their partners, and above all in the vast fictional prose work *Medusa* (1986) which in its resort to myth, fantasy and allegory in order to illuminate contemporary reality can be placed alongside recent novels by **Grass**, S. **Heym** and **Morgner**. In three sections mostly devoid of punctuation or paragraph divisions the central figure Marie Flaam – avatar of Joyce's Molly Bloom – undertakes with the help of her *alter ego* Gorga-Sappho, a reincarnation of Medusa, a traumatic journey in which the reality of the GDR appears as a series of grotesque visions, culminating in a Utopia where Marie merges with her matriarchal mentor and attains harmonious fulfilment with her male companion Naphtan. In here combining political and feminist criticism Schütz unites his two themes in a style driven headlong by a remarkable expressive energy, evident also in the novel *Katt* (1988), described as a 'Volksbuch'.

Schwaiger, Brigitte (1949–)

Brought up in comfortable circumstances, Schwaiger studied German, Spanish and psychology, then worked as a teacher, actress and secretary before becoming a professional writer in 1975. Her first novel, *Wie kommt das Salz ins Meer* (1977), which became a bestseller, is a feminist attempt to come to terms with the factors contributing to the failure of a premature marriage, and was followed by *Mein spanisches Dorf* (1978), an autobiography in the form of diary entries, letters, lyrical and narrative fragments, and *Lange Abwesenheit* (1980) in which a woman works through a disturbed relation to her father in an account of his last illness interrupted by flashbacks to childhood and an affair with an elderly man who had become a father surrogate. Schwaiger's works provide a popular, easily digested form of 'neue Subjektivität' imbued with a feminism which lacks the stridency of **Reinig** or the prolix emotional complexity of **Struck**.

Schwitters, Kurt (1887–1948)

Schwitters studied in the Academy of Arts in Dresden, and settled in Hanover: his many-sided talents have little equal in modern German culture (painter, designer, sculptor, writer of poetry and prose). He became associated with the *Sturm* circle in 1918 (**Walden** published two stories *Die Zwiebel* and *Franz Müllers Drahtfrühling*) and later with the Dadaists **Arp** and **Hausmann**. He incorporated into his writing various items from the world around him (clichés, proverbs, advertisements), just as in his collages and sculpture he used bus-tickets, pieces of newspaper, etc. The 'Anna Blume' poems show surrealist aspects; later Schwitters turned to concrete poetry. *Merz* is best defined as Schwitters's own brand of Dada (the term derives from the word 'Commerzbank' and is a fanciful extrapolation): it playfully refers to Schwitters's attempt to redefine art and non-art. Schwitters lived for many years in Norway; in 1937 he emigrated there and moved to England in 1940. He died in Ambleside in the Lake District. *Anna Blume und ich* appeared in 1965, facsimile *Merzhefte* in 1975. *Das literarische Werke* (four vols) was published in 1977, *Briefe aus fünf Jahrzehnten* in the same year. A novel by Richard Friedenthal (*Die Welt in der Nußschale* (1956)) gives an amusing portrayal of Schwitters ('Baby Bitter') in the internment camp on the Isle of Man.

Seghers, Anna (pseudonym of Netty Radvany, née Reiling, 1900–83)

Anna Seghers was a student of history, philosophy and art history; she gained a doctorate on *Jude und Judentum im Werke Rembrandts*. She joined the Communist Party in 1928 and published her novel *Der Aufstand der Fischer von St. Barbara* in the same year. The book is stylistically a fusion between elements of expressionism and 'Neue Sachlichkeit'; the theme of humanity will characterize most of her work. *Auf dem Weg zur amerikanischen Botschaft* (1930) contains a story dealing with the execution of Sacco and Vanzetti; *Die Gefährten* (1932) is unsubtly partisan, as is *Der Kopflohn* (1932). In 1933 she fled to France, in 1940 she moved to Marseilles (unoccupied). She became world-famous for her novel *Das siebte Kreuz* (1942), a description of the escape of seven prisoners from a concentration camp: only one survives. The novel *Transit* (1948), like the story *Der Ausflug der toten Mädchen* (1946), is based on a personal experience: here the struggle to gain a visa to be allowed emigration to Mexico. In Mexico Seghers became president of the anti-fascist Heine Club; she returned to East Berlin in 1947. Her later works (radio plays and several essays) are generally dedicated to promulgating the communist cause. Discussions with George Lukács revolved around the writer's freedom and commitment; three volumes of essays *Über Kunstwerk und Wirklichkeit* appeared in 1970 and 1971. *Gesammelte Werke in Einzelausgaben* were published from 1951 to 1953; *Erzählungen* in 1952, also in 1972; *Werke* (ten vols) in 1977; *Werke in Einzelbänden* (twelve vols) in 1976 and 1977; *Gesammelte Werke* (fourteen vols) from 1976 to 1980.

Seidel, Ina (1885–1974)

Born into a cultured medical family, Ina Seidel studied in Brunswick, Marburg and Munich, where she married her cousin, the writer Heinrich Wilhelm Seidel. Her first literary attempts were poems, essentially traditional, dealing with nature and religious (Protestant) feeling. Her most successful novel was *Das Wunschkind* (1930), a sensitive portrayal of female, specifically maternal, reactions to the times of upheaval in Germany during the Wars of the Liberation. *Lennacker* (1938) is a Christian novel in which the delirious hero dreams of his ancestors, twelve Protestant clergymen. *Das unverwesliche Erbe* (1954) portrays the female members of a family. Ina Seidel moved from Berlin to Starnberg in 1934; the essentially conservative and traditional nature of her writing alienated her from modernist writers; her last novel, *Michaela* (1959) deals with the situation of dissenting Germans under Hitler's Reich. She published her autobiography *Meine Kindheit und Jugend* in 1935; her biographies of figures from German Romanticism were widely read. *Gesammelte Gedichte*, consisting mainly of ballads and odes, appeared in 1949, then again in 1955 and 1958. Her father-in-law was Heinrich Seidel (1842–1906), a writer of humorous *Novellen* and children's stories, frequently using a Berlin setting. Her son, G. H. B. Seidel (1919–) uses the pseudonyms Christian Ferber and Simon Glas.

Sorge, Reinhard, later Johannes (1892–1916)

Sorge started writing at sixteen; at seventeen he left school, determined to live as a poet and dramatist. In 1911 he started writing *Der Bettler. Eine dramatische Sendung*, acknowledged to be one of the earliest expressionist works; the influence of Strindberg and Nietzsche is undeniable. The protagonist, incarnation of pure feeling, kills his insane father (Sorge's own father was mentally unbalanced) with poison, which the mother also drinks. He loves 'das Mädchen' in 'reiner Liebe', and becomes aware of his mission, 'durch Symbole der Ewigkeit zu reden'. The play was published in 1912 and awarded the Kleist prize. The next play, *Guntwar. Die Schule eines Propheten* was written in 1914 after a visionary experience on the island of Nordeney. Sorge married in 1913, became a Catholic (taking the name Johannes) and refused his wife intercourse. *Metanoite. Drei Visionen* was published in 1915. In that year Sorge studied theology in preparation for the priesthood; he was called up in May and was killed in July 1916 at the Battle of the Somme. Posthumous plays include *Der Sieg des Christo. Eine Vision* (1924), and *Der Jüngling* (1925); his poetry consists of the collections *Mutter der Himmel. Ein Sang in zwölf Gesängen* (1917), *Gericht über Zarathustra. Eine Vision* (1921) and *Nachgelassene Gedichte* (1925). *Werke* (three vols) appeared from 1962 to 1965. Sorge's confused Christianity, containing imperious visions and fervent humility, is reminiscent of that of Ludwig **Derleth**.

Späth, Gerold (1939–)

Born in Rapperswil on Lake Zurich Späth trained as an organ-builder and travelled in various parts of Switzerland before becoming a professional writer in 1968 and settling in his birthplace, where he found the model for the small-town settings of his works, comparable to the Seldwyla of his nineteenth-century compatriot Gottfried Keller. In a remarkably consistent *œuvre* he has proved himself a master of the picaresque novel in the tradition of Rabelais, Grimmelshausen and **Grass**: especially in *Unschlecht* (1970) in which the title-figure, after receiving his patrimony, is exploited by neighbours, runs away, travels Europe, marries an heiress, regains his property and returns in triumph; in *Stimmgänge* (1972), in which an organ-builder, having failed to make the fortune without which he cannot become his grandmother's sole legatee, writes his life story for his absent wife while confined to hospital by an injury; and in *Balzapf oder Als ich auftauchte* (1977) in which the fortunes of the Zapfen family are traced over four generations. In *Die heile Hölle* (1974), a short novel lacking the baroque extravagance of these works, Späth removes the mask of conformity from a middle-class family by giving an account of a critical day in the lives of each of its members. Both *Commedia* (1980), in which over two hundred portrait sketches ostensibly produced by their subjects precede the story of a guided tour of a castle museum which goes wrong, and *Barbarswila* (1988), which portrays one day in the lives of the inhabitants of a small Swiss town, achieve a panoramic effect by the accumulation of numerous vignettes. Späth's short stories have appeared in the volumes *Zwölf Geschichten* (1973), *Sacramento* (1983), *Sindbandland* (1984) and *Verschwinden in Venedig* (1986).

Sperber, Manès (1905–84)

Sperber was born in Polish Galicia and studied psychology in Vienna under Alfred Adler, who became the subject of his first book *Alfred Adler. Der Mensch und seine Lehre* (1926). He lived in Berlin between 1927 and 1933, when he edited a journal which propagated Adler's individual-based psychology. He had become a convinced communist before fleeing to France via Austria and Yugoslavia, but in 1937 he renounced communism, thus joining the ranks of other writers and intellectuals who suffered a similar disillusionment at about the same time. Having fought on the French side in 1940 and taken further refuge in Switzerland, Sperber eventually returned to Paris in 1946, where he worked in publishing while completing his *magnum opus*, the trilogy *Wie eine Träne im Ozean* (1961), which he had begun in 1940. Its three parts, *Der verbrannte Dornbusch* (1949), *Tiefer als der Abgrund* (1950) and *Die verlorene Bucht* (1955), trace the fortunes of a small group of communist revolutionaries who either survive as cynical exploiters of power or are forced into opposition. The central figure is Dojno Faber, a Galician Jew, student in Vienna and active communist who remains committed to and involved in the anti-fascist struggle in Spain, France and Yugoslavia, while losing faith in the party line as his comrades fall victim to internecine conflicts within the communist hierarchy. Having learned that his former wife and adopted child have died in Auschwitz he is left without illusions when France is liberated. Sperber's autobiography consists of the volumes *Die Wasserträger Gottes* (1974), *Die vergebliche Warnung* (1975), *Bis man mir Scherben auf die Augen legt* (1977), united under the title *All das Vergangene* . . . and his essays are collected in *Zur täglichen Weltgeschichte* (1967) and *Nur eine Brücke zwischen Gestern und Morgen* (1983). *Gesammelte Werke in Einzelausgaben* began to appear in 1981.

Sperr, Martin (1944–)

After training as a businessman and as an actor Sperr spent a short time in the theatre as an actor and production assistant before becoming a professional writer. His career suffered a severe interruption in 1972 when an accident led to a brain haemorrhage. Sperr belongs to a group of Bavarian dramatists, including also **Kroetz**, who have revived the *Volksstück* by injecting a strong element of social criticism in the manner of **Brecht**, **Horváth** and **Fleißer**. His reputation was established with the *Bayrische Trilogie* (1972), consisting of the plays *Jagdszenen aus Niederbayern* (1966) on the victimization of a homosexual driven to murder in a Bavarian village in 1958, *Landshuter Erzählungen* (1967) on the struggle between father and son over the future of a family building firm in which the son seeks to save the business by marrying the daughter of its chief competitor, and *Münchner Freiheit* (1971) set in 1968, in which the redevelopment of an area of Munich owned by a major brewery goes ahead despite student protests, the owners having done a deal with local politicians, a plot complicated by divisions within the ranks of both the student opposition and the brewing family. Sperr turned to the Third Reich for another play *Koralle Meier* (1970) in which a small-town prostitute, having been imprisoned for lending money to a Jew, is released on a word from a former customer who has become a Nazi. However, her attempt to take revenge on the mayor who denounced her misfires and she returns to prison and death. *Adele Spitzeder*, televised in 1972 and performed in the theatre five years later with the title *Spitzeder*, concerns a nineteenth-century folk heroine whose 'Dachauer Volksbank' was a gigantic confidence trick, and another historical play for television *Der Räuber Matthias Kneißl* (1971) follows the career of a bandit to capture and execution.

Spitteler, Carl (1845–1924)

Spitteler studied law and theology at Basel, after which he taught in Russia and Finland. In 1889 he worked for the *Neue Zürcher Zeitung*, in 1892 he gave this up to become an independent writer. He attempted prose (*Friedli der Kolderi* (1891); *Gustav, ein Idyll* (1892); *Conrad der Leutnant* (1898); *Imago* (1906)), also drama (*Der Parlamentär* (1889); *Der Ehrgeizige* (1892)), but it is as the author of vast epics, e.g. *Prometheus und Epimetheus* (1881) and *Olympischer Frühling* (1900–5) that he is best remembered. These monumental, cosmic visions owe much to Nietzsche, also Schopenhauer; they attempt a new mythology, a fantastic cosmogony not easily digestible. In 1924 Spitteler wrote a new version, in iambic hexameters, of *Prometheus und Epimetheus*, entitled *Prometheus der Dulder*. Spitteler is regarded as an outsider, a man whose work (like that of **Däubler** and **Mombert**) is remote from the modern experience and difficult of access. Freud, however, greatly admired *Imago* and used the title for the journal which he founded in 1912. Spitteler also wrote essays (on Nietzsche, Keller, Swiss neutrality). He received the Nobel prize in 1919. The *Gesammelte Werke* (eleven vols) appeared from 1945 to 1958, the *Kritische Schriften* in 1965.

Stadler, Ernst (1883–1914)

Stadler, an Alsatian, studied German and French literature, together with comparative philology, at Strasburg and Munich, and was a Rhodes scholar at Oxford from 1906 to 1908. Together with Otto **Flake** and René **Schickele** he edited the journal *Der Stürmer* (1902). From 1911 to 1913 he collaborated with Franz Pfemfert on *Die Aktion*. Stadler's early poetry (*Praeludien* (1905)) is characterized by neo-romantic and *Jugendstil* topoi: the influence of **Hofmannsthal** and **George** is apparent. The collection *Der Aufbruch* (1914), however, is acknowledged to be the most representative of the collections of early expressionist poetry (including 'Mensch, werde wesentlich'), where aestheticism is left far behind and a more urgent, humanitarian element is detected. From 1912 to 1914 Stadler was professor of German in Brussels; he was called up in 1914 and fell in October at Ypres. His name is frequently linked with those of G. **Heym** and **Trakl** as being one of the most outstanding of the 'Frühexpressionisten'. *Ausgewählte Gedichte* appeared in 1947; *Dichtungen* (two vols) in 1954; *Gedichte und Prosa* in 1964; *Dichtungen, Schriften, Briefe* in 1983.

Stehr, Hermann (1864–1940)

From a Silesian working-class background, Hermann Stehr worked as a primary-school teacher (from 1887) before devoting himself to writing. His early work, the stories *Auf Leben und Tod* (1898), *Der Schindelmacher* (1899), *Der begrabene Gott* (1905) show a fusion of realism and Silesian mysticism: Stehr was reprimanded by the education authorities for his unorthodox religious views and provocative stance on social matters. His most successful novel was *Der Heiligenhof* (two vols, 1918), set, exceptionally, in Westphalia and dealing with the Sintlinger family, farmers in a remote community. Central is the relationship between the father and his blind daughter Helene, who commits suicide. Mysticism and realism are interfused; the figure of Faber is based to a considerable extent on the author. Stehr settled in Schreiberhau in 1926 and became a close friend of **Gerhart Hauptmann**. Other novels convey a brooding sense of closeness to the earth (*Peter Brindeisener* (1924) and *Das Geschlecht der Maechler* (1929–44)). Stehr was hailed as a 'Künder deutscher Seele', and his 'volkische Erdverbundenheit' was greeted as exemplary by the Nazis, who appointed him to the *Reichsschrifttumskammer*. His play *Meta Konegen* (1906) met with little success; he also attempted poetry. The *Gesammelte Werke* (nine vols) appeared in 1924; a twelve-volume edition followed from 1927 to 1936. A considerable bulk of his work remains unpublished.

Sternheim, Carl (1878–1942)

Son of a Leipzig Jewish banker, Sternheim studied philosophy and art history in Munich, Leipzig and Göttingen. After his marriage in 1900 he met Thea Löwenstein, whom he married after his divorce in 1907. His second wife's wealth enabled him to live in style near Munich ('Bellemaison'), where he cultivated a fashionable salon. His early plays, *Der Heiland* (1898) and *Judas Ischariot* (1901) are undistinguished; the poems, *Fanale* (1901), are derivative. A group of plays, the best of which being *Don Juan* (2 parts, 1905–9), deal with the relationship between the sexes and have obvious autobiographical elements. In 1908 Sternheim and Franz **Blei** founded the journal *Hyperion*: it was Blei who encouraged Sternheim to continue writing, and the result was *Die Hose* (1911), a play initially banned by the censor, who insisted that the title be changed to *Der Riese*. It was to be the first in a cycle of social comedies bearing the title *Aus dem bürgerlichen Heldenleben*: Sternheim, with Molière as his model, unmasks the prurience, pusillanimity, cunning and self-deception of certain middle-class individuals. Theobald Maske, 'hero' of *Die Hose*, possesses an egotism which calls forth aversion and also admiration. Other comedies in the cycle are *Die Kassette* (1912), *Bürger Schippel* (1913), *Der Snob* (1914), *Der Kandidat* (1914), *1913* (1915) and *Tabula Rasa* (1916). The later play *Das Fossil* (1925) is also included in the 'Maske' tetralogy (with *Die Hose*, *Der Snob* and *1913*). These comedies are regarded as Sternheim's best; the language is precise, bordering frequently on *Telegrammstil*, deliberately stripped of metaphors, quirky and utterly original.

Sternheim reveals his satirical method in a famous essay on Molière: 'Ein Dichter wie Molière ist Arzt am Leib seiner Zeit. Des Menschen sämtliche, ihm von seinem Schöpfer gegebene Eigenschaften blank und strahlend zu erhalten, ist ihm unabweisbare Pflicht.' Similarities to the French dramatist are indisputable; the pose of the dandy, in which Sternheim indulged, brings Oscar Wilde to mind, and his castle and liveried servants show an aloofness hardly commensurate with the view of Sternheim as a champion of the left. A growing restlessness and valetudinarianism led to increasing strains within his marriage; in 1927 he divorced Thea and, in 1930, married Pamela Wedekind, daughter of the dramatist.

A collection of ironic stories was published in 1918 entitled *Chronik von des zwanzigsten Jahrhunderts Beginn* (two vols): the middle-class world is analysed with precision and disenchantment. The novel *Europa* (1919–20) continues the attack. The essays *Berlin oder Juste milieu* (1920) and *Tasso oder Kunst des Juste milieu* (1921) show Sternheim as a rationalist without illusions; linked by certain critics to certain expressionist writers, his cool and sober approach during the 1920s anticipates 'Neue Sachlichkeit'. Late plays (*Oscar Wilde* (1925); *John Pierpont Morgan* (1930)) are undistinguished; in the 1920s Sternheim also published collections of earlier *Novellen* (including *Fairfax* (1921) and *Libussa, des Kaisers Leibroß* (1922)). In 1934 Sternheim divorced Pamela Wedekind; he remained in Brussels until his death in 1942.

The attack on bourgeois smugness he shared with many other dramatists of his time, but he believed in no socialist Utopia; his work gave aid to no programme. It is proper to talk of a love-hate relationship with the middle class, hatred for its cant and hypocrisy, but admiration for its sheer tenacity. Conformism, the 'juste milieu' of which he writes, is certainly derided, and pusillanimous mediocrity is reviled above all. To break through the genteel in the German language was his aim, and in this he succeeded: his style is self-willed and concise. Despite his great gift of stage-craft, and his conscientious revision of earlier plays and stories, a sense of proportion is lacking, and frequent imbalance of judgement is perhaps connected with his many breakdowns. The later work is trivial, and often bathetic, but the 'Maske' plays are acknowledged masterpieces. A *Gesamtwerk* (ten vols) appeared from 1963 to 1976; *Gesammelte Werke* (six vols) from 1963 to 1968; *Briefe* (2 vols) in 1988.

Stramm, August (1874–1915)

Stramm entered post-office administration in 1893; in 1897 he worked as a postal official on the Bremen-Hamburg-New York line. He married Else Krafft, author of many popular novels, in 1902; the couple moved to Berlin in 1905. His early writing was derivative and unoriginal; in 1911–12, however, he found his own voice, and poetry and plays of startling originality were written. The plays *Sancta Susanna* and *Die Haidebraut* were written in 1912 and 1913, both experimental, daring and verging on the grotesque. At his wife's instigation Stramm approached Herwarth **Walden** in 1913, who immediately detected the poet's genius and modernity. From mid-1913 to mid-1915 no fewer than seventy-five poems, seven plays and two short monologues in prose appeared in *Der Sturm*. The 'Verlag der Sturm' published the posthumous collection *Tropfblut* in 1919: Stramm had been killed on the Eastern Front in 1915. Stramm is also the only writer to have had a facsimile manuscript of his work published in *Der Sturm*: the poem 'Schwermut' marked the tenth anniversary of his death.

Stramm is regarded as one of the most radically experimental poets of his generation, reducing language to abstract word-patterns, using daring neologisms and distorting syntax to convey compressed utterances. The reduction of language to abstract essences represents one extreme pole of expressionism, the other being the rhapsodic fervour of **Werfel**. Ultimate concentration is the aim. The collection *Du* (1915) as well as certain of the plays (*Erwachen, Kräfte, Die Unfruchtbaren*) deal with startling intensity with the relation between the sexes. A jerky, hectic quality is apparent in much of the writing: the collection *Weltwehe* (1922) contains a more mystic dimension (the influence of Ralph Waldo Trine may be noted here, a blood-stained copy of whose *In Tune with the Infinite* was found in Stramm's pocket after his death). Two volumes of *Dichtungen* appeared in 1920 and 1921; *Dein Lächeln weint. Gesammelte Gedichte* in 1956; *Das Werk* in 1963; *Kritische Essays und unveröffentliches Quellenmaterial aus dem Nachlaß des Dichters* were published in 1979, *Die Dichtungen* in 1990.

Strauß, Botho (1944–)

Strauß studied in Cologne and Munich, then, having abandoned a doctoral dissertation on **Thomas Mann** and the theatre, worked for the periodical *Theater heute* before joining Peter Stein's *Schaubühne am Halleschen Ufer* as literary adviser, contributing to the company's new versions of Ibsen's *Peer Gynt* (1971), Kleist's *Prinz Friedrich von Homburg* (1972) and Gorki's *Summer guests* (1975), all landmarks in the development of the post-war German theatre. In his first play *Die Hypochonder* (1972) he deliberately fails to unravel multiple plots, some with the features of a thriller, and allows one character to undergo a metamorphosis, a process which recurs in one variation after another throughout his later work. In *Bekannte Gesichter, gemischte Gefühle* (1974) three couples preparing for a dance tournament in an otherwise empty hotel pass into a dream world which is exposed as a mental illusion. *Trilogie des Wiedersehens* (1976) traces the meetings, conversations and unpredictable behaviour of visitors to an exhibition of paintings representing 'capitalist realism'. *Groß und klein* (1978), perhaps Strauß's most accessible play, presents the dissolution of a woman's identity as she fails to make contact with others in a series of disparate situations. *Kalldewey Farce* (1981), in which the title-figure may symbolize the suppressed unconscious endowed with positive and negative potential, satirizes modish feminism and the self-regarding nature of the 1970s psychoboom. *Der Park* (1983) brilliantly updates Shakespeare's *Midsummer Night's Dream*. In *Die Fremdenführerin* (1986) a tourist guide begins a half-hearted affair with a schoolteacher while remaining attached both to her former lover who appears in person and to her dream of a future lover with the features of Pan who appears in a vision. Of the three short plays *Besucher, Sieben Türen* and *Die Zeit und das Zimmer*, published together as *Besucher* in 1988, the first concerns a rehearsal dominated by an old pro, a subject treated also by **Dorst** and **Bernhard** in their recent work for the theatre.

In his prose Strauß adopts a more ruminatory approach to the same themes of self-absorbtion, identity crisis and obsessive emotional depen-dence/exploitation. In *Marlenes Schwester* (1975), containing the title-story and 'Theorie der Drohung', the severing of relationships leads not to the assertion but to the disintegration of the self, while in *Die Widmung* (1977) the narrator, bereft of his girlfriend, fails to come to terms with his new situation by writing about it. The father-daughter relationship in *Rumor* (1980) breaks down as the latter's restoration to health coincides with the former's degeneration. *Paare Passanten* (1981) offers notes of a strolling observer spiced with criticism of the media and other modern urban phenomena, a form to which Strauß returns in *Niemand anderes* (1987) with its numerous vignettes of persons in search of an ultimately satisfying relationship. His most ambitious and baffling work to date is undoubtedly *Der junge Mann* (1984); here what appears initially to be a *Bildungsroman* vaguely modelled on Goethe's *Wilhelm Meisters Lehrjahre* – the title-figure is shown working in the theatre, rehearsing two temperamental actresses and at the end renews contact with an old trooper – develops to become a phantasmagoria of disparate episodes belonging to various sub-genres united only by the German Romantic view of art as a 'progressive Universalpoesie'. The long poem *Diese Erinnerung an einen, der nur einen Tag zu Gast war* (1985) marks a break with post-war trends in German poetry in its cultivation of a tone of elegiac refinement.

No summary can do justice to the dazzling linguistic virtuosity and the imaginative and reflective power of his work, qualities which mark him off from other confessional authors grouped under the rubric 'neue Subjek-tivität'. Strauß appeared initially to merely demonstrate the incapacities and failures of the over-sophisticated without suggesting any distance between himself and his characters. His reputation has been based hitherto on his ability to convey the mood of a social group during a particular phase of history. However, as his work grows and deepens, he seems more likely to survive as one who registers, analyses and recreates by means of highly self-conscious experiments in fantasy a broader spiritual malaise.

Strauss, Emil (1866–1960)

Strauss studied in Freiburg, Lausanne and Berlin; he associated with many of the naturalists, including **Halbe** and **Gerhart Hauptmann**. From 1890 to 1892 he farmed near Schaffhausen, rejecting the life of the city; from 1892 to 1894 he lived as a farmer and teacher in Brazil. The stories *Menschenwege* and *Der Engelwirt* appeared in 1899 and 1901; a tragedy *Don Pedro* was written in 1899 (and revised in 1914). Strauss's most outstanding work was the short novel *Freund Hein* (1902), a sensitive account of a schoolboy with musical talents who, unable to grasp the rigours of mathematics, does badly at school and consequently is forbidden by his father to play the violin; he shoots himself. This theme is one that would be taken up by **Friedrich Huch**, **Hesse** and **Musil**. *Kreuzungen* (1904) deals, less successfully, with a man between two women. After his return to Europe, Strauss settled on Lake

Constance; he spent the years 1911 to 1915 in Hellerau (Dresden). *Der nackte Mann* appeared in 1924; the sensitive *Novelle Der Schleier* in 1920; *Das Riesenspielzeug*, a political parable, in 1934. The patriotic play *Vaterland* (1923) was not successful.

Strauss became a member of the Prussian Academy of Arts in 1926, left in 1931 but rejoined in 1933. He was silent during the Second World War; in 1949 he published the three stories *Dreiklang*. An autobiography, *Ludens*, appeared in 1955. *Gesammelte Werke* were published from 1949. *Freund Hein* was reissued in 1982. Strauss was largely forgotten until recently, when his rejection of the urban, and of authoritarian attitudes in education, made him popular once more.

· Strauss und Torney, Lulu von (1873–1956)

Daughter of an adjutant at the court of the Prince of Schaumburg-Lippe, Lulu von Strauss und Torney studied in Bückeburg, later using the princely archives for the collection of material. She began by writing poetry (*Gedichte* (1898), and *Balladen und Lieder* (1902)). Her interest in ballads brought her the attention of Börries von **Münchhausen**, and she published in the *Göttinger Musenalmanach* (1901–5). She also attempted novels (*Judas* (1911), reworked as *Der Judenhof* in 1937; *Der jüngste Tag* (1922), dealing with the Anabaptists in Münster). In 1916 she married the publisher Eugen Diederichs and settled in Jena; her right-wing stance became more pronounced, and she became a tireless champion of writers such as Hans **Grimm**, whose *Volk ohne Raum* she hailed as 'ein deutsches, geistiges Ereignis'. She wrote her play *Der Tempel. Ein Spiel aus der Renaissance* in 1921. It is as a writer of ballads that she is remembered: another collection, *Reif steht die Saat*, appeared in 1919. She also attempted historical and biographical writing: in 1936 she published *Eugen Diederichs Leben und Werk* and, in 1943, her reminiscences (*Das verborgene Angesicht*). She also translated from the French.

Strittmatter, Erwin (1912–)

Strittmatter worked after war service as a baker, farmer, mayor and newspaper editor.before becoming a professional writer. In 1959 he became secretary of the GDR Writers Union. He was initially encouraged by **Brecht**, who directed his verse play *Katzgraben* on the subject of land reform in 1953 for the *Berliner Ensemble*. Strittmatter has developed distinctive GDR versions of two popular fictional genres, the *Bauernroman* and the *Heimatroman*, giving them a socialist tendency which they had before totally lacked. These include *Ochsenkutscher* (1950) and *Tinko* (1954), both set in Lower Lusatia where Strittmatter grew up, the first during the years of the Weimar Republic, the second in 1948–9 during the transition. The strong autobiographical element evident here is also present in *Der Laden* (1983) which portrays a village idyll untouched by progress towards the Third Reich. More interesting for the Western reader, however, are Strittmatter's picaresque novels, which allow greater scope to a remarkably inventive if formally conventional narrative talent. In *Ole Bienkopp* (1963) which covers the years 1952 to 1956 the title-figure breaks with his aristocratic employers, travels the countryside selling beehives, marries, experiences the Second World War and returns home an advocate of land reform. Caught between reactionary farmers and party officials with no grasp of local conditions he eventually dies of exhaustion. *Der Wundertäter* in three volumes (1957, 1973, 1980) traces a village boy's growth and development from 1909 to 1943, when he deserts from the army in Greece, his activities after his return home in 1947 as journalist, chief clerk and party member, and his difficulties with the party bureaucracy during the 1950s. Just as Hermann **Kant** demonstrates how it is possible to be a member of the urban intelligentsia and a good communist, Strittmatter makes an official ideology palatable to the rural peasantry by combining nostalgia with an awareness of the need for change.

Struck, Karin (1947–)

Born in a Mecklenburg farming family which moved to the Federal Republic in 1953, Struck studied psychology, German and French before breaking off a doctoral dissertation and becoming a professional writer in 1973. In a series of works in which it is difficult to separate fact from fiction Struck has developed a form of confessional feminism marked by emotional candour, interest in different forms of sexuality (in *Lieben* (1977)) and in motherhood (in *Die Mutter* (1975)) and exploration of alternative life styles, such as the drug scene in *Lieben* and *Trennung* (1978). Other works are *Klassenliebe* (1973), *Kindheits Ende* (1982), *Zwei Frauen* (1982), *Finale* (1984) and *Glut und Asche* (1985), from which the first deserves to be singled out for its account in the form of a three-month diary of a triangular relationship involving the narrator, her medical-student husband, like herself of working-class origin, and her middle-class writer friend, a book typical of its time in its preoccupation with emancipation in all its aspects. *Bitteres Wasser* (1988) represents a new departure, being an account by a male narrator, an industrial worker, of his passage through the purgatory of alcoholism and its cure.

Stucken, Eduard (1865–1936)

Born in Moscow, Stucken studied linguistics and Egyptology in Berlin (1887–90) and travelled extensively in the East. His early writing is heavily indebted to popular neo-romantic trends (*Der Gral*, a play in seven parts

(1902–24); *Myrrha* (1908); *Merlins Geburt* (1913) and *Tristram und Ysolt* (1917)); his major achievement is an enormous novel, *Die weißen Götter* (1918–24) in three parts. This was greatly admired by **Gerhart Hauptmann**, who was impressed by the portrayal of the heliocentric Aztec civilization. Other novels include *Giuliano* (1933) and *Die segelnden Götter* (1937). Of his poetry, *Das Buch der Träume* (1916) and *Die Insel Perdita* (1935) deserve mention. Stucken also wrote scholarly works on astral myths, oriental mythology and Polynesian languages. Volume I of his *Gesammelte Werke* appeared in 1925; *Gedichte* appeared in 1938.

Sudermann, Hermann (1857–1928)

Born in Matziken (Memelland) Sudermann studied in Königsberg and Berlin, where he was in close contact with the naturalists. His greatest successes on the stage were *Die Ehre* (1890), *Sodoms Ende* (1891) and *Heimat* (1893). The first was an overnight success, a satirical portrayal of aristocratic *mores*; the second, more sensational, deals with seduction and suicide in Berlin artistic circles; the third, better known as *Magda*, describes the homecoming of a famous soprano from Italy to provincial German pettiness. This play helped both Sarah Bernhard and Eleonora Duse to world fame; it enjoyed great success in England, being uncompromisingly true to life by the English standards of the times. Sudermann was an energetic and prolific dramatist, but his popularity waned when the 'well-made play' fell into disfavour. His prose was greatly admired at the time; especially successful were the novels *Frau Sorge* (1887) and *Das hohe Lied* (1908). The book which has lasted best is *Litauische Geschichten* (1917), a collection of four stories dealing with the Memel countryside which Sudermann knew well (*Die Reise nach Tilsit, Miks Bumbullis, Jons und Erdme* and *Die Magd*). Six volumes of *Romane und Novellen* appeared in 1919; six of *Dramatische Werke* in 1923. *Miks Bumbullis* was published separately in 1958, and *Die Reise nach Tilsit. Prosa und Dramen* in 1971.

T

Thelen, Albert Vigoleis (1903–89)

Thelen, one of the more eccentric figures of his literary generation, settled in Majorca in 1931, where he became secretary of the diarist and connoisseur Harry Graf Keßler. During the Spanish Civil War he moved to France, then on the outbreak of the Second World War to Portugal, where he found refuge with the mystical poet Teixeira de Pascoaes, whose works he proceeded to translate. From 1947 he lived in the Netherlands and from 1954 in Switzerland. *Die Insel des zweiten Gesichts* (1953) is a picaresque novel based on the lives of Thelen and his wife during their five years in Majorca, introducing the real persons Keßler, Graf Keyserling and Robert Graves, who employs Thelen to type *I Claudius*, and a host of colourful minor figures including revolutionaries, tourists and matadors. The couple are eventually forced to move on when Franco's Falange takes over the island and German exiles are threatened with deportation. The sequel *Der schwarze Herr Bahßetupp* (1956) – both works were originally intended to form part of a larger autobiographical sequence – finds Thelen's persona in Amsterdam employed as interpreter/secretary to the title-figure who claims to be a professor of law attending a conference. Together they make a comic journey of discovery through Dutch society.

Theobaldy, Jürgen (1944–)

Theobaldy grew up in Mannhein, the scene of his first novel *Sonntags Kino* (1978), studied in Freiburg, Heidelberg and Cologne. Since 1974 he has lived in West Berlin except for a stay in Rome in 1977. He is both the most prominent practitioner and most articulate advocate of a trend in lyric poetry which may be defined as a combination of 'new subjectivity' and social realism characteristic of the generation which passed through the student movement, the ideals of which inspired the poems in his early collections *Sperrsitz* (1973) and *Blaue Flecken* (1974). Owing much to the American beat and pop poets publicized by **Brinkmann** and **Born** Theobaldy, along with the poets he has anthologized in *Und ich bewege mich doch. Gedichte vor und nach 1968*, concentrates on private everyday experiences conveyed in free verse which aims to reproduce the rhythms of natural speech. After *Zweiter Klasse* (1976) there is a development towards greater awareness of the German and international lyrical tradition, apparent in references to Rimbaud, Goethe, Hölderlin, **Trakl** and **Celan** (*Schwere Erde, Rauch* 1980) and in the classical verse forms adopted, at first sparingly in *Drinks. Gedichte aus Rom* (1979, revised version 1984 containing the cycle 'Midlands' prompted by a visit to England), more confidently in *Die Sommertour* (1983), inspired by Greece. In the novel *Spanische Wände* (1981, second version 1984) the failure of an academic couple to revive their flagging marriage on the Costa Brava is attributed partly to personal inertia, partly to the effects of time on the utopian hopes of the student movement.

Thiess, Frank (1890–1977)

Born near Riga, Thiess studied in Berlin and Tübingen, worked as editor, then as *Dramaturg* in Stuttgart, and theatre critic in Hanover. In 1923 he published two novels which brought him recognition: *Die Verdammten* and *Angelika ten Swaart*. They both deal with incest among the Baltic aristocracy and show a skilful handling of complex psychological states. Thiess devoted himself to writing after 1923; another successful novel was *Tsushima* (1936), dealing with the Russo-Japanese war of 1905; the two Caruso novels (*Neapolitanische Legende* (1942) and *Caruso in Sorrent* (1946)) should also be noted. After the Second World War Thiess was led to defend his stance on 'innere Emigration' when facing the strictures of **Thomas Mann** and others. He claimed he had invented the term, and attacked those who had left Germany for the 'comfort' of exile: Thomas Mann's vituperative reply (an open letter to Walter von Molo of 12 October 1945 in the *Augsburger Anzeiger*) asserted that all books printed in Germany between 1933 and· 1945 should be pulped. (It should be noted in this context that Thiess's historical novel *Das Reich der Dämonen* (1941), was only grudgingly permitted by the Nazis, as a veiled criticism of totalitarianism could be detected.) Thiess also published collections of short stories. *Verbrannte Erde* (1963) and *Freiheit bis Mitternacht* (1965) are autobiographical. *Gesammelte Werke in Einzelbänden* appeared from 1956.

Thoma, Ludwig (1867–1921)

Known above all as a humorous Bavarian writer, Ludwig Thoma studied forestry in Aschaffenburg, then law in Munich and Erlangen. In 1900 he became editor of *Simplicissimus*, having given up his legal practice. In 1906 he was imprisoned for six weeks for libel. He published frequent satires; in 1907 he edited (with **Hesse** and others) the periodical *März*. From 1908 onwards he lived in Rottach am Tegernsee, serving briefly as a medical orderly in the First World War. His best-known work is the *Lausbubengeschichten* (1905), a collection of humorous, often scurrilous stories; *Tante Frieda* (1907) was a successful sequel. The comedy *Die Lokalbahn* (1902) was also very popular; the more serious works (for example the 'Volksstück' *Magdalena* (1912)) were not. Thoma excelled above all in the pose of bluff, earthy Bavarian; the sharp, satirical element (anti-hypocrisy, anti-Prussian) is, however, also important. The story *Der Münchner im Himmel* (1911) sums up what is felt to be the quintessential Ludwig Thoma; it has been filmed, made into a cartoon and recorded numerous times. The *Gesammelte Werke* (seven vols) appeared in 1922 (eight vols in 1956); a six-volume edition followed in 1968. *Das große Ludwig Thoma Buch* was published in 1974, and *Das Schönste von Ludwig Thoma* in 1980.

Timm, Uwe (1940–)

Born in Hamburg, Timm studied philosophy and German literature in Munich and Paris, then sociology and economics. Resident in Munich, he has been involved in a publishing venture, the Autoren-Edition with Gerd **Fuchs** and others, and a literary group, the *Wortgruppe München*. His first novel *Heißer Sommer* (1974) is perhaps the most authentic fictional treatment of the student movement, here shown culminating in demonstrations against the Springer newspaper concern, the principal target of student protest against the politically motivated manipulation of opinion. Against this documentary background the transition from intellectual isolation to political engagement made by the central character, intended as an exemplary figure, is followed through in a manner which leaves the reader unconvinced that it will result in either psychological stability or effective action, an impression which indicates, no doubt contrary to the author's intention, the essential weakness of the movement. In *Morenga* (1978) Timm turned his attention to the uprising of the Hereros and Hottentots against German colonial rule in South West Africa (Namibia) between 1904 and 1907, recreating the experience of the conflicts from a multiple point of view and adopting a documentary style which successfully integrates historical records and the memories of those directly involved. *Kerbels Flucht* (1980), in which a Werther-like figure, in despair after the loss of his girlfriend, suffers increasing alienation from reality, can be related to works by **Born** and the early Botho **Strauß** characteristic of 'new subjectivity'. *Der Mann auf dem Hochrad* (1986), an affectionate portrait of the narrator's great-uncle who becomes a victim of his own belief in progress when the penny-farthing he rides is superseded by the bicycle, was followed by *Der Schlangenbaum* (1986) in which a German engineer is forced to abandon the construction of a paper factory in the South American jungle, a novel which combines several of Timm's earlier themes. His approach to social realism is defined in the important essay 'Realismus und Utopie' in *Realismus, welcher?*, ed. Peter Laemmle (1976).

Toller, Ernst (1893–1939)

Born near Bromberg (Posen), son of a Jewish dealer, Toller studied law in Grenoble, but returned to Germany in 1914 to enlist. In 1916 he became a pacifist, was badly wounded and declared unfit for military service. He continued his studies in Munich and Heidelberg; in 1917 he was arrested for anti-militaristic activities. On his release he joined the strike of munitions workers in Munich. Inspired by Gustav Landauer and Kurt Eisner he propagated an ideal, ethical socialism; his play *Die Wandlung* (1919) charts the path of the hero Friedrich from unthinking patriotism to a universal vision of love. The alternation of realistic and visionary scenes, and the final apotheosis, show Toller to be very much a representative of fervent, rhapsodic expressionism. Toller joined the Bavarian Soviet Republic; after Eisner's murder he became its leader, then, in the newly founded revolutionary formation, commander of the Red Guard in Dachau. His humanitarianism, however, deplored the use of violence, and he strove to prevent the worst excesses. In 1919 the Communist government in Munich was overthrown, and Toller was given five years' imprisonment. During this time he continued to write: *Masse Mensch* (1921) deals with the problem facing the middle-class idealist when faced with the realities of revolution and the need to use violence: the autobiographical element is transparent. The play uses nameless figures, chorus and dream sequences to powerful effect. *Die Maschinenstürmer* (1922) deals with an incident from the English Luddite movement. *Der entfesselte Wotan* (1923) is a parody of the rise of a tyrant like Hitler, and remarkably prescient: *Hinkemann* (1923) sees, much as Büchner did, the bedrock of pain and tragedy in existence which no political amelioration can overcome. *Hoppla wir leben!* (1927) is an expression of disillusionment at the Weimar Republic where, Toller sees, reactionary forces have not been eradicated. *Feuer aus den Kesseln* (1930) is an early example of documentary theatre. Toller also wrote poetry: *Das Schwalbennest* (1924) is so called after the swallows who built their nest in his prison cell. Toller became a tireless speaker and defender of pacifism and international brotherhood; he travelled widely and ceaselessly attacked the rise of fascism. Depressed, however, by the events in the Spanish Civil War (photographs of wounded horses affected him deeply), he committed suicide in a New York hotel. *Ausgewählte Schriften* appeared in 1959; *Prosa, Briefe, Dramen, Gedichte* in 1961; *Gesammelte Werke* (five vols) in 1978.

Torberg, Friedrich (pseudonym of Friedrich Kantor-Berg, 1908–79)

Having grown up in Vienna and studied in Prague, Torberg made a strong impact with his first novel *Der Schüler Gerber hat absolviert* (1930, second version under the title *Der Schüler Gerber* (1954)) on the suicide of a sixth-former. After the *Anschluß* Torberg moved to Switzerland, volunteered on the French side in 1939, then after the fall of France made his way via Spain and Portugal to the USA, where he remained for the next ten years. Two novels he then wrote, *Mein ist die Rache* (1943 in USA, 1947) and *Hier bin ich, mein Vater* (1948) belong to the small group of works by exiled writers which attempt to deal directly with exemplary situations in Nazi Germany and the countries it occupied (cf. **Heinrich Mann**, *Lidice* (1943), Kesten, *Die Kinder von Gernika* (1939), **Alfred Neumann**, *Es waren ihrer sechs* (1944)).

Both deal with problems of conscience faced by Jews under the pressures of Nazi persecution. His other pre-war novels concern early erotic experiences (– *und glauben, es wäre die Liebe* (1932), *Abschied* (1937)) and sport (*Die Mannschaft* (1937)). *Die zweite Begegnung* (1950) concerns the fate of a returned exile forced to flee again after the Communist coup in Prague in 1968, while *Süßkind von Trimberg* (1972) reconstructs the life of the only Jewish *Minnesänger*.

Törne, Volker von (1934–80)

Von Törne studied in Braunschweig and Wilhelmshaven, worked for three years on building sites, moved in 1962 to Berlin where he became editor of the magazine *alternative* and a leading member of *Aktion Sühnezeichnen*, an organization promoting reconciliation between Germany and Israel and the countries of Eastern Europe. He died of a brain haemorrhage during a lecture tour. His laconic, politically conscious verse in the Brechtian mode on the subjects of non-violence, social justice, disarmament and East-West understanding (cf. **Fried**, **Delius**, **Zahl**) appeared in several volumes between 1962 and 1981 and were assembled in *Im Lande Vogelfrei. Gesammelte Gedichte* (1981).

Trakl, Georg (1887–1914)

Born in Salzburg, Trakl studied pharmacy there and in Vienna; introverted and sensitive, he took to drugs and cultivated the pose of *poète maudit*, his models being Baudelaire, Rimbaud and Verlaine. Juvenilia (poems and plays) demonstrate a febrile, decadent attitudinizing; around 1910, however, Trakl found his own original poetic voice. A haunted, crepuscular, musical landscape of the soul is his, a world of evanescent beauty, suffused with decay. Trakl was befriended by Ludwig von Ficker, who published most of his poetry in *Der Brenner*. An intense, incestuous relationship with his sister Margarete, also a drug addict, brought an awareness of sin into his poetry, coupled paradoxically with a yearning for redemption. Trakl's first collection, *Gedichte*, appeared in 1913; the second collection, *Sebastian im Traum*, posthumously in 1915 (he had corrected the proofs). Remarkable above all in Trakl is the use of colour, the autotelic images, disembodied substantives and the ciphers of innocence who are preordained victims. The Kaspar Hauser figure meant much to him, almost to the point of self-identification.

Trakl's poetry exemplifies the transition from impressionism to expressionism. He remained aloof from literary coteries, was unhappy in Vienna and shunned large cities (during a visit to Berlin to his sister after her miscarriage of his child he met Else **Lasker-Schüler**). He was greatly admired by Karl **Kraus**, who detected his originality. In 1914 he enlisted in the medical corps: his last poems are unique war poems which see the conflict as a punishment upon an accursed race. The last utterance, 'Grodek', calls upon the sister for salvation. Appalled by the fighting on the Eastern Front, Trakl attempted suicide; he was sent to a military hospital in Cracow for observation, but ended his life there, presumably by an overdose of cocaine. His remains were later removed to Mühlau, Innsbruck. His sister shot herself in 1917.

Trakl is held to be one of the finest poets writing in German in the twentieth century. Although his range is narrow (autumn, evening, decay) his mastery is unquestioned. Incomplete selections of his poetry appeared in the 1920s and 1930s; the great critical, variorum edition (two vols) in 1969. *Der Wahrheit nachsinnen – viel Schmerz. Gedichte. Dramenfragmente. Briefe* appeared in 1981.

Tucholsky, Kurt (1890–1935)

Tucholsky studied law in Berlin, Geneva and Jena; in 1912 he made his literary début with *Rheinsberg. Ein Bilderbuch für Verliebte*, a light-hearted and tender love-story. He turned his attention increasingly to critical essays and satirical poems, some verging on the grotesque, which he contributed to *Vorwärts*, also to the *Schaubühne* (renamed *Weltbühne* after 1918). He became one of the most active polemical writers to the latter journal, attacking above all militarism, appeasement and anti-democratic attitudes. The *Fromme Gesänge* (1919) and *Träumereien an preußischen Kaminen* (1920) attack the infamous legend of a 'stab in the back' and the unsuccessful attempts made at liberalism. Tucholsky's literary criticism was perceptive and original; he was one of the first to review and draw attention to **Kafka**, **Benn** and **Brecht**. He became sick of Germany in 1924 and moved to Paris, where he lived for five years before moving to Sweden. *Deutschland Deutschland über alles* (1929) continues the crusade against Germany's failure to achieve true democracy. The novel *Schloß Gripsholm* (1931) was based on a summer holiday spent with Lisa Matthias ('Lydia') in Sweden; it was intended as a 'Fingerübung' for a more detailed book on women. The tone is light and ironic, but the 'Kinderheim' episode hints at the Nazi tyranny to come. In 1932 he collaborated with Walther **Hasenclever**, using the pseudonym Peter Panter, on a drama, *Christoph Kolumbus oder die Entdeckung Amerikas*. Growing disillusionment led to a withdrawal from the world of politics; Tucholsky turned to a reading of Schopenhauer and Kierkegaard. His health deteriorated, and he committed suicide at Hindås, near Gothenburg.

Tucholsky refused to write after 1932; only long after his death were the *Briefe aus dem Schweigen* and the so-called *Q-Tagebücher* published (1977 and 1978). The tone is sardonic and reveals a bitterly disillusioned writer. It is, however, as a writer of witty chansons, satirical ballads and trenchant reviews that Tucholsky is remembered. *Gesammelte Werke* (three vols) appeared in 1960 and 1961; *Ausgewählte Werke* (two vols) in 1965; a ten-volume edition of the *Gesammelte Werke* appeared in 1975; the *Gesammelte Gedichte* in 1983, also a *Kurt Tucholsky Chansonbuch*.

Tumler, Franz (1912–)

Born near Bolzano, South Tyrol, Tumler grew up in Upper Austria, became a writer in 1935 after a period as a schoolteacher, served in the army from 1941 to 1945 and moved to Berlin in the 1950s. He has succeeded in combining the traditional qualities of Austrian narrative with their roots in Stifter with the self-consciousness of modernist technique. A preoccupation with the special problems of his original homeland is evident in the *Das Tal von Lausa und Duron* (1935) and *Aufschreibung aus Trient* (1965). After a period of conformity to Nazi prescriptions Tumler wrote two novels on the disorientation produced by the aftermath of the Second World War (*Heimfahrt* (1950) and *Der Schritt hinüber* (1956)) and *Ein Schloß in Österreich* (1953), in which the castle and its inhabitants parallel the course of Austrian history between 1939 and 1949. Illumination of the present by reference to the past is a common feature of works otherwise as disparate as *Nachprüfung eines Abschieds* (1961), *Aufschreibung aus Trient* (1965), *Pia Faller* (1973) and *Volterra* (1962), the last a description of Italian landscape which looks forward to **Handke**.

U

Unruh, Fritz von (1885–1970)

Son of a distinguished family which had served king and country for generations, Fritz von Unruh was sent to a cadet school at the age of eight and chosen to be a fellow-pupil of two of the Kaiser's sons. He underwent a rigid training which was supposed to train him for war, but rebelled, writing subversive articles for the local paper. When he was an officer in the Imperial Guards at Potsdam he resigned and resolved to dedicate his life to writing. His first play, *Offiziere* (1912), produced by Max Reinhardt, reflects his situation at the time. Called up in 1914 he experienced the fighting at Verdun, which turned him into an ardent pacifist. He wrote the expressionist drama *Ein Geschlecht* in 1916, a play which sees that nationalism and war encourage violent aggressiveness which they cannot control, and yet which they obtusely expect to keep within limits. The Elder Son exemplifies amoral energy and radical nihilism: his vitalism turns to self-destruction. The Mother is killed by the Commander, but her vision of love inspires the Younger Son, who leads the soldiers to rebellion. *Opfergang*, a narrative (also 1916), written in a hectic and often fervent style, depicts the futility and waste of war. *Platz*, a play written in 1920, continues the expressionist style of writing; later work, however, is more sober in tone. During the Weimar Republic von Unruh saw himself as a public orator, whose eloquence was meant to inspire democratic ideals within his fellow men. (Typical is *Die Flügel der Nike* (1925)). In 1933 von Unruh was deprived of citizenship and driven into exile: he settled in America and earned his living as a painter. He attempted, after 1945, to communicate his lofty idealism to the youth of Germany, but remained, to his disappointment, without influence. Two autobiographical novels, *Der Sohn des Generals* (1957) and *Im Haus des Prinzen* (1967) are of interest for the vivid picture they give of Prussian militarism at its worst. The novel *Friede in USA?* (1967) is largely unreadable due to its inflated style and wooden characterization, although the sentiments are worthy and sincere. *Sämtliche Werke* (twenty vols) appeared from 1970.

V

Vesper, Bernward (1938–71)

Vesper, son of the National Socialist author Will **Vesper**, studied in Tübingen and worked with Gudrun Ensslin (later a member of the *Baader-Meinhof-Gruppe*) for the German CND and other causes associated with the student movement. From 1969 on he worked on the 'novel essay' *Die Reise*, which he left incomplete when he committed suicide in a mental clinic and which sold over a hundred thousand copies during the four years after its publication in 1977. This cult book by the *poète maudit* of 1960s student radicalism is divided into three narrative strands which are fragmented and shuffled together: the 'Einfacher Bericht' is an autobiography from childhood to the death of his father, which marked a turning-point in his life, the second strand is taken up with an account of the period of writing (1969–71) and covers his relationships with Gudrun Ensslin, their son Felix, other women and the disintegration of the extra-parliamentary opposition (APO), the third is largely an evocation of the stream of thoughts, images and associations induced by drugs taken in the company of an American artist whom he conveys from Yugoslavia to Munich, in which extreme states of mind find expression in a style of startling originality.

Vesper, Will (1882–1962)

Vesper studied German literature and history in Munich; he served in the army from 1915–18, after which he became a journalist and writer. He made his reputation before 1914 with his reworkings of legends (*Tristan und Isolde* and *Parzival* (both 1911)); he concentrated increasingly upon German themes: *Martin Luthers Jugendjahre* (1918) and *Die Nibelungensage* (1921) are good examples. From 1923 onwards he edited the periodical *Die schöne Literatur* (from 1931 known as *Die neue Literatur*); in 1933 he worked with Hanns **Johst** on the committee of the *Reichsschrifttumskammer*. His novel *Das harte Geschlecht* (1931) was an example of *Blut und Boden* writing, and he was welcomed by the Nazis, whose cause he embraced. He provided, in novels, plays and editorial work, patriotic literature which was readily accessible to a wide and undiscriminating readership. He continued to publish after 1945 (the stories *Seltsame Flöte* (1958); *Zauber der Heide* (1960); *Letzte Ernte* (1962)); he also edited the work of Rückert and Gotthelf.

Viebig, Clara (1860-1952)

Born in Trier, Clara Viebig attended a girls' school in Düsseldorf; she lived on family estates in Prussian Poland and went to Berlin in 1883 to study singing. In 1896 she married a Jewish bookseller. She began writing in the 1890s and became a prolific and popular authoress. The novels *Das tägliche Brot* (1902), *Einer Mutter Sohn* (1906) and *Die vor den Toren* (1910) deal with poverty and social deprivation in a Berlin setting; *Die Wacht am Rhein* (1902) and the stories *Kinder der Eifel* (1897) deal without fanaticism with patriotic themes. Her plays were unsuccessful. During the Third Reich she was constantly harassed by the authorities because of her Jewish husband; she lived alternately in Berlin and Silesia. Her *Ausgewählte Werke* (six vols) were published in 1911 (eight vols in 1922). The so-called *Berliner Novellen* appeared in 1952.

Vollmoeller, Karl (1878-1948)

Possessed of private means, Vollmoeller dabbled in literature, worked in films, constructed motor-cars and was an aviator. Influenced above all by D'Annunzio, **George** and Richard Wagner (he chose to live in the Palazzo Vendramin in Venice where Wagner had died), Vollmoeller published a neo-romantic *Parcival* (1903), a collection of poems which extol 'Monsalwatsch' as a city of sun and beauty. He achieved enormous success with his mystery-play *Das Mirakel* (1912), an example of monumental aesthetic religiosity, produced by Max Reinhardt (music by Engelbert Humperdinck) in Berlin in 1914. Other plays met with little recognition. Vollmoeller also wrote a *Novelle, Die Geliebte* (1920); a selection of his poetry was published in 1960. He emigrated to Los Angeles, where he died. He is best regarded as a gifted dilettante, but *Das Mirakel* exemplifies well the post-Wagnerian fusion of aestheticism and spiritual attitudinizing which characterized the time in which it was written.

Vring, Georg von der (1889-1968)

Vring studied art in Berlin, served as an officer during the First World War and earned his living from 1919 to 1928 as an art teacher. He made his reputation in 1927 with the novel *Soldat Suhren*, a successful war novel which, however, lacks the immediacy and power of the writing of **Remarque** and **Renn**. Vring devoted himself to writing after the publication of this book, and cultivated a relaxed, readable style. He was regarded as harmless by the Nazis; he published throughout the Third Reich and provided stories and novels that were unashamedly entertaining: *Die spanische Hochzeit* (1938), *Die kaukasische Flöte* (1939), *Primeln und Tulpen* (1941) and *Junge*

Liebe (1942) are good examples. Vring also wrote poetry: *Dumpfe Trommel, schlag an!* (1939) is a concession to the requirements of the age. He settled in Munich in 1951. He was an accomplished translator (from French and English). His *Gedichte und Lieder* were published in 1979.

Walden, Herwarth (pseudonym of Georg Lewin, 1878–1941)

Son of a doctor, Walden studied music and trained as a pianist. In 1903 he married Else **Lasker-Schüler** (this lasted until 1911); he founded the *Verein für Kunst* in 1904 to give modern authors a platform for their views. Walden worked as editor for several journals, frequently encountering opposition. His most important step was the foundation, in March 1910, of *Der Sturm*, the most important (and longest-lived) of the expressionist journals: it survived, in one form or another, until 1932. In 1912 he married Nell Walden, who assisted him in his work. Most of the foremost names of expressionism were contributors to *Der Sturm*; as well as literature, Walden encouraged expressionist painters, also the cubists and futurists: a *Sturm-Galerie* exhibited their work after 1912. The 'Erste Deutsche Herbstsalon' (1913) presented 336 items from 90 artists. *Sturm-Abende* (from 1916) were organized at which readings were heard from the work of poets and critics; an art school was also founded, as was a *Sturm-Bühne*. Completely indifferent to politics at first (this differentiating him from Franz Pfemfert), Walden turned increasingly to communism in the 1920s. His own original work includes the novels *Das Buch der Menschenliebe* (1916), *Die Härte der Weltenliebe* (1921) and *Unter den Sinnen* (1919); various plays include *Weib* (1917), *Trieb* (1918) and *Krise* (1931); a collection of poetry was entitled *Im Geschweig der Liebe* (1925). Walden emigrated to Russia in 1932, where he taught languages and worked on the exile journal *Das Wort*. On 13 March 1941 he was arrested by the secret police; he was taken to Lubjanka prison and from there to a prison-camp at Saratow, south-east of Moscow, where he died of heart failure on 31 October.

His *Gesammelte Schriften* include *Kunstkritiker und Kunstmaler* (1916), *Gesammelte Tonwerke* (1919) and *Moskauer Schriften 1933–1941* (1978).

Wallraff, Günter (1942–)

Wallraff trained as a bookseller before conscription in the West German army, an experience he made the subject of one of his earliest reportages. The problems he then faced in establishing his status as a conscientious objector led him in the mid-1960s to enter journalism as an investigative reporter and advocate of those too inarticulate or too hard-pressed to make their voice heard. Wallraff's method since has been to collect material on the spot by taking various jobs, sometimes disguised or under an assumed name, e.g. as a conveyor-belt worker with Ford, as a piece-worker with Siemens, as a dock worker in Hamburg and, for the bestselling *Ganz unten* (1985), as a foreign guest-worker. He has been a prominent member of the Dortmund *Gruppe 61* (see Max von der **Grün**) and helped to found the *Werkkreis Literatur der Arbeitswelt*, the group which broke off from it. Wallraff's type of investigative journalism continues the tradition established by Egon Erwin **Kisch** and the Workers Correspondence Movement of the 1920s. Concentrating on actions and situations he has developed a sober and matter-of-fact style. However, all of his campaigns have been marked by courage and commitment, and with some he has been associated with Heinrich **Böll**, coincidentally in his exposure of the *Bild-Zeitung* (*Der Aufmacher. Der Mann der bei 'Bild' Hans Esser war* (1977)) and directly in his report on the West German state security organization *Berichte zur Gesinnungslage des Staatsschutzes* (published with Böll's *Berichte zur Gesinnungslage der Nation* (1977)). Wallraff has also reported on the Greece of the colonels (*Unser Faschismus nebenan* (1975) with Eckart Spoo) and pre-revolutionary Portugal (*Aufdeckung einer Verschwörung. Die Spinola-Aktion* (1976)). Representative collections are *Die Reportagen* (1976) and *Bericht vom Mittelpunkt der Welt. Die Reportagen* (1984).

Walser, Martin (1927–)

Born on Lake Constance, where he has lived as a professional writer since 1957, Walser studied in Regensburg and Tübingen, wrote a doctoral dissertation on **Kafka** and was employed by *Süddeutscher Rundfunk* from 1949 to 1957. More recently he has been a guest professor at various American universities, one of which forms the background of his campus novel *Brandung* (1985). Walser's fictional œuvre has reached imposing dimensions but can be divided into two groups of novels and stories. In *Ehen in Philippsburg* (1957), the three novels of the Anselm Kristlein trilogy (*Halbzeit* (1960), *Das Einhorn* (1966) and *Der Sturz* (1973)) and *Fiction* (1970) he offers portraits of men (Hans Beumann in *Ehen*, Anselm Kristlein in the other works) whose desire to succeed in and conform to the system which they serve clashes with the frustrations and disillusionments which are an inevitable consequence of an intermediate position in the social hierarchy and of activities (middle management, public relations, advertising, freelance writing on fashionable topics, administration of a rest-home belonging to a private concern) which allow a limited freedom of manoeuvre. The initially idealistic hero enters a world in which business, art and sexual relations form a tempting and corrupting amalgam. Although drawn into the orbit of those who have profited from the West German economic miracle Kristlein is able to experience an idyllic love-affair and, having returned to the family fold and become aware of the precariousness of his position, makes a break with a way of life which had meant subjection to market forces which he had long hoped to control. *Die Gallistl'sche Krankheit*

(1972), although written between the second and third volumes of the trilogy, can be described as a transitional work precipitated by Walser's brief flirtation with the West German Communist Party; in it Josef Georg Gallistl overcomes the alienation produced by the pretence of living up to certain social norms by joining a group of young Communists. The second phase of Walser's fiction begins with *Jenseits der Liebe* (1976); this and all the succeeding novels with the exception of *Dorle und Wolf* (1987) about an idealistic GDR spy who falls victim to the institutionalized division of Germany form a cycle loosely linked by the principal setting of southern Baden-Württemberg, especially Lake Constance, and by certain figures who make multiple appearances in changing circumstances. The chief clerk of a dental accessories firm Franz Horn and his rival Horst Liszt of *Jenseits der Liebe* return in *Brief an Lord Liszt* (1982), the schoolteacher Helmut Halm, whose meeting with his old school acquaintance Klaus Buch initiates the action of *Ein fliehendes Pferd* (1978), perhaps the most successful of Walser's shorter works, becomes a visiting lecturer in the USA in *Brandung*, while the estate agent Gottlieb Zürn, who in *Das Schwanenhaus* (1980) fails to gain the commission to sell an art nouveau villa and thus save it from demolition, experiences a series of Kristlein-like professional and sexual adventures in a mood of increasing desperation in *Jagd* (1988). His cousin Xaver is forced to leave his employment as chauffeur for a job in industry in *Seelenarbeit* (1979), while even *Meßmers Gedanken* (1985), an aphoristic work which comes close to a personal confession, was on Walser's own admission originally intended for *Brandung*. The mid-life crisis, fear of sexual impotence (the principal theme of *Fiction*), sexual temptation, the alienation of offspring, professional set-backs, marital contretemps and reconciliations, male rivalries are themes which run through all these works conveyed in the headlong style marked by ironic awareness of the difference between outward mask and inner insecurity which has become Walser's hallmark.

Walser's plays include the two parts of a projected trilogy 'Deutsche Chronik' *Eiche und Angora* (1962), divided into three sections covering three phases of the period 1945 to 1960, in which the easy adjustment of Nazi fellow-travellers to the post-war situation is contrasted with the disorientation of a former concentration camp inmate whose failure to follow their example leads to his confinement in a lunatic asylum, and *Der schwarze Schwan* (1964), in which the son of a former concentration camp doctor fails in his attempt to unmask his father by means of the 'play within a play' device in the manner of Hamlet and commits suicide. In *Überlebensgroß Herr Krott* (1964) the title-figure, who owes much to **Brecht**'s Puntila and Baal, produces mayhem but proves indestructible thanks to the conformity of his underlings. The grotesque farces *Der Abstecher* (1967), *Die Zimmerschlacht* (1967) and *Ein Kinderspiel* (1970) are basically, like the novels, domestic dramas which expose middle-class self-deceptions. *Das Sauspiel* (1975), set in Nuremberg after the defeat of the peasant uprising in 1526, examines the role of the artist-intellectual, represented here by Dürer, Hans Sachs and Faust, in a time of political upheaval which offers analogies to the rise and fall of the student movement in the late 1960s. *In Goethes Hand* (1982) concerns Goethe's self-effacing amanuensis Johann Peter Eckermann, while *Die Ohrfeige* (1987, but written between 1981 and 1983) is a comedy which places a victim of unemployment against the background of the culture industry. Walser has also written numerous essays on literary and socio-political topics collected in, among other volumes, *Erfahrungen und Leseerfahrungen* (1965), *Heimatkunde* (1968), the Frankfurt poetry lectures *Selbstbewußtsein und Ironie* (1981) and *Liebeserklärungen* (1983). In *Über Deutschland reden* (1990) a subjective need is expressed to overcome Germany's division.

Walser's reputation may not yet be as high outside Germany as that of **Böll** and **Grass**, yet he, more than any of his contemporaries, prompts comparison with present writers in English-speaking countries on account of his uncanny ability to capture the manners, moods and neuroses of the middle classes by creating characters who are a constant prey to an unstable mixture of *Angst*, self-irony, realism and utopian aspiration.

Walser, Robert (1878–1956)

Son of a bookbinder in Biel (Canton Berne), Robert Walser studied banking in his home-town (1892–5), thereafter led a restless life. He attempted acting in Stuttgart, published juvenilia (poems) in 1898, associated with Franz **Blei**, visited Max **Dauthendey** in Würzburg, became (1903) secretary in an engineering firm, and a year later a bank official in Zurich. From 1905 to 1913 he lived with his brother Karl in Berlin; for a few months (in 1905) he took a course as a butler, and worked as a servant in Schloß Dambrau (Upper Silesia). The publisher Ernst Cassirer encouraged him to write, and three novels appeared in quick succession: *Geschwister Tanner* (1907), *Der Gehülfe* (1908) and *Jakob von Gunten* (1909). The first deals obliquely with Walser's Zurich experiences, the stifling routine to which the hero, Simon Tanner, refuses to conform; the second describes Walser's experiences in the engineering firm at Wädenswil. The most famous of the three, *Jakob von Gunten*, is in the form of a notebook, a boy's impressions of life at a school for servants run by the brother and sister Benjamenta. The book is remarkable in its insistence on humility and the rejection of power; the prose is limpid and ironic, and was greatly admired by **Kafka**, also **Musil**, who drew attention to similarities between these two writers. Walser quietly rejects the assumptions of Western civilization (particularly progress and ratiocination) and stresses in his writing withdrawal, adaptability and self-effacement. In 1913 he returned to Switzerland: *Kleine Dichtungen* and *Geschichten* date from this time (1914). The pieces are short, impressionistic and occasionally trivial ('Im Alltäglichen ruhen die Wahrheiten'). In 1921 Walser worked briefly as a librarian in Berne; his last book, *Die Rose*, appeared in 1925. In 1929 he was admitted to a sanatorium in Waldau, in 1933 to a mental home in Herisau. He lived there until 1956, dying on a walk to Rosenberg. Posthumous publications include the prose works *Prosa* (1960), *Dichtungen in Prosa* (1953–61), *Kleine Wanderung* (1963) and *Die Räuber* (1976). *Das Gesamtwerk* (twelve vols) appeared in 1978, as did the *Briefe*; *Sämtliche Werke* (20 vols) followed in 1986.

Walter, Otto F. (1928–)

Walter worked from 1951 to 1973 in various publishing firms, including that of his father in Olten, Switzerland, and has been a professional writer since. He has produced a series of novels, most of which are set in the fictional town of Jammers, in the north-western canton of Solothurn away from the tourist-haunted Alpine regions, on repressed guilt in close family relationships and on the conflict between progressive outsiders and a narrow-minded entrenched majority. In *Der Stumme* (1959), set on a road construction site on a Swiss pass, the title-figure becomes the innocent cause of his father's accidental death, while in *Herr Tourel* (1962) he is hounded out of a town where a year earlier he had had a secret love-affair with a girl who had later died in childbirth, the nature and extent of his guilt never having been established. In *Die ersten Unruhen* (1972) tension between local citizens and a group of 'immigrants' from Romansh Switzerland leads to open conflict on election day, in *Die Verwilderung* (1977) a car mechanic and a middle-class woman who together form a rural commune become the victims of small-town prejudice, and in *Wie wird Beton zu Gras* (1979) a demonstration against an atomic power-station is viewed from the perspective of a seventeen-year-old girl who makes her protest by commandeering a tank. *Das Staunen der Schlafwandler am Ende der Nacht* (1983) concerns the relation between fiction and reality in the life of a journalist-novelist, while *Zeit des Fasans* (1988) is the saga of a family of entrepreneurs, who for a time, although Swiss, have a stake in the Third Reich. Walter's plays are *Elio oder eine fröhliche Gesellschaft* (1965) and *Die Katze* (1967). His application of a wide range of modernist narrative techniques makes him, along with his compatriots **Frisch** and **Muschg**, much more than a conventional regional writer.

Wassermann, Jakob (1873–1934)

Son of a Jewish businessman, Wassermann decided at an early age to become a writer. He worked as a contributor to *Simplicissimus* and later achieved great popularity with his novels and stories which, refraining from modernist experimentation, keep well within the nineteenth-century realist tradition. *Die Juden von Zirndorf* (1897) rejects fanaticism (including religious) and stresses humanitarian tolerance; *Caspar Hauser oder Die Trägheit des Herzens* (1908) attacks the torpor and indifference of German provincial society; *Das Gänsemännchen* (1913) gives a most perceptive picture of a small German town in which the musician Daniel Nothafft is driven into shrill and bitter self-assertion. *Christian Wahnschaffe* (1919) has an expressionistic theme: the young man rejects his father's industrial wealth and goes to join the poor. The later novels, such as *Der Fall Mauritzius* (1928), *Etzel Andergast* (1930) and *Joseph Kerkhovens dritte Existenz* (1934) are best regarded as superior detective novels. Wassermann was enormously prolific, and reached record sales with his novels (**Thomas Mann** referred to him as the 'Welt-Star des Romans'); he lived in and near Vienna before moving to Altaussee (Styria). He also wrote essays; important is also the autobiographical account *Mein Weg als Deutscher und Jude* (1921), a sensitive analysis of the tensions between Teuton and Hebrew. The novel *Engelhardt oder Die zwei Welten* (1905, published posthumously in 1974) is also autobiographical. Wassermann was friendly with **Beer-Hofmann**, **Hofmannsthal** and **Schnitzler**; it was in his rooms in Munich that **Rilke** and Lou **Andreas-Salomé** became acquainted. Eleven volumes of *Gesammelte Werke* appeared between 1924 and 1931, seven volumes between 1944 and 1948. The *Tagebuch aus dem Winkel. Erzählungen und Aufsätze* was published in 1986.

Wedekind, Benjamin Franklin (Frank)(1864–1918)

Wedekind's father had been a doctor at the Sultan's court in Constantinople, was elected to the Frankfurt parliament, emigrated to the USA (where he married a German actress), returned to Europe, living briefly in Hanover (where his son Frank was born), then Switzerland. The young Wedekind wrote for the *Neue Zürcher Zeitung* and associated with the avant-garde writers in that city; he worked briefly as advertising agent for 'Maggi' soups, also as a secretary to a circus. In 1888 he was actor, *Dramaturg* and producer in Leipzig and Munich; in London (1894) he met Max **Dauthendey** and in Paris Strindberg and Lou **Andreas-Salomé**; he became secretary to Willi Grétor, the Danish art-dealer and forger. In 1896 he contributed to *Simplicissimus* in Munich, and spent a few weeks (1899–1900) in prison for a scurrilous ballad deriding the Kaiser. In the following year he worked for the cabaret *Die elf Scharfrichter* as an entertainer, accompanying his own chansons on the guitar. The fragmentary novel *Mine-Haha oder Über die körperliche Erziehung der jungen Mädchen* dates from 1900: Wedekind parodies the *Bildungsroman* and mixes a genuine concern for a liberal and progressive educational system with bizarre elements. In the same year he wrote *Frühlings-Erwachen*, produced by Max Reinhardt in 1904: the storm of protest from the authorities prevented its being performed again until 1912. The attack on hypocrisy and the pusillanimous deviousness, the unfeeling attitudes of teachers and parents in this play is again juxtaposed with grotesque caricature; a fantastic aspect ('der vermummte Herr', and the headless ghost) emphasizes the closeness of Wedekind to later expressionist, surrealist writers. Wedekind was supported by Herwarth **Walden** and Karl **Kraus**; he constantly ran into trouble with the censor for the frankness of sexual depiction in his plays and his anti-authoritarian attitudes. The next successes were the two plays *Der Erdgeist* (1895) and *Die Büchse der Pandora* (1902), the two 'Lulu' plays. Wedekind uses, in the prologue to *Der Erdgeist*, a circus technique (later to be endorsed by **Brecht**). Lulu is portrayed as 'das wilde, schöne Tier': she is both fascinating and revolting, yet her courage and integrity are also to be admired. The lesbianism of the Countess Geschwitz is portrayed by Wedekind with sympathy and compassion; the world of pimps, swindlers and prostitutes is well depicted. *Erdgeist* mixes farce and melodrama; *Die Büchse der Pandora* is marred by discursive *longueurs* and exhibitionism. Wedekind and his wife Tilly Newes frequently acted in these plays: a later film version (with Louise Brooks as Lulu) and Alban Berg's opera made the work world-famous.

Der Marquis von Keith (1901) depicts a swindler (Grétor) whose cynicism and cunning help him to survive: Wedekind never tired of portraying the charlatan who uses furtive ruse to get the better of his fellow men. The play was greatly admired by **Thomas Mann** who saw Wedekind acting the part of Keith. This, and the two 'Lulu' plays and *Frühlings Erwachen*, have kept their place in the standard repertoire: later plays (*Schloß Wetterstein* (1910); *Franziska* (1911) and others) have not. Wedekind's talents, eccentric and one-sided, did not develop or mature: Julius Bab called him 'ein tragischer Pierrot, ein Gehirnerotiker, ein mathematischer Phantast, der auf Augenblicke genial ist'. He remained in Munich, editing *Der Komet* from 1911. During the First World War practically all his plays were banned by the censor. His funeral was a remarkable and bizarre event; present were the brothers **Mann**, Brecht and **Lautensack** who attempted to film it.

Wedekind remained a freakish outsider, his talents more appropriate to cabaret, circus and Grand Guignol than conventional theatre. His attack on bourgeois morality is frequently linked with that of later (expressionist) dramatists, but his world of roués, criminals and cynics knows nothing of the inflated ideals of that movement. Nine volumes of *Gesammelte Werke* appeared from 1912 to 1921; *Ausgewählte Werke* (five vols) in 1924; *Prosa, Dramen, Verse* (two vols) in 1950 and 1964; *Mine-Haha und andere Erzählungen* in 1955; *Ich habe meine Tante geschlachtet. Lautenlieder* in 1960; *Gedichte, Bänkellieder, Balladen* in 1967. A three-volume *Werke* appeared in 1969, *Die Tagebücher. Ein erotisches Leben* followed in 1989.

Wegner, Armin (1886–1978)

Wegner studied law in Breslau, Zurich, Berlin and Paris; he also acted (under Max Reinhardt) and wrote for various journals. He published his first volume of poetry, *Im Strom verloren*, in 1903, to be followed by *Zwischen zwei Städten* in 1909. In the First World War he served as a medical orderly; in the 1920s he published several short stories and novels (*Der Knabe Hüssein* (1921)), which deal with travel experiences, particularly in Russia and the East. He became an ardent pacifist, helping to found the *Bund der Kriegsgegner*, writing (after witnessing the massacre of the Armenians by the Turks) to President Wilson and in 1933, to Hitler, deploring the Nazi treatment of the Jews: for this he was arrested. He was able to flee to England, thence to Palestine and Italy, where he taught at the University of Padua. He received many honours from the West German government and from Israel during the 1950s and 1960s; he died in Rome, where he had made his home. Wegner was most successful in his travel books; *Im Hause der Glückseligkeit* (1920), *Maschinen im Märchenland* and

Jagd durch das Tausendjährige Land (both 1932) should also be mentioned. Collections of his writing, *Fällst du, umarme die Erde* and *Odyssee der Seele* appeared in 1974 and 1976 respectively.

Weinheber, Josef (1892–1945)

Son of a Viennese butcher, Weinheber lost both parents and siblings within the space of six years and was brought up in an orphanage; these experiences he would later describe in the story *Das Waisenhaus* (1924). He became a post-office official in 1911, a job which he held for twenty years. He began publishing poetry in the 1920s (*Der einsame Mensch* (1920); *Von beiden Ufern* (1923); *Boot in der Bucht* (1926)); it was the collection *Adel und Untergang* (1934) that made his reputation. This consists of a cycle ('Antike Strophen'), a series of 'Variationen auf eine hölderlinische Ode' and a 'Heroische Trilogie'. Weinheber deliberately chose to model his poetry on the work of such writers as Hölderlin and **Rilke**: he was scornful of modernism and lamented the decadence of the age. The collection *Wien wörtlich* (1935) is a cycle of poems about old Vienna: some are in dialect. Weinheber had close connections with the Austrian Nazi party: he despised democracy and longed for the fusion of his country with Germany ('Ein deutscher Gruß aus Österreich' (1936)). He was encouraged by **Will Vesper** and invited to Germany, where he made speeches and broadcasts supporting the Nazi cause. The collection *Kammermusik* (1939) is probably his best, a cycle which explores the musicality of language and deals with specifically musical themes: 'Orgel' is dedicated to Anton Bruckner. There is much skilful poetry here which may be appreciated without reference to Weinheber's political aberrations. (He also wrote the obligatory poems to Hitler: 'Hymne an die Heimkehr' commemorates the latter's birthday, celebrated in the *Burgtheater*.) Weinheber lectured on language to students at Vienna University, stressing the mystical superiority of the German language. He died of an overdose of morphine on 8 April 1945. His *Sämtliche Werke* (five vols) appeared from 1953 to 1956 (revised from 1970); *Gedichte* followed (in 1978).

Weisenborn, Günther (1902–69)

Weisenborn began his writing career as a dramatist in Berlin with three plays in the 'neue Sachlichkeit' manner, the anti-war *U-Boot S4* (1928), the similar *SOS oder die Arbeiter von Jersey* (1929) and the adaptation in collaboration with **Brecht** of Gorki's *Die Mutter* (1931). A stay in Argentina from 1928 to 1930 inspired the novels *Die einsame Herde* and *Die Furie* (both 1937) and the play *Babel* (1946). After a further period of absence from Germany from 1935 to 1939 he combined work for the radio with clandestine activity for the 'Rote Kapelle' resistance group until arrest and imprisonment in 1942, an experience which led to the composition of his most memorable play, *Die Illegalen* (1946), in which a resistance fighter sacrifices himself voluntarily in order to ensure the survival of a group – a play which in plot resembles Brecht's *Die Maßnahme* but in form is devoid of alienation effects. *Memorial* (1947), an autobiographical account of his imprisonment in which two time levels are juxtaposed, was followed by *Der lautlose Aufstand* (1953), based on material assembled by **Ricarda Huch**, the first objective survey of anti-Nazi resistance within Germany during the Third Reich, and *Unternehmen Walküre 44* (1966), one of several plays by various authors on the officers' plot to assassinate Hitler of 20 July 1944. In *Der gespaltene Horizont* (1964) he continued his autobiography to include the years 1945 to 1964, when he was active in the theatre in Berlin and Hamburg and as editor of the periodical *Ulenspiegel*. His advocacy of nuclear disarmament is reflected in the oratorio-like *Göttinger Kantate* (1958) and the play *Die Familie von Nevada* (1958, alternative title *Die Familie von Makabah*). Weisenborn's novels, which also include *Die Barbaren* (1931), *Das Mädchen von Fanö* (1934), *Traum und Tarantel* (1938), *Der dritte Blick* (1956), *Auf Sand gebaut* (1956), are with the exception of *Der Verfolger*, which concerns post-war indifference to Nazi crimes, of less interest than his plays, which although they failed to remain part of the repertory are of considerable formal and thematic variety and include the chinoiseries *Fünfzehn Schnüre Geld* (1958) and *Das Glück der Konkubinen* (1962), besides *Die Neuberin* (1935), *Die guten Feinde* (1938), *Ballade vom Eulenspiegel, vom Federle und von der dicken Pompanne* (1949), *Zwei Engel steigen aus* (1954), *Lofter oder Das verlorene Gesicht* (1956), *Die spanische Hochzeit* (1949) and *Drei ehrenwerte Herren* (1951). Weisenborn has been overshadowed by his older contemporary Brecht, with whom he had much in common but could not compete in formal originality, astringency and intellectual force.

Weiss, Ernst (1882–1940)

Born in Brno, Moravia, son of a Jewish cloth-merchant, Ernst Weiss studied medicine in Prague and Vienna and worked as a surgeon. From 1912 to 1913 he was a ship's doctor, making several journeys to the Far East. He was friendly with Franz **Kafka** and supported him during the latter's first disengagement from Felice Bauer. In 1913 he published his first novel, *Die Galeere*, an account of a pioneer in radiology who learns of love and failure. Weiss served between 1914 and 1918 in the army, and saw action on the Eastern Front. *Tiere in Ketten* (1918, with its sequel, *Nahar* (1922)) is expressionistic in style, a vivid and often violent portrayal of sexuality and (literally) bestial experience. Weiss's most successful novel was *Boëtius von Orlamünde* (1928, retitled *Der Aristokrat*). The setting is a Belgian boarding-school for aristocrats; the action eschews the commonplaces of fiction and concentrates on three events, the breaking in of the stallion

Cyrus, the destructive fire and the escape to Brussels, where the narrator becomes a factory-worker and is present at the death of his father. The tone is subdued, but the psychological penetration and the intensity are undeniable. (The novel was, amazingly, regarded as a 'Sportroman' and awarded the silver medal at the Olympic Games in Amsterdam in 1928, the German flag being flown in Weiss's honour before some 25,000 spectators.) Weiss fled to Prague in 1933, and thence to Paris, where he lived until his suicide in June 1940, one day before the entry of German troops. The novel *Ich – der Augenzeuge*, published posthumously in 1963, depicts the life of a doctor during the Weimar Republic and Nazi Germany.

Weiss's medical and psychological skills, plus his imaginative empathy, created an *œuvre* admired by Hermann **Hesse**, **Stefan Zweig**, **Thomas Mann** and Franz Kafka. His *Gesammelte Werke* (sixteen vols) were published in 1982.

Weiss, Peter (1916–82)

Weiss, the son of a Jewish textile manufacturer, grew up in prosperous circumstances in a Berlin suburb and moved in 1934 from Germany via Britain to Prague, where he studied art. In 1939 the family settled in Sweden, where Weiss was employed as a textile pattern designer and art teacher, became a Swedish citizen in 1945 and married the stage designer Gunilla Palmstierna. For a time he made experimental and documentary films and from 1933 to 1962 painted in a style much indebted to the surrealists. His earliest writings in prose are semi-fictional explorations of the developing self against the background of family pressures (*Abschied von den Eltern* (1961)) or in the wider context of life in Sweden during the 1940s (*Fluchtpunkt* (1962), which culminates in a full awareness of identity and vocation on a trip to Paris in 1947) or precise and detached descriptive accounts of events in a restricted setting close to the French *nouveau roman* in style (*Der Schatten des Körpers des Kutschers* (1960, written in 1952) and *Das Gespräch der drei Gehenden* (1963)). Weiss's early plays develop the same theme of search for identity in the manner of Strindberg's late symbolist works (*Der Turm* (1962)) or grotesque knockabout farce (*Nacht mit Gästen* (1963)). At the same time he completed the play which made him internationally famous overnight, *Die Verfolgung und Ermordung Jean Paul Marats, dargestellt durch die Schauspielgruppe des Hospizes zu Charenton unter Anleitung des Herrn de Sade*, known generally as *Marat/ Sade*, which received its première in West Berlin in 1964 and was immediately translated and performed in Paris, London (a production by Peter Brook, later filmed) and Rostock GDR (a production by Hans Anselm Perten which with the author's approval stressed the long-term revolutionary implications of Marat's stance). The title-figures engage in a debate in which revolution and reaction, reason and unconscious drives, collectivism and individualism are opposed in the context of an enaction of the revolution which becomes a histrionic display of madness and excess complicated by a Chinese box structure adopted to convey three time levels. The result is an example of 'total theatre' in which the innovations of **Brecht** and Artaud are combined. Weiss went on to make three contributions to documentary with *Die Ermittlung* (1965), an oratorio in eleven cantos, a carefully arranged collage of extracts from the record of the trial in Frankfurt of former Auschwitz guards with music by Luigi Nono, *Gesang vom lusitanischen Popanz* (1967), in which the title-figure is an effigy representing the Portuguese colonial regime in Angola, and the *Vietnam-Diskurs* (abbreviation of a much longer title) (1968), a black-and-white treatment of the history of Vietnam in two parts covering the period from 500 BC to 1945 and that of the struggle against the French and the Americans. *Trotzki im Exil* (1970) which amounts to a rehabilitation of Stalin's rival, was followed by *Hölderlin* (1971) in which the title-figure, who eventually withdraws into feigned madness in order not to compromise his revolutionary ideals, is opposed to the poets and philosophers of Germany's classical age as a predecessor of Marx. With the three volumes of *Die Ästhetik des Widerstands* (1975, 1978, 1981) Weiss produced his *magnum opus* in which incidents and meetings of his own life are worked into an account by a working-class narrator born in 1917 of his experiences during the Third Reich. Forced to cut short the awe-inspiring programme of self-education he had begun with friends he leaves Germany, takes part in the Spanish Civil War, then moves on to Czechoslovakia, Paris and Stockholm, where in the years 1939–40 he encounters Brecht and becomes involved in his project for the dramatization of the life of a Swedish popular hero. The third volume, which traces the course of the resistance in Germany and the disintegration of the left in exile, almost ceases to be the 'Wunschautobiographie' which was the work's original conception as the narrator withdraws into the background. Even in the earlier volumes the presentation of incident takes second place to analyses of such works of art as the Pergamon frieze, Géricault's painting of the raft of the 'Medusa', Picasso's Guernica and **Kafka**'s *Der Prozeß*, which are made part of an all-embracing Marxist aesthetic aimed at justifying art in a period of repression. Resembling an erratic block in the West German literary landscape, *Die Ästhetik des Widerstands* marks the end of a phase which began long before the so-called 'Stunde Null' of 1945, forming as it does a résumé of the literature of exile. The four *Notizbücher* of 1981 and 1982, covering the periods 1940–1971 and 1971–1980, throw much light on the progress of this monumental work.

Wellershoff, Dieter (1925–)

Born in the Lower Rhineland Wellershoff served in the army from 1943 to 1945, studied German literature, art history and psychology, completed in 1952 a doctoral dissertation on the poet Gottfried **Benn**, which was followed by the critical study *Gottfried Benn – Phänotyp dieser Stunde* (1959). He read before the *Gruppe 47* in 1960 and spent 1973 as writer in residence at the University of Warwick. His earliest impact was as an author of radio plays which consist mainly of psychological portraits in monologue form collected in *Das Schreien der Katze im Sack* (1970), but include also social criticism conveyed through the medium of a criminal investigation in *Wünsche* (1970). Meanwhile as reader for the publishers Kiepenheuer und Witsch he gathered together and promoted a number of young writers including **Herburger**, **Brinkmann** and **Born** who before they developed in different directions became associated under the label of the Cologne school of new realism, a theoretical concept devised and elaborated in a number of important essays. Having declared his allegiance to an international prose avant-garde in *Der Gleichgültige* (1963), he advocated in *Literatur und Veränderung* (1969) and *Literatur und Lustprinzip* (1973) a combination of psychological insight into characters under emotional pressure and precise evocation of everyday objects and surroundings as practised in the French *nouveau roman*, believing that the author by entering the subjectivity of his principal figures widens his own awareness and that of his readers. Other essay collections and theoretical works include *Wiederherstellung der Fremdheit* (1967), *Fiktion und Praxis* (1968), *Transzendenz und scheinhafter Mehrwert* (1972), *Das Verschwinden im Bild* (1980) and *Der Roman und die Erfahrbarkeit der Welt* (1989). After *Ein schöner Tag* (1966) about the breakup of a family he produced three novels *Die Schattengrenze* (1969), *Einladung an alle* (1972) and *Die Schönheit des Schimpansen* (1977) in which men are driven by various circumstances to commit serious crimes followed by flight or suicide. *Die Sirene* (1980) traces the collapse of a scientist's ordered mental world under the influence of the title-figure, a female voice on the telephone. The long *Der Sieger nimmt alles* (1983) covers twenty years in the life of a businessman who after a deprived childhood studies economics, marries into a firm, undertakes shady deals which fail and dies alone from a heart attack in a hotel alienated from wife and son. Wellershoff is also the author of short stories (*Ein Gedicht von der Freiheit* (1974) and *Die Körper und die Träume* (1986)), plays mainly for theatre and television and the autobiography *Die Arbeit des Lebens* (1985).

Werfel, Franz (1890–1945)

Born in Prague, son of a wealthy Jewish businessman, Werfel became a publisher's reader in Leipzig in 1910 and quickly established himself at the centre of a group of early expressionist writers. The publication of his first collection, *Der Weltfreund*, in 1911 made an enormous impact; it has been claimed that the expressionist movement began with these poems. The last of them, 'An den Leser', represents the declamatory, rhetorical aspect of the movement. *Wir sind* (1912) continues, and exceeds, the ecstatic tone:

the attempt at sublimity dangerously teeters upon the bathetic. Werfel fought on the Russian Front during the First World War; his pacifist play *Die Troerinnen* (1915, based on Euripides) caused a sensation. Werfel settled in Vienna after the war and married the widow of Gustav Mahler. His story *Nicht der Mörder, der Ermordete ist schuldig* (1920) is typical in its attack on authority, on the patriarchal principle above all, cause (in Werfel's eyes) of war and oppression. The important play *Spiegelmensch* dates from this time: it is a criticism of the solipsistic aspects of expressionism, the cult of subjectivity. Werfel achieved great popularity during the 1920s, despite the strictures of Karl **Kraus** and Kasimir **Edschmid**, the latter sharply criticizing the 'prophetische Umarmungsrufe' with the 'weltlichen Hosiannas und den Caféhaus-Gebärden'. *Der Abituriententag* (1928) is a short novel dealing with failure at school and culpability; *Barbara oder Die Frömmigkeit* (1929) is a *roman-à-clef* dealing with Werfel's own experiences in the war, and conditions prevailing in Vienna immediately afterwards; *Die vierzig Tage des Musa Dagh* (1933) describes an episode from the massacre of the Armenians by the Turks. Werfel's humanitarianism became increasingly marked, even obtrusive; he travelled frequently, often to Italy (the novel *Verdi* (1924) had praised the sanity of the Italian as opposed to Wagner's dangerous imperiousness). In 1938 Werfel fled Austria; in Lourdes he vowed he would write a novel on Bernadette Soubirous should he escape the Nazis (his interest in Catholicism was always fervent, although he was never baptized). He escaped to the USA: *Das Lied von Bernadette* (1941) became a best-seller. Later novels are avowedly utopian (*Stern der Ungeborenen* (1946)). The collection of essays *Zwischen Oben und Unten* (1946) expresses the tensions felt between Werfel's Jewishness and the Catholic faith. *Gesammelte Werke* (eight vols) appeared between 1921 and 1936; *Gesammelte Werke in Einzelausgaben* appeared from 1975.

Weyrauch, Wolfgang (1907–80)

Weyrauch studied in Berlin, was a journalist and publisher's reader from 1933, served in the army from 1940 to 1945 and was editor of the satirical magazine *Ulenspiegel* from 1946 to 1948. He is a neglected figure remembered largely for his coinage of the term 'Kahlschlag' (clearance of terrain) in the anthology of prose by thirty contemporary writers *Tausend Gramm*, which he edited in 1949, in order to define the break with a debased literary language necessary to describe the physical reality and spiritual situation after 1945. Weyrauch had produced novels and stories before this date, but he came into his own when West German literature was able to gain contact with foreign models, especially the American short story – *die minute des negers* (1953, broadcast 1954) can be related like works by other writers at this time to Ambrose Bierce's 'Incident at Owl Creek Bridge' – and other forms including those in which fantasy and fable

Gedichte and *Ausgewählte Werke* appeared in 1951 and 1953 respectively; *Gedichte. Musik der Kindheit* in 1981.

Wohmann, Gabriele (1932–)

The daughter of a clergyman, Wohmann studied German literature and music in Frankfurt, then spent three years as a schoolteacher on the North Sea island of Langeoog and in Darmstadt, where she has remained since becoming a professional writer. Wohmann's world is obsessive and claustrophobic owing to the radical introspection of the central-figure/narrator, who, whether male or female, undertakes a microscopic analysis of the surrounding world and of the sensations which contact with it produces. Wohmann is not a satirist in any conventional sense, although her works contain much material for a critique of the everyday aggressions and deceptions in middle-class professional and personal relationships. Nor is she a feminist who places the problems of her female protagonists at the door of unfeeling, domineering men, as male protagonists, in e.g. *Jetzt und nie* (1958), *Schönes Gehege* (1975) and *Frühherbst in Badenweiler* (1978), are endowed with a sensitivity and desire to withdraw into the illusion of an alternative identity evident in her female narrators. Such figures neither engage the reader's full sympathy nor do they become the vehicle for the author's views. Only the child in *Paulinchen war allein zu Haus* (1974) becomes a focus for the satire of those who fail to provide her with the understanding and support she needs. Wohmann's vast output also includes the novels *Abschied für länger* (1965), *Ernste Absicht* (1970), *Ausflug mit der Mutter* (1976), *Ach wie gut, daß niemand weiß* (1980), *Das Glücksspiel* (1981) and *Der Flötenton* (1987), numerous volumes of short stories, from which the selection *Ausgewählte Erzählungen aus zwanzig Jahren* appeared in two volumes in 1979, five volumes of poetry and several plays mainly for radio and television.

Wolf, Christa (1929–)

Born in Landsberg an der Warthe (now Gorzów Wielkowski) Christa Wolf moved to Mecklenburg in 1945. She studied German literature in Leipzig and Jena from 1945 to 1953 and joined the SED, becoming later a candidate member of the party's central committee. After a spell as co-editor of the periodical *Neue deutsche Literatur*, during which she was active as a reviewer and essayist, she became a professional writer in 1962. After *Moskauer Novelle* (1959) on the revival of a relationship between a woman doctor from East Berlin and a Russian interpreter in Moscow she turned in *Der geteilte Himmel* (1963) to the delicate topic of an affair between a woman training to become a teacher and an industrial chemist which comes to grief when the man leaves the GDR for the West after difficulties with the planning authorities; she, however, having briefly joined him and attempted suicide, returns confirmed in her commitment by her experience of work in a GDR railway carriage factory. The success of this novel was not matched in the GDR by *Nachdenken über Christa T.* (1968), the life story of a young woman, from childhood, through flight at the end of the Second World War, work on the land and study to premature death from leukaemia. The theme – the tension between the social development of the GDR and the title-figure's withdrawal from constraints on personal growth – and the form – a collage of memories of a number of acquaintances, flashbacks, reflections of the writing process, held together by the diffuse subjectivity of the narrator – ensure the novel controversial status as a radical departure from socialist realism. The threatened private sphere has continued since to be a major preoccupation of Wolf's fiction and essays, from the story 'Ein Juninachmittag' (1967) to *Sommerstück* (1989). Having in the story 'Unter den Linden' come to terms with a crisis typical of her generation with the aid of dream reflections, she joined other GDR authors (**Sarah Kirsch, Morgner**, de **Bruyn**) in contributing to the anthology *Blitz aus heitrem Himmel* (1974, published in the Federal Republic under the title *Geschlechtertausch*) on the theme of sex change, and offered in *Till Eulenspiegel* (1972) a Marxist interpretation of the folk figure. In the semi-autobiographical *Kindheitsmuster* (1976) the narrator reconstructs her early life during the Third Reich by skilfully juxtaposing three separate time levels in an attempt to answer the question: 'Wie sind wir geworden, wie wir heute sind?' *Kein Ort. Nirgends* (1979) presents the fictional encounter in 1804, as a prelude to their suicides, of the writers Heinrich von Kleist and Caroline von Günderode, whose artistic sensibilities alienate them from their surroundings. *Kassandra* (1983) in which the title-figure reviews her life in an inner monologue and identifies military power with the patriarchal order, was accompanied by the Frankfurt literature lectures *Voraussetzungen einer Erzählung: Kassandra*, an account of the germination of the story during a journey to Greece in 1980. *Störfall. Nachrichten eines Tages* (1987) consists of ruminations on the threat to the future of humanity inspired in the narrator by the Chernobyl disaster, while *Sommerstück* (1989) traces relationships between refugees from the city and their contact with the locals in a rural retreat. Wolf's stories are collected in *Gesammelte Erzählungen* (1974, 1980) and her essays in *Lesen und Schreiben* (1971, extended in later editions). *Was bleibt* (1990, but written in 1979) is a controversial account of surveillance procedures in the GDR.

Wolf, Friedrich (1888–1953)

Wolf studied medicine in Munich: he was a ship's doctor from 1913 to 1914 and served in the medical corps in the First World War until he was interned as a conscientious objector. He joined the Saxon Workers and Soldiers Council in 1919: his first play, *Das bist du* (1919) is an expressionistic, politically committed work which culminates in the statement: 'Die Welt wird umgestürzt werden von oben bis unten, von unten nach oben, daß sie neu werden kann. Nichts ist unmöglich!' In the 1920s Wolf worked as a country doctor, later he settled in Stuttgart. He joined the Communist Party in 1928; his greatest success in the theatre was *Cyankali* (1929, filmed in 1930), a play concerning a young woman who dies after an abortion, chosen because of the hopelessness of the European situation. (Wolf would later, in 1931, be arrested for ostensibly performing an abortion in similar circumstances; he was freed after mass demonstrations.) Wolf's motto became 'Kunst ist Waffe', and his plays unashamedly agitprop theatre. The play *Die Matrosen von Cattaro* (1930) describes the fate of a naval mutiny in 1918; *Professor Mamlock* (1934), first performed in Yiddish in Warsaw, deals with a Jewish doctor, a patriot with a Prussian sense of duty, who is slandered and vilified; he finally commits suicide. The play was a great success and became the most famous of all exile dramas. In 1933 Wolf fled to Switzerland; he went to Moscow where he became, in 1943, one of the founders of the *Freies Deutschland* group of anti-fascist writers. In 1945 he returned to East Berlin and became active in theatre and radio; he deliberately sought to distance himself from **Brecht**, whose formalism and concept of epic theatre he disliked. From 1950 to 1951 he was the East German ambassador to Poland. *Dramen* (two vols) appeared in 1946 (five vols from 1947 to 1955); *Ausgewählte Werke* (fourteen vols) appeared from 1953 to 1960; *Gesammelte Werke* (sixteen vols) from 1960 to 1967. *Friedrich Wolf. Ein Lesebuch für unsere Zeit* appeared in 1961; a two-volume edition of *Werke* in 1973.

Wolfgruber, Gernot (1944–)

After a period as an apprentice and a programmer Wolfgruber studied from 1968 to 1974 in Vienna, where he lives as a professional writer. He belongs to a generation of Austrian social realists, Michael **Scharang**, Franz Innerhofer, Josef Winkler, who have focused on the struggles of young men at the mercy of varying pressures from family, employment and the affluent society in general on the border between the working and the lower middle classes (cf. also the West Germans Gerd **Fuchs** and Wilhelm Genazino). In the novels *Auf freiem Fuß* (1975), *Herrenjahre* (1976), *Niemandsland* (1978), *Verlauf eines Sommers* (1981) and *Die Nähe der Sonne* (1985) these pressures lead respectively to crime and imprisonment, over-extension of resources and bereavement, marriage breakup, professional disaster and madness.

Wolfskehl, Karl (1869–1948)

Descended from a family of rabbis and patrician Jews, Wolfskehl studied German language and literature in Berlin, Giessen and Leipzig. In 1893 he met Stefan **George** and edited with him the collection *Deutsche Dichtung* (1901–3). His first publication was an anthology of poetry *Ulais* (1897); he also published rhapsodic, mystical dramas (*Saul* (1905); *Thors Hammer* (1908); *Sanctus und Orpheus* (1909)). He became a close friend of Stefan George, and his house in Schwabing became the meeting-place for members of the George-*Kreis*, also the *Kosmiker* (Alfred Schuler and Ludwig Klages). He was one of the most active contributors to the *Blätter für die Kunst* (writing much fervent, expressive prose), which he also edited with George; Wolfskehl emphasized the Dionysian element as opposed to George's restraint and control. In the 1920s and early 1930s he published hymn-like poetry (*Der Umkreis* (1927); *Die Stimme spricht* (1934)); in 1933 he left Germany for Switzerland, Italy and finally, to get as far away from Germany as possible, to New Zealand. Wolfskehl had seen himself as a 'Mithüter des deutschen Geistes': the turbulence of the Book of Job seemed appropriate to him as a portrayal of the plight and suffering of the Jews (*Hiob oder die vier Spiegel* appeared in 1950). He died in Auckland in 1948. *Zehn Jahre Exil. Briefe aus Neuseeland* were published in 1959; two volumes of *Gesammelte Werke* in 1960. Various letters (illuminating are those to the Dutch poet Verwey) have also been published.

Wollschläger, Hans (1935–)

Born and brought up in Westphalia, Wollschläger studied music there from 1955 to 1957 and settled in Bamberg in the following year as a professional writer. He translated the works of Edgar Allan Poe with his mentor Arno **Schmidt**, then the Anna Livia Plurabelle chapter of James Joyce's *Finnegans Wake* (1970) and the whole of *Ulysses* (1975), an achievement for which he has received unstinted praise. He shares with Schmidt religious agnosticism, reflected in his non-fictional works *Die bewaffneten Wallfahrten gen Jerusalem. Geschichte der Kreuzzüge* (1973) and *Die Gegenwart einer Illusion. Reden gegen ein Monstrum* (1972, extended 1978), and an interest in the late nineteenth-century author of exotic adventure stories Karl May, whose biography he has written (*Karl May. Grundriß eines gebrochenen Lebens* (1965, extended 1976)). Wollschläger's chief work to date is the novel *Herzgewächse oder Der Fall Adams. Fragmentarische Biographik in unzufälligen Makulaturblättern*, written from 1959 to 1962 but not published until 1982. The central figure Adams, born of Jewish parents in Aden in 1900, resident in Bamberg from 1905 to 1935, emigrates to London and becomes a war correspondent who takes part in a bombing raid over Cologne in 1942, then returns to Germany in 1950 to compose 'Herzgewächse' which combines the history of the human race with autobiography. In a state of growing paranoia he conjures up the mephistophelean figure of a Nazi war criminal who has become a weapons dealer and international gangster, with whom he develops a symbiotic relationship. The style of this *magnum opus* is marked by a multiplicity of time levels, historical, literary, mythological and philosophical allusions and verbal play which form an intricate network of dazzling complexity comparable to works of similar modernist virtuosity by Joyce, **Thomas Mann** and Arno Schmidt.

Wondratschek, Wolf (1943–)

Wondratschek studied literature, philosophy and sociology in Heidelberg, Göttingen and Frankfurt, was writer in residence at the University of Warwick in 1971–2 and now lives in Munich. A miniaturist involved in the pop scene, he has an ear for the spoken cliché, the fragmentary wisdom that can be picked up in public places, and an eye for the images of the mass media, comics and pulp literature which he assembles into collages without clear plot-line and little overall sense. As a best-selling poet he has developed an accessible song-like style in which instead of the political commitments of the late 1960s mockery and resignation find expression. The collections of poetry *Chuck's Zimmer* (1974), *Das leise Lachen am Ohr eines andern* (1976), *Männer und Frauen* (1978) and *Letzte Gedichte* (1980) are assembled in *Chuck's Zimmer. Alle Gedichte und Lieder* (1982) and have since been followed by *Die Einsamkeit der Männer* (1983, Mexican sonnets inspired by Malcolm Lowry) and the cycle *Carmen oder bin ich das Arschloch der achtziger Jahre* (1986). Representative prose collections are *Omnibus* (1972) and *Menschen Orte Fäuste* (1987). Wondratschek has also produced numerous radio plays, of which *Paul oder Die Zerstörung eines Hör-Beispiels* (1969) marks a turning-point in the development of radio drama in Germany.

Z

Zahl, Peter-Paul (1944–)

After an incident in which he exchanged shots with a policeman Zahl was sentenced in 1974 to four, then in 1976 to fifteen years' imprisonment. His writing in custody provoked a widespread discussion concerning his status as a prisoner claiming political motives for his actions and he was released in 1982. Having joined the Dortmund *Gruppe 61* in 1966, he wrote numerous essays attacking established culture, then his first novel *Von einem, der auszog, um Geld zu verdienen* (1970), a portrait of the radical underground of the late 1960s. The similar *Die Glücklichen* (1979), set in the underworld and alternative scene of Berlin Kreuzberg in the 1970s, has a strong picaresque and utopian element evident in the progress of the central figures from petty crime, prostitution and drug abuse to the establishment of a commune and the successful outcome of a battle against a drug dealer. Zahl's poems, in *Schutzimpfung* (1975), *Alle Türen offen* (1977) and *Aber nein sagte Bakunin und lachte laut* (1983), are politically engaged in the laconic Brechtian mode.

Zech, Paul (1881–1946)

Son of a village schoolmaster in West Prussia, Zech grew up with farming relatives in the Sauerland; he went to school in Wuppertal but broke off his studies and worked for two years in the coal-mines of the Ruhr and the steelworks of Belgium and northern France. As a union representative he travelled to Paris where he became acquainted with contemporary French poetry. In 1910 he moved to Berlin, became friendly with Else **Lasker-Schüler** and made contact with the *Sturm* circle. From 1913 to 1920 he was assistant editor of the expressionist journal *Das neue Pathos*. His stories, poems and plays lie very much within the expressionist orbit, and deal frequently with his experiences as a miner (*Der schwarze Baal* (1917); *Das schwarze Revier* (1909); *Schwarz sind die Wasser der Ruhr* (1913)): influenced by Van Gogh, he sought to share the hardships of the life of the proletariat, and keenly advocated social amelioration. He was arrested in 1933 and imprisoned in Spandau; upon his release he emigrated to Prague, and from there to Paris and South America. The more important works of his exile include the prose works *Die grüne Flöte von Rio beni* (1955) and *Deutschland dein Tänzer ist der Tod* (1981); the collection of poems *Bäume* *am Rio de la Plata* (1936) should also be noted. Zech lived in poverty and earned his living mainly as a translator from the French; he also wrote articles for many Latin-American journals. He fervently wished to return to Europe, but collapsed in the street in Buenos Aires and died in hospital there. *Vom schwarzen Revier zur Neuen Welt. Gesammelte Gedichte* appeared in 1983.

Zuckmayer, Carl (1896–1977)

Zuckmayer was the son of a wealthy manufacturer; he went to school in Mainz, enlisted in the army in 1914 and served throughout the war, becoming an ardent pacifist. He contributed to Pfemfert's *Die Aktion* and, with his play *Kreuzweg* (1921), exhibited crassly expressionist elements. This mode of writing was not, however, suited to his talents, and he achieved his greatest success when remaining within the traditions of naturalist drama. His most popular play was *Der fröhliche Weinberg* (1925), a *Volksstück* set in his native Rhineland and displaying a robust feeling for the rightness of the natural order. Other successes followed: *Schinderhannes* (1927) and *Katherina Knie* (1928). Another triumph was *Der Hauptmann von Köpenick* (1931), a satirical attack on the cult of the uniform and the Prussian insistence upon obedience. Zuckmayer also provided the script for the film *Der blaue Engel* in 1930 based on Heinrich Mann's *Professor Unrat*. In 1933 he was forced to leave Germany (his mother was partly Jewish) and he settled in Austria; after 1938 he fled to the USA via Switzerland and Cuba. The play *Des Teufels General* (1946) deals with the problems facing the general who, an opponent of Hitler, has sworn an oath of allegiance to him. *Der Gesang im Feuerofen* (1949) deals similarly with resistance and betrayal. In the USA Zuckmayer worked as a farmer in Vermont (1940–6). He returned to Germany and achieved a limited success with *Das kalte Licht* (1955), a play dealing with a nuclear physicist and his defection. Zuckmayer was at his best in the portrayal of unsophisticated people: he was less successful when venturing into the realms of intellectual argument. His prose is likewise grounded in a realist tradition and avoids experimentation. *Als wär's ein Stück von mir* (1966) is an informative autobiography. *Gesammelte Werke* (four vols) appeared from 1947 to 1952 and again in 1960; *Meisterdramen* in 1966; *Dramen* in 1967; *Meistererzählungen* in 1967; *Gedichte, Dramen, Prosa 1914–1920* in 1981.

Zweig, Arnold (1887–1968)

Son of a Jewish saddle-merchant, Zweig was born in Glogau; from 1907 to 1915 he studied at various universities before enlisting. His early novels and stories, particularly the *Novellen um Claudia* (1912) and *Die Bestie* (1914), show the influence of Freud; the experiences at the front however (1915–18) made Zweig a committed pacifist and communist. In 1918 he joined a revolutionary soldiers' council; an interest in Judaism (he had earlier written the plays *Abigail und Nabal* (1909) and *Ritualmord in Ungarn* (1914)) led to his editorship of the *Jüdischer Rundschau* in 1923. His most famous novel is *Der Streit um den Sergeanten Grischa* of 1927, a book dealing with the fate of an escaped Russian prisoner of war, his capture, trial and subsequent execution. The book is characterized by its impressive ability to deal with the complex economic and social factors that led to the outbreak of the First World War, also by its humanity. Zweig later grouped the novels *Erziehung von Verdun* (1935) and *Einsetzung eines Königs* (1937) to form a *Grischa* trilogy. In 1933 Zweig was forced to emigrate, and reached Palestine. *Das Beil von Wandsbek* (1943) is a skilful portrayal of life under Nazi rule, and shows how the butcher Teetjen is employed to kill, his success and his downfall. The novel refuses to condemn the German people as a whole, and is refreshingly free of crude moralizing. Zweig returned to East Germany after the end of the Second World War and was president of the Academy of Arts from 1950 to 1953. His *Ausgewählte Werke in Einzelbänden* (sixteen vols) appeared from 1957 to 1967.

Zweig, Stefan (1881–1942)

Born into a wealthy Viennese Jewish family, Stefan Zweig dedicated himself at an early age to writing; in the decade before Hitler's seizure of power he was one of the most widely read authors in the German language. The most successful stories (*Angst* (1920); *Amok. Novellen einer Leidenschaft* (1922); *Verwirrung der Gefühle* (1927)) are characterized by a tightly-knit narrative and polished style; his essays on literary and historical figures are a good example of *haute vulgarisation*. *Jeremias* (1917) is an anti-war dramatic poem; *Volpone* (1925), freely adapted from Ben Jonson, was Zweig's greatest stage success. In 1935 Zweig collaborated with Richard Strauss on the opera *Die schweigsame Frau*. His *Novellen* and biographies were translated into most European languages, also Japanese; his popularity and stylistic ease (with a frequently exotic setting) led to comparisons with Somerset Maugham. In 1934 he emigrated to England; his only novel, *Ungeduld des Herzens*, appeared in 1939, and the famous *Schachnovelle* in 1942. Zweig moved to Brazil, where he and his wife committed suicide in Petropolis (near Rio de Janeiro) after the fall of Singapore. Important is his autobiographical *Die Welt von gestern. Erinnerungen eines Europäers* (1944), which gives a (somewhat idealized) depiction of life in Europe before the First World War. Two volumes of *Gesammelte Erzählungen* appeared in 1936; *Ausgewählte Novellen* were published in 1946; *Ausgewählte Werke* (two vols) in 1960; *Die Dramen* in 1964; *Jubiläumsausgabe* (ten vols) in 1981; *Gesammelte Werke in Einzelbänden* from 1982; *Werke* (five vols) in 1983.

Zwerenz, Gerhard (1925–)

Zwerenz became a soldier in 1943, a policeman in the GDR after repatriation from the Soviet Union in 1948 and a student of philosophy under Ernst Bloch in Leipzig in 1952. Having been associated with an anti-Stalinist group centred on the philosopher Wolfgang Harych which also included Erich **Loest** he left the GDR in 1957 when some of its members were imprisoned. His first works were about the social upheavals of the GDR in its infancy (*Aufs Rad geflochten. Roman vom Aufstieg einer neuen Klasse* (1959)) and the uprising of 17 June 1953 (*Die Liebe der toten Männer* (1969)). His later work consists of a picaresque novel *Casanova oder Der kleine Herr in Krieg und Frieden* (1966), autobiographical works *Kopf und Bauch* (1971), *Der Widerspruch* (1974), *Das Großelternkind* (1978), two books on Kurt **Tucholsky**, a biography (1979) and a short novel *Eine Liebe in Schweden* (1980), *Die Quadriga des Mischa Wolf* (1975) on the Guillaume spy affair which led to the resignation of Chancellor Willi Brandt, the book version of the film (directed by **Fassbinder**) *Die Ehe der Maria Braun* (1979), two dystopias *Salut für einen alten Poeten* (1980) in which the government forbids citizens to exercise their memories, and *Der Bunker* (1983) a vision of nuclear war and its aftermath, and a series of semi-pornographic satires, some written under pseudonyms, *Erbarmen mit den Männern* (1968), *Tantenliebe, Die Zukunft der Männer, Rasputin* (all 1970) and the twelve volumes of *Erotische Kalendergeschichten* (1983). From Zwerenz's prolific output the stories collected in *Heldengedenktag* (1964), some autobiographical, some set in the Second World War, and the notorious *Die Erde ist unbewohnbar wie der Mond* (1973) on which Fassbinder based a play, on a real estate fraud in Frankfurt involving a Jew, are worth singling out. He has also produced poems, *Galgenlieder von heute* (1958), *Gesänge auf dem Markt* (1962) and *Die Venusharfe* (1985) and numerous polemical essays and diaries, mainly on the division of Germany, *Ärgernisse. Von der Maas bis an die Memel* (1961), *Wider die deutschen Tabus* (1962), *Der plebejische Intellektuelle* (1972), *Antwort an einen Friedensfreund* (1982) and *Die DDR wird Kaiserreich* (1985).